A New World Order

"Democrism"—The Third Economic System

Theory and Practice

A New World Order

“Democrism”—The Third Economic System
Theory and Practice

Viswanathan Ekambaram

KALPAZ

First Published, 2017

Published by

Kalpaz Publications
C-30, Satyawati Nagar,
Delhi – 110052
E-mail: kalpaz@hotmail.com
Ph.: 9212142040

Printed at: G. Print Process, Delhi

Cataloging in Publication Data—DK
Courtesy: D.K. Agencies (P) Ltd. <docinfo@dkagencies.com>

A new world order : "democrism" : the third economic system theory and practice.
pages cm
ISBN 9789386397072

1. Management—Employee participation. 2. Employee ownership. 3. Economic development.

HD5650.N49 2017 DDC 331.0112 23

Dedication

I dedicate this book to very soul of sacrifice Mr N. Veerabhathiran, an ordinary manual worker who helped my education throughout my academic career and financed me generously to publish all my books. It is he who sacrificed his whole life to save not only me but also all my six brothers and my only sister from the very deep sea of appalling poverty.

The author (at centre) with Nobel Laureate Amartya Sen (at left) during the World Economic Congress held in New Delhi, India, at 1983

Contents

Volume – II
Causes for Human Problems

Volume – III
People's Direct Ownership of Capital (Democrism)

Volume – IV
Economic Justices and Rights

Volume – V
Justices of Democrism

Acknowledgements

I would like to express my gratitude to the many people who saw me through this book; to all those who provided support, talked things over, read, wrote, offered comments, allowed me to quote their remarks and assisted in the editing, proofreading and design.

I would like to thank Veerabathiran, T.V. Vasudevan, I.A.S. E. Raghavan and Professor Dr E. Chandrasekaran for enabling me to publish this book. Above all I want to thank my wife, Professor Nirmaladevi and the rest of my family, who supported and encouraged me in spite of all the time it took me away from them. It was a long and difficult journey for them.

I would like to thank Michiel Bijikerk (Holland), Col. SP Singh and Deenadayalan and above all Javed Sulan of Kalpaz Publications for helping me in the process of selection and editing. Thanks to Amit Garg my publisher who encouraged me.

Last and not least: I beg forgiveness of all those who have been with me over the course of the years and whose names I have failed to mention."

– Professor Viswanathan Ekambaram

Foreword

Dr K. Venkatasubramaniam, Former V.C. Pondicherry University

> The book “A New World Order” is quite interesting as it deals with all crucial economic issues which need our immediate attention.

Professor S.N. Sen, University of Pune

> To sum up, the book deals with many important problems which merit to be discussed at an International conference by both Indian and Foreign Economists and, I suggest that the author should go ahead with his proposal of putting forth his publication at the forthcoming World Economic Conference.

Dr K. Sitaraman Swami, Ph.D (USA), F.R.E.S (UK)

> “A New World Order” is an excellent treatise for solving poverty, and other economic evils and political evils such as ‘Star Wars’.

Brig. T.V. Manoharan, Ministry of Defence, New Delhi

> I am sure the book “A New World Order” will be one of the finest ever in the world and will bring out Socio-Economic problems in the world.

Pramod Yadava, Professor in Molecular Biology, School of Life Sciences, JNU, New Delhi

> A very good model in principle. It needs to be subjected to thorough scrutiny in silico and then adopted for real implementation. It will have to follow due democratic approvals and processes. I am an independent protagonist of one world and doing away with all issues related to international borders which give basis for the state to invest beyond their means in defence and make stockpiles of armoury.

Preface

"Creation of Ideal Society is within our reach"

In solving poverty and unemployment, the very basic structural problems of mankind, both Capitalism and Socialism have miserably failed even after experiencing more than one hundred years. These systems can wait for one more 100 years but not poverty and unemployment. Now these systems have taught us that the capital should be owned neither by a few nor by the State but by 'all' – the Third Theory of Economic System.

When the capital is owned by 'all' a 'Democratic Economy' will emerge and it can be easily created by just enacting one law: "One Share To One Person". In Democratic Economy "All Industries will be owned by Each and Each Industry will be owned by All". The people, on the Direct Ownership of Capital, will automatically establish Tax-Free, Interest-Free and Corruption-Free Economy and War-Free and Terrorism-Free Society.

On the direct assumption of capital the people will not allow their industries to produce any weapons of mass destruction. The way for any conventional or nuclear war and terrorism will be completely eliminated. The people, the owners of capital, will not allow themselves to suffer in poverty and unemployment. The Theory of Democrism is the only option left for mankind to establish an Ideal Society within fifty years. If we wish we can.

Professor Viswanathan Ekambaram,

CEO, International Socio-Economic
Research Bureau. India
Cell: 91 94446 35017,
E Mail: economist1943@gmail.com

VOLUME: I

Evolution of Societies Towards Perfection

Chapter – I

The Authority of Natural Law Struggles for New World Order

"Each work has to pass through these stages—ridicule, opposition, and then acceptance. Those who think ahead of their time are sure to be misunderstood" **—Swami Vivekananda**

The intuitive mind is a faithful servant. We have created a society that honors the servant and has. **—Albert Einstein**

"Violence is not necessary to destroy a civilisation. Each civilisation dies indifference to the unique values which created it" **—Nicolas Gomez**

The attempt and struggle to establish a better ordering of human society than the destructive and cruel chaos in which mankind have hitherto existed is by no means modern. The origin of attempt executed to conceive an Ideal Society has been emerged even before the dawn of history. So many leaders, the so called men of reincarnations, great thinkers, philosophers, scientists and political and revolutionary leaders have tried but in vain. For this noble cause of attainment of an Ideal Society, Lord Buddha (The Holy Dhammapada), Sri Krishna (The Holy Bhagavat Gita), Jesus Christ (The Holy Bible), Prophet Mohammed (The Holy Koran) and so many men of reincarnations tried on the religious pedestal. Men of wisdom like Socrates (Socrates dialogues), Plato (Republic), Rousseau (Social Contract), Karl Marx (Das Capital), John Maynard Keynes (General Theory of Employment, Interest and Money), Thiruvalluvar (The Holy Thirukual) attempted on intellectual arena.

And the revolutionary leaders like Mira beau (Leader, French Revolution), Lenin (Leader, Russian Revolution, 1905-1917), Abraham Lincoln (American Civil War- 12th April 1861 to 13th May,1865), Mao Tze Tung (Long March of Red Army from 16th October,1934 to 19th October,1935), Mahatma Gandhi (The bloodless War of Independence (1920-1947), struggled on the battle fields.

Igniting their hearts with a spirit of undaunted courage, tireless perseverance, restless struggle and utter sacrifice with pristine purity, men constituting all sectors of wisdom such as politics, religion, economics, social philosophies, ethics, and science and technology tried to establish an Ideal Society by changing one formation of society into another during the long process of time. What are they we are still lacking for?

The treasures of wisdom originated even before the dawn of history have been accumulated in our book shelves. No one restricts us to turn the pages of Holy Bhagavat Gita, Holy Bible, Holy Koran, Holy Dharmapata, Holy Guru Grantha Sahib, Holy Vedas, Social Contract, Das Capital etc., to find a solution for socio-economic miseries of mankind. No one is twisting our hands for not exploiting and extracting the boundless natural resources to put into use for eradication of poverty. No one prevents our economists to circulate requisite volume of money the economy needs for smooth operation of economic machinery as the economists opt for. No one is going to agitate against us to codify any appropriate law for the establishment of better Order of Society. Everything in the world is under our own control and direction. Neither supernatural power nor any external force exerts any mysterious control on our intellectual strength to restraining us from creating an ideal society that we want to establish from time immemorial. Still we are not a success!

Evolution of Human Societies

From the genesis of civilisation so many men of wisdom preached and codified uncountable rules and regulations in religious, political, and social domains suitable to the then prevailing conditions. Evolution to create an ideal society. But the people did not satisfy on the creation of such societies as their views and visions were high and justifiable. As per Natural Law, for example, Darwin Theory, every system should undergo continuous and perpetual change until it reaches its perfection and eternality. The indisputable example is the Evolution of Man from the period of Paleolithic age. According to Interpretation of History explicated by Karl Marx every society should have been changed consistently and continuously by the struggle of radical revolutionists still it would reach its perfection.

But Karl Marx disastrously arrived a conclusion that the ownership of capital should be entrusted in the hands of 'State' under the guise of 'proletariat dictatorship' that would be managed by one party system. Since the economic thought was at its infantry stage during the period of Karl Marx, he might have been come to the conclusion that proletariat dictatorship would prevent the economically powerful capitalists and it would lead the working class to create an egalitarian society. On the other hand, when the 'State' captured the national capital, it crushed the working class and blocked them behind an 'iron curtain' and locked them in a 'prison economy'.

Marxian Socialistic Mode of Production pathetically failed to lead the mankind towards its perfect evolution as the socialists preached. People now are realising that they have yet to discover a new system that will lead them towards an ideal society. What is that system?

Chapter – 2

Modes of Production and their Evolutions to Create an Ideal Society

"Philosophers have so far only changed their interpretation of the world; the point however is to change the world" —**Karl Marx**

'Mode of Production' means how socially needed goods are produced by the different industrial organisations on the basis of their 'capital ownership'. The capital ownership may be in the form of 'sole trading business', 'partnership', 'cooperative society', Joint stock company', 'multinational corporation (MNC)' etc.

Modes of production and Karl Marx

Basic and Super structures of societies

It is the supreme historical discovery of Karl Marx that all the societies are established on two structural factors. One is basic structure and the other is super structure. The basic structure is the foundation of society, that forms the 'mode of production'. The basic structure is exclusively owned by the capitalists or those who own the capital. The super structure of society is built upon the basic structure of society, and it forms the fabrication of society such as legal system, education system, religious practices, custom and conventions, cultural formations etc. It is invariably controlled to the views and visions of the 'capital owners' at the basic structure.

The Basic structure: The basic structure of any society is laid on the factor that 'who primarily owns the 'capital' of the industry. Capital denotes not just 'machines and tools and factory buildings'. Moreover the capital not only assists labours and increases their productivity but it also possesses enormous 'economic power' that will explicitly control all socio-economic and political activities of a society.

The Super structure: On the other hand the 'super structure' of the society that has been raised upon the basic structure consists of various aspects of society such as the fabrication of education, religion, customs and conventions, political systems, judiciary and legal systems. It is those capitalists who are in possession of basic structure design the elements of the super structure of society in the way in which they should protect themselves and not the common people. With the help of capital and production of various goods and services the capitalists even demoralize the well-established culture of the society for their aim of 'maximisation of profit' in terms of money. Such form of societies always exhibit inequalities, undemocratic, arrogant, chaotic and full of complexities. Most of the philosophers, therefore, warn the people that the creation of 'just society' will ever be a 'will- o'- the- wisp'.

"Private capital tends to become concentrated in few hands. The result is an oligarchy of capital the enormous power of which cannot be effectively decided even by a democratically organised political society".

—Albert Einstein

Chapter – 3

Emergence of Capitalism and its Total Collapse

"Capitalism is a mode of production based on private ownership of the means of production. Capitalists produce commodities for the exchange market and to stay competitive must extract as much labour from the workers as possible at the lowest possible cost. The economic interest of the capitalist is to pay the worker as little as possible, in fact just enough to keep him alive and productive." **—Mind Hunt**

"To understand any modern society it is essential to probe beneath its surface and illuminate its fundamental economic laws of motion, as Marx did for capitalism." **–Excerpts from: "Death of Stalinism"**

On the outburst of technological and scientific inventions in the field of production of goods and services emerged widely and deeply from the eighteenth to the nineteenth century. It was called as Industrial Revolution. Major changes in agriculture, manufacturing, mining and transport had a profound effect on the socio-economic and cultural spectrums in United Kingdom, European countries and USA.

The top 15 Inventions of Industrial Revolution that changed the world:

1. The Steam Engine by James Watt in 1769,
2. Cotton Gin by Eli Whitney in 1793,
3. The Steam Boat Service on Hudson River by Robert Fulton in 1807,
4. Locomotive Engine – Rocket- by George Stephenson in 1829,
5. Telegraph by Samuel F.B. Morse in 1836,
6. Sewing Machine by Elias Howe by 1844,
7. Improves and markets Howe's Sewing Machine by Isaac Singer in 1851,

8. Transatlantic Cable by Cyrus Field in 1866,
9. Dynamite by Albert Nobel in 1867,
10. Telephone by Alexander Graham Bell in 1876,
11. Phonograph, Incandescent Light Bulb and Motion Picture by Thomas Edison in 1877, 1879 and 1892,
12. Induction Electric Motor by Nikola Tesla in 1888,
13. Diesel Engine by Rudolf Diesel in 1892,
14. First Airplane by Orville and Wilbur Wright in 1903,
15. Model T Ford Car and Assembly Line by Henry Ford in 1908 and 1913 and
16. Nuclear fission by Sir John Douglas and Ernest Walton in 1932 and then Enrico Fermi.

Allying the scientific inventions the capitalists produced goods in huge volume for accumulation of profit and wealth. These goods could not be produced in village and cottage industries. The production of these goods required 'factory system of production' in huge quantities and they had to be distributed all over the world. The factory system of production required the investment of enormous capital. It created a new class known as 'capitalists' from the feudal landlords and wealthy persons. They started gigantic factories for production of goods in mass.The above mentioned inventions paved the way for the 'emergence of capitalism' in England and other Western European countries. To dump the overproduction they established colonies worldwide

Moreover the term 'capital' implies not only huge machines and factory buildings but also supreme 'economic power'. With the help of this 'economic power' the capitalists can control all the political powers of any government. They breed brutal economic power even to change or destroy the long cherished and esteemed culture, religion and education of any society for their monetary benefit and for their own survival in the business competitions with other countries.

Working class at the mercy of capitalists

Since the working class is indispensably depending on the capitalists for their wage income and to protect their 'right to live' they have to work for the interest of capitalists and for their aim of maximisation of profit and accumulation of their wealth. So the working class, the true representative of society, will easily succumb to change their life values such as culture, custom and conventions, method of education, norms of socio-political laws, life style etc. for the satisfaction of few capitalists. Such capitalistic societies will not represent the Just Society for which the people have been struggled for years together.

After industrial revolution the mankind realised that they could not establish an Ideal Society for which they have been dreaming for since the genesis of civilisation. This is because of the fact that despite the abundant volume of production of invented goods there is no justifiable system of distribution. The capitalist mode of production is aiming at maximisation of profit but not executing equality to establish Just Society. Both Socialist and Capitalist Modes of Production have failed in the justifiable distribution of goods and stabilisation of employment which is the exclusive object of production.

World War I and II were fought with the scientific goods invented during industrial revolution. All the world governments misused the inventions to commit horrendous crime on mankind by killing millions and millions of innocent people for their transitory victory. The nuclear fission and its consequent invention of Atom Bomb by Albert Einstein and Robert Oppenheimer, despite their objection of usage on mankind, were dropped on Hiroshima by the Capitalist America killing millions of people in seconds.

Now not only Socialist and capitalist Modes Production but also Islamic Mode of Production have manufactured atom bombs, the weapons of mass destruction, and heaped them in their military arsenal. Can anyone even guess such modes of production lead the mankind towards an Ideal Society in future? Is this the object of scientists to invent nuclear fission for mass destruction and nuclear holocaust? Whither are we going?

It is the Capitalistic Mode of Production that has transformed the wonderful scientific inventions into weapons of mass destruction during two world wars and now the mode of production helps the terrorist groups day in and day out to carry out terrorist activities and kill millions of innocent people. In the same direction of capitalist countries many socialist, democratic and even poor Islamic countries too marching on and on towards global destruction. Neither Holy Bible, nor Holy Koran and nor Holy Bhagavat Geeta can stop them by their divine preaching. All the countries desire to claim pride on testing atom bombs, various forms of ballistic missiles. No country want to put even one step forward towards the creation of an Ideal Society in the midst of wonderful scientific inventions presented for the welfare of mankind.

The Capitalist mode of production is a way using capital to produce a particular commodity as a sole proprietorship or Partnership or Private Limited Company or a Joint Stock Company or Global Corporate Company. The corporate companies in order to accumulate huge volume of capital issue millions of shares to the public. But the public are allowed to claim stake only less than 49 per cent and retain majority of shares, more than 51 per cent, to exert control over the management of the company. The shares of these companies are being permitted to marketing in the 'Share Market' for monetary benefit without producing anything and thus induce the public to indulge in gambling. The success of these corporate companies is determined by their profit exploited from the consumers. To expose huge volume of profit these companies involve various illegal and manipulative activities and even produce destructive weapons like RDX, AK47 for distributing them to the terrorists purely for monetary benefits. They also produce very harmful chemical goods that will pollute the air, water and land. Moreover production of adulterated, substandard and health hazardous goods are very common in these companies. Only these companies have spoiled the Ozone layer in the atmosphere. Their main purpose is to earn maximum profit by hook or crook at the expense of human health. Moreover most of the terror outfits have invested their black money in the stock markets and use the dividend received to carry out their terror activities. Huge volume of black money is circulated in bullying the stock price to translate it as the success of these companies and stimulate the common public to indulge in stock market gambling. One day when the artificial bubbling economy burst out most of the millionaires become slum dogs and commit suicide. This trend is prevailing everywhere in the world. Billions and billions of dollars are speculated in the gamble of stock markets in the name of investments.

The mankind has been now puzzling and trembling for what to do in the midst of total collapse of economic systems, nuclear proliferation, climate changes, terrorist activities and ever spreading pollution. These are all horrible consequences as we are following the chaotic and incompetent modes of production of capitalistic and socialistic systems blindly for a long period of time. Then what is the justifiable mode of production now left with us at last to establish an Ideal Society? Is socialism a true alternative?

Chapter – 4

Emergence of Socialism and its Total Collapse

"The totality of production relation constitutes the economic structure of society, the real basis upon which a legal and political superstructure arises and to which definite forms of social consciousness correspond. The mode of production of the material means of life determines, in general, the social, political and intellectual process of life"

—Karl Marx: 'Critical of Political Economy'

"Socialism is the Big Lie of the twentieth century. While it promised prosperity, equality, and security, it delivered poverty, misery, and tyranny. Equality was achieved only in the sense that everyone was equal in his or her misery." **—Mark J. Perry: "Why Socialism Failed"**

Collapse of Socialistic mode of production in USSR: No socialist country in the world ever succeeds in its object of establishing an Egalitarian Society or Ideal Society by executing Socialist Mode of Production. Honestly speaking it was Mikhail Gorbachev, the Soviet leader, who attempted to transform and reform the Socialist society in democratic way instead of proletariat dictatorship in the second half of 1980s. So he introduced **Glasnost** (openness) which was the policy of maximal publicity, openness, and transparency in the activities of all government institutions in the Soviet Union, together with freedom of information.

The Impact of Glasnost and Perestroika

In order to continue his political and economic reforms Mikhail Gorbachev introduced **Perestroika** (restructuring- Russian: Перестройка) in June 1987. Its literal meaning is "restructuring", referring to the restructuring of the Soviet political and economic system in democratic way by allowing the people to voice their political and economic liberty. When thousands of political prisoners and many dissidents were released in the spirit of glasnost and perestroika, Gorbachev's original goal to reform the Soviet Union was not achieved. In1991, the Soviet Union was dissolved following a failed coup by conservative elements that were opposed to Gorbachev.

(Time Magazine, 4 June 1990 page 19 and Goodbye to the USSR)

Picture 1: Stalin's body buried alongside the Kremlin wall.

During a period of destalinisation undertaken by Khrushchev Stalin's body was removed and buried alongside the Kremlin wall.

Picture 2: Stalin's Statue toppled in Hungary.

'Stalin- terror' horrified all the socialist countries. He knows only brutality to implement Socialism instead of economic techniques in democratic ways. In Hungary his statue was toppled and someone had placed a sign over Stalin's mouth that read "RUSSIANS, WHEN YOU RUN AWAY DON'T LEAVE ME BEHIND!"

By the 31st December, 1991 the Soviet Union collapsed and the Soviet Socialism was overthrown. The Union was dismantled into 15 independent states by abolishing the Treaty of the Union of the 1922. Socialist mode of production failed in its own mother land in creation of an Ideal Society dreamt by Karl Marx because of the basic and emphatic fact that no one knows how to operate economic machinery using economic techniques in production, distribution, banking system, exchange and market system and equilibrating the macro level of income and expenditure, and proper circulation of money and in equilibrating the inflow and out flow of money in respect of producers and consumers.

When Mikhail Gorbachev introduced Glasnost (1985) and Perestroika to alleviate workers mental and physical agony by injecting political democracy in order to create an ideal society the people utilised the great opportunity to annihilate the dictatorial socialistic mode of society. The USSR was fragmented and the member states declared their independence to choose their own model of democratic society. **–Mikhail Gorbachev**

Emergence of Communism in China and its total collapse

Dr Sun Yat Sen's Liberal Democratic Mode of Production

In China a 'dictatorial form of society' based on the 'autocratic mode of production' was followed during the period of emperor Quing Dynasty that declares:

"All lands under Heaven belong to the emperor, all people under Heaven belong, are subjects of the emperor"

Since the society was slavery Dr Sun wanted to establish a new society on three democratic principles of Abraham Lincoln that held the 'government of the people, by the people and for the people'.

On 1 January 1912, Sun Yat-Sen announced the establishment of the Republic of China in Nanking, and he was inaugurated as the Provisional President of the Republic. It was Dr Sun Yat Sen who gained freedom for China but not Mao. Mao just introduced 'Socialistic Mode of Production' in China in 1946 after 34 years as an economic policy of China. But Chinese government intentionally declares that it is Mao who gained freedom for China, completely overthrowing the name of Dr Sun Yat Sen.

Dr Sun's economic policies were greatly influenced by the economic thoughts of **Henry George.** Accordingly Dr Sun replaced the autocratic government by the republic government on the 'People's Three Principles' **(nationalism, democracy and social reform)** and liberated the corvee farmers from the clutches of the emperor. But this transformation of society did not satisfy the radicals to establish an ideal society as it was lacking effective 'Democratic mode of production' and unable to prevent western and American imperialism from exploitation of industrial workers.

Dr Sun Yat Sen got Independence for China not Mao

At the demise of Dr Sun the Nationalist Party headed by Chiang Kai-shek captured the reins of the government. He had alliance with Communist Party of China which was started in 1921. He was unable to establish an Ideal Society and China was reeling under appalling poverty. **Henry George** blamed much of China's economic ills on bad government and on imperialism. So the Communist Party of China determined to introduce the Socialistic Mode of Production, in harmony with that of Socialist Russia, to create an Ideal Society replacing the then decayed and wretched society. It inevitably necessitated the Community party to launch a counter revolution to overthrow Chiang Kai-shek from the power. Mao attacked the nationalists led by Chiang Kai-Shek and gained absolute control over the country. Mao declared on October 1, 1949 the establishment of People's Republic of China less than One Party System to create a just society.

Mao introduced Socialistic mode of production

In order to establish an Ideal Society Mao wanted to inject socialistic mode of production in China. So he followed the strategy of Stalin by abolishing private property and execution of direct ownership of national capital and wealth by the State in authoritarian way. For which in 1958 Mao started the **"Great Leap Forward" (1958-1960)**. Since Mao did not know how to operate the economic machinery to implement the Socialistic mode of production he resorted to dictatorship like Stalin and other Bolshevik masters of Russia. Mao was also considered to be one of most brutal dictators of the twentieth century though he was worshipped by millions Chinese. It had been estimated that he was responsible for well over 70 million deaths during the period of Great Leap Forward.

Chinese students fought for democratic mode of society

(a) **Collapse of Communism**: In the early 1980s, the communist ideology was crippling toward its ultimate collapse as that of USSR. The soaring price level, the increasing unemployment, the appalling poverty, the unbridgeable economic disparity, the unparalleled corruption among bureaucrats of communist leaders, huge accumulation of wealth in billion dollars by the sons of these bureaucrats and so on.

(b) **Francis Fukuyama**: He was policy decision maker of U.S. State Department. In winter 1989 in the University of Chicago he delivered a speech titled **"Are We Approaching the End of History"** on the collapse of communism. He told his audience the collapse of Communism was leading "not to an 'end of ideology' or a convergence between capitalism and socialism…but to 'an unabashed victory of economic and political liberalism." It was not an ideology that had ended but "history as such" (Francis Fukuyama: 'The End of History and the Last Man'-New York Free Press 1992).

Fukuyama took the thesis into bold new terrain, arguing that deregulated markets in the economic sphere, combined with liberal democracy in the political sphere, represented "the end point of mankind's ideological evolution and…final form of human government" (Fukuyama: "The End of History").

(c) Communism at turmoil: It was not that China's leaders, then led by Deng Xiaoping, were committed to protecting the state-owned factories and farm communes that formed the foundation of the Communist state. (Naomi Klein-"The Shock Doctrine" - p. 184)

(d) Ignorance on the operation of economic machinery: On the approach of ultimate collapse of communist economy the Chinese leaders, like the other Western Socialist leaders, do not know how to execute the chaotic and complex economy towards perfection. They are well versed only on the imposition of 'proletariat dictatorship' and 'military rule' to crush the voice of the people.

(e) Introduction of free-market economy: In order to save the Chinese economy from 'depression' Deng was enthusiastically committed to converting to a corporate-based economy – so committed that, in 1980, his government invited **Milton Friedman [Milton Friedman** (July 31, 1912 – November 16, 2006) was an American economist, (Chicago School of Economics)] to come to China and tutor hundreds of top-level civil servants, professors and party economists in the fundamentals of **free-market theory**. (Naomi Klein-"The Shock Doctrine'-p. 185)…..His central message was "how much better ordinary people lived in capitalist than in communist countries". (*ibid:* p. 185)

(f) Deng at his debacle: But in the late eighties, Deng began introducing measures that were distinctly unpopular particularly among workers in the cities-price controls were lifted, sending prices soaring, job security was eliminated, creating waves of unemployment and deep inequalities were opening up between winners and losers in the new China….

(g) Huge corruption: Many Chinese citizens wanted more freedom in the market, but "reform" increasingly looked like code for party officials turning into business tycoons, as many illegally took possession of the assets they had previously managed as bureaucrats. (*ibid:* p. 186)

(h) Failure of Friedman and students' unrest: Friedman did not have the desired results. The pictures in the official papers of the professor offering his blessing to party bureaucrats did not succeed in bringing the public onside. In subsequent months, protests grew more determined and radical. The most visible symbols of the opposition were the demonstrations by student strikers in **Tiananmen Square**. These historic protests were almost universally portrayed in the international media as a clash between modern, idealistic students who wanted Western-style democratic freedom and old-guard authoritarians who wanted to protect the Communist state.

(i) Wang Hui: Wang Hui, one of the organisers of the 1989 protests, and now a leading Chinese intellectual of what is known as China's "New Left". In his 2003 book, **China's New Order,** Wang explains that the protests spanned a huge range of Chinese society-not just elite university students but also factory workers, small entrepreneurs and teachers. What ignited the protests, he recalls, was a popular discontent in the face of Deng's "revolutionary" economic changes which were lowering wages, raising prices, and causing "a crisis of layoffs and unemployment" (Wang Hui: "China's New Order: Society, Politics, and Economy in Transition"-Harvard University Press, 2003, 45, 54). According to Wang "These changes were the catalyst for the 1989 social mobilisation" (*ibid*).

To save the Chinese economy Deng opened the flood gates of globalisation. He ardently greeted the 'capitalistic Wal-Mart' to enter the 'communist China'. A total collapse of ideologies.

One of the partners of Procter & Gamble – the distributor of Wal-Mart-expressed: "One well-stocked '7-Eleven' could knock out 30 (Iraqi) stores, a 'Wal-Mart' could take over the country" (Thomas B Edsall and Juliet Eilperin, 'Lobbyists Set Sights on Money Making Opportunities in Iraq), Washington Post, October 2, 2003.

Protests against communism at Tiananmen Square and great Massacre

The Chinese students, intellectuals, government officials and workers were molded in the same school of thought and wanted to infuse democratic dose in the society ejecting the harsh socialistic mode of society. In 1989, they saw the collapse of a number of communist governments around the world. At the same time the visit of Gorbachev to China ignited the hearts of the students to proclaim the pro-democracy slogans. The student demonstrations between 1987 and 1989 for greater democracy and anti-corruption were strongly supported by **Hu Yaobang**, the general secretary of the Communist party. In 1989, upon his death, 100,000 people gathered at Tiananmen Square on the eve of his funeral. The government wanted to use the policy of oppression with the help of military. To suppress the protests, the military massacred thousands of students. It was called as the Tiananmen Square protests of 1989, referred in the most of the world as Tiananmen Square Massacre.

The protests failed because they lacked a unified cause or a powerful leadership; the participants fragmented into various groups; they included disillusioned Communist Party of China members and Trotskyites as well as free market reformers, who were generally against the government's authoritarianism and voiced calls for economic change and democratic reform within the structure of the government. The students did not have adequate knowledge on how to operate economic machinery with the help of effective and predetermined economic system based on 'democratic principles' basically 'each industry for all and all industries for each', which is the only remedy

Tiananmen Square, Beijing, China, 1989

Art students put finishing touches of "Goddess of Democracy" statue.

Student Protesters – Mao's picture at the background

Tank Man

Student-Protesters for Democratic Economy

Struggle against the Chinese Army, the PLA.

Tiananmen Square, 1989.

now available as alternative to the decaying pitalism and socialism. I call this economic system as "Democrism – The Third Theory" or Democratic Mode of Production that is illustrated in the next chapter.

The Revolutions of 1989 (also known as the Fall of Communism, the Collapse of Communism, and the Autumn of Nations) are the revolutions which overthrew Soviet-style Communism state in Eastern-bloc European countries. The events began in Poland, and continued in Hungary, East Germany, Czechoslovakia, Bulgaria and Romania. Romania was the only bloc European country to overthrow its communist regime violently. But the Tiananmen Square protests of 1989 failed to overthrow communism in China.

Chapter – 5

Emergence of 'Democrism' to Save Mankind (Democratic Mode of Production)

"Our Founding Fathers well understood that concentrated power is the enemy of Liberty and the rights of man. They knew that the American experiment in individual liberty, free enterprise, and republican self-government could succeed only if power were widely distributed. And since in any society social and political power flow from economic power, they saw that wealth and property would have to be widely distributed among the people of this country..."

"This is not a new policy. Jefferson and Adams, Webster and Lincoln, Cleveland and Wilson - all understood its importance. But it is a policy that needs strong new emphasis in an age where its basic truth has sometimes been forgotten and removed from public discourse"

—Ronald Reagon, Oct.1980 on "Expanding Ownership"

It is the supreme command of the Natural Law that all the celestial systems in the universe should undergo evolution until they reach perfection and eternality. For example, the Solar System and the living organisms on the earth have attained perfection after billions and billions of years of evolution. **Dr Salvador Moya-Sola** of Miquel Crusafont Institute of Paleontology in Barcelona said that it took 13 million years of evolution for **Pierolapithecus catalaunicus** to become common man who attained perfection and eternality.

Not only natural organisms and elements but also man made inventions and systems should move towards perfection for their survival. For example, the invention of airplane by Wright brothers is moving on its evolutionary path towards its perfection and perhaps it may tend to be infinity. So many social elements like customs and convention and political elements like form of governments are undergoing evolution towards perfection. Though democratic form of political government is not perfect people accept it as it is somewhat better than any other systems at present.

But our bone of contention concerns with different Economic Systems and their disastrous and devastating Modes of Production. All the countries throughout the world at first followed Foraging Mode of Production and then derived step by step towards Dictatorial Mode of Production, Dictatorial Mode of Production, The Antique Mode of Production, and The Feudal Mode of production and/or The Liberal Mode of Production by the force of geographical and political compulsions.

After Industrial Revolution the socialistic countries like Russia and China followed the Socialist Mode of Production in which capital was owned by the State and the other democratic countries like UK, USA, the West European and Asiatic countries followed the Capitalist Mode of Production in which capital was owned by a few wealthy persons. The object of evolution that occurred in the modes of production towards socialist and capitalist modes of production was to achieve perfection and eternality to establish an Ideal Society.

But the two modes of production have now failed throughout the world. The USSR dismantled into 14 states and the socialism was abandoned both in Russia and China. Both Russia and China have permitted private ownership of capital widely replacing its strategic economic mechanism of State Ownership.Though all the socialist countries move towards privatisation by evolution they could not evolve an Ideal Society because huge volume of capital is locked in the hands of few individuals in private sector economy. It is these few people have the economic power to decide whether they have to lead the society towards an Ideal one or an exploited one. It is naked truth that the sole aim of capitalists in private sector is to accumulate their private wealth but not promote the society to achieve its goal of Just and Ideal Society. Then what is the remedy? And where does the remedy lie?

The end of evolution will not end at private sector economy i.e. capitalist market economy in capitalist democratic countries or socialist market economy in socialist and dictatorial countries to attain its perfection. The evolution should move still further towards 'Democratisation of Economy' to reach its eternality and perfection. If so what do I mean by the concept 'Democratisation of Economy'? And what does I indicate its characteristics should be and how do I lead the mankind towards a Just or an Ideal Society by the economic theories and techniques by refining the present fiscal and monetary policies?

Hereafter I wish to use the word "DEMOCRISM" instead of Democratisation of Economy. I use DEMOCRISM as the Third Theory assuming Capitalism and Communism/Socialism as first and second theories.

Distinction between Democracy and Democrism: Democracy is associated with a political system. It denotes a particular type of government which is created by the people by franchising their right to vote to elect their governing representatives directly or indirectly through a political party system. **President Abraham Lincoln** in his **Gettysburg speech** (19 November, 1863) defined democracy as the 'Government of the People-by the people-for the people'. On the other hand Democrism is the word coined by me to denote an economic system for differentiating it from Capitalism and Communism.

Meaning of Democrism: Democrism denotes 'economic government or economic rule of the people-by the people-for the people'. It requires establishment of strong ECONOMIC GOVERNMENT and its method of formation is illustrated in point No. 2. In Democrism everyone /every worker will have share in the capital of all the industries and every industry will be owned by all workers. In other words 'Each Industry for All and All Industry for Each". It will lead to "PEOPLE'S DIRECT OWNERSHIP OF CAPITAL". What would be the resultant and natural consequences if the people have direct ownership of capital?

Each Industry for All and All Industries for Each

In Capitalism a very few people own all capital share of a country;

In Socialism no people own no capital share of a country; and

In Democrism every people own equal capital share of a country.

What does it mean?

First of all if a country ventures to launch an industry all the workers of the country will contribute a capital share out of their wage income. In the same line of ideology all the industries of the country will be started by the workers according to their wage income. Moreover a 'National Investment Fund' will be created by the working people. This national Investment Fund will be utilised to buy all the 'capital Share' of the existing corporate companies at 'par value' over a period of time without disturbing the existing capitalists. In the due course the 'capitalist classes, will be wiped out in the country and there will be only a working class that will directly administer the capital creation and accumulation of the country. Thus, not only the new companies but also the existing companies will be directly owned the people. This will lead the economy to the 'Industrial Justice' of 'Each Industry for all and All Industries for Each.'

Implementation of Democrism by "Economic Government"

Moreover to empower the workers to rule over their country economically (i.e. administration on the what to produce, how to produce, and for whom to produce and their justifiable distribution, determination of employment, national income, poverty alleviation etc.,) an 'Economic Parliament' like 'Senate' will be constituted anew to run the government actively apart from the present passive Political Government. In the political government the representatives of people for parliament are elected from the districts or states of a country. Whereas in the 'Economic Government' the representatives of people or workers will be elected by industry wise. For Example, let's assume there are 100 industries in a country like railways, iron and steel industry, textiles, information technology, construction, cottage and village industries, agriculture etc. and 10 billion workers are engaged in these industries. According to prorata of workers population of each industry the representative of workers will be elected to the Economic Parliament of the government.

To uphold democratic administration the 'head of the government' in the name of 'Economic President or Economic Prime Minister' as the case may be, will be elected by the 'workers-representatives'. To assist the 'head of the government' an expert 'Economic Commission' from various fields of industries will be appointed with the approval of the 'Economic Parliament'.

Capital Justice

By the enforcement of People's Direct Ownership of Capital or the Democratisation of Economy there will be only one economic system in the world created by the general will of the people on the basis of Capital Justice. Capital justice means distribution of national capital to all the workers equally or according to their wage. Because it is the people not only produced consumption goods but also capital goods. It is the capital goods that provides 'right to work' to the people and thereby 'right to live' and its provision of which radiates as the foundation of all political constitutions. Since the People's Direct Ownership of Capital assures one's right to live no one has the liberty to marketing the share capital. All share markets in the world will be abolished. It is the crux of capital justice in Democrism.

Property Right to Proletariat only

The workers produce not only consumption goods but also capital goods. But in both capitalist and socialist economies the workers are paid wage-income to buy consumption goods only. The value of money to buy capital goods is exploited by capitalists in the name of profit in capitalist economy and by the State in the name of common wealth in socialist economy.

On the establishment of People's Direct Ownership of Capital the entire wealth of the nation will be distributed to all workers according to their wage. By virtue of this distributive justice all workers will have 'Compulsory Property Right'.This will ensure the 'economic justice' of 'Property Right to Proletariat Only'. When each and every worker equally or justifiably shares in the national wealth they will secure 'economic security', 'Job Security' and

'Economic Freedom'. Subsequently their 'fear about future' will automatically disappear.

Administration by the workers (Administrative Justice)

Since each industry is directly owned by all the workers the administration of each industry cannot be looked after by all the workers as the nation as a whole. The administration of each industry will be entrusted in the hands of the manager-workers of that industry. These manager-workers should keep transparency and maintain accountability not only to the workers of that industry but also to the whole working class of the country. This is the 'administrative justice.'

Industrial Peace

There will be no room for any industrial dispute like 'strikes and lock outs' in any Industry as management of the industry has been directly entrusted in the hands of the workers themselves. No workers indulge in industrial disputes against themselves. There will be smooth flow of production and distribution with an accelerated tempo in all industries. Since each industry is owned by the workers, no worker will be treated as a commodity to buy for 'wage-price' as it has been practiced in the capitalist and socialist economies. The workers will be treated with utmost dignity and humanity.

Investment by workers only and Investment Justice

Capital is the stock and investment is the flow. Capital is one of the two factors of production in binary economics. Capital is already taken into account in the CAPITAL STOCK of a country. It is also termed as stock of accumulated labour in the past. Basically it is used as a source to determine the volume of employment, volume of production and volume of income. Whereas investment is a flow towards capital stock over a period of time. Investment is created out of one's income and more often it emerges from one's savings.

The capital stock maintains the employment of present workers and their wage income. Therefore it is the indispensable duty of the present workers to create investment out of their wage income to provide employment opportunity for all future employees waiting for job. Today's employees cannot find job as the 'Yesterday' employees had not created adequate investment and the 'Future' employees will not find job if the 'Yesterday' employees could not have created new investment out of their savings. Thus, the investment unites all the employees inseparably in time link of 'Yesterday, Today and Tomorrow' and thus nurtures **'Industrial Fraternity'** among the workers. Therefore it is the Investment justice that demands all the workers to pursue the path of economic cooperation for the creation of adequate investment and upholds the 'Time Link' not to be broken at any cost. The 'Time Link' can be preserved only by the working class but not by any few capitalists or the State. Therefore the basic economic concept should be developed as follows:

"Work according to Energy,

Wage according to Work and

Investment according to Wage."

Investment according to Wage

The economic system of 'People's Direct Ownership of Capital' put every worker under economic obligation for creating investment according to his wage for generating employment opportunities for his future generation. For the creation of National Investment, every worker will contribute a specified share of his wage income. In other words every worker will contribute an Investment Share according to his wage. For instance if a company is floated by issuing 100 billion shares of $1 each, all the shares will be distributed only to the workers of the country according their wage. This process will be continued perpetually whenever share are issued. No individual will be allowed to swindle as many shares as he can buy with his money power. The shares will be issued usually according to the three income groups i.e. lower, middle and higher income groups.

Dual Income

On the "People's Direct Ownership of Capital" we know that all the workers will own a share of capital in all the countries. Therefore the profit earned by all the industries or the 'national profit' will be directly owned by all the workers of the country. It will lead the workers to get wage-income for their work and dividend-income for their capital share i.e. for their contribution of investment. For distribution of wage we have to follow **'efficiency justice'** and for the 'dividend' we have to adhere to 'Distributive Justice.'

Distributive Justice

For the contribution of 'investment according to wage' the workers assume full economic responsibility not only for the growth of economy but also for the creation of new employment opportunities for their successors. In the creation of investment low-income workers bear more 'Investment Burden' than middle and higher income workers. They have to sacrifice even the consumption of their bare necessities. The same condition of economic scarification prevails higher to middle-income group than to higher income group. The 'Investment Burden' or Economic Scarification varies from one income-group to another. The distributive justice of dividend payment equilibrates the economic scarification of all the workers. Now the economic doctrine develops as follows:

"Work according to Energy,
Wage according to Work,
Investment according to Wage and
Dividend according to Investment Burden"

Creation of Egalitarian Society

When all the workers contribute a particular percentage of shares of income as investment to the National Investment according to their wage income, the 'Investment burden' of the low income group of workers will be greater than the 'Investment burden' of the high income group of workers. For example, if low income group of people contribute $3,000 per annum as investment out of their annual wage income of $30,000, their investment burden would greater than that of high income group of people who contribute $10,000 per annum as investment out of their annual wage income of $120,000 because the low income group of people have to sacrifice even the consumption of necessities as their saving power is nil at that wage income and on the other hand the high income group of people need not sacrifice any consumption of goods but only to convert their savings into investment. Therefore, the low income group of people bear greater 'investment burden' for the development of the national economy than the high income group of people. Then it is the economic justice that the 'more dividend' should be paid to the low income group of people than the high income group of people on the basis of 'investment burden'. **More the investment burden means, more the dividend and less investment burden means less the dividend. This distributive justice of dividend will lead the economy towards Egalitarian society.**

First of all the higher dividend received by the 'low-income group' and the lower dividend received by the 'middle-income group' and similarly the dividend distribution between middle-income and high-income groups will reduce the 'Income Gap' between the three income groups. Secondly, in Democrism the concept profit will not be used as a tool of exploitation of workers but as a 'mechanism' for the establishment of Egalitarian Society'. Now the basic economic concept will widen its domain of principle as follows:

"Work according to Energy,
Wage according to work,
Investment according to Wage,
Dividend according to Investment Burden and
Equality according to Dividend"

Classless Society

Establishment of Classless society is the fundamental object of all economic systems. There are two economic approaches to create classless society. One is 'Negative approach' and the other is 'Positive approach'. After October revolution the Bolshevik masters in communist countries did not have any economic technique to establish classless society without violence. They simply abolished 'the right to property' in the constitution and forcefully confiscated the property of rich and appropriate it as 'State Ownership'. Thousands of rich and capitalists brutally murdered under the guise of creating 'Classless Society'.

In democratic capitalist countries 'right to property' has been made one of 'fundamental rights' of constitution mainly to protect the property of rich people. According to Keynes the capitalist system will operate unless economic disparity prevails between rich and poor because it the rich people who finance the required capital for the industries to create employment opportunities.

The 'People's Direct Ownership of Capital' i.e. Democrism follows 'Positive Approach' to create 'Classless Society'. In the system of 'People's Direct Ownership of Capital', all the capitalists become workers and all the workers become the capitalists. Moreover the class distinction between 'producers and consumers' and 'employers and employees' will also disappear instantly without any violence. Therefore the 'People's Direct Ownership of Capital' is the only positive economic technique to create a classless society.

Since the theory of democrism follows Positive approach by ensuring equal share of capital wealth to all to establish classless society, the equal ownership of capital wealth to all the workers will provide them inalienable economic power, economic security and economic equality, by which they can protect themselves from exploitation and lead the mankind towards an Ideal Society. Now the economic doctrine develops to reach its ultimate goal as:

"Work according to Energy,
Wage according to Work,
Investment according to Wage,
Dividend according to Investment Burden,
Equality according to Dividend and
Ideal society according to Equality"

Tax - Free Economy

For effective operation of economy the 'People's National Profit' the diagram in divided into three segments such as

1. Income-compensation profit,
2. Tax-compensation profit and
3. Producers' deficit money-inflow (income) compensation profit.

Income compensation profit

It means the first segment of National profit will be kept apart for distribution of dividend according to investment burden of the poor people. In order to fill the income-gap between low-income and high income groups a considerable portion of this national profit will be italicized not only for increasing the purchasing power of poor people but also employed for the establishment of egalitarian society. The execution of this technique has already been explained above

Tax-compensation profit

It denotes the second segment of National profit. This portion of national profit will be directly allotted to the government to meet its expenditure. This profit is nothing but the government revenue which is so far earned in the form of direct and indirect taxes from the people. All kinds of taxes will be abolished in the economy and the people will directly contribute a part of their National profit to the government for its expenditure. There will be "tax-free" economy in the country. By doing so, a huge volume of money spent for collection of taxes will also be wiped out. Moreover corruption involves both in the collection of taxes and in the evasion of paying direct taxes and economic immorality of tax payers for paying the tax will automatically disappear. People will behave with high economic honesty.

Producers' deficit money-inflow compensation profit

It means the third part of National Profit to uphold the stability of economy at all levels of employment. In monetary terms stability of economy means equilibrium between out-flow of money during production of goods and inflow of money on the sale of goods produced at a particular time at static economy and the monetary equilibrium all levels of money supply in a dynamic economy. If the producers fail to get the expected money income from sale of goods, the stability in volume of employment, production and income of workers will fall. The economy will be crunched into recession and the workers will lose their employment and thereby their 'right to live'... If industries suffer to get 'expected income' by sale of goods the third part of National profit will be set into flow towards the industries to compensate their deficiency of 'expected income' to sustain the level of employment and production. In other words it is the workers who help themselves to sustain their 'right to work'. To put into real terms unemployment will never arise due to deficiency in effective demand i.e. due to failure of consumers to buy the goods produced for them, as deduced by John Maynard Keynes.

Maintenance of stable economy

The vital factor that underlies in all economic systems is to maintain the economic machinery in perfect condition perpetually to ensure stable economic growth with required accelerated tempo especially to wipe out poverty and unemployment. The smooth operation of economic machinery requires 'a perfect and sustained monetary equilibrium' in the circular flow of money between producers and consumers. "The rate of money-flow (for example, ₹ 100 billion) from the producers to the consumers when the production of goods takes into effect in a particular duration of time should be equal with the rate of money-flow (the same ₹ 100 billion) from the consumers to the producers when the consumption of goods takes into effect in the same duration of time."

If the consumers create 'a time lag' in spending their money income of ₹ 100 billion the producers will face deficiency (for example, ₹ 10 billion) in their required money income of ₹ 100 billion, and it will force the producers to reduce the volume of production by ₹ 10 billion in the next round of production and the level of employment accordingly. In order to wipe out the " deficiency of ₹ 10 billion in the producers' required income of ₹ 100 billion" to sustain the economic activities in the next round, the third portion of the 'National profit' i.e. "Producers' deficit money-inflow of profit" will be utilised to fill the 'Monetary gap' of producers even if the goods are not sold. Goods may perish but not the life of workers due to unemployment as it is now happening in capitalism and socialism. If we want to put into Keynesian terms unemployment will not arise due to lack of effective demand when the third portion of National profit is properly used.

In democratisation of economy the very concept of profit will be expelled from the 'factor of exploitation of workers' but will operate as an economic crusader retrieving the workers (people) from clutches of taxation, economic inequality and economic disequilibrium. In other words the concept of profit will be used here as an 'economic technique' or as 'economic stabilizer' or as 'an economic equilibrator' 'to maintain dynamic stability in economic activities such as volume of employment, production and income instead of an 'exploiter' by capitalists as in the capitalist economy.

Prosumer-Society

On the democratisation of an economy and subsequently in consequence of the principle "Investment according to wage", all the consumers (workers) will become the producers. So the economic discrimination between consumers and producers will naturally disappear. A PROducer cum conSUMER society, known as PROSUMER Society will newly emerge in the economy. In the prosumer society we can deduce that all the consumers will naturally become the producers of the commodities which they want to produce. The people as a whole will determine what to produce, how to produce and how much to produce and they will bear the 'risk factor' of production to maintain economic stability.

Just Price

A Just Price is a price of a commodity determined by consumers themselves who want to buy that commodity in a prosumer society since all the consumers are the producers in a prosumer it is the consumers themselves who will fix a price of the commodities which they want to consume. Therefore it is the Just Price. The consumers will not agitate against the price that they have fixed. There will be no tussle between demand and supply forces initiated by producers and consumers in the fixation of price. There will be contentment and consentaneous general will among the consumers in fixation of the price instead of competitiveness. It is Just Price because there is no room of ambiguous feeling the price level is higher or lower.

Moreover it is the just price because even if the price fixed is considered to be much higher than the cost of the goods, it will yield higher margin of profit. Higher the profit means higher distribution of the dividend; higher the dividend means higher the dividend-income to the consumers who are in the parenthesis of low and middle income groups. What the consumers pay more in the form of 'marginally increased price' will be immediately compensated more than that in the form of 'higher-dividend-income'. A rise in price-level will always tacitly help the consumers to fill their 'income-gap' instead of exploiting them. The profit created will be drained to the consumers as they are the producer as well in the Prosumer Society. We have already seen there is 'tax-compensation profit' in the domain of National profit of the people. If the price-level is reduced to the point where it will cover only the 'government expenses', the people will get no dividend to enhance their income along with wage-income. The 'profit-free price level', though it will be comparatively low, will not help the low-income group of people to harvest the benefit of the 'dividend-income' to increase their total income. So the people will tend to push up the price-level up to a point where the national profit will be enough to yield 'higher rate of dividend' than the 'marginal increase of price-level.'

The higher volume of dividend than the 'marginal increase of price level' in respect of low income group of people will be termed as 'income gain' for them. We can term the 'income gain' as "Income Equilibrator" because it reduces the income gap between low and high income group of people as 'dividend will be distributed according-to-Investment-burden'. At a particular point on the curve of price level the poor will receive more dividend than the rich. Thus, the 'Income equilibrator' transfers a portion of money-income of rich to the poor bit by bit. This gradual transfer of money income will reduce the income gap between poor and rich and will tend to attain economic equality. The economic equality cannot be attained at a single stroke of lightning. The combined socio-economic circumstances should be taken into account. In the name of equality we should not crush and squeeze the rich. A universal harmony and consensus should prevail among the people in the attainment of equality.There are various points on the curve of price line at which the rate of dividend will be greater than the 'marginal increase of price level' such a point on the curve of price line determines the 'Just price' of the economy at a particular level of production.

Interest-free economy

In consequence of democratisation of economy the just price will act in smooth concerted way by increasing total income along with wage-income and increased dividend payment. Since any increase in the price level will increase the payment of dividend the total income, i.e. wage plus dividend, of the poor will increase their purchasing power. Moreover, the just price is determined by the universal consensus of consumers only. So, if the price level increases it is increased so in order to widen the profit margin and it will be effective to pay higher 'dividend – income' to the poor people. Therefore any increase in price-level will increase the purchasing power of the poor people but not forfeit it.

The vicious wage-price spiral inflation will not emerge in the democratisation of economy. Here there is no "market price" determined by the interaction of demand and supply forces, but only the 'just price' determined by consumers themselves. Therefore the mode of operation of the economy will be "inflation-free' of any kind.

Administration of Natural Resources

In the democratisation of economy it is the people, only the people, will take utmost care and absolute control over the allocation and allotment of Natural Resources. The natural resources are not only very scarce but also remain very source of all production and distribution of goods and services of any economy. The people will take exclusive control over the natural resources and assume full liberty and authority in their allocation to the various production and economic activities quashing government's participation in any way or in any form.

When the natural resources come under the direct control of the people, they will not allow the natural resources for the production of destructive goods like nuclear weapons which are now threatening the very existence of human race and such hazardous commodities like ganja, opium and other narcotic drugs which are harmful to human health. At present the narcotic drugs are widely spreading their wings throughout the world, especially among the youth, and posing hazardous risk to the very life of the people. Since there is worldwide network in trafficking and strong nexus among the politicians, executives and underworld dons in the business of narcotic drugs for monetary benefits ignoring the welfare of the society and taking no thought of the health of future generation, the enforcement of laws and execution of punishments seem to be ineffective and impotent on checking and abolishing of the flourishing of the trade day by day. The only solution now remaining at last is the democratisation of economy and entrust the natural resources in the hands of the people.

Saving of the Planet from Global Warming under People's Direct Ownership of Capital

Climate Justice and Equity: For a number of years, there have been concerns that climate change negotiations will essentially ignore a key principle of climate change negotiation frameworks: the common but differentiated responsibilities.

This recognises them historically that

(a) industrialised nations have emitted far more greenhouse gas emissions (even if some developing nations are only now increasing theirs);

(b) rich countries therefore face the biggest responsibility and burden for action to address climate change; and

(c) rich countries therefore must support developing nations adapt—through financing and technology transfer, for example.

This notion of climate justice is typically ignored by many rich nations and their mainstream media, making it easy to blame China, India and other developing countries for failures in climate change mitigation negotiations.

Development expert, **Martin Knorr**, calculated that taking historical emissions into account, the rich countries owe a carbon debt because they have already used more than their fair quota of emissions. Most scientists (if not most politicians) now believe that man's consumption of fossil -fuels and planetary deforestation activities are causing carbon buildup in the atmosphere and triggering global warming. The questions are how long, how fast, and how much damage is being done. **The scientist Flannery** believes that we are rapidly approaching the point where irreversible temperature changes will melt the ice caps, cause mass extinctions, and destroy coastal cities. Weather Makers is his call to act.

Elimination of nuclear weapons

If we deeply contemplate to find out the root cause for the production of "Weapons of Mass Destruction" (WMD) like nuclear weapons, ballistic missiles, poisonous chemical weapons, we deduce the fact that it is the State, only the State, having the ownership of capital, produces such kind of weapons throughout the world in the name of 'self-defense' or 'military balance' or to enjoy the dignity under the guise of 'super power'. These weapons are produced by the State without the knowledge and approval of the people, though the capital used for the production of such weapons, is ravished from the tax payments of the people.These weapons convert the whole world as 'open battle-field' and kill millions of innocent people. The people who pay the tax for their own welfare are not aware of the conversion of productive capital into destructive capital. They are always being kept in utter darkness.

The only solution for the people to save themselves from the nuclear holocaust is the immediate execution of democratisation of economy i.e. 'peoples' direct ownership of capital. Because on the direct ownership of capital people will not allow at any cost their capital and their industries to produce the 'weapons of mass destruction', and thereby to destroy-themselves. No summit meetings on reduction of nuclear weapons, bilateral or multilateral treaties on non-proliferation of nuclear technologies will ensure world peace. I believe the only hope for human survival and scope for the world peace anchor on the democratisation of economy apart from solving poverty and unemployment.

Elimination of Terrorism

The Statement, 'One man's terrorist is another man's freedom fighter', has become not only a cliché but also one of the most difficult obstacles in coping with terrorism. The matter of definition and conceptualisation is usually a purely theoretical issue but in the struggle against terrorism, the problem of definition is a crucial element in the attempt to coordinate international collaboration.

The destructive weapons in the hands of wrong persons induce them to indulge in terrorism. If there is no destructive weapon there are no terrorist activities. For instance, the terrorists cannot hijack planes with bare hands with the intention of destroying the twin towers of World Trade Centre in New York and terrorise the whole world by killing three thousand people at a stroke of lightning. In stationary vehicles, in flying planes and in suitcases arms and ammunitions and deadly explosives are used to kill innocent people. We can find no terrorists with bare hands to fulfill his political ends. There is a notion among people that Saudi Arabia is the epicentre of global terrorism where huge monetary resources are available in the name of heavenly law. The arms and explosives constitute the basic element for terrorism.

The production of such deadly weapons cannot be properly controlled and cannot be prevented to pass into hands of terrorists in the capitalistic mode of production whose only aim is profit motive but not social welfare. Before shifting the epicentre of terrorism from the Saudi Arabia to other parts of the democratic countries, we have to close all the venues and mode of production and distribution of destructive weapons. Even human suicide bombers cannot turn into terrorists unless they are equipped with explosives. The capitalistic mode of production is never effective to keep the self-interested capitalists under control in the production and distribution of such destructive weapons required by the terrorists. May the aim and pattern of terrorism be any design; the accessibility to the destructive weapons by the terrorists should be wiped out completely for the eradication of terrorism in the world.

Only in the democratisation of economy the people as a whole would have absolute ownership of natural resources and control over the allocation of them for production and distribution of such terrorist-weapons. The individual consumers will be served with only consumption goods; no terrorist group or the state will gain access to procure natural resources for the production and distribution of weapons that terrorists require. Sooner the democratisation of the economy sooner will be the world peace on the eradication of terrorism. If the views and visions of the people in this regard are clear and courageous, the result will be peace and prosperous.

Chapter – 6

Real and Electronic Moneys-
to Solve Human Problems

Dual Monetary System – An Economic Technique
To Implement The Theory of Democrism

"You can make even a parrot into a learned political economist all he must learn are the two words 'Supply' and 'Demand'" —**Anonymous**

"A review of this nation's economic history reveals that bankers, in concert with traitors in Congress, gained control of the money system, set up private "national" banks, began implementing its mechanisms of usury and were then taken down". —**"Thomas Jefferson on Monetary Policy".**

There are two economic techniques to administer economic machinery to maintain a perfect circular flow of money between producers and consumers at all levels of employment: one is **'multi economic technique'** and the other is **'mono economic technique'.**

In the 'multi-economic technique' only one kind of money would be used in circulation to maintain perfect operation of circular flow of money i.e. to uphold monetary equilibrium in circular flow of money between producers and consumers. All the global economists pursue 'one money system' in circulation known as 'Mono-Monetary System'. Mono-Monetary System means using only one kind of money. At present the existing 'consumption money' is used to operate both the production and distribution activities of any economy.

In Mono-monetary system we use the present money which has to assume responsibility to operate two self-contradictory functions such as 'medium of exchange', a dynamic one and 'store of value', a static one. Since money has 'store of value' and the people are fascinated with 'money illusion', they always prevent the flow of money into 'expenditure stream' at the rate at which money flows in their 'income stream'. This ever prevailing disequilibrium in the flow of money explodes all economic problems and the economists are crushing their brain to find a solution for how to solve it. This problem arose since the genesis of classical economy. This store of value of money not only prevents the spending of money by consumers at the rate required by producers but also stimulates the people to hoard and heap 'black money to run a parallel economy with huge volume of billions and billions of dollars in each country as the value of money will not diminish in short period. Moreover it also encourages corruption in all sectors of economy.

On the existence of single money in circulation – mono monetary system-to controlling and regularising all conflicting and muddling economic activities which are numerous heterogeneous. So that the economists are forced to practice 'multi-economic technique' through government budgetary policies and the Central Bank Monetary policies. This system has been extensively and indispensably used in all countries after Keynesian revolution though it could not succeed in its venture.

On the part of government it uses three types of budgetary methods known as deficit, surplus and balanced one to exert direct control over the expenditure and income of people through taxation, public borrowing, manipulating price level of goods, redistribution of income, offering subsidies, bailing out the collapsing industries by paying poor man's taxation etc. People are agitating why the governments pay billions and billions of dollars to save one man's wealth from the tax revenue of billions and billions of poor people. It is the fate of 'capitalist economy' i.e. capitalistic mode of production.

The government use three types of budgets known as deficit, surplus and balanced one to exert direct control over the expenditure and income of people through taxation, public borrowing, manipulating the price of goods, redistribution of money income etc.

On the other hand the central bank through its monetary policies by administering Bank Rate, Open Market Operations, Cash Reserve Ratio, repo rates etc., to exert indirect control over the supply of money through commercial banks. Usually the government and the central bank never cooperate with each other in controlling supply of money and goods and stabilize the required monetary equilibrium between producers and consumers. Both the techniques have failed throughout the world because people always behave in the market according to their erratic psychology but not in the desired direction of Government and central bank. In the midst of so many fiscal and monetary policies the economists ultimately confuse the administration of world economic systems. Consequently it is the poor people who are suffering at the end.

On the other hand, Democrism (the economic system of People's Direct Ownership of Capital) adopts only one economic technique known as

'Mono-Economic Technique'. I term this technique as 'DUAL MONETARY SYSTEM' to effectively control replacing both the central bank's monetary and government's budgetary policies which are heterogeneously destructive for consistent operation of economic machinery. In the Dual Monetary System new money known as 'Investment Money' will be put into circulation in addition to the existing Consumption money. I have scheduled a separate chapter for 'DUAL MONETARY SYSTEM' in which I have explained how the 'Investment Money' will operate the economic machinery with full steam.

(a) Stabilisation of economic equilibrium

When the investment money comes into circulation it will stabilize the economy at all levels employment. Its main object is to prevent the erratic psychology of consumers in spending erratically the consumption money which is badly in need of producers as money income by selling their goods to equilibrate with their money expenditure on producing the goods. In short it will assure the producers for maintaining their required 'monetary equilibrium' to sustain the volume of employment at all levels of production.

(b) Separation of dependency of 'goods flow' on 'money flow'

One of the serious impediments in the operation of economic machinery is the dependency of goods flow on the money flow i.e. G! = f (M !). The producers venture into production primarily for maximisation of profit in terms of money. The producers cannot realise their expected money income unless they sell the goods produced to the consumers. In other words the producers cannot realise their expected money income (inflow of money) unless they succeed in propelling the produced goods to flow towards the consumers. Since the consumers are in billions in numbers swarming the markets and are spending the money erratically and many a times hoarding the money, or creating time lags in spending the money the producers are horribly constrained to harvest the required money income to sustain the volume of production in succeeding rounds and are compelled to operate the economic machinery divergent velocities. This makes the producers to push the economic activities into recession and then depression. John Maynard Keynes attributes this economic terrorism to 'lack of effective demand' for goods. The interdependency of money flow and goods flow impedes the economic sustainment.

(c) Strategic performance of Investment Money

The only solution to sustain the level of employment and production is to separate money flow from goods flow and there by empower the producers to get monetary equilibrium between their money expenditure and their expected money income. In this juncture the DUAL MONETARY SYSTEM (DMS) occupies the predominant economic responsibility to keep the economic machinery to run in uniform velocity. Under Dual Monetary System new money known as "INVESTMENT MONEY" will be put into circulation without disturbing the present circulation of "CONSUMPTION MONEY". When the Investment Money comes into circulation, at the very same moment it absorbs the Consumption Money from consumers who have hoarded or created time lags in spending it. The Investment Money exchanges the stagnated Consumption Money which is indispensable for producers to operate the economic machinery with required acceleration. This economic technique will drive the 'money-flow and goods flow' to circulate in separate orbits according to the need of producers and consumers. In other words even though consumers do not spend money for the purchase of goods produced, the producers will get required volume of money for smooth operation of economy for spending for the factors of production to maintain the volume of production, employment and income of workers.

When the Investment Money comes into operation, the outdated and ineffective numerous fiscal and monetary policies will disappear. I have reserved a separate chapter to explain how the dual monetary system will operate the economic machinery.

(d) Interest-Free Economy and Creation of required Investment

One of the vital functions of Investment money is to create required investment for solving poverty and unemployment. The investment money will function as 'Side -Stream' to flow off investment from the main 'Income-Stream' of consumers (workers/people) to the 'Investment pool' of producers (workers/people). For example, if an economy requires one trillion dollars for investment the economic commission of workers will put into circulation the investment money to that equivalent amount during a period and the investment will absorb the consumption money from the people by the same amount of one trillion dollar without paying an interest.

The investment money so absorbed from the people will be credited in INVESTMENT ACCOUNT of the workers in the INVESTMENT BANKS operated by the existing commercial banks as their subsidiary units. The workers will contribute 'Investment according to their wage'. The investment money cannot be used as 'medium of exchange' to buy commercial goods and services in the market. It will be used as an economic technique to absorb the required consumption money which is firmly gripped by the consumers due to their money illusion or kept for speculative motive in terms of John Maynard Keynes.

The investment money will release the arrested consumption money to flow towards producers to maintain aggregate monetary equilibrium between expenditure and income of producers. This aggregate monetary will sustain the economic growth at all levels of employment.

(e) Corruption - free economy

In mid-November, 2009 the United Nations, the World Bank and other watchdog groups gathered in Doha, Qatar, in an effort to curb world political corruption costs and grant concrete authority to enforce the 141-nation UN anti-corruption agreement.

Lost monies hidden in corruption move from country to country and are placed in anonymous investments estimated to total up to $6 trillion.

"There's an estimate that $20-$40 billion a year, in terms of corruptly stolen assets, leaves developing countries to go to developed countries each year."

—OkonjoIweala, managing director of World Bank, said (Reuters).

The enactment of 'anti-corruption laws' and 'International agreement on anti-corruption' will not eliminate corruption. In India, 80 per cent of elected representatives, educational institutions and government officials are listed to be most corrupted people. Why they throng for corruption and why they are so hungry for gulping bribe? I think no man of wisdom so far contemplated correctly for the reason of it.

The basic reason rests on the bottom line of corruption is that if a man gets bribe he can spend that money to buy goods and services. Suppose the economic system is such that no man can spend his black money or corruption money or bribed money even to buy a single safety pin, he will not go for getting any corruption money. If he cannot buy anything with corrupted money, the money with him will be nothing but a waste paper. We want an economic technique that will convert all the corruption money to be useless or mere waste paper. What is that economic technique? It is nothing but launching 'Investment Money' into circulation under DUAL MONETARY SYSTEM. As soon as the Investment Money is launched into circulation it will regulate the erratic flow of consumption money into expenditure stream towards producers to maintain 'monetary equilibrium in respect of producers'. How this technique will work and eliminate corruption at its very origin?

1. Every worker/every person will have a Savings Bank Account as well as investment account in its bank for the principle of Democrism "Investment according to Wages". (All the persons should be the depositors in his bank especially middle-income and rich people as they are the indispensable persons who always indulge in corruption in huge volume. These persons are always in the domain of politics and bureaucracy.
2. There should be transparency and accountability in every one's bank account. Therefore the monthly and annual income should be specified in each account periodically as everyone's income changes though insignificantly in a year for example.

3. Beyond all perceptions it is indispensable to establish a 'business internet network' among the banks in coordination with distributive centres like super markets. A software technique will execute the internet network system.
4. **The application of technology (Investment money):** Suppose if a person goes to a computerised market to buy goods he will pay the bill. As soon as he paid the bill by debit/credit card (electronic money) the amount will be debited from his bank account. When he uses corrupted or black money to buy goods beyond his accounted money the bank account will send alarming signal to the distribution centre that corrupted money is used to buy goods and stop billing the account. With zero time lapse the purchaser with corrupted money (black money) will be caught by police.
5. In consequence as the people could not use the corrupted money to buy goods and services, the money received as corruption would automatically become waste paper to be discarded in the dustbin. Moreover these corrupted people will be severely punished. Even if they give the corrupted money as gift to others no one will receive it. They know what kind of fate will be waiting for them. There will be no receiver and giver for corrupted money. The world societies will automatically become a just and ideal one.

In their book Wikinomics (2006), Don Tap Scott and Anthony Williams explore the potential of Peer production for advancing business enterprise. As they observe, the emerging consensus is that business models that are based on mass production are slowly being eclipsed by new models based on mass collaboration.

Throughout history corporations have organised themselves according to strict hierarchical lines of authority. Everyone was a subordinate to someone else—employees versus managers, Marketers versus customers, producers versus supply chain subcontractors, companies versus the Community. There was always someone or some company in charge, controlling things, at the "top" of the food chain. While hierarchies are not vanishing, profound changes in the nature of technology, demographics, and the global economy are giving rise to powerful new models of production based on community, collaboration, and self-organisation rather than on hierarchy and control.

Volume: II

Causes for Human Problems

Chapter – 7

It is the Cause – I (Introspection)

*"Of all human sciences the most useful and most imperfect appears to me to be that of mankind; and I will venture to say the single inscription on the Temple of Delphi (Know thyself) contained a precept more important and more difficult to be in all huge volumes that moralists have ever written"**

"All the powers in the universe are already ours. It is we who have put our hands before our eyes and cry that it dark" **–Swami Vivekananda**

We, the people of all the countries, in violation of the supreme commandment of Economic Justice of holding one's due Capital under one's own control, have entrusted it, by our utter ignorance, to a few individuals in the name of Capitalism and to the State in the name of Socialism, and that ignorance has caused the basic reason for all the global socio-economic problems such as poverty, unemployment, economic disparity, economic insecurity, economic slavery, the ever threatening the nuclear holocaust and ever pervading terrorism.

I like to mention a famous quotation that if a fool throws a stone into a deep sea it will be formidable for thousands of intellectuals to take it away. We have committed such foolish act at every successive social transformations and social changes in the history of mankind.

Capital, the basic factor of one's employment and one's right to live, is like a diamond in the economy. Without knowing the value of it, in the Capitalistic society we have thrown it into the sea of capitalists and in the Socialistic society into the sea of State. By the reason of this even by the

* Jean Jacques Rousseau: "A Dissertation on the Origin and Foundation of the Inequality of Mankind."

thousands and thousands of intellectuals a solution could not be drawn out to eradicate even the very basic problems of poverty and unemployment.

It is as much dangerous to entrust our capital in the hands of a very few capitalists as it is entrusted in the hands of State because of the fact that capital is not merely a 'factor of production' to produce goods and services but also it possesses enormous 'Economic Power'. With the help of this economic power either the few capitalists or the State or the both will easily and efficiently exert control over the liberty and socio-economic-politico rights of people and design the law, art, culture and conventions, religion and education of society according to their views and visions. The economic power, moreover, has the authoritative and controlling power over all elements of political system, especially over the democratic rights of the people.

When the people entrust the capital to a State in the name of Socialism, the State immediately oppresses the 'Liberty' of the people who have created the State. Similarly when the people hand over the capital to a few capitalists in the name of 'Capitalism' the capitalists suppress the 'Equality' of the people. On the collision of the two opposing doctrines of capitalism and socialism the 'Fraternity' among the people has been depressed throughout the world.

It is the Himalayan blunder in the history of mankind that the people have handed over their capital in the custody of the 'Capitalists' or the 'State' due to the misguidance of their political masters. The unprincipled 'surrendering of Capital' by the people has become the invisible root cause for all their socio-economic problems. If it is so, a question subsequently arises 'to whom' capital would have been handed over for the benefit of mankind?

The answer is very simple. It is the 'man'. By the word 'man' I mean 'the working class as a whole'. If the capital is distributed among the working class equally no one will object it because it is their creation. The 'equal capital distribution' will be the supreme justice of all justices and it will be beyond all limits of contradictions. The working class should have 'Direct Ownership of Capital' because it is the working class who are the creators of all goods and services, of all principles and practices; because it is the working class who operate the societies and are operating in the society; because it is the working class who command the laws of society and are abiding by the laws of society; because it is the working class who constitute the governments and are transforming the same governments; because it is the working class who form the societies and in turn the societies form the working class.

It is the working class that exclusively represents the man. Man is the economic justice; the man is the social justice and the man is the political justice. Man is perennial and 'immortal' and indivisible even by time factors. Since there is no element superior than man in the world, the capital which upholds one's right to live in the world should be entrusted with the man only.

When the capital comes under the 'Direct Ownership of People', 'DEMOCRSIM' will emerge in the world as 'THIRD THEORY'of mankind assuming Capitalism and Socialism as First and Second theories. This 'THIRD THEORY' will perform as a guidepost to the people to establish an IDEAL SOCIETY for themselves for which they have been struggling since the time of genesis of civilisation.

Chapter – 8

It is the Cause – II (Economic Reasons)

We, the people, have to be pre-equipped with a comprehensive knowledge on the 'three economic truths' to find a solution for our hitherto tantalizing socio-economic problems such as poverty, unemployment, economic disparity, terrorism and nuclear war etc. and to lead the mankind towards an Ideal Society.

1. **The first truth:** It unfolds why manifold and heterogeneous economic systems such as Capitalism and Socialism have emerged among us and have divided the mankind accordingly.
2. **The second truth:**: For the second truth we have to understand what is the 'Technical modus operandi' of the different economic systems that they pursue to operate their economic machineries.
3. **The third truth:** For third truth we have to know 'how should an economic machinery operate in perfection' to solve our problems.

Among the three economic truths, the 'determinant factorial truth' is the third one for all human problems. It is not exaggeration to say that we are unnecessarily carrying on our head the poverty and unemployment, in particular, for not operating our economic machinery in perfection. We cannot shift the blame on anybody but on our utter ignorance.

The basic cause for emergence of various economic systems

The economic systems vary with each other in the name of different 'isms' on the determinant fact of 'who owns the capital'. If the national capital comes under the 'State Ownership' (i.e. owned by the State) we call it 'Socialism' or 'Communism'; on the other hand if it goes to the acquisition of 'Individual ownership' (i.e. owned by a few individuals) we name it

'Capitalism'. At present economic scenario the national capital, in considerable level is owned by the 'State' as well as by a 'few individuals' and we comfortably call it 'mixed economic system'.

The chemistry of capital ownership and various 'isms': On the question of whether the capital is owned by the 'State' or by a 'few individuals' and at what 'ratio', various economic 'isms' have emerged in the world.

In order to illustrate the differentiation between various 'isms' let me explain by a simple example. For instance we may take for consideration an 'automobile industry'. On completion of work, we can assume that all workers have the factory switching off all the machines. And the factory is now standstill.

Now the factory building, various machines, raw material, semi-finished goods, the stock of finished goods and other tools and instruments of the automobile industry enterprising in an inactive condition. If these 'capital stock' is owned by the 'State' it called as 'Socialism', on the contrary if it is owned by 'a few individuals' it is termed as 'Capitalism'

Irrespective of the ownership of capital by the 'State' or by 'a few individuals' the automobile industry ventures only to produce the cars as its finished goods. One different vibration of object is that the 'State' proclaims that it produces the cars for the welfare of the people whereas the few capitalists pronounce that the production is concentric for 'maximisation of profit' for their self-motivation despite the interest of society. Therefore, the chemistry of capital ownership and the 'motivation of production' determine various 'isms' though the production of finished goods and mode of technologies are the same and invariable.

What capital is today owned the 'State' may be owned by 'a few individuals' tomorrow and vice versa? Whoever owns the automobile industry, in our example, will produce the same finished goods, the cars, engaging the same machines and technology. No one can alter this automobile industry to produce 'computers' instead of 'cars'. Therefore, the kind of economic systems or 'isms' are decided only by the 'determinant factor' of 'who owns the capital'.

Basic questions of capital ownership: The capital ownership under 'capitalism' has been a historical evolution since the advocacy of 'individualism' by Adam Smith, the father of economics, but the 'State Ownership' of capital under 'proletariat dictatorship' was skillfully projected basically by Karl Marx, the revolutionary thinker, in the name of 'scientific materialism'. But the very elementary question tantalizing the mankind is 'who should own the national capital according to economic justice' to solve all the socio-economic problems of mankind.

Now I wish to preserve the vital question of 'who should be the justifiable owner' – whether it is 'a few individuals' or 'the State' or 'the workers as a whole under economic democracy i.e. industrial democracy'- in the forthcoming chapters.

Operation of Economic Machinery: At present I intend to concentrate my mind on two pressing problems. One is 'how is now our economic machinery operating in the direction of psychological factors of people? And the second is 'how should our economic machinery operate perfectly in harmony with economic justice?'

Chapter – 9

It is the Cause – III Defective Operation of Economic Machinery

A. How does it operate?

We cannot be victorious unless and until we understand the technical operation of economic machineries of all the systems, which behave uniformly identical but by disorderly. Prior to putting one step forward in our discernment we have to be aware of the fact that the 'law of economic mechanical operation' is distinct from the 'economic systems' such as capitalism and communism. In other words what I want to emphasise is the 'mechanical operation of economy' is the invariably identical whatever may be 'kind of economic system'. The ownership of capital may vary but the mechanical operation of the systems is the same. The intrinsic point is that there are no different mechanical operations for different economic systems. In order to illustrate the economic system and functional distinction let me take the simple 'physic-psycho' differentiation of man.

B. Psychological and physiological factors

Fundamentally the people are distinguishing themselves in characteristic qualities of their mind. In this evolution of thought the distinction may flourish in the name of religion, language, culture and conventions and socio-economic-political concepts. If we take the domain of language the people are again resort to various sub-divisions according to their different mother tongues in the name of English, Chinese, Spanish, Germans, and Dravidians and so on and so forth. Similarly on religious thought people are divided into Hindus, Christians, Muslims, and Buddhists etc. All over the world people are living in different segments and societies on the basis of the 'principle of thoughts'.

This psychological differentiation is natural and moral compulsion. But there is no physiological differentiation among men whatever may be their 'pursuit of thought'.

On visualisation of a man we perceive externally one head, two hands, two legs etc. and internally one heart, two lungs, two kidneys, a stomach, a small and large intestines, the blood veins and so on. Though men are differentiated by their 'thought' their 'organs and their functional operations' are harmoniously same. Every man in the world whoever he may be has the same 'functional operation of organs' such as 'the blood circulatory function', 'respiratory function', 'digestive function', 'excretory function' etc. are identical and homogeneous.

Though the 'Law of nature' constitutes the 'physiological functions' of man to be homogeneous, the 'Law of Thought' designs the 'psychological functions' to be heterogeneous.

In accordance with the man's physiological and psychological designs all the economic systems collectively as well as individually differ in their philosophy pertaining to 'who should own the capital' but all are similar in their 'operation of economic machinery' which explicitly denotes 'the circular flow of money' between producers and consumers.

Not only man but also all living creatures have attained perfection in their evolution. Man is mortal not because of his perfect physical structure but because of the defection or imbalance occurred in his 'functional operation of organs'.

Similarly man is infected with severe economic problems not because of the differentiation in the ownership of capital which formulates various 'isms' but because of the everlasting imbalance occurred in the functional operation of economic machinery in the form of 'imperfect circular flow of money between producers and consumers. How is this 'imbalance in perpetuity' existing in the 'operation of economic machinery' in the form of 'circular flow of money between producers and consumers'?

Keynes blames it primarily for the 'erratic psychological behaviour of consumers' in the market in spending their money- income in buying goods and services and thereby keep the producers in suspense to equilibrate their expected money income and real expenditure. The 'income-gap' primarily causes for poverty and unemployment.

Chapter – 10

It is the Cause – IV
Ten Basic Causes for Our Economic Problems

The Functional Law of Economic Machinery

The functional law of economic machinery is defined as 'a monetary equilibrium between the producers and consumers at levels of money supply'. Further the 'monetary equilibrium' denotes the money income and expenditure equilibrium between producers and consumers at all levels of employment or production or money supply.

The primary fact is that the 'functional law of economic machinery is an independent factor of economic systems. Whenever a country changes its economic system either capitalism or socialism, the functional law of economic machinery will not change. In other words one country can change the 'ownership of capital of an industry' but it will not lead to change 'requisite the monetary equilibrium between producers and consumers'. Whatever may be the economic system, the sustaining of the 'monetary equilibrium' is indispensable for smooth operation of the economic machinery. It is similar to the 'law of organic function of man' which is always constant whoever the man is in the religious or cultural platform. For example, man can change his religious colour but he cannot change his 'law of blood circulation' which is universally harmonious to all human beings.

A primary fact is that though the 'operational function of economic machinery' is independent factor of 'economic system', according to Keynes it is also 'dependent factor' of psychological behaviour of people.

In short how world economy does operate? The consumer-people are in multitudes. We cannot expect that they would behave rationally in the market in spending their money income to buy goods and services. Usually the consumers are controlled by their erratic psychological behaviour influenced by their religion, customs and conventions and mostly by fraudulent and immoral advertisements. When the consumers spend their money income erratically in the market it affects the 'expected income' of producers and they in turn reduce the level of production and employment. Whatever may be the economic system the economy of all the countries is always under the threat of monetary disequilibria between producers and consumers, which spread out all the socio-economic problems in the world?

The present defective operation

"Man is born free and everywhere he is in chains". He now realises that he has 'no right to live' anywhere; no constitution has offered him 'right to live' in its 'fundamental rights'.

Man wants to live in societies only to safeguard his 'right to live'. In these civilised societies man first wants to produce something useful to other members and then he wants to get his share from others to ensure his 'right to live'.

The 'Economic Functional Law' says: "Man should produce goods according to his energy and then distribute it justifiably according to his work (or need)". The circular operation in equilibrium between production and distribution is deeply rooted in the economic functional law and it constitutes the very basic foundation of it.

In the present scientific age a 'corporate systems of production in large factories' have been evolved rapidly. Huge and gigantic machines are put into operation. Mass production, mass employment and mass distribution have been occupied the economic activities. We can notice 'mass ness' everywhere. Under these circumstances we have to discern how the economy is operating with its inseparable defects in line with following 'Operational law of Economic Machinery'.

(i) **Mass employment:** Workers are hurrying and rushing to factories in masses day and night;

(ii) **Mass production**: Goods and services are produced in masses and in large scale;

(iii) **Equilibrium between outflow of goods and money:** In every factory it is assumed safely that at a particular time 'the rate of outflow of goods' and 'outflow of money' towards consumers are in equilibrium. It is further assumed or expected that the workers or the consumers with the help of their money-income exchange their wage-income in the commodity market to buy goods and services to ensure equilibrium between them.

(iv) **Consumers erratic psychology:** In the real and practical world the economy is not operating as we have assumed. Since the consumers are numerous and they have no economic coordination in spending money, the goods produced are not bought in the market at the rate at which they are produced. In consequence of that the producers are unable to sell the goods at the rate at which they produced for consumers. Since the goods are stocked in the market the producers have to reduce the level of production and employment. Therefore unemployment and poverty will always be a threatening problem to the global economy.

(v) In theory, according to the 'functional law of economic operation' what volume of money the producers set into expenditure steam towards the consumers at the time of production, they will expect at least the same volume of money from the consumers by selling the goods to carry on the second round of production. In other words the producers will expect at least equilibrium between their actual expenditure and actual income. But in practice this monetary equilibrium (Producer's Expected Income and Producer's Actual Income-Keynes) is not realised due to defects in our 'monetary system'.

Two Kinds of Monetary Systems

The most mysterious and highly complicated to understand is the 'operation of monetary system' in any economy. I wish to distinguish the monetary system into parts. One is 'Mono-Monetary System' and the other is 'Dual Monetary System'.

The Mono-Monetary System means the application of only one kind of money for production and consumption purposes simultaneously both for exchange of factors of production and commodities in the factor and commodity markets. Since there is only one kind of money the producers have to use the same money for the production of goods in the factor market and for distribution (sale) of produced goods in the commodity market. They have to get what kind of money they spent for production by selling the goods in order to carry out the second round of production sustaining the same level of employment.

Similarly the consumers (workers) have to spend what kind of money which they receive from the producers in the factor market to spend the same money in the commodity market to buy goods and services. By doing so the consumers set to flow in the 'expenditure stream' the same kind of money which the producers want to use it to equilibrate their 'expenditure and expected income' to proceed further production at the same volume of employment.

Irrespective of economic systems, the same kind of money is used both by the producers and consumers for different purposes i.e. for production and consumption. Usually and habitually the consumers are spending their money income with erratic psychological behaviour. Sometime they create 'time-lags' in spending the income, some other time they are 'hording or saving' the money and most of the time they indulge in 'gambling'. Such act of consumers prevents the producers to get 'what kind of money' they require for production. The producers, therefore, indulge in cut-throat competition to grab the money from the consumers.

At present all economic systems lack proper and competent economic technique to control the consumers' to spend their precious money-income rationally to ensure 'a monetary equilibrium between their rate of income and rate of expenditure at all levels of income'. This intrinsic monetary technical fault (Mono-Monetary System) is prevailing perpetually at every corner of the world and causes for all global economic issues.

Dual Monetary System

Dual Monetary system is an economic technique to control the erratic circulation of money. In this system there would be two kinds of money known as Consumption money and Investment money. The main function of Investment money is to control the 'circular flow of consumption money' which is in existence used both by the producers and consumers to execute their economic operations.

The Investment Money, if it comes into circulation it will keep 'a perfect circulation flow of money (consumption money) between consumers and producers' to operate the economy smoothly at all levels of employment. The main function of Dual Monetary System is to illumine 'how should an economy operate?' At present it is not our concern. We are now basically concentrating on 'how is our economy operating?' I have explained 'the operation of Dual Monetary System' in the chapter: 32.

The defective 'Economic Exchange'

By the term 'economic exchange' I mean two kinds of exchange of money executed by the producers and consumers. In other words one is 'production exchange' and the other is 'consumption exchange'.

In the 'production exchange' the producers use the consumption money i.e. the existing money in circulation, as a means of exchange in factor market for purchasing 'means of production', especially labour, to produce goods and services. In turn the consumers (labour) use the same money in the 'commodity market' to buy goods and services for their consumption.

If the consumers commit blunder as usual in spending the money at the rate at which they receive it, the producers will face short of income to produce the same level of production and cause for depression. In our present economic systems a same kind of money is used as 'medium' for all kinds of exchanges which are conflicting with each other. For example, the producers want 'high price' and more income than expenditure whereas the consumers want 'low price' and less expenditure than income. Neither the producers nor the consumers economically prudent and rational to maintain a 'monetary equilibrium between their income and expenditure'. This state of function cause the global economy to behaves erratically and irrationally, since the genesis of economic thought.

Money performs both 'constructive and destructive functions' simultaneously. Money always manifests itself to be 'la belly dame sans merci' (Beautiful girl without mercy). So it ever displays both the contradictory characters of 'hero and villain', 'virtues and vices' and 'dynamic and static'at the same time.

Money is beautiful, charming, essential and indispensable for the people to execute their socio-economic activities but in the same vein it spreads out all kinds of sins and economic viruses to endanger stable and sustainable economic development which we expect to solve our problems.

Money is entrusted with to perform two contradictory functions namely, 'medium of exchange' and 'store of value'. 'Medium of Exchange' is dynamic in character that promotes economic growth whereas 'Store of Value' is static in behaviour that prevents the economic activities come to halt.

The producers though they are very few have great economic sensibility and power of responsibility on effectuating the money to perform only 'the medium of exchange'. As long as the money functions only as the medium of exchange, the producers will continuously as well as progressively realise 'an equilibrium between their money expenditure on production and money income on sale' and operate economic activities without any risk and future apprehension on market behaviour despite the strong influence of the erratic psychology of innumerable consumers.

But the 'operational tragedy' of economy is that the money also functions as 'store of value' which conveniently induces the consumers, especially who are in the parenthesis of higher – income group, to hoard or save the money not to flow into the 'income – stream' of producers to continue their economic activities in subsequent rounds of production. The 'monetary and fiscal policies' of central banks and the government budgets respectively always fail to restore 'perpetual equilibrium between the income and expenditure' in respect of the producers to run the economy smoothly because of the fact that the 'erratic psychological behaviour of consumers' is tossing the producers vehemently like tsunami tide not to maintaining required economic equilibriums – real and monetary. This is the way how our global economies are crushed to operate harshly forever.

Imbalance between Savings and Investment (Leakage and Injection) Lack of Confidence

Economic activity is depicted as a circular flow of money. Spending by one individual becomes part of the earnings of another individual, and vice-versa. In practical world, however, people have become less confident about the future, and it is held that they cut back on their outlays and hoard more money. So once an individual spends less, it reduces some one's income and he in turn also cuts his spending. A vicious cycle is set in motion. This economic situation continues still equilibrium between income and expenditure reaches at lower level of income. The decline in people's confidence causes them to spend less and to hoard (leakage from circulation) more money; this lowers economic activity further, thereby causing people to hoard more, etc.

Ineffective 'Interest' technique : The neo classical economists and even the modern economists, some extent, believe that the 'interest technique' will convert the 'savings' into 'investment'. Investment is the "producers' money" by which they will buy or create capital goods to wipe out the unsold consumption goods to maintain equilibrium between overall production and consumption. No doubt the 'injection' of investment goods will increase further production, income and consumption.

Since saving enables the production of capital goods, saving is obviously at the heart of the economic growth that raises people's living standards. On this **Ludwig Von Misses** writes as follows:

> "Saving and the resulting accumulation of capital goods are at the beginning of every attempt to improve the material condition of man; they are the foundation of human civilisation".

Psychology of the producers

In the practical world of economic operation the 'interest technique' is ineffective because there is no particular rate of interest that will equilibrate all the savings with investment. The economies are experiencing a huge 'investment gap' as the investors are exhibiting more economic-concern over their long term 'expecting profit' (marginal efficiency of capital) rather than the 'existing market rate of interest'. A company's success is determined in terms of its profit. Therefore the profit has become the determinant factor of investment rather than 'rate of interest'. Since future is uncertain due to stiff competition of multi-national corporations, sudden disappearance of local corporations, change of government policies, unforeseen technological changes, unstable consumers' taste etc., the national producers feel insecurity in converting all the national savings into investment. This huge 'investment gap' has intensified unemployment and poverty in many countries. This is the way how the present economies are operating.

Misuse of Savings

Theoretically speaking the national savings should become national investment to restore the 'circular monetary - equilibrium between producers and consumers'. But the potential savers especially upper-middle-income people, rich and affluent, and supper-income people misuse their savings for economic gambling in stock markets, for social evils in night clubs, aiding for terrorism, funding for democratic elections, settling political scores, corrupting the bureaucrats, criminalising underworld dons, aggravating wars for material and human destruction[1] etc. Moreover huge volume of savings is kept in the form of black money to run a parallel or informal economy[2] and government mainly by the corporate sectors.

[Informal or parallel economy is economic activity that is neither taxed nor monitored by a government; and is not included in that government's Gross National Product (GNP); as opposed to a formal economy.

Pragmatically it is way how the global economies are functioning. There is no even near equilibrium between the rate of money-income and the rate of money-expenditure both in respect of producers and consumers, which is required to maintain a perfect circular flow of money.

Interdependency of "Money - Flow and Goods – Flow"

In our money using economy the 'medium of exchange function of money' plays a crucial role to explain how is the global economies are operating. In any economy 'the perfect circular-flow of money from producers to consumers and then from consumers to producers at the constant rate' is an economic necessity to sustain the level of production, the level of employment and the volume of income in the short run.

The basic economic fact is that it is the producers who occupy the pivotal role of determining the volume of production and the level of employment. The producers take risk in their venture of production only for 'maximisation of profit in terms of money'. The producers, therefore, always endeavour to achieve their 'monetary equilibrium'. It means an equilibrium between the rate of outflow of money and rate of inflow of money' at all levels of production to harvest their 'expecting profit'. We may define it as "Producers' Monetary Equilibrium".

The basic economic fact is that it is the producers who occupy the pivotal role of determining the volume of production and the level of employment. The producers take risk in their venture of production only for 'maximisation of profit in terms of money'. The producers, therefore, always endeavour to achieve their 'monetary equilibrium' which means equilibrium between the rate of outflow of money and the rate of inflow of money' at all levels of production to achieve their 'expecting profit'. We may define it as "producers' monetary equilibrium".

In our money exchange economy the producers could not realise their monetary equilibrium as soon as they produced the socially needed goods. Since the money flow and goods flow are inter-dependent the producers could not realise their 'expected money income' unless they sell their goods at a particular price. In other words the producers 'rate of production of goods and rate of sale of goods' should be at equilibrium. It is defined as 'producer's real (goods) equilibrium'.

It has ever been formidable task for the producers as a whole to realise 'real or goods equilibrium' because of the fact that the goods equilibrium is decided by the consumers in the 'commodity market'. In the commodity market the consumers are not buying goods at the rate at which they are produced in the industries. The consumers spend their money income erratically in the market; they create 'time lags' between income and expenditure; they hoard or save the money when their income rises; when their marginal income increases their marginal propensity to save also increases even more than the increase in marginal income. They consume or buy fewer goods.

The consumers are not economically rational or prudent to uphold equilibrium between their rate of money income and money expenditure. Since the consumers' expenditure is the producers' income, the producers experience 'income gap' to equilibrate their expenditure. In consequence of the 'income gap' they reduce volume of production, level of employment and volume of workers' income. The recession in economic activities continues as a vicious circle. It results in poverty and unemployment. This is authentic economic situation how is our economic activities are put into operation towards chaos and confusion. It is always true the producers are unable to equilibrate their money income and expenditure at all levels of employment or production. The practical 'monetary – disequilibrium in respect of producers' is the root cause for all problems.

Volume: III

People's Direct Ownership of Capital

(Democrism)

Chapter – 11

"People's Direct Ownership of Capital" – Why do we Want?

Denial of the natural justice of 'Right to Live' under Capitalism and Socialism

"Access to capital ownership, asserted Kelso, is as fundamental a human right as the right to the fruits of one's labor. Furthermore, Kelso argued, the democratisation of capital credit is the "social key" to universalizing access to future ownership of productive wealth, so that every person, as an owner, could eventually gain income independence through the profits from one's capital."

—Norman G. Kurland: Director,
Centre for Economic and Social Justice.

Capital triggers and intensifies wars

We, the people of all the countries, unanimously hate intensely the wars which germinate in any form or for any cause. Naturally we are peace loving people. Despite our strong desire for establishment of peace, innumerable wars have been fought all over the world and billions and billions of innocent people apart from soldiers, have been brutally killed and massacred and the skeletons of these people have been heaped like mountains in graveyards. What cause underlies for these wars? The answer may be attributed to a single word – 'the capital'. It is the 'Ownership of Capital' by a few capitalists or the 'State' that attributes for all kinds of war that negates one's 'Right to live' in the name of patriotism in particular.

Let us for time being set aside the wars fought before Industrial Revolution. The factory system facilitated for the production of 'weapons of mass destruction' that can be employed from the land, from the ocean and from the air. The whole world turned into open battle field for the nuclear bombs, ballistic missiles, supersonic jets, various kinds of military rockets and the military satellites orbiting the earth. Whatever might be the causes of First and Second World Wars, but their consequences were horrible that pushed the mankind to the very verge of its extinction from the earth planet. Why?

Wars before and after Industrial Revolution: Before the industrialisation the wars were fought on a particular battle fields and between two hostile warriors only. The range of destruction was very narrow and limited in coverage because the warriors used only spears and swords. The weapons were manufactured in cottage industries or by the warriors themselves. Natural boundaries like mountains, rivers, oceans and great deserts prevented the enemies to enter into an independent country.

After industrial revolution, weapons of mass destruction were produced with the help of highly sophisticated technologies with help of huge capital in factories owned by a few capitalists and the 'State'. The natural bounties disappeared and the whole world became open battle field. These weapons were maneuvered only by the highly skilled technocrats. The technocrats used these weapons on the common innocent people to terrorize the enemy-governments to surrender immediately. For example, in World War II USA used nuclear atom bombs to bombard on millions of Japanese civilians and terrorised the government to surrender without fighting in the battle field. Nowadays the battle fields are disappeared and the whole world has become open battle field in the face of mighty ballistic missiles and nuclear atom bombs. They can be produced only with the help of scientists and huge capital owned by the 'State' and a 'few capitalists'. As long as the capital is owned by the 'State' and 'few capitalists' we cannot escape from nuclear holocaust. Originally Capital was created by the working class to assist them to increase their productivity of consumption goods. As soon as the capital went into the illegal ownership of 'State' and 'Capitalists' it was used for the production of mass destructive weapons. If we scrutinize the expenditure of the world governments we can detect that a large portion of government expenditure has been allocated for 'military upgradation' than for the 'promotion of education' and 'elimination of poverty'.

Economic Theory of War

First "if the accumulation of destructive capital increases the temptation for war will increase and vice versa". The destructive capital means the capital that is used for the production of destructive weapons used by military forces. Secondly the difference in economic ideology of a country prompts it to increase its military power to show its ideological success over the other country and spread its ideology over other countries through war. For example,

USA and Russia used war as a weapon to spread their capitalistic and socialistic ideologies over other countries. The pages of recent past history will illustrate the fact and also the reason for accumulation of nuclear weapons and other variety of scientific weapons of mass destruction. Thirdly, on the globalisation of world economy the capitalist rich countries invest huge volume of their excessive capital in poor and developing countries. In order to protect their huge capital from nationalisation by the beneficiary countries a mighty military force is required by the investing countries. For instance the American war and threatening of war over Arabian countries to protect her huge capital invested in exploration of petrol and fuel industries. Now American capitalists are investing billion and billions of dollar in I T industries of India and other developing countries. The American capitalists believe that they can protect their capital by their country's military power. If any country try to nationalise these industries it will result in war. Fourthly, the over production of industrial goods by rich countries force them to dump their over production in poor countries through their military power.

Economic reason for two World Wars: Virtually after Industrial Revolution in most of the European countries the capital was owned by a few individuals. Since the very aim of capitalism was 'maximisation of profit' the workers were paid less and it resulted in deficiency of effective demand which caused for 'over production'. These European countries occupied the poor countries by their military power and converted them as their 'political colonies' and with the concept of 'Free Trade', they dumped their over-production in the colonies and also exploited the wealth of the colonies. India was the notorious example for that.

With the help of exploited wealth these 'mother countries' strengthened mainly their military power. The safety and security of the other 'Dictatorial European countries' which had 'State or less individual Ownership of Capital' were in jeopardy and unprotected in front of the mighty capitalist countries. On detection of the geographical track these countries found that there were no countries in the world to occupy them as their colonies for exploitation in order to increase their wealth and thereby their military power. These lately wakened dictatorial countries sniffed the fact that their 'political and military supremacy' would be pulled down rapidly on the downward track. In order to surpass the supremacy of the Capitalistic European Countries the 'Dictatorial European Countries, found no other alternative except 'war' on the Capitalistic European Countries and on their colonies all over the world. The 'lust for supremacy' over the other countries forced them to wage two world wars. Napoleon and Hitler waged war against all European countries because for the sake of supremacy.

Ayn Rand emphatically points out the genesis for the two world wars in his book 'Capitalism' as follows:

> "...... World War I was started by monarchist Germany and Czarist Russia, who dragged in their freer allies. World War II was started by alliance of 'Nazi' Germany with the Soviet Russia and their attack on Poland" *

In this nuclear age we witness a political and economic turbulence all over the world for a mad race for military equilibrium and economic supremacy. Both the Capitalism and Socialism have no blueprint to terminate the opportunity for Third World War. The rich capitalist and socialist countries want to become richer and richer by pushing the vast majority of poor countries to become poorer and poorer as per World Economic Reports.

At present the silent turbulence boiling in the poor countries will burst into a Third World War which will be fought between the rich northern countries and the poor southern countries of the world and result in nuclear holocaust. That is why the USA is very keen on preventing the proliferation of nuclear technology among the southern countries using its military might.

Economic Fraternity

The only way left for the mankind to prevent the ever threatening danger of nuclear war is the execution of economic equality among the global countries. In this perception rich countries should extend their helping hand to poor countries to pull them up from poverty and to help them to reach up to their standard ofof economic development step by step. Reducing the economic imbalance between rich and poor is the vital concept of "Economic Fraternity". But the capitalist countries will not permit the economic equality within and without but fight for upholding their economic supremacy which will be the ultimate cause for the Third World War.

The economic fraternity is as intrinsic concept as liberty and equality in the application of the theory of justice. Without the basic structure of economic fraternity the super structure of liberty and equality of justice will collapse. The theory of justice depends on two principles which ascertain the "social advantage of people" in any society.

The first principle explains the 'advantage position' of people **by birth** and by **derivation. By the term derivation I mean the derived advantages** of social welfare measures from society**. The second principle** explains the unavoidability of '**economic fraternity'** among the people structuring economic justice.

According to the first principle considerably a few billionaires and multi-millionaires and moderately some rich people who are put into

* Ayn Rand - "Capitalism: The Unknown Ideal" (New American Library, 1967) p. 37.

'more advantaged position' *by* ***birth*** such family wealth, social status and right parents and by welfare facilities ***derived from society*** like high qualitative education, special healthcare and rich social environment.

In contrast, a vast majority of people are put into **'less advantaged position'.** They are lacking good education, adequate healthcare, decent employment and reasonable social environment. They have to work very hard to compete with others to wipe out their poverty and to earn decent income to ensure their right to live and to maintain a reasonable value of social status. They are in the cover of Darwin's principle of **"survival of fittest".**

The people who put into more advantaged position enjoy derived benefits from society at the cost of the poor people who are put into less advantaged position. For example, in India the government spends 1,500,000 to 2,000,000 rupees apart from tuition fees to produce a doctor. This huge expenditure is borne by the vast majority of poor people who are put into less advantaged position, in the form of tax payment. Such doctors who are produced at the cost of poor, don't like to go to rural areas to serve the poor but want to stay in the cities or to go abroad to further enhance their 'more advantaged position' and enhance their **'economic power'.** By this economic power they become richer and richer and make poor, 'poorer and poorer'.

The principle of "Economic Fraternity" is applicable widely at global level. The countries in the northern hemisphere like US, UK, European and Gulf countries are put into more 'advantaged position' than the countries in the southern hemisphere, by nature and by derivation. According to the 'first principle' of justice, the countries like US have extensive fertile land, huge volume of scarce minerals, numerous perennial rivers, suitable climate for living and working conditions by 'Nature' and numerous colonies for exploitations of natural resources in the countries of poor southern hemisphere by 'Derivation'.

A solution for the second principle of justice can be found by the implementation **"Economic Fraternity".** The economic system of Democrism can implement the economic fraternity by applying its concept of "Distributive Justice". The people who put into "less advantaged position" will get more volume of dividend than the people who put into "more advantaged position". In other words the poor and low income group of people will get more dividend than the high income group of people on the concept of "Investment Burden". Since the investment burden of low income groups of people is more than the high income groups of people the former groups will get more dividend than latter income groups on principle of distributive justice. This destructive justice leads for implementation of "Economic Fraternity", the basic structure of justice.

Similarly this concept will be extended to global level. To implement economic fraternity the developed countries should extend their helping hand to poor countries in south hemisphere to pull them up economically step by step within a time period to reach their economic standard to par with them. This paradigm will be executed only by economic system of Democrism. This implementation will be the only long-term solution to prevent World War III and lead the mankind towards an Ideal Society.

We, the people, therefore, have no other alternative except to forfeit our capital from the capitalists as well as from the 'State' and to retain it under our 'Direct Ownership' to coordinate with the command of Natural Laws to save the mankind.

(a) Consequences of world wars and destructive capital

"The First World War was fought between 1914 and 1918. During the span of 4 years the war was fought violently 120 million seconds. Nearly 48 million people (including soldiers) were dead and wounded. In other word, in every 10 seconds 4 people were killed either dead or wounded.*

In the Second World War when the war was virtually approaching its end, on 6th August, 1945 an Atom Bomb by name 'Little Boy' – a new war machine that the mankind hitherto never experienced – was dropped on Hiroshima. Within 10 seconds one million innocent people were killed.

The First World War took 10 seconds to kill 4 people but the second world war, at its end, took 10 seconds to kill one million innocent people. The annihilation depends on the density of population of a city on which an atom bomb drops on. The Super Powers like USA and Russia, have now heaped in their arsenal million times more powerful atom bombs than the one that was dropped on Hiroshima.

No doubt the atom bombs that dropped on Hiroshima and Nagasaki were invented by the nuclear scientists. The billion dollar question is whether the scientists produced them with their bare hands or in cottage industries or in sophisticated industries created by huge capital. No capitalist will ever afford such huge capital for the production of weapons of mass destruction because their aim is always 'maximisation of profit'. Only the State can siphon huge capital for the production of atomic bombs only with the help scientists to threaten the other countries and to enjoy the status of 'super powers'.

Though the atom bombs are the brain-children of atomic physicists the capital required to manufacture them is funded only by the governments secretly against the wishes of the people. As long as the capital is owned by the governments, irrespective of Socialist or Capitalist governments, they spend

* Nehru, Jawaharlal: "Glimpses of World History": p. 637.

huge capital for the production of atom bombs in order to achieve military supremacy over other countries or to attain at least an equilibrium in military power. Extensively it is the hard-core radical politicians brain wash the people under the guise of 'patriotism', 'National security' and 'National pride' for the production of atom bombs and other ballistic weapons. Since most of the atomic scientists are the government scientists they have to produce atom bombs at the insistence of governments in the name of national security.

"In 1943 the Manhattan Project Laboratory at Los Alamos, New Mexico, with Robert Oppenheimer as its director, was assigned the task of developing an atom bomb. The first test at Alamogordo on July 16, 1945, was an outstanding success (the desert sand was fused to glass for hundreds of yards around the site). In August two atom bombs were dropped on Japan".

"Hiroshima inaugurated not only a new age of science but a new kind of scientists - the government servants whose knowledge and talent are an important part of the national arsenal. Furthermore, the scientists were now much more conscious of their social position and responsibilities. This was true in all advanced industrial countries, put particularly in the United States and the Soviet Union. Presumably, Soviet scientists were satisfied to follow the dictates of government leaders, but after World War II, Oppenheimer and other American scientists entered into a great debate over the human, political and social implications of atomic science and a profound searching of their own consciences. Oppenheimer resisted the building of the hydrogen bomb - a much more devastating weapon than the bombs used against Japan in the early 1950's, and he made important enemies. When Oppenheimer's security clearance was withdrawn in 1954, a great outcry from his colleagues expressed more than personal indignation. The Frankenstein myth appeared to be true, and the monster had locked the scientist out of his own laboratory. Certain branches of scientific research are not only secret today, they are expensive secrets; the cyclotrons and reactors of the 1960's are far beyond the means of any university or other institution without government support".*

I can arrive two conclusions from deducing the above historical facts:

Firstly, we have to free the atomic scientists from the clutches of governments.

Secondly, we have to forfeit our capital from the hands of governments and to keep it under our own control and possession.

Unless we, the people, forfeit our own capital from the governments and restore 'people's direct ownership of capital' we could not prevent the governments from the mad race for producing 'weapons of mass destruction' ranging from AK-47 to atom bombs (of 20,000 megaton attack).

---

* Cantor, Norman F. – "Western Civilisation: Its Genesis and Destiny" III –1970; pp. 528-529.

When we pay the tax-money to the governments, we intend tacitly that they would spend it to solve our poverty; but they do not do so. **In a speech on April 16, 1953, President Eisenhower said as follows:**

"Every gun is fired, every warship launched, every rocket fired signifies, in the final sense, a theft from those who hunger and are not fed, those who are cold and are not clothed ...

The cost of one modern heavy bomber is this: a modern brick school in more than thirty cities...... We pay for a single fighter with a half million bushels of wheat. We pay for a single destroyer with new homes that could have housed more than eight thousand people............

This is not a way of life at all, in any true sense. Under the cloud of threatening war, it is humanity hanging from a cross of iron......."

Professor Dallas W. Smyth of Illinois said,

"Billions for defense but not a cent for socialism. It is not socialism to have the government spend 50 billion dollars for weapons; it would be socialism if the government spent the same amount for education or for public works".

When we entrusted our capital to the capitalist as well as the socialist governments we constituted a tacit 'Economic Contract' with governments. The first and foremost element of the 'Economic Contract' was that the governments should utilise our capital to solve our basic economic problems such as poverty, unemployment, economic disparity etc. But the governments in violation of the Economic Contract have spent our capital to destroy our own survival by engaging in the production of weapons of mass-destruction. The governments with the help of scientists produce variety of ballistic missiles and nuclear bombs and test them day in day out to display their scientific genius and military power to other governments. The accumulation of such deadly weapons have now pushed the mankind to the very verge of nuclear holocaust. We, the people of all the countries, therefore, want to recover our capital from the governments and to keep it under our own control and ownership to preserve a perpetual world peace, our birth right.

The cause for dropping atom-bomb on Japan

There are two theories for dropping atom bomb on Japan. The first is to take retaliation on Japan for its attack on Pearl Harbor. The second is to prevent Socialist Russia to capture Japan.

The first theory does not sound reasonable because

Hitler committed suicide on 30th April, 1945. Immediately on 7th May the Germans agreed to unconditional surrender. Moreover Mussolini and his mistress were killed on April by anti-Fascist Italian partisans. Japan's position was now completely helpless, and the emperor supported a party in the Japanese government that wished to seek a negotiated peace. The Second World War was more or less approaching to its end.

The second theory sounds well because

On 16th July 1945 President Harry S. Truman - who had assumed office on Roosevelt's death on 12th April, - was informed that an atom bomb had been successfully tested in New Mexico. The US military found that no other weapon was so awful in destructive power as that of the atom bomb. At the same time the military forces of Socialist Russia were rapidly advancing towards Japan – the border country of Socialist Russia to capture it.

The Capitalist America was now in great distress that the Socialist Russia would not only capture Japan but also convert it a Socialist state. To uphold its supremacy America thought that it had no other choice except to execute two things:

1. To prevent immediately the invasion of Socialist Russia on Japan;
2. Instead, it had to capture Japan without sacrificing any more lives of American soldiers in the invasion of Japan.

In order to fulfill the above aims, the Capitalist America was left with only one option that was to use the awful new weapon - the atom bomb - on the civilians to force Japan to immediate surrender. Persuaded by the military strategy, Truman decided to use the bomb and it was dropped on the Japanese city Hiroshima on 6th August, 1945. About 80,000 civilians were killed immediately. Nearly 200,000 died later of radiation or were maimed for life.

On the sudden turn of events, Soviet Russia sensed that Japan would go out its hand though it was within its reach. So two days later, on 8th August, Russia declared war on Japan and crossed the Manchurian frontier as the Japanese army remained committed to a fight to the finish.

Since there was a race for supremacy between Socialist Russia and Capitalist America to capture Japan and moreover Russian army crossed the Manchurian frontier, the Capitalist America was forced to act swiftly. So, a second atom bomb – Fat Man - was dropped on Nagasaki on 9th August, 1945 by Capitalist America. Nearly 70,000 civilians died immediately. The following day the Japanese government offered to surrender. On 14th August the terms laid down at Potsdam were accepted and the Second World War was over.

The truth is still solid and sound that the atom bombs were dropped on Japanese cities not because Japan would succeed in the Second World War but because the governments of Capitalist America and Socialist Russia were arrogantly desirous to show their supremacy over the other as their economic systems were quite contradictory with each other. Both Capitalism and

Communism wanted to prove that it was their system that ultimately led the Second World War towards victory. This ideological conflict between the America and Russia, at the end of the war, resulted in nuclear holocaust of Japan.

There is no assurance to the people of all countries that another nuclear war will not burst out due to the ideological conflicts between the countries or to show their supremacy or for some other reasons the time will decide. Not only America and Russia but all the nuclear countries do not now wish either to destroy all their nuclear weapons or dismantle the industries which produce such weapons of mass destruction. Under these circumstances and ground realities how can we believe and console ourselves that yet another nuclear war will not threaten mankind and cause to vanish the very existence of mankind on the earth. So, we, the people of all the countries, declare to forfeit our capital from the few capitalists and the State and to keep it with ourselves. When we have 'direct ownership of capital' we will not allow our capital for the production of nuclear weapons or any other weapons of mass destruction.

Economic Justice in jeopardy and in peril

When we handed over our capital to a few capitalists, we were under strong presumption, that they would in certain sense, solve at least our basic problems of poverty and unemployment. On the contrary, since the very basic aim of capitalists is 'maximisation of profit' they execute all kinds of nefarious designs to exploit the labourers and treat them like other business commodities. So with the enrichment of new technologies the capitalists always intend to replace the workers or minimise the labour force by sophisticated machines. The capitalists have never shown any interest to promote the economic justice in solving the human problems like poverty, unemployment, economic inequality, unequal distribution of income and wealth etc.

But now the capitalists in some way or other have promoted the welfare of society only by way of promoting their own self-interest. In other words if and only if the capitalists are assured that their self-interest would be promoted then alone they will allow the betterment of welfare of other members of society. The welfare of huge majority of society is always considered to be a 'dependent factor of a few capitalists' in the system of private ownership of capital.

In other words the Welfare of Society (WoS) operates as 'function of Interest of Capitalists (IoC)'. We can write it as

WoS = f (I oC) .... (1)

The Interest of Capitalists, in turn, depends on their 'Maximisation of Profit (Max. oP). So the equation becomes

IoC = f (Max. o P) .... (2)

The Maximisation of Profit (Max o P) by the capitalists results in the 'Exploitation of Working class' (EoW). It may written as

Max. oP = f (EoW) .... (3)

The Exploitation of Working class (EoW) creates 'Misdistribution of National Income' (Md. o NI)

EoW = f (Md. o NI) ....(4)

The degree of misdistribution of national income exposes how the workers are exploited in a country. Generally speaking in most of the countries the top 10 per cent of population enjoys 80 per cent of the national wealth and only just 20 per cent of national wealth is distributed to a vast majority of 90 per cent of population. The mal-distribution of national income has always kept the vast majority of people to suffer with low purchasing power and in due course it results in over production. Due to overproduction the producers are forced to reduce their volume of production and level of employment. On finding the disequilibria that the goods are not consumed at the rate at which they are produced the producers are forced to close their industries. The very aim of capitalists, the maximisation of profit, not only crushes them but also the whole society. Therefore, the private ownership of capital will be dangerous to the whole society and the national capital should be equally distributed among the people for the welfare of the mankind. So, Bertrand Russell says:

> "Private ownership of land and capital is not defensible on the grounds of justice or on the grounds that is economical way of producing what the community needs"
>
> — Russell, Bertrand : "Political Ideals" (p. 35)

Equally the Marxian theory of "State Ownership of Capital" lacks perfection and threatens human rights. Marxian theory is formed on adamant and inflexible principle and it will not coordinate with the changing world conditions. It preaches a kind of 'economic fundamentalism' which wants the elements of society to remain in rigidity forever. So Loucks rightly states:

"Errors in the theoretical of Marxian thought are so serious and so basic that they cannot be corrected by interpreting or modernizing Marx not can they be considered superficial"

— Loucks: "Comparative Economic Systems" (p. 166)

Poverty in the midst of plenty

The World is not poor but the people are poor

"Being unwanted, unloved, uncared for, forgotten by everybody, I think that is a much greater hunger, a much greater poverty than the person who has nothing to eat." –Mother Teresa

4.1. Global Poverty: Year after year, like a thunderbolt of heaven, the World Bank alarms consistently that 80 per cent of global population is reeling under appalling poverty in the midst of plenty.

Almost half the world – over three billion people – lives less than $2.50 a day.

At least 80 per cent of humanity lives on less than $ 10 a day

More than 80 per cent of the world's population lives in countries where income differentials are widening.

The poorest 40 per cent of the world's population accounts for 5 per cent of global income. The richest 20 per cent accounts for three-quarters of world income.

4.2. Death due to poverty: According to UNICEF, **26,500-30,000 children die each day due to poverty**. And they "die quietly in some of the poorest villages on earth, far removed from the scrutiny and the conscience of the world. Being meek and weak in life makes these dying multitudes even more invisible in death."

4.3. Forfeiture of education: Based on enrolment data, about **72 million children of primary school age** in the developing world were not in school in 2005; 57 per cent of them were girls. And these are regarded as optimistic numbers. Nearly a billion people entered the twenty-first century unable to read a book or sign their names.

4.4. Weapons at the cost of education: Less than one per cent of what the world spent every year on weapons was needed to put every child into school by the year 2000 and yet it didn't happen.

4.5. Wealth Distribution: In 2005, the wealthiest 20 per cent of the world accounted for 76.6 per cent of total private consumption. The poorest fifth just 1.5 per cent. The poorest 10 per cent accounted for just 0.5 per cent and the wealthiest 10 per cent accounted for 59 per cent of all the consumption.

4.6. Poor man's burden: The GDP (Gross Domestic Product) of the 41 Heavily Indebted Poor Countries (567 million people) is less than the wealth of the world's 7 richest people combined.

4.7. World gross domestic product (world population approximately 6.5 billion) in 2006 was $48.2 trillion in 2006.

4.8. The world's wealthiest countries (approximately 1 billion people) accounted for $36.6 trillion dollars (76 per cent).

4.9. The world's billionaires — just 497 people (approximately 0.000008 per cent of the world's population) — were worth $3.5 trillion (over 7 per cent of world GDP).

4.10. Low income countries (2.4 billion people) accounted for just $1.6 trillion of GDP (3.3 per cent).

4.11. Middle income countries (3 billion people) made up the rest of GDP at just over $10 trillion (20.7 per cent).

Financial control

5.1. The total wealth of the top 8.3 million people around the world "rose 8.2 per cent to $30.8 trillion in 2004, giving them control of nearly a quarter of the world's financial assets." **In other words, about 0.13 per cent of the world's population controlled 25 per cent of the world's financial assets in 2004.**

5.2. For every $1 in aid a developing country receives, over $25 is spent on debt repayment.

5.3. 51 per cent of the world's 100 hundred wealthiest bodies are corporations.

5.4. The poorer the country the more likely it is that debts repayments are being extracted directly from people who neither contracted the loans nor received any of the money.

5.5. In 1960, the 20 per cent of the world's people in the richest countries had 30 times the income of the poorest 20 per cent — in 1997, 74 times as much. The shocking fact is when 26,500 children die per day on account of poverty the world spend $4.72 billion per day for military strength.

Global military expenditures hit $1.04 trillion in 2004 ($975 billion in inflation-adjusted 2003 dollars), nearing the historic peak of 1987-88, **to. Prep.**

In a world where billions of people struggle to survive on $1-2 per day, governments spend on average $162 per person on weapons and soldiers. ...

Bertrand Russell writes in his book 'Political Ideas' (p. 72) as follows:

> "The world in which we exist ......will pass away, burnt up in the fire of its own hot passions; and from its ashes will spring a new and younger world, full of fresh hope, with the light of morning in its eyes".

Forbidden of Right to Live and Right to Work

Throughout the length and breadth of the world we can notice the youth both in rural and urban areas bearing great agony in their eyes, having no value for their education are wandering desperately on the streets in seeking employment. The unemployment has pushed them to strip away their dignity, self-respect and equal status among others not only in the society but also in their own family. Everywhere they are treated as insignificant trivial and above all less than a human being. In the economic systems, both in capitalism and socialism, they feel that they have deprived of the possession of 'Right to Live' at all.

Origin of terrorism and economic crimes

It is partly true that unemployment generates economic insecurity among the youth. But by and large it victimizes the youth an easy prey to drug addiction, trafficking, terrorism, and other socio-economic evils.

The universal accepted fact is that capitalism cannot solve unemployment. The function of capitalism is such that if we want to adhere with capitalism we have to live with unemployment at certain level. The advocates of capitalism have now proved that full-employment in capitalism is only a myth and mirage. Hence as long as capitalism is prevailing in the world, so long as the socio-economic evils will also be pervading in the world as its by products and they will be deteriorating all the well-nurtured cultural fabrics of society. If we want capitalism, we have to learn to live with terrorism and other socio-economic evils.

Economic Equality is a Mirage

It is evident throughout the world, the economic inequality among the people not only within the country but also between the countries is going on widening with an accelerated momentum. In 1982, the per capita income of developed countries in average was 42 times more than that of developing countries like India and China, but the gap was still widening 56 times in 1989. As the gap is going on increasing the poor countries are becoming still poorer and rich countries are more richer. It is natural not only among the people but also among the countries to develop strong feeling of jealousy and hatred, and an impression of inferiority complex and a sentiment of economic slavery. In the complex and confused modern economic systems, the concept and reality of 'economic equality' is rushing over beyond the orbit of one's reach. In this context, our strategic fiscal and monetary policies are reducing to be insignificant to face the challenges. Hence Jawaharlal Nehru rightly blames the capitalistic system of economy for the economic equality:

> "Normally speaking it may be said that the forces of a capitalist society, if left unchecked, tend to make the rich, the richer and the poor, the poorer, and thus increase the gap between them"
>
> – Nehru, Jawaharlal: "The Years of Power" (1960) p. 294

It would be faulty conclusion that the economic inequality is inseparable function of capitalism alone; even in communist countries we can notice wide economic disparities among the people. Professor P.T. Baur states:

> "..... But there are evident wide differences in income in communist countries after decades of communist rule. And in Soviet Union (a country often thought to be dedicated to the removal of economic differences), the differences in income and living standards are quite as pronounced as

in some market oriented societies and this after more than half a century of mass coercion". – Baur, P.T.: "The Grail of Equality"

The economic equality is one the three basic necessities of 'Equality, Liberty and Fraternity' for the establishment of an Ideal Society. But neither capitalism nor communism do not know any effective economic technique to ensure us 'economic equality'. Hence I venture to say it is futile to allow our capital to remain in possession of some individual capitalists or the State.

Incompetence of Providing Right to Work

Invariably the 'Declaration of Independence' of all the countries proclaim that man has 'Right to Live'. On the introduction of 'Division of Labour' in the modern production system, no one can produce all the goods that require even to lead a very simple life, or a single whole commodity one needs.

On the Division of Labour, everyone is trained to produce only a part of a commodity for which he can receive his wage and with which he has to buy the necessary goods in the market to lead his life. Since a man cannot produce whatever he wants to live, his 'Right to Live' solely depends upon his 'Right to Work'. But no Constitution of any country is powerful enough to provide 'Right to Work' as one of the 'Fundamental Rights' because the economic systems that the countries pursue are basically defective and incompetent to face the economic challenges. In the absence of 'Right to Work' irrespective of what kind of economic system a country follows, the employers never consider man as a man and not even as a commodity. On the other hand they treat man as a 'rental commodity' that can be engaged by paying wages as 'rent'. The defect of economic systems have reduced man and humiliated him as mean and ignoble thing. With full of depression in his heart, P.A. Samuelson exhibits the real condition of man as follows:

"Since slavery was abolished, human earning power is forbidden by law to be capitalised. A man is not even free sell himself; he must rent himself at a wage" – Samuelson, P.A.: "Economics" (p. 52)

Absence of Stable and Just Price

Universally in all economic systems - whether it is market oriented economy or State controlled economy - the prices in the market are behaving erratically and disorderly. Especially the prices of consumption goods of poor people are always enhancing. But the income of poor people is not increasing as much as the increment of price of their consumption goods. Consequently, this economic phenomenon is horribly crushing the purchasing power of the poor. Hence the fact is universally accepted that 'the poor people are born in poverty, live in poverty and die in poverty'.

Whenever the governments declare that they have contained or reduced the rate of inflation it seems always to the benefit of the rich. The economic systems, existing now, do not know any economic techniques to sustain a just price level at stable for the welfare of the vast majority poor.

Deceits and Injustices to Working Class

In Jerusalem I heard the Israeli Supreme Court say: "It is better ten guilty persons be acquitted than that one innocent person be convicted".

This legal justice should not be confined only to the courts of justice but it should be equally extended to govern both the economic justice and economic systems. The economic systems, on the contrary, conveniently permit the economic criminals to escape from punishment and in turn punish the innocent workers who perform their social duty.

The utmost duty of a worker is to produce socially needed goods and services only; but it is not the duty of the worker to bear the responsibility whether the goods and services he produced are sold out. On the other hand it is the duty of the consumers to buy the goods and services that are produced for their consumption at a just price and at the rate at which the goods and services are produced for them.

On the contrary, the consumers, as a whole, behave in the market, guided by their erratic psychological factors, create time lags in purchasing the goods that are produced for their consumption and sometimes neglect the goods to buy at all. These negative and duly non-responsive factors affect the economy severely and ultimately result in the stagnation of goods in the markets. Due to the stagnation of goods in the market an equal volume of goods stagnated are not produced in the subsequent round of production. On the reduction of production of goods the workers who have fulfilled 'the production – duty' of the economy, have to lose their employment. The unemployment of a worker not only affects his 'Right to Live' but also of the whole family that depends on him. The unemployment of a worker ruins the education of his children, their future ambition in life and their morality and social dignity and their future economic security.

The present economic systems are not efficient enough to secure and the "Right to Live" of the workers who have honestly accomplished their 'production-duty'. To strengthen my argument I like to quote the words of Prof. Mrs. Joan Robinson below,

> "It is true, with adequate organisation there need be no unemployment … There is always something useful that can be done even with a man's bare hands"
>
> – Professor Mrs. Joan Robinson: "Economic Philosophy" (p. 114)

Joan Robinson too finds fault on the economic systems for wide range of unemployment; in other words, the economic systems that we pursue now are the primary reasons for the failure to provide "Right to Live" to the workers throughout the world. In the present economic systems and economic conditions 'employment' and 'Right to Live' are synonymous or just the same.

What is the basic cause, today, throughout the world, for billions of youth are crushed by the burden of unemployment?

Severe unemployment problems

"Every person, in equivalent to his standard of education and technical training that the society has offered to him, can produce socially needed goods with his bare hands or with the help of small and simple capital that he can afford by himself and thus create 'self-employment' opportunities and secure right to live by himself. The creation of self-employment creates an expectation in the mind of the worker that the society i.e. the consumers should behave with a sense of 'economic responsibility' by consuming the goods at the rate at which he produces, at a reasonable price to sustain the livelihood of the worker. But every self-employed youth knows that the 'economic responsibility' is absolutely lacking in the minds of consumers. What is deeply rooted in the minds of unemployed youth is 'a fear about the future' that the consumers or the society that he belongs to would not perpetually and automatically accept the goods at a reasonable price that he produces by 'self-employment'. The 'fear about the future' in the minds of the youth who wants to venture in 'self-employment' is reasonably justifiable. Due to 'fear on the future' the unemployed youth are not venturing in self-employment competing with the highly sophisticated industries. It is then whose fault if the youth are unemployed? The present economic systems have no economic techniques or 'action programmes' to evacuate the 'fear of the future' in the minds of the unemployed youth and to induce 'economic responsibility' in the minds of society to save the 'self-employed' youth from the competition of well-organised industries.

I have to point out it is the fault of the economic systems for the cause of unemployment and moreover I wish to state that the capitalists and equally the governments should not lay blame on the 'fate' of the youth for their unemployment. On the other hand, the capitalists and the governments are persistently blame the fate of the youth and try to escape from their 'economic responsibility'. So we have no other alternative except to forfeit our capital from the them and retain it with ourselves as we know perfectly well how to solve our unemployment and other economic problems.

Financial Gambles

The basic intention leading for the invention of money is it should be used as a 'medium of exchange' in buying and selling goods and services. On the contrary, our present economic systems have invariably paved way for the money not only to be used as a 'medium of exchange' but also at a large extent as a 'Medium of Economic Gambles' throwing away the honesty and morality of societies to the winds. The multi-millionaires, today, have idly and futilely invested billions and billions of money in the stock markets as a medium of gambles uprooting the very noble function of money. The electronic media and the newspapers extensively propagating the stock market indices for the benefit of the rich gamblers, the economic criminals, who want to earn quick and easy money without shedding even a drop of sweat. The present economic systems have accepted this kind of economic gambles without any shyness.

In addition, in the cradles of civilisation, especially in the places of sports and games like cricket stadium, Tennis courts, Football grounds, Boxing arenas billions and billions of money are set into circulation as a 'medium of gambles'. With the help of the 'capital-power' the capitalists today have vigorously transformed the noble arts, skillful sports, beautiful games and wonderful cultures into easy-money-earning centres instead of promoting these symbols of civilisation. The capitalists in the name of 'promoters' have developed strong hatred not only in the minds of 'players' but also in the minds of 'audience'. This kind of economic gambles is now rapidly spreading like dangerous virus in all four corners of the world. For example, the 'Statesman' in its 10th October 1978 issue states as follows :

"Britain is a gambling nation. Nearly 94 per cent of population indulge in an occasional flutter on races, at the gambling tables, on foot-ball pools or on a variety of other sports. Thirty-nine per cent of all Britons are habitual gamblers. In 1977, an estimated $ 800 million were stated on races and gamblers. In 1977, an estimated $ 800 million were stated on races and other sports".

Instead of producing socially needed goods and services and creating employment opportunities, the capitalists are utilising 'our capital' for economic gambles extensively and demoralising our long cherished cultures and civilisations throughout the world.

The capitalists now adopt a new business strategy to exploit the consumers: 'First kill the civilisation and then sell the goods'. The capitalists know the consumers will become an easy prey for sexual exposition. So they in all their advertisements use 'women in half naked beauty' to enchant consumers to buy their commodities. We know the capitalists are misusing 'our capital' to 'sexually assault' the consumers to maximise their profit at the cost of cultural destruction and spreading demoralisation. With deep mental agony I like to state that millions of young women have now turned as prostitutes as a source of employment and the International Labour Organisation (ILO) now recommends to accept prostitution as 'flesh industry' which contributes reasonable amount of foreign exchange for many countries.

Class distinction and failure of economic machinery

In lieu of promoting fraternity among the people the present economic systems create various class distinctions such as 1. Proletariat and capitalist, 2. Consumer and producer, 3. Savers and investors. The class distinction between proletariat and capitalist is always underlying at the bottom of strikes, lock outs and innumerable industrial disputes. The class distinction between 'consumers and producers' is attributable for the failure of determination of 'just price' in the market and for uneven distribution of goods among the people. The class distinction between 'savers and investors' is harmfully preventing the requisite acquisition of investment to eradicate poverty and unemployment expeditiously in the world. The present economic systems are full of contradictions without which they cannot function. Our capital in the possession of few capitalists and the State is the root cause for all class distinctions. Once the capital comes under the 'direct ownership of people' all the class distinctions will disappear.

Aim of maximisation of profit destroys morality of society

In the present economic systems the industries project their 'volume of profit' as the 'balance of judgment' of their determination of 'industrial success.' The industry which earns more profit is considered to be more successful. The mental attitude forces the even to destroy the natural environment extensively in order to produce goods cheaply. With the sole aim of maximisation of profit, the capitalists have no even an iota of concern over the future welfare of society, the physical and moral welfare of the people. And they use their investment only for the production of goods which yield high profit even at the cost of welfare of people and rare natural resources. Gus Tyler, exhibits the mean mind of capitalists as follows:

"The profit making corporate world is shamefully, almost criminally, wasteful. It is concerned with company profit now and not with social survival of tomorrow. Hence it produces whatever will sell good, bad or indifferent; it will use whatever resources as possible – no matter the damage to the environment. It does this not out of misanthropy nor miserliness but to survive and surpass in a system that equate profit with success"

— **Tyler, Gus: "Scarcity"** (p. 226)

Let us take Japan for example. Once she was highly disciplined and honourably cultured society. As soon as capitalistic mode of production gained the grass roots among the entrepreneurs, moral turpitude and corruption spread among the people widely like spread of virus. According to recent statistics, 1.8 billion people have subjected to alcoholic addiction. Forty-five per cent of Japanese women are habitual drinkers. In average every Japanese drink 15 gallons of alcohol per year.

— **Sen, K.K. "Comparative Economic Systems"** (p. 51)

In 1974 itself, USA has spent $ 26 million for the advertisement of alcoholic drinks, in term of Indian rupee it amounts to 78,000 crores; Britain spends $ 200 million per year for the drink advertisement. Though the drink addiction would spoil the families and the younger generation, the capitalists will be going on producing various kinds of alcoholic drinks because their only object is monetary profit but not moral benefit of society.

Destruction of Universal 'Fraternity-Justice'

In a civilised society according to the noble principle of fraternity the person who is put in 'more advantaged position', utilising such a position, should assume it his moral obligation to bring up the person who is put in 'less advantaged position' equally up to his position. By this way of moral obligation the persons who are in 'more advantaged position' should try to create an 'equal society'. This is the crux of 'Fraternity-justice'. This fraternity justice applies not only to the individuals but also to the countries for the benefit of the world peace and prosperity.

Applying this principle as yardstick for measuring the quality of 'fraternity-justice', the developed countries in the world, with the help of their abundant capital stock, sophisticated technology, scientific knowledge and technical know-how should strive hard to bring up the less developed countries equally up to their standard in order to promote economic equality among the countries. This, I wish to state, is the very essence of the fundamental principle of 'Universal Fraternity-Justice.'

On the contrary, at the advent of Industrial Revolution the developed countries i.e. the countries which were put in more advantaged position, converted the poor countries i.e. the countries which were put into less advantaged position, into their 'market places' to absorb their over production and to plunder the wealth of these countries and turned them into their 'political colonies'.

The capitalists of the very same developed countries today, utilising their excessively abundant capital, have established multinational corporations throughout the world, and with the help of these giant corporations the capitalists plunder the wealth of the poor countries by paying low wages to the workers and convert these countries into their 'Economic Colonies'. At first these poor countries were 'Political Slaves' of capitalists of developed countries and after attaining independence they have now become 'Economic Slaves' because of the fact they do not know how to solve their economic problems. The mammoth capital dumped in the poor countries are now under the protection of mighty military power of the developed countries and so that they cannot nationalise these capital and have to remain to be 'ever economic slaves'.

On the creation of 'Economic Colonies' by the multi-national corporations of developed countries, economic disparity has now deeply and widely created between developed and poor countries and it has bifurcated the world into 'rich north' and 'poor south'. The poor countries in the southern hemi-sphere of the world are now pointing accusing finger towards the rich countries in the northern hemi-sphere for their poverty, unemployment and for all other economic and political turbulences. They are now waiting for the world-wide bloody revolution to raze off unevenness. This may lead the mankind towards 'Third World War' and nuclear holocaust and day-to-day terrorism as common and universal strategy for immediate solution.

Since our capital is appropriated by the capitalists of multinational corporations they are at liberty to plunder the working class of all the countries and to hamper the efforts to promote universal fraternity. On the other hand they induce the countries to conflict with each other to gain a control over the governments to establish their corporations and to accumulate their wealth. Since the opportunities to cherish universal fraternity is perpetually prevented it will lead to Third World War for the benefit of the capitalists. So we, the people, have to forfeit our capital from these capitalists to save the world from total annihilation.

Sacrifice of liberty and equality

In his book "Principles of Social and Political Theory" Ernest Barker says that justice co-ordinates both liberty and equality.

"Justice is a joining or fitting together not only of persons, but also of principles. It joins and knits together the claims of the Principles of Liberty with those of the Principles of Equality".

— **Barker, Ernest: "Principles of Social and Political Theory"** (pp. 169-170)

Justice is something having high moral qualities that join together not only the people but also the principles. Justice should co-ordinate all reasonable expectations from the Principle of Liberty with those of the Principle of Equality. In other words justice is a collection of human rights that can be achieved from the Principles of Liberty and Equality. According to the grammar of Justice, in a society, people should be entrusted with liberty and economic equality as inalienable life elements. On the other hand, if any society is incapable of providing both of them simultaneously, such society will destroy itself in due course of time because liberty cannot survive without equality and equality cannot prevail without liberty. Liberty and equality are inter-dependent elements.

For example, unless we are entrusted with political as well as economic liberty we cannot distribute income and wealth equally to the people.

Similarly, if we are constrained from equality in income and wealth we cannot protect our liberty.

The capitalist as well as the socialist societies are not now established on the noble concepts of justice. Capitalism has proved inefficient to execute any economic technique to distribute income and wealth equally among the people. Owing to this stupidity and misdistribution of income it collapsed pathetically during 1930s throughout the world and more or less all the countries oppressed by 'Great Depression'.

Similarly, Socialism is still in a state of incompetent how to entrust political and economic liberties and rights to the people. People in the socialist countries have been subjugated to one party's dictatorial rule. The appropriation of liberty of the people has revolutionised the people to overthrow Socialism in 1992 Russia and other European countries.

The very survival of capitalism and socialism depends on their ideological cooperation in promoting liberty and equality but not on conflicts and contradictions. But on contrary their ideologies have been framed at diametrically opposite poles. Due to this confliction, it is not the systems, but it is the mankind that is ultimately going to be wiped out. So Robert K. Heilbroner warns the mankind stating as follows:

"Socialism and Capitalism will have to adjust their differences in ideology and national purpose show of the fond belief that the economic doom of the other is rapidly approaching"

— Heilbroner, K. Robert: "The Making of Economic Society" (p. 220)

Absence of Action Programme 'Towards One World'

The people of all the countries now realising the necessity of living in a Global Village, in the socio-economic-political environments, shattering all narrow domestic walls like religion, race, language, culture, nation etc. instead of fighting among themselves perching on hatred on each other. But the capitalists and socialists have no plan of action or pragmatic principle to lead the mankind towards the ultimate object of establishing "One World, One Government and One Humanity" translating the noble thoughts of the people into realistic action. Instead they indulge in fanning the fire of strife in the name of religion, language, patriotism and fundamentalism.

The reasons I listed above for forfeiting our capital both from the capitalists and the State, though, they are few now and multiply into many in future. They exhibit how capitalism and the socialism have simultaneously and equally failed in solving our problems. In this atomic age the crying need to save the mankind is to formulate a new socio-economic system overthrowing the present systems of capitalism and socialism. William O. Douglas*, the justice of supreme court of United States, like other thinkers, insists the need for such a new socio-economic order.

"The central problem of our time - one that is shared by all races and nationalities - is to discover the things, qualities and interests that people have in common so that durable institutions can be designed for mankind's survival"

— **Douglas, William O. "The Anatomy of Liberty"** (p. xxiii)

Upholding the Economic Justice the only alternative left before us to establish an Ideal Society for which we are longing for, is to forfeit our capital from the capitalists and the State and to retain it with ourselves. Since we have committed an historical blunder long before in entrusting our hard earned capital in the possession of some capitalists or the 'State', it is our utmost obligation to forfeit our capital from them in democratic way or if necessity demands in revolutionary ways by introducing some pragmatic 'economic techniques' to establish 'People's Direct Ownership of Capital'. In consequence of this a new economic order known as 'Democrism' would emerge in the world coordinating all the merits and benefits of both capitalism and communism. I venture to say we can achieve this by adopting a new economic technique known as 'Dual Monetary System' without forcing detriment on anyone physically or mentally. Since the operational technique of Dual Monetary System requires a detailed analytical study I have reserved a separate chapter No. 32.

The conceptualisation of new economic system - "Democrism" I assure, will, in the direction of justice, solve our socio-economic problems 'from poverty to nuclear war' and lead the mankind towards 'One World, One Government and One Humanity'. Now I am going to explain how to establish 'Democrism – The Third Theory' assuming capitalism and communism as first and second theories.

Chapter – 12

The Law of Economic Democracy

"Economic democracy is a socioeconomic philosophy that proposes to shift decision-making power from corporate shareholders to a larger group of public stakeholders that includes workers, customers, suppliers, neighbours and the broader public. No single definition or approach encompasses economic democracy, but most proponents claim that modern property relations externalise costs, subordinate the general well-being to private profit, and deny the polity a democratic voice in economic policy decisions. In addition to these moral concerns, economic democracy makes practical claims, such as that it can compensate for capitalism's claimed inherent effective demand gap."

Smith, J. W. (2006). *Economic Democracy: A Grand Strategy for World Peace and Prosperity.* ISBN 1933567023.

Democracy, generally speaking, is a loose word to portrait a form of government. It has been established in most of the countries by evolution through a long process of time. It is a transformation of government from 'Might is Right (to rule) to Right is Might (to rule)'. Here 'Might' means the Might of a person to rule over others and 'Right' means the Right of the people to rule over themselves.

The term Democracy is widely and conveniently used in politics mainly to protect vested interests. The definition of Democracy 'the rule of the people, by the people and for the people' lacks effective power of the people as a whole. The true intention of the definition is not followed honestly both in parliamentary and presidential form of governments but the definition is protected by the vested interests for their safeguard and benefit to curtail the voice of the people against injustice and cruelty.

In the multi-party system the democracy is reigning as the 'rule of the majority, by the majority and for the majority'. The ruler's i.e. ruling party, of majority and sometimes of less than majority occupy the reins of power with the help of money power of capitalists exclusively. No President in USA or Prime Minister in other countries and the Members of Parliament or Senate cannot be successfully elected (or contested) without the help of the money power of capitalists. For the sake of statistics and in theory though the rulers in democracy are elected by the majority of people but in practice by the capitalists at the backdrop. So people can exercise their power only at the time of election but the capitalists at all times over the government. If the government loses the confidence of the capitalists it will be dethroned though it is claimed that the government is elected by the people. So in modern democracy no government will go against the whims and fancies of capitalists to sustain in power for the stipulated period. The capitalists rule over country through 'their government' politically and economically.

Political Rule and Economic Rule of Democracy

"Political rule for the workers and Economic rule for the capitalists" or "Political rights for the workers and Economic rights for capitalists" has been the guiding principle of all the countries for the formation of constitutions which is supposed to protect democracy. All the constitutions are written by the capitalists or the politicians and legal experts blessed by the capitalists with sole aim of protecting the economic rights of minority capitalists from majority workers.

The framers of constitution with nefarious designs do not like the majority workers to enjoy Economic Rights that may endanger the interests of the minority capitalists. In the name of 'Property Rights' and 'Protection of Property Rights' they have entrusted all Economic Rights in the hands of minority capitalists. In the Property Rights, the framers of constitution have prohibited the operation of 'Distributive justice' which requires equal distribution of wealth and income among all the workers. In the same line of thought the framers have allowed the minority capitalists to accumulate wealth and income in disproportionate manner and to exercise their cruel 'economic power' over vast majority of workers and made them 'economic slaves'. A kind of economic slavery is prevailing all over the world irrespective of capitalism and communism. Here arises a distinction between Economic Democracy and Political Democracy. The former which is powerful and real for the minority of rich capitalists and the latter which is impotent and imaginary (delusive and deceptive) for the majority of poor workers.

When the Democracy is coordinated both by political and economic democracies, it is foolish and treachery that one for the rich and the other for the poor. Since allocation of two kinds of democracy is historically authentic we cannot be idle and mute spectators on seeing the collapse of very meaning of true democratic principles. Now I like to demonstrate how to entrust economic democracy along with political democracy to vast majority of workers.

Creation of Economic Democracy

Capital should not be considered as a mere instrument to produce goods and services. In strict usage of the term, an enormous economic power is compressed in capital. With the release of economic power capital will exert control over all the socio-economic-political activities of the people. The kind of ownership of capital determines what economic system a country follows. If the ownership of capital is given directly to the people as a whole on the 'distributive justice of equality' we can say the economic system follows 'Economic Democracy'. In other words Economic Democracy means direct creation of capital by the people and for the people. Everyone will have equal share of national capital and thereby equal economic power to protect themselves.

As the political democracy rests on the principle of **'one vote to one person'** so the economic democracy on 'one share to one person'. 'Right to equality' prevails in politics when we exercise 'one vote to one person'. And similarly 'Right to economic equality' can be restored when we exercise 'one share to one person' in creation of capital.

The concept of 'one share to one person' is concentric on the establishment of industries in democratic ways. It renders equal opportunity to all the workers (persons) to participate in the establishment of industries with equal value of shares. Let me explain in detail.

In the modern economic set up the capital for establishment of industries is acquired by issuing 'capital shares' in millions to the public. A few rich groups are allowed to buy more than 51 per cent of total capital shares by "interest bearing debt" from private commercial banks and vast majority of common people are left to buy only a meagre number of shares. Bu in the democratic economy the people or the workers would be empowered to buy (or allotted) equal number of shares on the equality principle of 'one share to one person'.

Suppose the establishment of a new automobile industry requires capital to the worth of ₹ 10 billion and the industry divides the capital into 1 billion shares of ₹ 10 each. Assume there are 1 billion workers in the country working in various industries.

On the issue of shares the 1 billion workers will buy the 1 billion shares of ₹ 10 each on the concept of 'one share to one person'. Now the automobile industry will accumulate the required capital of ₹ 10 billion from 1 billion shareholders. Now assume the industry employs 10,000 workers including workers well trained in business and industrial administration, whom we call 'works-managers'.

Since the 1 billion 'worker-share holders' of the industry cannot directly participate in the management of the new industry, they will entrust the management to the 'works-managers' of the company and the 1 billion worker-shareholders will take responsibility for smooth operation of the industry by keeping an equilibrium between volume of production and volume of consumption to sustain the level of employment, production and income. The profit earned by the industry will be distributed as dividend to all the 1 billion worker-share holders.

The works-managers should keep transparency and accountability in the management of the industry. They are accountable in the management of the industry not only to the workers of the industry but also to all the workers who are the shareholders of the industry. The establishment of all forms of industrial and business organisations in a country by this principle of democratic justice will be a continuous process whenever people buy goods and services in the markets second by second, minute by minute, hour by hour, day by day, month by month and year by year till the attainment of full employment in the economy.

Democratic mode of production

"One share to one person" establishes 'Democratic mode of production'

"Many shares to one person" creates 'Capitalistic mode of production' and

"No share to any person" organises 'Socialistic mode of production'

In practice we realise the people have to sacrifice 'Equality' at the altar of "Capitalistic mode of production and "Liberty" at the crushing feet of 'Socialistic mode of production'. However, the three noble dictums of democracy "Liberty, Equality and Fraternity" can be entrusted to people only in the 'Democratic mode of production'.

Instead of pursuing the distribution of 'many shares to one person' as in capitalism and 'no share to any person' as in socialism if the countries enact a law in the distribution of shares as 'one share to one person', the global economic scenario will change and the conflicts and the contradictions of the present economic systems will disappear. In their place of capitalism and communism a new economic system known as Democratic Economy will emerge and lead us towards 'One world' and 'One Economy' and perhaps towards world peace.

In the midst of explosive knowledge and high intellectual framework we need not to indulge in bloody revolutions but a general will to enact a law, just a law, is enough to transform the destiny of mankind from poverty to property, from unemployment to full-employment, from inequality to equality, from corruption to honesty, from economic insecurity to security, from competition to co-operation, from economic fluctuation to stability, from terrorism to tranquility, from fear of nuclear holocaust to the hope of world peace and much more. Once again I stress to say that the one law is **"one share to one person".**

In the Democratic Economy since all the workers will become the capitalists 'a classless society will be established without class struggle, Since all the workers will distribute national capital among themselves equally they will acquire equal economic power by which they will reap and restore the basic economic rights such as

'Right to Economic liberty',

'Right to Economic Equality',

'Right to Economic Security',

'Right to Participate in the Management',

'Right to own one's share of capital',

'Right to Work' and so on.

These economic rights are more powerful than the passive political rights such as 'Right to Speak', 'Right to Expression', 'Right to assemble', 'Right to vote', etc.to establish true Democracy envisaged by Abraham Lincoln and many champions who dreamed and struggled for effective Human Rights to create a just society.

VOLUME: IV

Economic Justices and Rights

Chapter – 13

Declaration of Capital Ownership Justice and Human Rights

Think free
Act free
Be free

it's your right

We the people, solemnly and sincerely, declare that it is the Universal Justice that only the Creators have the Right to claim absolute ownership on their creations and the Right to utilise such creations only for the benefit and welfare of the society in which they are inseparable members.

And that among the human creations the 'Capital' alone is the basic element for the very survival of humanity and genesis for the all human rights and modern civilisation.

Since the 'Capital' - the very basic factor of one's **"Right to Live"** and "Economic Security" - is collectively created by the people, the 'Right to own one's creations' empowers the people to distribute the capital directly and equally among them as per Natural Law.

That by securing the 'Economic Justice' of **'Right to own one's due capital'** (Democrism), we, the people are legitimately endowed with certain unalienable rights in consequence of owning Capital Right and among them are Right to live, Right to work, Right to equality, Right to liberty, Right to live with fraternity, and Right to participate in the management one's working concern and that of political government.

And that on achieving these rights the Natural Laws have further entrusted us the requisite authority to recapture our own capital which is now illegitimately and fallaciously in possession of some capitalists or in possession of 'State', by peaceful and democratic ways or in case of opposition by revolutionary ways because our oppressing poverty and unemployment and ever threatening nuclear holocaust could not wait patiently until the capitalists as well as socialists would find out solution leisurely in the endless time of future.

That on the basis of different composition of ownership of capital different systems of economy are instituted among us. The national capital is created by the people, only by the people and for the people. Since the people were unorganised and lacking intellectual administrative coherence in the production and distribution of goods and services in the complicated confusing economic setup, the people's capital was allowed to maintain in the hands of a few individuals and thereby a Capitalistic System of Economy was thrust among us and alternatively when the capital was handed over to the 'State', Socialistic System of Economy was imposed among us. We, the people handed over the capital either in the possession of a few individuals or the State with unequivocal hope that they would lead us towards an ideal society.

On the contrary, if both the systems realise that it is a formidable task for them to establish an ideal society even after consuming a reasonable span of time we naturally possess the supreme 'Right to forfeit our capital' from them and to keep it under our absolute control to establish a **'New Economic System'** and to organise it in such a manner to protect our socio-economic justices and to uphold our economic rights which underlie as basic structure of an 'ideal society'. By retaining our capital in our possession as per Natural Law we march towards a justifiable economic system in which 'People's Direct Ownership of Capital' is ensured out of all contradictions and it is the system which is vibrating perennially through all socio-economic changes from time immemorial.

Why do we demand 'People's Direct Ownership of Capital?'

By the term 'Direct Ownership of Capital' I effectively mean 'equal distribution of capital among the working people' or 'distribution of capital according to wages'. In other words we want to proceed one step forward to make perfect the universal truth of principle " Work according to ability; Wage according to work" by adding with "Capital according to wage" because both consumption and capital goods are manufactured by the workers and their wage should cover the value of both consumption and capital goods. Only the workers are entitled to buy both consumption and capital goods to uphold economic justice. On the contrary, if the production and ownership of capital goods are forfeited from the workers by a few 'capitalists' or the 'State' the workers will lose their 'Right to work' and consequently their 'Right to live'.

Right to live

On the outburst of Industrial Revolution during 1750s the mode of production and distribution was completely shuffled by the introduction of huge and complicated machines and division of labour. The village and cottage industries were replaced by factory system. Technological development and miraculous scientific inventions introduced a new concept of 'mass-ness' in the socio-economic sphere. There appeared mass production, mass consumption, mass distribution, mass education, mass communication, mass transportation etc. The village and cottage industry workers felt horrible and shocking on witnessing the 'mass-ness'. In the mass-ness they saw the price was cheap, the quality of goods was superior and there was variety of new goods. These workers realised that they would not produce goods competitively to the factory-made goods with their small and rude capital on which their 'right to work' and 'right to live' were depending on. Since their capital became futile they had to disown the basic concept of life 'own one's capital' to protect 'right to live' and 'right to economic security'.

Transfer of ownership of capital

On the destruction of village and cottage industries 'the direct ownership of capital by the workers' was transferred to the 'direct ownership of capital by the capitalists', a new powerful class emerged on the invent of industrialisation. The new capitalist class produced goods for all consumers for profit motive which resulted in naked exploitation of workers. The working class had to depend on the few capitalists for their work, for their wages and for their life and to sacrifice their 'right to work' and 'right to live' once they enjoyed in their villages.

Basic and Super Structures of Society

On the transfer of 'ownership of capital' which was the basic structure of any society, the 'super structure of society' which comprised of all the socio-economic-political elements of society such as mode of production, right to work, right to live, right to economic security, culture and conventions, concepts of religion, education, life style, formation and mode of governments, laws and regulations were also changed simultaneously in the same breath. There was change everywhere and in every element of life. People especially the working class found themselves in a new world full of embezzlement. The working class realised darkness around them and felt that they had become 'economic slaves' of a few capitalists. In the chaos and confusion of industrialisation the working class was mystified about their and drowned in utter ignorance of how to retaining their 'capital right in the creation of new capital' in the new factory system of production.

Misguidance by Adam Smith and Karl Marx

In the cottage industrial system the workers were able to create or buy their required capital individually because of their simplicity and cheap in value. But in the factory system mammoth and complicated machines were introduced in different types to produce a single commodity. The workers lost their individuality in creation of such machines which required huge volume of money and wealth. But by extending the basic economic principle from 'work according to ability and wage according to work' to 'capital according to wage' such huge and scientific machines could have been created. And the principle 'capital according to wages' could have smoothly, securely and peacefully transferred the cottage system of production to the factory system ensuring the workers to uphold their 'the capital right of owning one's own capital' which would protect their 'right to work' and 'right to live'. The workers of all the countries would have gained 'economic democracy' along with 'political democracy' and empowered to solve all of their socio-economic problems to establish an ideal society.

During the period of transformation of economy from cottage to factory system the economic systems were in the state of crude and infancy and the economic thoughts were mostly based on theoretical arguments instead of rational facts. An array of theoretical arguments were presented on the question of who should have the 'right to capital' first by Adam Smith (1723-1790) and then by Karl Marx (1818-1883). Both of them completely neglected the working class to regain their 'right to own their share of capital in the establishment of industries under the factory system also'. The reason for dereliction or abandonment of working class from getting their democratic right to own one's capital during that period might be insufficient infrastructure of economy like banking system and the complete ignorance of people not knowing the epicenter of all economic problems. And the ignorance is still prevailing throughout the world in the midst of knowledge explosion and great scientific wisdom.

Economic Affidavits

In the early period of economic-technological ignorance the lack of sufficient economic infrastructure and uncontrolled economic activities might have forced Adam Smith in his book 'An Inquiry into the Nature and Causes of Wealth of Nations'(1776) to declare a 'Capitalistic Economic Affidavit' that if the workers surrendered their due ownership of capital to a few capitalists that those capitalists would turn the sand into the gold and lead the workers towards an 'ideal society'. The capitalists used the advocacy of Adam Smith for their advantage by forfeiting the capital goods from the workers by brutal exploitation in the name of maximisation of profit. By insulating legal identity and economic justification for the maximisation of profit a few capitalists retained the lion's share of income and vast majority of workers were paid poorly and pushed into appalling poverty.

On ascertaining the exploitation of workers had been the breeding source of capital, Karl Marx vigorously engaged in a crusade for the workers' capital right. So he aggressively presented a counter affidavit in the name of Socialism in his magnum opus the 'Das Capital'(1867) and it was called as 'Socialistic Economic Affidavit' in which he advocated "workers' capital right" as if the capital should be owned directly by the working class. It was so preached that the factory workers would develop an assumption that each factory would be directly owned by that factory workers and the farmers assumed that each agricultural land would be owned directly by the farmers. The innocent socialists thought that 'each factory for that factory workers and piece each land for that land farmers'. Having such a thought of capital ownership deeply rooted in their mind the so called socialists led the bloody October Revolution in Russia in 1917.

On the success of the revolution the workers seized the factories and the farmers the lands by physically eliminating the factory owners and the land-lords. Since there was no guiding road map to ensure the working class to retain their 'direct ownership of capital' the revolution generated chaos and confusion, and caused for the collapse of whole economy. Lenin proclaimed 'All Powers to Soviets' and forfeited the national capital for the 'State Ownership' instead of 'Workers' Direct Ownership'. Stalin then suppressed the voice of the working class for their 'Direct Ownership of Capital' with his strong iron hand and raised iron curtain to prevent any entry of economic and political democratic principles into the country. The same episode was staged in succession in China by **Mao Tse-tung** through his **'Long March'** in 1934-36 and the 'War of Liberation' during 1937-1949. In all the Socialist countries the workers were denied the 'Right to Direct Ownership of Capital'.

However, the people's thought of socialism and Marx's thought of socialism was contradicting with each other. People were always kept under the illusion that they would retain their 'Right to Direct Ownership of Capital' in the socialistic pattern of society. But after the Revolution they experienced the reality was entirely different. At that time the economy was very young, the infrastructure of economy was very weak and the workers and farmers were illiterates. Though Karl Marx was targeting for the establishment of 'Direct Ownership of Capital', due to lack of adequate economic techniques to execute the noble principle, he was forced to preach on political platform that the workers should surrender their capital to the 'State' under Proletariat Dictatorship and that State would lead the working class towards an 'Ideal Society'. The socialist leaders followed the Marxian ideology word by word as gospel truth because they were also lacking knowledge on any scientific economic technique to execute "Workers' Direct Ownership of Capital".

Marx was forced to seek last resort to political violence to solve economic problems of 'who should own the capital'. Hence **'Proletariat Dictatorship'** and 'Statism'.

Both Adam Smith and Karl Marx had been in perfect coordination in abandoning the working class in retaining its 'capital ownership' when the question arose 'who should own the capital'. Adam Smith's 'Individualism' favoured a few capitalists and Marx's 'Socialism' advocated 'State' to preserve 'capital right' in their absolute possession by forfeiting the capital from the workers. Though the capital goods and consumption goods were produced by the workers they were permitted to receive wages up to the value by which they could buy only consumption goods. Both the capitalists and the State exploited the workers by forfeiting adequate money in the form of 'profit' and 'taxation' from the 'gross wage income' of workers to purchase capital goods. Workers' 'net wage income' was very meager by which they could lead only a poor life with inadequate consumption goods. Even now both the Capitalistic and Socialistic Economic Systems do not allow the workers to retain their 'capital right' and to own their due capital. With the historical experience of exploitation of workers by the capitalism and socialism we have now arrived at the following conclusion:

"We, the people, are now realising our Himalayan blunder that in contrary to the 'Economic Justice' of retaining our capital under our own direct ownership, we have stupidly surrendered it either to a few capitalists in some countries on the strong provocation of Adam Smith or to the State in some other countries on vigorous incitement of Karl Marx that they would lead us towards an 'ideal society' and that historical blunder in the past has been now exploding violently for all our socio-economic evils in every corner of the world, in the form of acute poverty, drastic unemployment, ever-widening economic disparities between men and men and between nations and nations, economic insecurity, vicious soaring of price levels and inflations, vehement class struggles, ever-pervading corruptions and economic gambles in the domain of share markets, annihilation of morality for capitalistic advertisements, polluting the atmosphere and destroying even the ozone layer in the guise of economic prosperity, widely triggered terrorism and above all the ever threatening nuclear holocaust to destroy our long preserved civilisations.

The capital will be divine as long as it will be in the direct possession of the workers the actual creators, and it will be devil as soon as it is owned by a few capitalists or the State, the exploiters.

Mode of production and the structure of societies

It is the truth and only the truth that the different kinds of capital ownerships determine different 'modes of production' and in turn the different modes of production determine different **'structures of society'.**

At the genesis of industrial revolution when the capital had been exploited by a few capitalists they developed a basic structure of 'Capitalistic mode of production' and established on its base a flexible super structure of 'capitalistic society', full of inequalities, insecurities and collapse of human moralities whereas when the capital had been forfeited by the 'State' it developed yet another basic structure of 'Socialistic mode of production' and established on its base a rigid super structure of 'socialistic society', full of restrictions on human rights and liberties and collapse of democratic principles. On the other hand if the capital is regained by the workers under the 'principle of direct ownership of people' (Democrism), it will develop a deep and wide basic structure of 'Democratic mode of production' and establish on its base an 'Ideal society' full of socio-economic equalities, liberties and fraternities. In short

"Capitalism is popular and popularly defective,

Socialism is destructive and destructively popular, and

Democrism is justifiable and justifiably acceptable."

Chapter – 14

Universal Declaration of Economic Justice

vs.

We, the people of the world, declare these facts to be the universal truths, only the truths and nothing but the truths that by exploiting our utter ignorance on the intricate operation of economic complex machineries during the sudden outburst of Industrial Revolution, both Adam Smith (1723-1790) and Karl Marx against the **'Economic Justices'** of retaining 'one's capital under one's direct ownership', misguided us to surrender our capital, created exclusively by us, to some capitalists in the name 'Capitalism' and to the 'State' in the name of Socialism, swearing solemnly in their respective written Economic Affidavit known as 'Wealth of Nations'(1776) and the Counter Economic Affidavit 'Das Capital' (1867), and that they the capitalists and the dictators of proletariat - would lead us towards an Ideal Society for the establishment of which we, the people of the world, have been struggling for thousands of and thousands of years since the dawn of history.

Due to our utter ignorance, we, the people of the world, had no other alternative except to believe the **'Economic Affidavit'** of Adam Smith or the 'Counter Economic Affidavit' of Karl Marx without least proportion of suspicion and therefore sincerely and honestly handed over 'our capital' to the capitalists in some West European and North American countries and to the 'State' in the East European and some Asian countries. Even now we are still ignorant that the capital which we handed over comprises inherently an enormous Economic Power' by which we can uphold not only all our 'Economic rights' especially our 'Right to live', 'Right to work', 'Right to participate in the management', 'Right to Economic equality' 'Right to Economic liberty' **and 'Right to Economic security'** etc. but also our fundamental 'Political rights' such as 'Right to speak', 'Right to expression', 'Right to assemble', 'Right to worship', 'Right to live with dignity', 'Right to live in peace', 'Right to govern ourselves' and so on. But to our utter disappointment even hitherto, neither the capitalists nor the socialists do not lead us towards an Ideal Society in their respective own countries and we have no iota of hope that they will fulfill their promises at least hereafter in the midst of highly complicated socio-economic conditions and ever threatening nuclear holocaust.

Considering all the historical facts we want 'People's Direct Ownership of Capital' as the only last resort over throwing the both capitalism and socialism because we have been witnessing severe socio-economic evils beyond our control in every corner of the world, in the form of acute poverty, drastic unemployment, ever-widening economic disparities between men and men and between nations and nations, viciously soaring price levels and inflations, vehement class-struggles and industrial, ever-pervading corruptions and fierce economic gambling in share markets, economic insecurity, war on a countries morality waged by capitalist advertisements to cheat the consumers, polluting the pure atmosphere and destroying ozone layers in the pretext of economic prosperity, inducing arms-race in the name of self-defense and balancing of military power and above all the ever threatening nuclear holocaust the ultimate end product of human conflicts.

The capital will be Divine as long as it will be in the possession of the people who are the actual creators and same capital will be Devil as soon as it goes in the possession of the "State" or a few "Capitalists" - the suppressors of working class. When we relinquished our 'Right to Capital' to the credibility and the honesty of the capitalists or the State we made agreements in the name of 'Constitution' that they would establish for us an Ideal or Just or Well-ordered Society and they accepted our agreements and established their 'Economic Systems' in the name of Capitalism or Socialism on the principle of their different 'Capital Ownership'.

Since Industrial Revolution the capitalists rejuvenating the form of capitalism have waged a vulgar and vindictive war in the 'socio-politico-economic fields' arming with complicated economic techniques and they have now ultimately presented us a defective capitalistic modal of society, full of contradictions and complexities, in some part of the world and after October Revolution of 1917 the Socialists imposed on us a destructive socialistic modal of society, full of violations and rigid regulations of human rights and liberties, in some parts of the world and ultimately both of them keep millions and millions of us in utter 'poverty in the midst of potential plenty' and now lead us to the brink of nuclear holocaust, the ultimate end-product conflicts between men and men and nations and nations, though we have more in harmony than in conflict.

We, the people, cannot endure such intolerable deceptions and hollow promises of capitalism and socialism for a long time to reach our **'promised land'.** So we proclaim that the Natural Laws have endowed us with 'the Socio-Economic Justices' to uphold certain unalienable rights; among them are the Right to live, Right to work, Right to own one's capital, Right to secure socio-politico-economic equalities and that of liberties, Right to live with fraternity, Right to acquire equal investment, Right to participate in the management of one's working concern, and that to achieve these fundamental rights for the establishment of an Ideal Society, the Natural Laws have further entrusted us with an omnipotent power to solve our problems by ourselves by forfeiting our capital from the possession of the deceptive capitalists and the arrogant Socialists (State) in peaceful and democratic ways or in revolutionary ways if we are opposed, since our poverty and unemployment and nuclear holocaust could not wait any more to annihilate us till the capitalists and socialists would find out solutions leisurely in the long stretch of indefinite future. Capitalism and Socialism can wait but not poverty.

We, the people of the world, solemnly and sincerely declare that it is the Universal Justice that 'only the creators have the 'Right to claim absolute ownership on their creations' and the Right to use such creations only for the welfare of the society in which they are inseparable members'. Since the 'Capital' is created solely by the people collectively, the 'Right to own one's creations' enforces the **Natural Laws** to distribute the capital directly to the people who have created it, and as the capital is now fallaciously handed over to a few 'capitalists' or to the 'State' who use them for their own benefits against the people's 'Right to live' which we have witnessed during the two World Wars and the nuclear bombardment on the innocent people of Hiroshima and Nagasaki killing millions of people within few seconds.

That to secure the **'Right to own one's due capital'** economic systems are instituted among the people. The absolute fact is that if the capital is owned by a 'few individuals' as in Capitalism or by the 'State' as in Socialism, just an opportunity given by the people to possess the capital by them. This opportunity is derived by a few individuals or the State is only transitory from the consent of the misguided people who created the capital, on two conditions. The first condition is that the capitalists or the State, should lead the people towards an Ideal and Well - ordered Society and the second vital condition is that if both the capitalists and the Socialists are incompetent after consuming a reasonable span of time to fulfill their obligations. We, the people, have unequivocal 'Right to forfeit our capital' from the present illegal possessors by peaceful ways or by revolutionary ways if necessary, and retain it in our own possession and control, and to form a 'New Economic System' which can be organised in such a form as seems to be the best for the safety and happiness of the people and lead the mankind towards an Ideal Society. Thus, the 'People's Direct Ownership of Capital' will not only be beyond all the contradictions but also a perennial instinct that vibrating constantly in all our socio-politico-economic justices. Why do we demand 'People's Direct Ownership of Capital? Why do we want to hasten the people to eliminate the capital ownership of a few capitalists or the State? The reasons are manifesting themselves below as historical facts:

1. That the two-third of world population is still living in utter poverty or in inadequate nutrition. Despite the working class have created and accumulated huge volume of capital-potentialities and sophisticated technologies with which we can produce more goods than the actual requirements for eradication poverty. But our economic systems are crippling with paradoxical element of **'Poverty in the midst of plenty'** justifying the views of J.M. Keynes;
2. That young men and women in billions have been roaming in the streets with great mental agony and dashing hopes in their eyes in search of employment and demanding their 'Right to live' throughout the world;
3. That the **unemployment** has not only created economic insecurity but also pushed the youth into moral degradation to become easy victims to violence, socio-economic-political and religious and patriotic terrorisms, drug trafficking and narcotic addicts and moreover unemployment has deprived of one's self respect, dignity and hope on the future;
4. That gulf of **economic disparity** is ever-widening day by day between men and men and between nations and nations. The noble concept of 'equality' seems only to be a mirage in our modern economic systems;
5. That every member of a society has 'Right to live' but it has been deprived of us. Though the 'Right to live' in the modern economic systems depends on one's **'Right to work'** no constitution in the world is competent enough to provide the 'Right to work' as a

fundamental right and it is because of the fact that the economic systems are defective and inefficient to assure us such vital rights;

6. That the ever **soaring price levels** and their erratic movements in the markets not only threaten the decision-making of producers but also crunch the purchasing power of the poor terribly. They have 'to born in poverty, to live in poverty and to die in poverty'. There is no prudent mechanism in our economic system to assure a just and sustainable price-level in the market;
7. That the present economic systems against the 'General will' of the people permit the riches to operate illegally a parallel economy propelled by huge volume of **black money** which empowers them to exert control over all of our socio-economic-political institutions, prevents 'equal opportunity' to the poor and induces envy and greed, and bias and prejudices among the people, and hostility and hatred in the minds of poor on noticing the luxurious and bombastic life style of life of riches. The economic systems allow the riches to establish themselves an insulated 'Island of Paradise' in the midst of vast 'Ocean of poor', though the **'Declaration of Independence'** of America (1776) for example proclaims that "We hold these truths to be self-evidence that all men are created equal .....". The Declarations of Independence of all the countries have now turned to be the symbols of mockery as they are exercising defective and ineffective economic systems;
8. That the **mal-distribution of income** and wealth by our economic systems forfeits our economic liberty and thereby justifies the immortal words of **Rousseau** that 'man if born free and everywhere he is in chains';
9. That our economic systems have no mechanisms to save our honest workers who perform their duties in producing socially-needed goods from the irrational consumers who often commit blunders in the markets in buying goods produced for them. If the consumers do not buy the goods the fault of consumers is shifted on the workers to lose their employment because of lack of effective demand created by consumers. **By losing their employment the workers cease to sustain their 'Right to live'**. Our economic systems provide predominant importance to the production and distribution of goods rather than to the creation and sustenance of level of employment. As soon as goods are not sold the workers will be ceased of employment and their wage income which is very source of their livelihood. For our present economic systems material goods are superior than the life of workers. In the words of **J.M. Keynes** that our economic systems determine the level of employment and income of workers by the effective demand for goods by the consumers.

Lord Acton says **'man knows how to produce and not how to distribute'**. Our economic systems do not develop any scientific strategy to distribute goods and income equally among the people in the midst of plenty and this ignorance keeps a vast majority of people under utter poverty. The world is not poor but the people are poor because of defective economic systems. The people are not for economic systems but it are the economic systems for the people. If the economic systems are not competent enough we should overthrow them immediately to save the mankind.

10. That our economic systems are invariably termed as 'Evil-provokers and evil-promoters'. They are permitting the speculators to hoard a huge volume of money for indulging in 'economic gambling' not only in stock-markets but also in foot-ball grounds, cricket stadiums, tennis courts, boxing rings etc. Money in invented to function as a 'medium of exchange' but our economic systems have assigned money to perform yet another function the 'medium of economic gambling'. Once Pliny told as soon as money was discovered the seeds of sin were sowed in the world. The present economic systems have converted money as 'source of sins and virgin of vices'. Next to biblical snake, money is now tempting all the people to indulge in various vices and sins.

VOLUME: V

Justices of Democrism

Chapter– 15

Workers' Administration Justice and Industrial Democracy

(A detailed study is presented in chapter 30 "How workers can rule a Nation Democratically by themselves")

In the economic system of 'DEMOCRISM' or **'Democratisation of Economy'** when the national capital is directly owned by the people or the working class as a whole every industry of the nation would be directly owned by the people. But the workers of the country as a whole cannot administer directly every industry. On realisation of such practical difficulties it would be prudent that the administration of each industry would be invariably entrusted in the hands of the workers who are working in that particular industry. It is the 'administrative justice' for which the working class has been fighting for years together as their one of their **'fundamental economic rights'.**

The worker is not a 'cog among cogs' of a rotating wheel of gigantic machines in an industry. He is not like a replaceable cog if one cog is damaged in a wheel as the capitalists think. Each worker is a human being who has absolute right to live in the world. The capitalists invest only their wealth in the industries but the billions of workers invest their labour, their future dreams and ambitions, the welfare of their family members, the excellence of education of their children and their future fundamental demands in their industries. Therefore in order to protect the workers and their economic security, 'the administrative justice' emphasises that the **'industrial management'** should be entrusted in the hands of workers of that factory. This is the only way to establish 'industrial democracy' in every industry. Cyril Smith, the staunch advocate of **'industrial democracy'** states as follows:

"I believe that industrial democracy is necessary, right and moral. Not only do liberals believe that a form of industrial participation is essential to the future welfare of our economy but also that is morally right that people who invest their life and strength in the future of a firm should have the 'right to participation' in its decision-making process. Nothing is more debilitating than to feel you are simply a cog in a wheel a cog that could be easily replaced"

—Cyril Smith: "Industrial Participation" (p. 152)

The industries will operate efficiently and effectively if and only if the administration of industries are entrusted exclusively in the hands of the workers. It will induce the workers to behave with high degree of responsibility. In consequence it will erase the industrial problems such as strikes and lockouts. If the industries are owned by the workers against whom they will strike? The workers will acquire a sense of economic security and stable employment stability. The workers will secure 'economic freedom' only if they are assured 'industrial democracy' in every industry widely and deeply. This eternal fact has been extensively pronounced by all socio-economic thinkers like Harold J. Laski in the following words:

"Citizens should be free from constant fear of unemployment and insufficiency. Economic liberty implies democracy in industry. This means that the workers should have a share in the administration of productive system"

— Harold J Laski: "A Grammar of Politics" (p. 147)

In the same line of thought Bertrand Russell, the great thinker, insists the important of industrial self-government as follows:

"The approach to a system free from...evils...is perfectly possible to proceed step by step towards economic freedom and industrial self-government"

— Bertrand Russell: "Political Ideals" (p. 36)

It is an accepted fact that the natural flow of administrative power of industries into the hands of workers will occur as soon as the capital is directly owned by the workers. Then the 'industrial democracy' will flourish in all the industries which produce goods and services. The service industries include even the educational institutions such as schools, colleges, universities, training centres etc. The administration of the educational institutions will be entrusted in the hands of the teaching staff.

Managerial staff: One vital point we have to note is that all the workers of every industry cannot look after the administration of the respective industry. Each worker will be specialised in a particular job under **division of labour.** Therefore, each industry will appoint a well-trained and educated 'industrial managers' to look after the management of the industry on behalf of the workers of that industry. There are numerous universities (like IIMs) which train and educate industrial managers throughout the world. Nowadays the management of all the industries are entrusted in the hands of these industrial managers.

In democratisation of economy the industrial management will be under the custody of the industrial managers. These managers are accountable to the workers of the industry in respect of production, marketing, pricing policies and in important **'decision makings'**. These managers should keep 'transparency' with workers in all the industrial matters. This is the essence of industrial democracy established on administrative justice.

Chapter – 16

Capital Ownership Justice and Distributive Justice

"Man is born free, and everywhere he is in chains. Many a one believes himself the master of others, and yet he is a greater slave than they. How has this change come about? I do not know."

—**Rousseau, Jean Jacques – 'The Social Contract'** (p. 100)

Economic Slavery and Ownership of Capital

Rousseau reserves no hesitation to admit his inability because of the reality that he witnessed the complications that deeply rooted in the premature socio-economic order that was existing during his time. But in the midst of knowledge explosion at present I can deduce the reason for the socio-economic slavery of the people. I know the answer for the slavery. It is both very simple and highly complicated to explain in the present context of permutations and combinations of socio-economic orders. The answer is very simple on the fact that as soon as the man surrenders his capital to a few capitalists in the name of capitalism or to the 'State' in the name of 'Socialism' especially after industrial revolution man has become a slave to the capitalists or the 'State'. On the other hand the answer is very complicated that requires deep acumen to find out exact faults and defects that have deeply anchored in every segments of socio-economic order like religion, customs and conventions, education, law, politics, and psychological behaviour of man; these socio-economic segments have still been propelling the views and visions of man to surrender his capital to the capitalists or to the 'State' instead of retaining it with himself to regain **'the economic power of capital'** to get rid of any kind of slavery. The surrender of capital is the utter ignorance of man that has ever been witnessed in the long stretch of the history of mankind.

A new kind of slavery known as **'Economic Slavery'** came to surface over the social fabrication during the Industrial Revolution. During this period of Industrial Revolution huge machines came to play a vital role in the production of goods and services. The owners of such huge machines in other words the capital, emerged as the masters of the society and the rest of members of society, a vast majority of workers, turned into 'economic slaves' in all the capitalist societies.

After the Industrial Revolution when these huge machines were directly owned by the 'State' the same workers in the name of socialism again became as 'economic slaves' in all socialist states.

This is the process of slavery what Rousseau says that man is born free and everywhere he is in chains. How do we have to shiver into pieces these 'chains of slavery' which are still binding the workers physically and mentally even in all democratic societies. The answer perches on the elucidation of the people to understand 'What is **Capital Justice**?' and on the finding out an 'economic technique' of 'how to entrust the capital directly to the people which is solely created by them?'

'What is Capital Justice?'

I venture to state the only reasonable approach to solve any problem is first and foremost to understand the problem, and to understand such a problem we have to stand under the problem with perfect view and vision of justice and without being a traitor to our own conscience. So it commands me to keep my thought perpetually in a balanced attitude without taking even a least privilege neither towards capitalism nor socialism. I believe myself I can settle with this pre-requisite condition before writing my concepts in the interest of justice and welfare of mankind. And now let me define the idea of 'Capital Justice'.

"'The Constitution of Natural laws' codifies the 'Economic Justice' being the basic structure of economic system on which the beautiful and pleasing elements of the super-structure of a well - ordered society are constructed".

Having the liberty of reason I wish to state that according to 'Economic Justice, the capital of a country is created by the people and for the people and hence it should be directly owned by the people'. Once the capital, which is now owned by a few or by the State or by the both, comes under 'People's Direct Ownership', consequently each worker is assured a direct share of national stock of capital. It leads to **'Each Industry for All and All Industries for Each'.** This is the crux of 'Economic Justice'. I announce it the **"First Economic Justice of Democrism"**, the supreme theory of all social and scientific theories.

"On the direct ownership of capital by the people in conformity with 'Economic Justice' , a new economic system known as 'DEMOCRISM' will emerge on the basis of **'Economic Democracy'** demolishing all the socio-economic evils that are futilely pervading in every economy due to its faulty formulation. For the sake of simplicity, I am assuming the Capitalism and Communism as First and Second theories and introducing my 'Democrism' as 'Third Theory' to differentiate it with present theories".

Right to Own One's Due Capital

The **"Declaration of Independence"** of United States of America proclaimed on 4th July, 1776 states as follows:

> "We hold these truths to be self-evident that all men are created equal, that they are endowed by their Creator with certain unalienable Rights, that among these are Life, Liberty and the pursuit of Happiness".

The 'Declaration' emphasises that among all human rights, one's 'Right to Live' is supreme, and it cannot be forfeited by anyone or by any force without the consent and confirmation of Justice. In the name of war or in the name of patriotism or in the name of religion or in the name of law or in the name of caste, creed and conventions no one has any divine or earthly authority to forfeit one's **'Right to Live'** on the earth. Even if a man dies due to appalling poverty it implies that the man's 'Right to Live' has been forfeited and the whole society should take collective responsibility.

In the modern economic systems no one can produce whatever he wants without the help of others. On the introduction of division of labour in the factory system of production, one can produce only a particular part of a commodity and he has trained and educated only to do the particular job. Under these economic conditions one's 'Right to Live' exclusively depends on one's 'one's **"Right to work".** In turn one's Right to Work always remains as a dependent factor of volume of capital or investment flow. If the volume of capital becomes insufficient, one's Right to Work will be affected and consequently his 'Right to Live' will also be confiscated. Since the supreme duty of every civilised society is to provide 'Right to Live' to each and every member. Moreover the 'Right to Live' is exclusively depending on the volume of capital. The society, therefore, should justifiably provide one's due volume of capital to uphold his unalienable 'Right to ensure his 'Right to Live'. This is basic concept of **"Capital Justice".** (Upholding **'people's Direct Ownership of Capital'** to ensure one's 'Right to Live' with dignity and security is the basic principle of Capital Justice')

Generally in economics we classify the goods produced as 'Consumption goods and Capital goods' depending of their usage by the final consumers. If the goods like 'cars' are used for personal usage by the consumers they are called consumption goods whereas if the same cars are used for 'hiring purposes, as taxis, to earn an income they are called capital goods. I am not erroneous to say that both the consumption and capital goods are produced by the workers as a whole. No one dares enough to advocate that the consumption goods are produced by the 'consumer-workers' and the capital goods are produced by the 'capitalists' or by the 'State', in capitalism and socialism respectively. Both kinds of goods are produced by the workers and only by their workers according to their ability as per 'Work Justice' (i.e. work according to ability).

The Wage Justice declares 'Wage according to Work'. The work includes the production of both consumption and capital goods as a whole. But the workers are not paid wages to equivalent value of the volume of capital and consumption goods that they produced. Both the capitalists and communists pay wages to workers equivalent to the value of consumption goods only. They have been nakedly exploiting a huge volume of workers' wages in name of profit by which they purchase capital goods which are solely produced by the workers. No one has derived neither 'divine authority' nor 'temporal authority' to forfeit a part of workers' wages in the name of 'capital' without the 'General Will' of workers or legal approval of working class.

The Power of Capital

The capital not only possesses huge productive capacity to produce goods and services but also enormous **'economic power'** like nuclear energy of an atom. With the economic power both the capitalists and the State can control all the socio-economic-political activities of the working class and subjugate them as 'economic slaves' and always threaten their 'right to live'.

I find no words to register my mental agony that a great 'distributive injustice' has been enforced on working class by negating distribution of capital against legal and moral grounds. This 'distributive injustice' exhibits the inherent defects that have been deeply rooted in our economic systems. Invariably all the economic and social thinkers have fiercely demonstrated such defects and distributive injustice. For instance, **John Maynard Keynes,** who is still considered to be the most intelligent among the economic thinkers, writes in his revolutionary book **"The General Theory".**

"The outstanding faults of economic society in which we live are its failure to provide for full employment and its arbitrary and inequitable distribution of wealth and income"

— John Maynard Keynes

Thus, Keynes has established the fact that the capital too should be equally distributed among the people to rectify the faults of our economic systems. I wish to state that if both the consumption and capital goods are distributed among the people in satisfaction of justifiable views and visions of Keynes, it will lead the society towards **'Democratic Economy'** i.e. 'DEMOCRISM', a new economic system.

The ultimate fact is the capital should be distributed among the people in coordination with **'Distributive Justice'** "All Industries will be owned by Each Worker and Each Industry will be owned by All Workers". In the establishment of such industries neither the capitalists nor the state would be allowed to claim any capital ownership. The creation of all the industries would be "by the people, for the people and of the people" **This would be called as 'Democratic Economy' or "DEMOCRISM" - The Third Theory – assuming Capitalism and communism are first and second theories.**

Understanding of Capital Justice or Democrism

The crux of the problem of understanding "DEMOCRISM" rests on the two theoretical pillars: Firstly, the process of distribution of national Capital (i.e. Capital Stock of a nation) to the people and secondly, the creation of 'new investment' of the people, by the people **Output Ratio:** Suppose the national capital of country amounts to $ 3,000 billion and the country produces $ 1,000 billion worth goods and services in a year. It indicates **the Capital : Output Ratio** of the country is 3 : 1. In other words in order to produce $ 1 dollar of goods the country requires $ 3 dollar worth of capital.

Again let me assume the annual income of a 'hypothetical worker' is $100,000 and he spends all his income for the purchase of consumption goods. Since the capital : output ratio is 3 : 1 for the production of $ 100,000 worth of consumption goods, $ 300,000 worth of capital goods would have been used. Siilarly according to the total income of all the workers, a capital stock should have been used three times of income. Generally speaking for the production of a particular amount National Income, a particular volume of Capital stock would have been used and it determines Capital : Output Ratio. This Capital Stock is legally entitled to the workers only but it has been fallaciously handed over to a few capitalists or the State. This is fallible of infallible justice. In order to uphold 'Economic Justice' the capital stock also should be distributed to all the workers according to capital : output ratio. This mode of proportional distribution of national capital to all the workers will guarantee and ensure an active powerful **'Economic Democracy'** among the people than the passive and week 'political democracy' to protect one's liberty.

In the modern production system since 'the capital' has occupied the position of the hub in the production of goods and services and moreover it determines one's 'right to work' and 'right to live' no worker is entitled to merchandise his capital to other workers. No worker is permitted to hold a share of capital more than his country's 'capital : output ratio'. Marketing of capital share in democratic economy is forfeited because of the fact it will lead to sell one's 'right to live', 'right to work', **'economic security'**, and 'economic equality'. Justice warns man not to sell economic liberty even if he can sell his political liberty.

Distribution of Capital: Capital is inseparable block. It cannot be divided into convenient parts to distribute to the workers according to their wage-income. It forms huge industries. The workers can only claim a **'capital right'** in the national capital stock and a **'dividend-income'** according to their share of capital. The capital goods cannot be distributed to the workers as consumption goods. But every worker can claim a certain value in the national capital to ensure their capital right. The value of capital would be distributed to the workers equally or according to their income. The distribution of capital is just a 'book-keeping entry' to assure every worker that they have a capital right in the national capital.

Every worker will have a **'Capital Account'** in his bank and a 'capital - share-value' according to his annual income will be credited. The workers will be strictly restricted to bargain his 'share of capital' to other workers as it is now practiced in the 'share-market'. The 'share-gambling' involved in the share market would be completely abolished. On the other hand, there will be only **'commodity market'**. Since one's share of capital represents one's 'right to live', 'right to work' and economic liberty and security the sale of capital will not be permitted at any cost in the **'People's Direct Ownership of Capital'** i.e. "Democratic Economy".

In the distribution of national capital to the people the 'capital : output ratio' would be taken as guideline to ensure 'capital to each worker according to his wage'. Right from ordinary village workers to the top-most managing director of a huge company the ratio would be strictly followed in the capital distribution as it preserves 'distributive justice'. No one would be afforded undue advantage to claim more capital – share than the one's income ratio. The aggregate national capital would be distributed to all the people without any discrimination of one's labour. This is the idea of 'Democrism' i.e. **'Economic Democracy'**. I wish to take liberty to express such kind of distribution would uphold the noble concept of 'Capital Justice'.

Mahatma Gandhi emphasises this capital justice in his own fashion of spiritual style as follows:

"We should aim at getting only what the rest of the world gets. Thus, if the whole world gets milk, we may also have it. We may pray to God and say: "O God, if you wish me to have milk, give it first to the rest of the world"

—Gandhi, M: "Speeches and Writings of M. Gandhi" (p. 384)

If any one wishes to portray his argument that the above example presented by Gandhi in the distribution of milk can only be coordinated to the 'distribution of income' but not the **'distribution of 'capital – wealth'**, Gandhi replies them as follows:

"Earn your crores by all means. But understand that your wealth is not yours; it belongs to the poor. Take what you require for your legitimate needs, and use the remainder for society ......But I have visions that the end of this war will mean also the end of the rule of capital. I see coming the day of the rule of the poor, whether that the rule be through force of arms or of non-violence".

— **Gandhi, M: "Harijan",** Feb. 1, 1942

The views and visions of Gandhi are placidly warning the capitalistic society that the capital – wealth should be honestly handed over to the people within the frame of supreme justice; otherwise, he cautions, that the poor would take even the deadly arms to uphold their legitimate right to own their capital through non-violence as the **'rule of poor through bullet'** instead of **'rule of poor through ballot'** that could be the only solution for all evils suppressing the poor.

Now I explain the basic concept of Democrism in ordinary terms. In Democrism in order to ensure a sense of security regarding the 'capital ownership' in the minds of every worker, 'a capital account' would be opened in his name and his legitimate due capital would be credited in his capital account.

The capital in the view of a common man may look like a commodity as machines and factory buildings. But it is not so in real sense. The capital contains in its core an enormous 'Economic Power' only by which one can save and ensure one's 'right to live' in the world, which is valued as supreme right of all the socio-economic-political rights. No worker, therefore, would be permitted to sell or buy one's share of due capital. Capital is not a marketable commodity because if the sale of capital 'in the form of share' is allowed among the workers, it is nothing but allowing the workers to sell their 'right to live', 'economic liberty', **'economic equality'**, 'economic security' and so on. The sale of capital would lead the workers towards their economic slavery; no political revolution can uplift them. That is why Rousseau says in his Social Contract ; "Man is born free and everywhere he is in chains".

It is Universal law that the natural force of all evolutions is to lead all imperfect systems towards their perfection overcoming one hindrance after another hindrance in its process. If the hindrances are many and powerful the natural force of evolution will consume more span of time to overcome them. "Perfection" is the law of nature; and "Evolution" is its mechanism. As per the 'natural force of evolution, the capital should be owned by all the workers to attain its perfection and to uphold capital justice. In this context we know that our economic systems are crippled with imperfection and struggle hard to move towards perfection, and therefore we have no other alternative except to wipe them out not to plunge the world into destruction.

As a matter of fact if both the imperfect capitalism and socialism want to move towards their 'perfection' as a rule of nature they have to restore the 'capital' to people and to ensure 'People's Direct Ownership of Capital' the ultimate end product of perfection in the formation of economic systems. The People's Direct Ownership of Capital would be out of all theoretical and moral contradictions and constitute a perfect economic system known as 'DEMOCRISM'. On the establishment of Democrism the capital will be owned neither by a few capitalists as in Capitalism nor by the State as in Socialism but the people of all the countries. This **"People's Ownership of Capital"** will be the rule of the nature and the natural force of evolution of any economic system. Nobody or no power in the world will resist it.

Chapter – 17

Socialistic Justice and Creation of Classless Society

"Classless society, in Marxism, the ultimate condition of social organisation, expected to occur when true communism is achieved. According to Karl Marx (1818–83), the primary function of the state is to repress the lower classes of society in the interests of the ruling class. However, after the class struggle has resulted in the victory of the proletariat and the establishment of a socialist society, there will be no further need for such a repressive institution; with the disappearance of classes, the state is expected to "wither away." **– Article, Encyclopedia, Britannica**

The supreme object of all socio-economic philosophies of mankind hither to discovered is to eliminate discrimination between man and man in his socio-economic fabric of society which he has created for his welfare. To achieve this aim Democrism i.e. people's direct ownership of capital strives vehemently to implement the 'socialistic justice' to abolish the class discrimination which appears primarily in the form of 'labour and capitalist', employee and employer', 'consumer and producer', 'depositor and investor' and 'haves and have - not's'.

Dual approach: In the domain of socialistic justice there are two approaches to establishing classless society – one is 'negative approach' and the other is 'positive approach'. In the **'negative approach'** no one would have 'right to property' but in the **'positive approach'** everyone would have 'right to possess equal property' and the 'national wealth would have been distributed equally or proportionately to all according to wages'.

Each for All and All for Each: In the 'negative approach' since no one have the property right the people would have sacrificed their 'economic security, economic power', 'economic equality', and 'right to work'. Socialism follows the 'negative approach' and suppresses the 'economic rights of people'. In the 'positive approach' the 'national property' or 'national capital' will be distributed to all the workers equally or proportionately according to their wages. There by 'each industry will be owned by all workers and all industries will be owned by each worker'. On the justifiable (equally or proportionately) distribution of property to all workers a powerful classless society will be established and the workers will be empowered with all economic rights 'each industry will be owned by all workers and all industries will be owned by each worker'. On the justifiable (equally or proportionately) distribution of property to all workers a powerful classless society will be established and the workers will be empowered with all economic right.

For the establishment of **classless society,** Socialism follows 'negative approach' whereas 'Democrism' or **'Democratisation of Economy'** follows the 'positive approach'. Socialism desires the 'State' to be empowered whereas the 'Democrism' wants the 'people' to be economically powerful.

Socialism is an empty glass bottle and the Democrism is a clean watered bottle but on the outlook both will appear as same as crystal clear. Whether both systems are same like glass bottles? Socialism is an illusion. However, the question is when we have 'positive approach' why should we follow the 'negative approach' to destroy ourselves?

1. Negative approach of Socialism : Due to historical necessity and naked exploitation of workers Karl Marx hurriedly advocated the 'negative approach' in the attractive name of 'Socialism' by which he demanded 'abolition of the right to property' to all. Karl Marx strongly believed that the classless society would be established if and only if the national capital was transformed to the 'State ownership' under the **'Proletariat dictatorship'**. The negative approach of **Karl Marx,** in due course of time by the modernising socio-economic-political evolution, anchored the root cause for the abolition of socialism throughout the world.

Stalin, behind the **'Iron Curtain'** in USSR and Mao, in the name of 'Cultural Revolution' in China crushed billions of workers in the name of establishing classless society blaming the cold and hot wars of surrounding capitalist countries specifically the USA which was known for upholding democratic values.

1. (a) Economic power of capital: The people have to bear in mind that the **capital is not merely one of the factors of production but it has energized with immense 'economic power' by which one can overrule all other socio-political powers.** Accumulation of capital in few hands is always dangerous and hazardous for any civilised society. It is an accepted truth that the accumulation of capital more and more in few hands it will provide a power of ruthless brutality and killer instinct to its owners. Without realising the economic power of capital the working class entrusted it to the 'State' on the advice of Karl Marx for the creation of classless society. On forfeiting the capital ownership from workers the 'State' acquired enormous socio-economic political power and crushed the very working class which created the capital. The working class in all socialist countries had to surrender both their economic liberty and economic security to the 'State'. The 'proletariat dictatorship' had become 'Communist party dictatorship' because the workers found that they had no 'right to equal capital ownership' but it had been forfeited by the party. The socialist workers slowly realised that they had been more deeply drowned into the muddy slavery than before.

The uncontrolled economic power is always dangerous. In this juncture I wish to point out the words of Harold J Laski:

"…..Power as such, when uncontrolled, is always the natural enemy of freedom. It prevents the exercise of those capacities which are released for activity by the absence of restraint. Wherever it is possessed in excess, it tilts the balance of social action in favor of possessors"

— Harold J. Laski: "Liberty in the Modern State"

1. (b) Consequences of 'negative approach' of Karl Marx: Since 1917 consistently for 75 years the Russian working class had been brutally suppressed by Bolshevik masters to restore the 'victory' of October Revolution. During the Revolution, the workers mistook that the national capital would be entrusted to them under the sensational and powerful slogan of 'the factories for workers and the farms for peasants'. But after the revolution the national capital was forfeited by the small coterie of Bolshevik masters in the name of 'proletariat dictatorship' against the wishes of the working class. Since the proletariats realised that their dream of 'capital ownership' was shattered into pieces they did not show any interest to work hard and to uplift national economy. So the State engaged secret agents and engaged military force to extract work from the proletariats. Even though the proletariats were crushed harshly to 'forced labour' like in the 'prison economy', the Russian economy marched towards depression year after year. Huge volume of money was spent on military and the 'military might' in World War II and the 'orbiting of first man –**Yuri Gagarin** - in space' was proclaimed as **'victory of Socialism'** when billions of proletariats were starving. The Russian economy failed in all sectors especially in agriculture.

It was **Michael Gorbachev** who realised the indispensability of political and economic liberties to proletariats and 'capital ownership to them' to induce productivity for 'taking off economy into sustained growth'. To give impetus to his 'counter-revolutionary thoughts' against Karl Marx, in 1992 he injected a small dose of capitalism and introduced **'Glasnost' (openness)** and **'Perestroika' (restructuring)** into the **orthodox socialist economy**.

As soon as the people of Soviet Union breathed the fresh air of the political and economic liberties they utilised the long waiting opportunity to muster their revolutionary strength and shattered the Union of Soviet Socialist Republics (USSR) into various independent states; they wiped out the slavery under the 'proletariat dictatorship' which falsely aimed to create classless society by the negative approach of Karl Marx. People did not wish even to attach the word 'Socialist' as a prefix to 'Russia'. The people's fury was so vigorous to consider that Marxian approach would be dangerous for their socio-economic liberties and economic development.

Moreover, the name of USSR was also changed as **'Commonwealth of Independent States' (CIS).** The word Socialism which was embodiment for 'classless society' was buried in its own soil due to negative approach of 'Socialism' or **'Statism'** (The Theory of Capital Ownership by State).

1. (c) Lack of Economic Justice: There is no convincing economic justice for making of State ownership of for people's capital; it never established on the 'General Will of the People'. Nationalisation or State ownership of capital is nothing but a collaboration of 'Policy and Decision-making System' of government for simplifying the rule over the economy. It is not the exclusive and the only justifiable way to proclaim nationalisation of capital for the establishment of 'classless society' capital. **The mere 'property right' without 'equal ownership of capital' is futile.** The mere 'property right' will strive to protect the huge wealth of a few capitalists to exploit the workers and will not help the poor to acquire legally eligible volume of capital according to economic justice.

2. (a) Positive approach of Democrism: The positive approach should rest on 'Economic Justice' and **'General Will** of the people'. Since the capital is created only by the working class it should be naturally owned by them alone. So 'Democrism' necessitates equal distribution of national capital or national wealth directly to the people (workers) as a whole. Every worker will be entrusted with constitutional right over the share of national capital equally or proportionately according to their wages. The workers will be endowed with inalienable 'property right' on their legal acquisition of a share in the national capital. The mere 'property right' without 'equal ownership of capital' is futile. The mere 'property right' will strive to protect the huge wealth of a few capitalists to exploit the workers and will not help the poor to acquire adequate capital according to their wages.

2. (b) Property right and equal distribution of capital: Positive approach emphasises equal distribution of national capital to the people at first and then legal protection to such capital ownership by enforcing **'property right' in the constitution**. When the national capital is distributed in the form of 'shares' to the workers, all the industries will be owned by every worker and every worker will own a share in all the industries. This justifiable distribution of capital will eliminate the discrimination between 'labourers and capitalists', 'depositors and investors', and 'producers and consumers' and pave the way for the establishment of 'Classless Society'. This is the real 'Socialistic Justice' to satisfy the aspiration of working class.

By this positive approach, people will equip themselves with 'equal economic power' and they would be powerful enough to protect their all socio-economic-political rights and liberties by their own. Hence 'Democrism' or 'Democratisation of Economy' is the only realistic way to establish stable and powerful classless society in the world.

A social class is, basically, a group of people that have similar social status. The relative importance and definition of membership in a particular class differs greatly over time and between societies, particularly in societies having a legal differentiation of groups of people by birth or occupation.

Many scholars view societies as stratifying into a hierarchical system of "socioeconomic classes" based on economic status, wealth, or income. From ancient history until the development of trade and industry, many historians and economists used a bi-partite model to view societies as consisting of an upper class of the immensely wealthy and powerful, and a lower class of the poor and weak. The development of urbanisation and trade, and later of industrialisation, resulted in the emergence of an increasingly powerful economic middle class of artisans, merchants, manufacturers, and highly paid professionals.

Chapter – 18

Interest-Free Economy and Workers' Investment Justice

"Those who swallow down usury cannot arise except as one whom Shaitan has prostrated by (his) touch does rise. That is because they say, trading is only like usury; and Allah has allowed trading and forbidden usury. To whomsoever then the admonition has come from his Lord, then he desists, he shall have what has already passed, and his affair is in the hands of Allah; and whoever returns (to it) - These are the inmates of the fire; they shall abide in it. —**Surah al-Baqarah** 2:275

"The most powerful force in the universe is compound interest"

– **Albert Einstein**

"Compound interest is the eighth wonder of the world. He who understands it, earns it he who doesn't pay it." – **Albert Einstein**

1. (a) Bearing Economic Responsibility: In Democrism when the national capital is directly owned by the people, every worker will claim equal share in the accumulated capital of all the industries. If the workers want the **'Capital Right'** in the national capital created by the past workers, the present workers should equally bear an 'Economic Responsibility' for **creation of 'new capital.'** Why?

Firstly, in Democrism if the workers in the capacity of capitalists do not create new capital in the form of investment the economy will stagnate and all other economic activities such as the marginal increase in the level of employment, production, consumption and income will come to a grinding halt.

Secondly, the people should be aware of the fact that the capital is not only just one of the factors of production and a great source of economic power; but also it is an unbreakable **'Time Chain'** which links 'workers of yesterday, today and tomorrow'. It is 'time chain' because yesterday's investment becomes today's capital and today's investment becomes tomorrow's capital. Therefore, it is utmost duty of every worker to preserve 'this time chain of capital' to sustain the economic development.

I wish to explain the working of 'the time chain of capital' by an example. Let us assume that a worker in a factory is working with an average capital of $100,000. This volume of capital is not brought into factory by the worker. This volume of capital has already been created in the factory by the workers of yesterday so that he has been able to get a job in that factory. 'Since the 'workers of yesterday' has already created capital the 'workers of today' are now acquired an opportunity to work.. Similarly if and only if the 'workers of today' create new capital the 'workers of tomorrow' will get job opportunity. This is an irrefutable economic truth. Hence the life of all workers are tied inseparably with **'labour - fraternity'** by 'yesterday, today and tomorrow'. If 'the workers of yesterday' had not been created any capital 'the workers of today' would not have been got any work for their livelihood. Therefore, it is the indispensable 'economic duty' of 'workers of today' to create new capital or 'investment, for 'the workers of tomorrow' to get job opportunity to live in the world. It is the 'Investment Justice'.

1 (b) Operation of Investment Justice : 'Investment justice' denotes that each and every worker will create 'new investment' according to his wage. Whenever a worker buys goods and services in the market he will also buy 'investment goods' in the form of shares. The worker will buy such 'capital shares' bit by bit in the market and the value these capital shares will be deposited immediately in his bank for which he will receive dividend. (For detailed study refer Chapter No. 32). The investment justice extends the Marxian ideology from **'work according to energy and wage according to work'** to 'Investment according to wage'.

1. (c) Investment burden: As per investment justice every worker will assume that it is his indispensable **'economic duty'** to create 'new investment' according to his wage for the employment of coming generation and we can notice a kind of 'economic sacrifice and responsibility' in the creation of new investment. In the **creation of investment** out of one's wage the 'low-income worker' has to bear 'more investment burden' whereas the 'high-income worker' will bear 'less investment burden'. For instance, if a worker who earns $2,000 per month invests to buy 'new capital shares' for $200 which proportions to 10 per cent of his income he has to sacrifice some of his essential demands for necessities; on the other hand if a worker who earns $10,000 per month invests to buy 'new capital shares' for $1,000 which proportions to the same 10 per cent of his income, he may not forgo any of his essential demands but only some of his comfort or luxurious goods. The 'investment burden' of the former worker of low income – group is greater than the latter worker of higher income group.

We can view this 'investment burden' in another angle of 'economic justice'. That is in regard to the future economic growth of a country, in generating employment opportunities to the forthcoming generation and in assuring them 'right to live', the workers of low-income group bear greater 'economic burden' than the workers of high-income group.

1. (d) Dividend Income: Though discrimination may prevail in the 'investment burden' between different income groups of workers it is true that the workers of all income groups will own a 'capital share' in all the new and expanded industries which are created out of their investment and moreover all the workers claim 'dividend income' from profit earned by all the industries. In Democrism the dividend income will be distributed to the workers according to their 'investment burden' to alleviate their monetary sufferings for their 'economic sacrifice'. In other words, the workers who bear 'greater investment burden' will receive 'higher dividend' than the workers who bear 'less investment burden' to compensate their economic sacrifice. I have dealt with in detail on the working of this mechanism in the next chapter of 'Distributive Justice'. Now the economic ideology of Democrism (Democratisation of economy) will be conceptualised as follows:

'Work according to energy,...First commandment of Democrism

Wage according to work,...Second commandment of Democrism

Investment according to wage...Third commandment of Democrism

Dividend according to Investment burden"...Fourth commandment of Democrism

Chapter – 19

Distribution of National Dividend to All Workers

All men are created equal

"In the individual body the head is not high because it is the top of the body, nor the soles of the feet low because they touch the earth. Even as members of the individual body are equal so are the members of society"

— **Mahatma Gandhi: 'Harijan',** July 13

Working for economic equality means abolishing the internal conflict between capital and labour. It means the leveling down of the few rich in whose hands is concentrated the bulk of the nation's wealth on the one hand. And a leveling up of the semi-starved naked millions on the other. A nonviolent system of government is impossibility as long as the wide gulf between the rich and the hungry millions persists. The contrast between the palaces of New Delhi and the miserable hovels of the poor labouring class cannot last one day unless there is a voluntary abdication of riches and the power as the richest in the land....

— Quotes of Mahatma Gandhi from SARCAJ

In the creation of societies a 'social contract' has been formulated according to the 'General Will' of the members of society to ensure that all men are created equal. To empower the socio-economic-political equality among men legal entity has been assured in all the 'Political Constitutions' of democratic countries. For instance, 'The Declaration of Independence of USA', The Charter of Human Rights of France' and 'The proclamation of Human Rights and Liberties of UN', and the Constitution of democratic countries in the world declares even in their preamble that all men are created equal.

Differentiation in human efficiencies

Though all men are created equal their productive and creative efficiencies vary from man to man in the production of goods and services. Though every man is the best in his specific work in the division of labour, the value of productive efficiency varies from man to man. For example, in an industry the contributive value of a productive engineer is highly estimated than the ordinary worker. Similarly in a university the contribution of knowledge and research work of a professor for cause of education has higher distinction than the contribution of a clerical worker. Since the contributive value varies from man to man they are monetarily rewarded accordingly despite the fact that all men are created equal. The differentiation in wage is accepted as 'permissible economic inequality'. So in the same line of thought Karl Marx has already advocated 'wage according to work'. Great thinkers like Bertrand Russell says that the **'Economic Justice'** accepts the discrimination in economic benefits.

'I cannot be prepared to maintain that economic justice requires an exactly equal income for everybody. Some kinds of work require a larger income for efficiency than other do.'

—**Bertrand Russell: 'Political Ideals'** (p. 27).

Brutality of inequality

(a) **Lack of equal opportunity:** We should be aware of the fact before justifying the 'economic justice' of 'income inequality' that the high-income group people will make the low–income people as their easy victim and exploit them comfortably with their excessive money power and prevent the 'equal opportunity' not to be utilised by all. The equal opportunity varies between rich and poor. Tawny in his book 'Equality' says:

"The son of a poor man creates opportunity through talent, but the son of a rich man has opportunity thrust upon him" – **Tawny: "Equality"**

(b) **Provocation of envy:** The workers who are equipped with professional education and qualitative efficiency will amass wealth when they engage in production but the workers having less efficiency professional skill will earn only meager income and they will ever be in poverty, misery and in loss of self-respect. Though the efficient workers earn their wealth in justifiable way, the poor workers who are at the diagonally opposite corner develop misery, envy and inferiority complex on viewing the comforts of rich workers. Karl Marx really worries on such richness:

'Accumulation of Wealth at one pole is at the same time accumulation of misery, agony of toil, slavery, ignorance, brutality, mental degradation at the opposite pole' – **Karl Marx: 'Capital'** Vol.1. (p. 209)

In the same vein of thought **E.F. Schumacher** distresses:

'They (the riches) corrupt themselves by practicing greed and they corrupt the rest of the society by provoking envy'.

Whatever may be the dignity and spectrum of society if economic inequality prevails it will promote the rich to be more richer and poor to be more poorer. Under the crushing weight of poverty the poor workers will fail to maintain their rich characters and high moral values and they will be forced to become brutal instruments of extremists. Mathew Arnold is correct in his view of such societies:

'A society of unequal's materialises our upper class, vulgarizes our middle class, brutalizes our lower class'.

Necessity for Economic Equality

In the present chemistry of economic systems though the 'permissible economic inequality' is unavoidable on the justifiable concept of 'wage according to work' it would be a hidden destructive factor for the construction of 'just society' because of the fact that vast majority of people are poor who constitute a society. So creation of 'economic equality' is indispensable to uplift the economic status of poor to obtain socio-economic liberty and to bring out their immense creativeness despite the 'permissible economic inequality' based on 'wage according to work'. It is also said:

'Economic equality will not only bring justice and social freedom, but it will also release immense resources of ability now running into waste'

– F.M. Durbin : 'Economic Equality'

Moreover

"Equality is desired because the surplus of production should be used not to provide luxuries for a few but to abolish poverty, with its evil consequences of ill-health, squalor, ignorance, ugliness and waste of hundreds of millions of human lives".

– Lewis: 'The Principle of Economic Planning' p. 30

Creation of Equality in the midst of Inequalities

It seems to be paradoxical dogma that creating equality in the midst of inequalities like 'poverty in the midst of plenty'. However, the establishment of equality is a must on the basic principles of 'economic justice' which requires any person not to sacrifice anything that is legally entitled to him and not to be distressed at any degree but with the 'General Will' of the people. In the establishment of equality both the Capitalism and Socialism, the prime economic systems, have failed in their endeavour for many decades. In this regard I wish to quote the words of G.D.H. Cole:

"It is not possible for men to be socially or politically equal as long as there exist among themselves differences of wealth and income. The achievement of the ideal economic equality remains a mere dream so far and it is equally of both the present the present capitalist as well as socialist society"

– **G.D.H. Cole: 'A Guide to Modern Politics'** (pp. 489-490)

The Nature and Object of Distributive Justice

It is imperative that in attempting to establish 'economic equality' among the people we have to be scrupulous that it is based on 'distributive justice'. It implies that the system of redistribution of income should be acceptable as justice in the view of both the most efficient workers and the workers who receive high rewards for their efficiency in the production of goods and services. In other words it should be universally acceptable both to the low and high income groups that the redistribution of income is justifiable to establish 'economic equality'. Hence the social system should be designed to satisfy all the members of society. John Rawls writes as follows:

"The social system is to be designed so that the resulting distribution is just however things turn out"

– **John Rawls: "The Theory of Justice"** (1985) p. 275

Redistribution of income : In socialism the distribution of income implies 'wage according to work' and in Democrism redistribution of income implies 'dividend according to investment burden' in addition to wage income. I am explaining this concept in the following paragraphs.

Just economic system: It is an accepted economic justice when economic inequality prevails between worker and worker on the basic concept of 'wage according to efficiency of work'. But at the same time 'economic justice of inequality' should not affect the overall welfare and inherent quality of the society. On the other hand if this 'justifiable economic inequality' seems to harm the society we cannot consider it a just one. Therefore, a just economic system can be reckoned on its ability to lead the society to its ultimate principle of 'equality' though its first principle accepts the inequality on the concept of 'wage according to the efficiency of work'.

Two principles of Distributive justice : The first principle of distributive justice is based on the concept of 'wage according to (efficiency of) work'. Though it is acceptable it leads the society towards inequality. To bridge the gap between poor and rich the second principle of distributive justice requires the distribution of **'dividend according to investment burden'.** The second principle will operate only in 'Democrism' i.e. Democratisation of economy or 'Economic Democracy' which will establish 'egalitarian society' in the process of accelerated economic growth..

Three factors of distribution: How long the establishment of 'egalitarian society' will take place depends on three factors: (1) the accelerated of momentum of economic growth; (2) the volume of national profit contributed by all industries to distribute the dividend; and (3) the proportion of dividend to be distributed between different income groups i.e. Poor and rich workers, according to 'investment burden'.

Operation of Democrism for the creation of equality

In Democrism i.e. Democratisation of economy when the total accumulation of national capital comes under the direct ownership of the people, all the industries will be owned directly by all the workers. Under such economic situation the total aggregate profit earned by all the industries (Gross National Profit) will be directly owned to the workers only. But in the present economic systems the profit is used as a legalised factor to exploit the poor and to direct the rich to lead a luxurious life without contributing any work and to empower them to exert control over the government to become rich to be richer and poor to be poorer. On the other hand in Democrism the national profit will be used to perform three factors of economic activities such as

1. Creation of Egalitarian society,
2. Creation of Tax-Free Economy and
3. Economic stabilizer of employment and income of workers.

Note:

A basic income guarantee (or basic income) is a proposed system of social security that periodically provides each citizen with a sum of money. In contrast to income redistribution between nations themselves, the phrase basic income defines payments to individuals rather than households, groups, or nations, in order to provide for individual basic human needs. Except for citizenship, a basic income is entirely unconditional. Furthermore, there is no means test; the richest as well as the poorest citizens would receive it. The US Basic Income Network emphasises this absence of means testing in its precise definition, "The Basic Income Guarantee is an unconditional, government issued guarantee that all citizens will have enough income to meet their basic needs."

In everyday usage, the phrase basic income is often inaccurately conflated with means tested guaranteed minimum income alternatives such as a negative income tax. A basic income of any amount less than the social minimum is referred to as a partial basic income. Similar proposals for "capital grants provided at the age of majority" date to Thomas Paine's Agrarian Justice of 1795, there paired with asset-based egalitarianism.

"History of Basic Income": Basic Income Earth Network (BIEN), retrieved on 18 June 20.

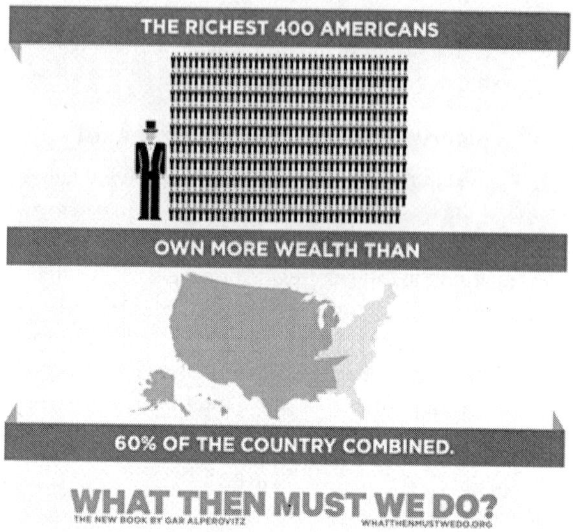

Chapter – 20

Production Justice and Right to Work

"In our glorious fight for civil rights, we must guard against being fooled by false slogans, as 'right-to-work.' It provides no 'rights' and no 'works.' Its purpose is to destroy labour unions and the freedom of collective bargaining... We demand this fraud be stopped.

–Martin Luther King, Jr

"Nearly all men can stand adversity, but if you want to test a man's character, give him power."

– Abraham Lincoln

"It is the eternal struggle between these two principles - right and wrong. They are the two principles that have stood face to face from the beginning of time and will ever continue to struggle. It is the same spirit that says, "You work and toil and earn bread, and I'll eat it"

– Abraham Lincoln

Origin of the concept of "Right to Work"

The phrase "the right to work" was coined by the French socialist leader Louis Blanc in light of the social turmoil of the early 19th century and rising unemployment in the wake of the 1846 financial crisis which leads up to the French Revolution of 1848.

– Revolutions of 1848: A Social History by Priscilla Robertson, 1952, Princeton University Press.

Meaning of 'Right to work'

(a) Of all human rights the 'right to work' occupies an indispensable position to keep every citizen of a society to exercise his 'right to live' that is endowed by the law of nature.

(b) When man invented and perfected the skill and art of 'production' for converting the 'natural resources and goods' into 'artificial consumable goods', the 'right to work' became indispensable for his existence with other members of society in which all are equal.

(c) By the term 'right to work' I insist strongly that man can exercise the right to convert the natural goods into consumable goods without poisoning or damaging the natural resources which are preserved by nature by billions of years. For example, man should not damage the ozone layer by emitting CFC (Chlorofluoro carbon), pollute ocean and under-ground water, destroy green forests, poison the enriched natural soil with toxic chemicals, kill or destroy other living creatures that cannot be reproduced.

The law of nature allows man to exercise his 'right to work' to extract natures invaluable and scarce treasure without poisoning or damaging them. If not Nature warns man that it will get fury by losing 'equilibrium of her factors' and destroy mankind until she gets her 'equilibrium between her elements. By the concept of 'right to work' the quality of society is valued by 'how man preserves nature's treasures but not how he exploits them invariably.

(d) **Constitutional meaning of 'Right to Work'**: Since the 'right to work' leads to 'right to live' it should be empowered by constitutional legitimacy and lew enforcement. The constitution, therefore, should provide legal protection to 'right to work' as follows:

(i) When an involuntary unemployed person who registered his name in the 'employment exchange' for suitable employment according to his education and training which the society offered to him, he should be employed within six months;

(ii) If the government fails to employ him within six months, it should pay him a suitable compensation to lead his life with dignity and social honour. In addition if the involuntary unemployed does not satisfy on government's action, he/she can file a criminal suit against the government as it has violated his/her fundamental right to get a suitable job to the entire satisfaction of judiciary;

(iii) Moreover the government should be aware of the fact that the unemployed person assures the government that he would produce socially needed goods and services at the beginning itself and only after some period he demands his wages to buy the goods and services from the society to uphold his 'right to live';

(iv) Right to work under Capitalism, Socialism and Democrism:

(a) The societies or the countries which pursue 'capitalistic mode of production' or 'capitalism' of any kind (liberal, monopoly, casino, supreme etc.) are forbidden to endow their citizens the 'right to work' or the 'right to live' because the very aim of capitalists is 'maximisation of profit' but not to provide 'maximisation of welfare to the people'. In view of capitalists the workers are commodities to buy for wages and they are not human beings.

Robert B. Reich, (author of "Aftershock", "The Work of Nations" and "Beyond Outrage") Chancellor's Professor of Public Policy at the University of California at Berkeley, who was Secretary of Labour in the Clinton administration writes in his article "The Fable of the Century" (April 5, 2012) as follows:

"Imagine a country in which the very richest people get all the economic gains. They eventually accumulate so much of the nation's total income and wealth that the middle class no longer has the purchasing power to keep the economy is going full speed. Most of the middle class's wages keep falling and their major asset – their home – keeps shrinking in value."

In the capitalist countries, the corporate sector considers that the workers have no 'right to work' to claim and thereby no 'right to live'. The capitalists think that they are entitled to throw away the workers out of work at any time because for their vision the workers are not equal members of any civilised society except for a few rich people who have 'capital ownership'. The capital ownership has developed such barbarian thought in the minds of employers irrespective of 'capitalists' or 'States'.

V. Democrism under 'people's direct ownership of capital' is the only effective and powerful economic system that may offer the inalienable 'right to work' to all people because of the following facts :

(a) When the people directly owns the capital the distinction between 'employer and employee' and the 'capitalist and worker' will automatically disappear, and every employee will ensure 'right to work' to himself as an employer.

(b) Since the employees create necessary capital required for the economy, the employees possess absolute economic power to bestow 'right to work' on them;

(c) Since the employees create adequate 'effective demand' to stabilise volume of income of employers/employees even by diverting their national profit to fill the 'expected income gap' of employers to stabilise the volume of employment, the employees, therefore, ensures themselves 'right to work'.

(d) Of all economic systems Democrism only has an effective economic technique i.e. Dual Monetary System to operate economic machinery efficiently towards 'full employment' so that workers would be legally assured 'right to work' with constitutional guarantee.

Economic Duty of Producers and Consumers

In an ideal society, the prime duty of each work (producer) is to produce socially needed goods and services for the consumers to assure their 'Right to Live'. Similarly, the essential duty of each consumer is to consume goods and services at the rate at which the producers (workers) are producing them to sustain their level of employment and thereby restore their 'Right to Work'.

Meaning of Production Justice

In any just society both the consumers and producers have endowed with mutually equal economic duties to depend on each other to live in the world. It is the fact that the procurers are producing goods and services on the implied instructions of the consumers to satisfy their demand at required volume. But as the consumers are innumerable if they create 'time lags' in buying the goods or reject them summarily the produced goods will stagnate in the market. Due to the stagnation of goods in the market the innocent workers having the sense the economic duty have to fail to sustain their employment and wage income. It will not only severely affect the workers but also the family depending on them to lose their 'Right to Live'. Therefore what the workers insist in the name of "production Justice" is that their 'Right to Live' should not be under the threat of eminent danger even if the consumers commit faults in buying the goods. In other words the 'Production Justice' should basically uphold the sustenance of employment and income of workers despite the faults committed by some other consumers.

The aim of Production Justice

In an ideal society both the producers (workers) and the consumers are obliged to live with mutual duties and responsibilities for economic welfare. Only on the implied directions of the consumers the producers (workers) are producing socially needed goods and services for the utilisation of consumers. On the contrary, if the consumers create 'time lags' or summarily reject the goods to purchase at the rate at which they are produced, these goods will stagnate in the market, and the producers will fail to get their expected volume of income to continue the production. The innocent and the honest workers (producers) who produce the goods will be thrown out of the employment. Moreover, their unemployment will severely affect the 'right to live' of their dependent family. In this context what the 'Production Justice' insists is that even if the consumers commit blunders in the market the sustainability of employment and income of workers (producers) should not be affected at any cost. The producers' stable employment and income should not be a dependent factor of consumers' behaviour in the market. This is the vital object of 'production justice'.

Two Conditions of Production Justice

Production Justice is the interaction of two combatible conditions. Firstly, the workers (producers) should perform exclusively their economic duty of producing socially needed goods and services for the consumers. Secondly, if the consumers commit serious blunders in the market to buy the goods at the rate at which they are produced for them, such blunders should not stand as obstacles for the employment and income or 'right to live' of the workers who have performed their productive duties honestly. Because of the fact that the producers economic duty is only to produce socially needed goods for consumers but not investigate them whether they have purchased such goods at the rate at which they have produced.

Economic Responsibility: Producers Vs. Consumers

Generally in all our economic systems, whatever may be the industry, the producers venture into production only after making through scrutiny of economic factors and forecasting future market conditions and technological changes. The producer's exercises are plan oriented activities. On the contrary the consumers never exercise such planned spending during their consumption or purchasing goods because they are not only heterogeneous in thinking but also make innumerable independent decisions in the market. Moreover no economic system has any economic technique to coordinate and guide the consumers decision-makings in harmony with the planning of producers to run the economic machinery smoothly.

Time Lags and Right to Live: (Goods Vs. Man)

On behaving erratically in the market the consumers either reject or create time lags in purchasing goods. It causes over production. In order to eliminate over production the producers reduce the volume of production and level of employment. In other words to avoid wastage of goods due to overproduction the producers make the workers to go waste as unemployed persons and thereby cause to forfeit their 'right to live'. In the present economic systems the producers are striving to sustain the level of employment rather their the level of employment. For them, goods are important rather than man and their right to live. This is the way in which our economic systems are operating in the world. Which is important? Production of goods up to 'effective demand' or protection life of workers despite waste of goods.

Goods are produced for men but the capitalists say that men are produced for goods. That is economic system in which we are living in the world. So Prof. Kenneth J. Galbraith advises the capitalist economists to save man despite the goods are going to waste.

"Income and employment rather than goods have basic economic concern"

– **Kenneth J. Galbraith: 'Affluent Society'** (p. 227)

In the same streak of thought of Prof. Galbraith, Robert K. Wetzel says:

"Freedom of choice (of consumers) can only be meaningful if man's economic well-being is not threatened by starvation or annihilation"

– **Robert K. Wetzel; 'The Philosophy of Freedom'** (p. 54)

Basic concept of Production Justice:The basic concept of production justice is that no worker should live in destitute or unemployed as long as he is willing to work and to produce socially needed goods. In this regard I like to quote the words of Bertrand Russell:

"No one ought to be allowed to suffer destitution so long as he or she is willing work........"

"A man's pay should not cease through the accident of his work being no longer needed, but should continue so long as he is willing to work, a new trade being taught him at the public expense, if necessary"

– **Bertrand Russell: 'Political Ideals'** (p. 30)

Chapter– 21

Tax - Free Economy

"Taxes are equal, is a dogma which I'll prove at once," exclaimed a Tory boor, "Taxation hardly presses on the rich, And likew"Taxes are equal, is a dogma which I'll prove at once," exclaimed a Tory boor; "Taxation hardly presses on the rich, And likewise presses hardly the poor"

– Anonymous

"We contend that for a nation to try to tax itself into prosperity is like a man standing in a bucket and trying to lift himself up by the handle".

– Winston S. Churchill

"This is a question too difficult for a mathematician. It should be asked of a philosopher"(when asked about completing his income tax-form)

– AlbertEintein

"Certainty? In this world nothing is certain but death and taxes."

– Benjamin Franklin

"We contend that for a nation to try to tax itself into prosperity is like a man standing in a bucket and trying to lift himself up by the handle"

– Winston S Churchill

"This is a question too difficult for a mathematician. It should be asked of a philosopher"(when asked about completing his income tax-form)

– Albert Eintein

"Certainty? In this world nothing is certain but death and taxes."

– Benjamin Franklin

For all governments irrespective of Socialism and Capitalism a huge volume money is required to maintain and promote the welfare activities of people such as public works, Healthcare, Education, Internal and

External defense, Law and order, etc. To fulfill their welfare obligations governments require a huge volume of income which has been acquired from the people in the form of direct and indirect taxes. The governments find no other economic technique except for taxation for their revenues.

Creation of Parallel Economy: It is the obligation of 'household sector' to contribute a share of its 'wage income' and the 'business sector' a share of its 'profit-income' to the common pool of government revenues.

Income and Spending Flows

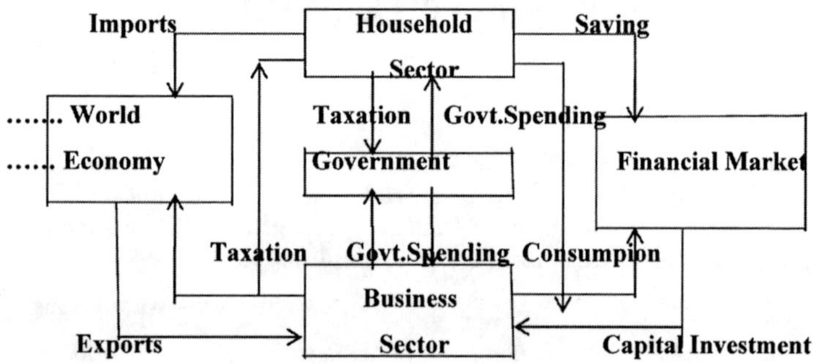

Circular Flow of Money

In the above figure of 'circular flow of money' in the economy we can notice that the government gets it revenue from the household and business sectors in the form of **taxation** levied on **'wage income'** and **'profit income'** of these two sectors. Whenever the government increases the taxes it the household sector that shows its intense disapproval in the form of strikes and agitations and the business sector on the other quietly indulge in evasion of taxation by accumulating **'black money'** by which it empowers the operation of a 'parallel economy'. Though government has no other alternative to taxation for its revenue, both the sectors show aversion on the 'taxation technique' of the government.

Inducement for corruption: Corruption is widely prevailing among the government servants whenever they estimate the taxes and receive the taxes. There is nexus between the bureaucrats and the politicians in swindling the 'tax money' from the people. Especially the politicians are powerful enough to exploit the people through the taxation. They exploit the people extensively to gain money power to strengthen their party and to capture the government in order to exploit the citizens legally with the help of political power. No politician has the pure intention of serving the people. It has prompted

George Bernard Shaw to say that 'politics is the last resort of scoundrels'. No doubt all politicians are scoundrels because of the weakness of the system.

Misdistribution of resources: Moreover the taxation system generates confusion in the market in fixation of prices. This confusion distorts misdistribution of rare natural resources. Therefore it is said as follows:

"Most taxes create distortions in the market system by forcing suppliers and demanders to face different prices. These distortions, in turn, misallocate resources, thereby creating allocation inefficiency"

– Richard W. Tresch: "Public Finance – a Normative Theory" (p. 120)

The black money created to evade taxes is extensively used by the rich to buy luxurious good and to aid the militant and terrorist agencies to purchase destructive goods in hundreds of billions of dollars. The production of these goods divert the rare natural resources which cannot be reproduced for going to waste.

Mal-distribution of Tax-Revenue: More or less all the world governments are implicitly run by the rich behind the curtain. So the governments are trapped to become instrumentals of rich to allocate their considerable portion of tax income to protect the rich and to maintain the economic disparity but not to uplift the poor to move towards the rich. The economists like Frank Ackerman and Andrew Zimbalist blame the governments in this regard as follows:

"Government spending very often is of greater benefit to the rich man than to the poor. They conclude that the government spending serves not to redistribute resources to the poor but to maintain the existing unequal distribution of expenses and the capitalist institutions that generate it"

—Frank Ackerman and Andrew Zimbalist:
"The Capitalist System" (p. 306)

Taxation is not the only main source: The great fault of all governments is that they are conceiving fallaciously that the taxation is the only main source of public revenue. The taxation technique has entrenched economic immorality and tempted the tax payers to indulge in corruption in instead of promoting 'economic duty' for the welfare of people. It is the justifiable economic system which encourages the people to participate in the public revenue with sense of economic responsibility by some other economic techniques instead of taxation.

Role of Contributive Profit in Public Revenue: In the democratic economic system i.e. Democrism all the 'direct and indirect taxes' will be abolished. I have already mentioned in the previous chapter that a portion of national profit will be allotted for 'Contributive Profit'. The welfare Justice implies the direct contribution of people to the public revenue for their welfare according to their ability to pay. Accordingly people will allocate and allot the **'contributive profit'** to the government to meet its public expenditure. Moreover, it is the people who will decide 'how much' to pay to the government from their 'contributive profit' for its expenditure but not the government. The government will not dictate the people how much they have to pay to meet its pre-determined expenditure.

Deciding authority: In the present economic systems it the government which first decides its 'expenditure' and then coerces the people to pay taxes to meet its expenditure. But is 'Democrsim' it will be people who will first decide what should be expenditure of government and they will contribute it from their 'contribute profit' at one payment. Here the people will be the deciding authority in fixation of government expenditure but not the government itself. The government should spend the people's money within the ambit of people's contribution from their 'contributive profit'. For its spending the government should not only be accountable to people but also keep transparency with the people. Under these economic climate it is the people who will exercise economic rule over the government but not vice versa. Such economic situation will truly empower the people to retain **'economic democracy'.**

Moreover, people will be empowered with constitutional rights that they may prosecute the government if it spends the people's money for selfish motives, or lavishly or announce fascinating and populist schemes to garner vote bank at the time of elections or against welfare of the society.

Absence of expenditure for tax collection: Since the people pay their contribution directly to the government the huge expenditure for the collection of taxes hitherto prevailed will be completely wiped out. Moreover true democracy will emerge when people rule over themselves instead of ruling over by a political party or alliance of political parties with a majority vote. It is often quoted that the best government is that governs least.

Chapter– 22

Price Determination Justice and "Prosumer Society"

"My father always told me that all businessmen were son of bitches but never believed it till now"

– John F Kennedy, "A Thousand Days" by Arthur Schlesinger Jr. [1965]

"Thou sellest thy people for nought, and dost not increase thy wealth by their price". **– Bible**

"One man's wage increase is another man's price increase".

– Harold Wilson (British Prime Minister: 1916-1995)

"And if thou sell ought unto thy neighbour, or buyest ought of thy neighbour's hand, ye shall not oppress one another" **– Bible**

Just price and Democrism

On attempting to find out the root cause for all human problems Pundit Jawaharlal Nehru at the end come to the conclusion that it is the ignorance of man on the just distribution of goods and services which he produced for himself. So he blames the society as follows:

"Society has leant how to produce but not how to distribute what it has produced"

–Jawaharlal Nehru: "Glimpses of World History" (p. 1371)

Effective Demand and Distribution of Income

The world thinkers, at last, learned on crunching of 'Great Depression' during 1930's that poverty and unemployment would not be solved by mere accumulation of capital and extensive volume of production of goods and services. The world also learned that it is fallacious that **'supply creates its**

own demand' as per **Say's law** and the unemployment cannot be solved automatically as there is no any 'in-built rectifier or solution finder' in the economy. It is **John Maynard Keynes** who diagnosed the operation of capitalistic system as erroneous and prescribed equitable distribution of income to create adequate effective demand for goods produced to solve unemployment. So he wrote that 'the level of employment and income is determined by the level of **effective demand'.** The level of effective demand depends on the quality and quantity of equitable distribution of income. 'More **the equitable distribution of income** means more the level of effective demand and less the level unemployment; less the equitable distribution of income means less the level of effective demand and more the level unemployment'. Because equitable distribution of income is the determinant factor of level of effective demand and volume employment.

Nature of Production and Distribution

The common basic factor of all economic systems is to produce goods and distribute them. But our economic systems operate detrimentally in production and unjustifiably in distribution. Bertrand Russell says:

"Economic systems are concerned essentially with production and distribution of material goods. Our present system is wasteful in the production side and unjust on the side of distribution".

– **Bertrand Russell: "Political Ideals"** (p. 35)

All the great thinkers like Jawaharlal Nehru, John Maynard Keynes and Bertrand Russell blame that our economic systems fail to distribute the goods produced in the just manner. The goods produced are distributed unjustifiably because 'there is no control, no plan of action, and whatever occurs is economic life is the result of innumerable independent decisions'. **(Prof. Mrs. Joan Robinson: 'Introduction to the Theory of Employment')**

The basic cause for all defects perpetrated in our economic systems is attributed to the erratic behaviour of innumerable consumers in the market, absence of centralised control over the consumers, absence of systematic planning in spending among the people and absence of economic responsibility in the behaviour among the consumers.

Class Distinction Between Producers and Consumers

In our present economic systems both the producers and consumers have serious conflicting psychology in nature. So they separate themselves into two distinct classes and indulge in sharp economic struggles in the market. The producers are always maneuvering for high prices for their commodities in the market to achieve 'maximisation of profit', the very purpose of production. On contrary the consumers struggle for the distribution of goods at low prices for 'maximisation of utility'.

Due to the conflicting behaviour of producers and consumers it seems to be impossible to fix a 'just price' for commodities. Moreover the conflicting behaviour consumes unnecessarily long span of 'time lags' in the determination of price level of commodities. This 'time lag' always prevents the equilibrium between the rate of production and rate of consumption. Since the goods are not to be distributed to the consumers at rate at which they are produced the producers decelerate the rate of stable production, the level of required employment and the volume of consumers' income and other economic activities. In consequence, these adverse factors discourage 'the risk bearing of producers' to venture in the production at the rate at which the economy requires to solving unemployment.

Two negative factors

On one hand the consumers behave erratically in the market due to ignorance on the production of goods and services and they are always kept in the dark chamber not to know the production activities. On the other hand the producers use all the unjustifiable market strategies to exploit the consumers in order to accumulate their income in the name of maximisation of profit as soon as possible. These two negative psychological factors of consumers and producers decelerate the wheels of economic activities and cause for unemployment and poverty. Not only the consumers and producers but also the governments do not show any serious concern over these negative factors and the poverty of the people.

Absence of economic techniques

The present economic systems are both attempting and tempting to induce the conflicting psychological factors of producers and consumers in determination of price and thus distribute the goods erratically. Our economic systems are invariably powerless to equip us to design an 'economic technique' to determine a 'just price' by our self. They have left us at the mercy of producers to buy goods under the misguidance and the influence of hundreds of fascinating advertisements through numerous medias consistently surrounding us. Nowadays retailers like **'Wal-Marts'** become monopolies and spread their wings over the countries and dictate the prices of goods through local and e-markets benefited by 'credit cards'. They say 'don't come to market we come at your door steps' to exploit the consumers. In the 'electronic revolution' the local and 'multinational corporations' are misusing the 'internet communications' to exploit the people throughout the world. What we require by virtue of economic justice is a 'justifiable market system' for distribution of goods and services among us at a 'just price' using the 'electronic revolution' in a justifiable manner.

Prosumer Society

The only way to create such a justifiable market is to establish 'people's direct ownership of capital' i.e. 'democratisation of capital'. When the capital is directly owned by the people 'the economic discrimination between producers and consumers will disappear. It will make all the consumers to become direct producers and all the producers to become direct consumers. A 'PRODUCER cum CONSUMER society' known as 'PROSUMER SOCIETY' will emerge in all economies in the world.

The principle of Just Price

The principle of just price depends on two factors. The first factor connotes the determination of price and the second factor the impact of the price. According to the first principle the price level of all the goods and services will be determined by the consent of all the consumers who consume them. The second principle prescribes that even if the people think that the price level is fixed more than the total cost of production for a particular cause the excess money paid will increase the volume of profit and this marginal profit will be redistributed to the poor more than what they paid in excess.

In the Democratisation of economy under an 'Economic Contract' the consumers themselves in the capacity or producers will determine the price of all commodities and distribute them among themselves. This is the 'Price Determination Justice'. This is the 'Just price' because it will not affect any one. If anyone thinks that a particular price level will affect the producers it will do so because all these producers are consumers and in the capacity of consumers all the producers will be benefited. Therefore in the Prosumer society no one will be affected on the price level whatever it may be. Hence it is the **Just Price.**

When the distribution of national production is justified the poverty and unemployment will be eliminated as early as possible for which the national capital should be directly owned by the people under the principle of Democrism. This is the ultimate economic justice.

Chapter – 23

Corruption-Free Society; How to Create? War on Corruption By Dual Monetary System

"Corruption is authority plus monopoly minus transparency"

– Unknown

"Power tends to corrupt; absolute power corrupts absolutely"

– Lord Acton

"Communism has never come to power in a country that was not disrupted by war or corruption, or both". **– John F. Kennedy**

"I will not let anyone walk through my mind with their dirty feet"

– Mahatma Gandhi

"To oppose corruption in government is the highest obligation of patriotism."
– G. Edward Griffin

Corruption is widely acknowledged to distort markets, undermine the rule of law, damage government legitimacy, and hurt economic development. The global anticorruption movement has gained ground since the mid-1990s, but its key agents -developed and developing countries, international organisations, and MNCs — must do more to prevent and punish misbehaviour systematically.

Corruption is both a major cause and a result of poverty around the world. It occurs at all levels of society, from local and national governments, civil society, judiciary functions, large and small businesses, military and other services and so on. Corruption affects the poorest the most, despite rich or poor nations.

The issue of corruption is very much inter-related with other issues. At a global level, the "international" (Washington Consensus-influenced) economic system that has shaped the current form of globalisation in the past decades requires further scrutiny for it has also created conditions whereby corruption can flourish and exacerbate the conditions of people around the world who already have little say about their destiny.

A difficult thing to measure or compare, however, is the impact of corruption on poverty versus the effects of inequalities that are structured into law, such as unequal trade agreements, structural adjustment policies, and so-called "free" trade agreements and so on. It is easier to see corruption. It is harder to see these other more formal, even legal forms of "corruption." It is easy to assume that these are not even issues because they are part of the laws and institutions that govern national and international communities and many of us will be accustomed to it—it is how it works, so to speak.

When asking why poor countries are poor, it is quite common to hear, especially in wealthier countries that are perceived to have minimal corruption (at least domestically) that other countries are poor because of corruption. Yet, corruption is not something limited to third world despots. Rich countries too have been involved in corrupt practices around the world.

As Professor **Robert Neil** from Trinity College, Cambridge University writes in Public Corruption; **The Dark Side of Social Evolution** (London: Anthem Press, 2002), (p. 209)

"Rich countries and their agencies ... commonly have been and are accomplices in corruption abroad, encouraging it by their actions rather than impeding it...."

Specific problems he highlights include:

1. The impact of Cold War corruption: (supporting dictatorships, destabilizing democracies, funding opposition, etc.);

Firms from rich countries bribing rulers and officials from developing countries to gain export contracts, particularly in the arms trade and in construction (even justifying it by suggesting bribery is "customary" in those countries, so they need to do it too, in order to compete);

The "corruption-inducing effects of the purchase, by the rich countries and their international corporations, of concessions in Third World countries to exploit natural deposits of oil, copper, gold, diamonds and the like." Payments made to rulers often violate local (and Western) rules, keeping corrupt rulers in power, who also embezzle a lot of money away.

"Bribery may be pervasive, but it is difficult to detect. Many Western companies do not dirty their hands, but instead pay local agents, who get a 10 per cent or so 'success fee' if a contract goes through and who have access to the necessary 'slush funds' to ensure that it does. Bribery is also increasingly subtle...... Until recently, bribery was seen as a normal business practice. Many countries including France, Germany and UK treated bribes as legitimate business expenses which could be claimed for tax deduction purposes".

– Dr Susan Hawley, Exporting Corruption;
Multinationals and Bribery, the Corner House, June 2000.

The drug trade

Neil suggests that international law and national laws in rich countries that prohibit drugs may serve to "produce a scarcity value irresistible to producers, smugglers and dealers." Governments and civil society in the third world are often "undermined, sometimes destroyed" by the violence and corruption that goes with the drug trade. "This is probably the most important way in which the policies of rich countries foster corruption and violence. Yet the effect on the Third World seems scarcely to enter discussion of alternative drug policies in the rich countries." Legalizing drugs, a system of taxation and regulation, comparable to that applied to tobacco and alcohol might do more to reduce corruption in the world than any other measure rich countries could take, he suggests.

Globalisation, Multinational Corporations, and Corruption

Corruption scandals that sometimes make headline news in Western media can often be worse in developing countries. This is especially the case when it is multinational companies going into poorer countries to do business. The international business environment, encouraged by a form of globalisation that is heavily influenced by the wealthier and more powerful countries in the world makes it easier for multinationals to make profit and even for a few countries to benefit. However, some policies behind globalisation appear to encourage and exacerbate corruption as accountability of governments and companies have been reduced along the way. For example, Dr Hawley also lists many of impacts that multinationals' corrupt practices have on the "South" (another term for Third World, or developing countries), including

1. They undermine development and exacerbate inequality and poverty,
2. They disadvantage smaller domestic firms,
3. They transfer money that could be put towards poverty eradication into the hands of rich,
4. They distort decision-making in favour of projects that benefit the few rather than the many,
5. They also increase debt; Benefit the company, not the country; Bypass local democratic processes; Damage the environment; Circumvent legislation; and Promote weapons sales.

"For multinationals, bribery enables companies to gain contracts (particularly for public works and military equipment) or concessions which they would not otherwise have won, or to do so on more favourable terms. Every year, the Western business pays huge amounts of money in bribes to win friends, influence and contracts. These bribes are conservatively to run to us $80 billion a year – roughly the amount that the UN believes is needed to eradicate global poverty".

— **Dr Susan Hawley, Exporting Corruption; Privatisation, Multinationals and Bribery,** the Corner House, June 2000.

ROOT CAUSES FOR CORRUPTION

1. Contradictory Functions of Money: The genesis of all causes for corruption and huge accumulation of 'black money' throughout the world sprouts from the very concept of money which has to perform two contradictory functions simultaneously known as 'medium of exchange' and 'Store of Value'.

2. Medium of Exchange: Money, at the very outset, was discovered to perform the only function of 'medium of exchange'. When the money was used to perform exclusively as the 'medium of exchange', the velocity of the flow of money in the income and expenditure streams was always at equilibrium. The economy was effective and dynamically stable at that instance.

3. Money illusion and hoarding: When the money was happened to perform 'store of value' also, it induced the natural instinct of 'money illusion' of the people and so that the people tempted to hoard the money in the form of coins or gold or jewels or in some other valuable metals and they buried the wealth under the ground because they knew the hoarded wealth would not loss its value over a period and more over no banking system was developed at that time.

4. Medium of corruption: The 'store of value' converts the 'medium of exchange' into 'medium of corruption'. In other words the hoarded money, benefited by 'store of value' not only prevents the dynamic function of 'medium of exchange' of money but also promotes as an instrument for corrupt practices. Induced by 'money illusion' Judas betrayed even the Jesus for thirty silver coins assuming its value would exist for a long period of time. This corruption is the mother of all corruptions witnessed in the history of mankind. History has recorded thousands of wars are waged by kings for the acquisition of 'hoarded wealth' because of its 'store of value'.

5. Oil and Corruption: Even now the USA is waging shadow and real wars on the 'Oil Rich' Arabian countries for acquisition of 'hoarded wealth of oil' and in later stages it converts the oil into dollars.

6. Global phenomenon: The 'money illusion' patronised by the 'store of value' results in corruption and pervades all over the world irrespective of poor and rich countries. Even the holy epics in all the languages have depicted the spectrum of corruption.

7. Nexus for illegal activities: Nowadays a strong bonding nexus for corruption prevails between 'rich people in corporate sectors politicians and bureaucrats' for acquisition of billions and billions of dollars for running economic activities for the benefit of rich.

8. The sanctuary of Swiss Banks: In order to conceal their illegal wealth and black money the ' men of leaches' deposit their black and corrupt money in the banks of some other foreign countries especially in 'Switzerland' which is proving full protection and maintain secrecy for the deposits of corrupt money wherever it comes from. India is considered the second topmost country which deposits billions and billions of dollars of black money in Swiss banks by nearly 2000 rich persons though 80 per cent of Indian population living under the poverty line.

9. Compensatory Interest payment: Though the 'deposited corrupt money' would lose its real value due to influence of inflation in due course of time, the corrupt people are under the impression the interest 'interest' payment will compensate the loss of money value and their corrupt money will maintain the 'value of monetary equilibrium'.

How to wage a war on black money? In my economic theory of Democrism under the aegis of the **'DUAL MONETARY SYSTEM'** (DMS) the 'Investment Money' will prevent the circulation of black money at its very germination. In brief:

The economic strategy of DMS is once the 'Investment money' comes into circulation it will prevent the money income of any person over and above his 'specified and known source of income' or the black money of a person to flow into 'expenditure stream' by forfeiting its 'store of value'.

On the deprivation of 'store of value' billions and billions of dollars now operating in the parallel economy will lose its face, value and they would become just waste papers to be thrown away into the dust bin and there would be no taker for it.

Economic Strategy for the 'War on Black Money'

(a) In the operation of 'Democratic Economy' each and every consumer will be allotted a 'Capital Account' or 'Investment Account' in a particular bank as the consumers like.

(b) Each account will be designated as with a specific 'capital account number'.

(c) Each consumer will be provided with 'Consumption Goods Identification Card'.

(d) The Consumption Goods Identification Card will be furnished with the following details:

1. The photos of and the names of family members;
2. The name of the bank with the members account number;
3. The family's statutory annual income as well as monthly income;
4. Necessary details of the family members; and above all a 'debit/credit card' to all members of family with photo identity;
5. These electronic money cards will have the 'identical family capital account and capital account number' to facilitate easy transaction; and the value of the movable and immovable property of the family.

Under Dual Monetary System when the 'Investment Money' comes into operation it will check the black money not buying or selling any goods and services. It's one of the primary duties is not only create necessary investment without "Interest" but also to inspect the perfect circulation of 'Consumption Money' and to prevent illegal circulation of black money and restrain completely the corruption and such kind of dowry system that is now practicing in India and spoiling many families.

How the Investment Money erases corruption

For example, let's assume a family's monthly income amounts to $100,000. According to **'Investment Justice'** we have already seen that every worker should contribute certain percentage of his income for investment. Let the investment ratio of the family may be 20 per cent. When a worker spends $100,000 in a month for purchasing goods and services he would get $80,000 worth of consumption goods and $20,000 worth of 'investment money'. Investment or capital is a national wealth and no one buy it in small quantities of tools and machines.

Moreover, we have to keep in mind that the workers produce not only 'consumption goods' but also 'investment goods' simultaneously. No one can purchase consumption goods and investment goods separately. Consumption goods are for immediate consumption of a family whereas the investment goods for the producers to create new industries and employment.

In the operation of Dual Monetary System when a consumer pays $100,000 in the market it is assumed that he buys $80,000 for consumption goods and provides $20,000 for purchasing investment goods in his name.

In the market the sellers credit $20,000 to the 'Investment Account' of the worker as a legal assurance that the worker has purchased his due investment goods. This business operation will be executed on the information furnished in the workers family card and all the goods and service markets are computerised and linked with the banks. The workers can verify their accounts at any time in the bank or through internet facilities.

Moreover, if a consumer has $20,000 in his investment account in a particular month it will indicate that he has spent $100,000 in the market. The consumer can operate his business anywhere in the world because of the 'internet facilities and computer technologies' as it is now functioning with 'credit/debit cards'.

Abolition of corruption: Suppose a consumer gets $30,000 as bribe in addition to his monthly income of $100,000. His total disposable income will amount to $130,000. If he spends all the $130,000 he would be provided with $104,000 consumption goods which are higher than his legal $80,000 worth of consumption goods by $24,000 and the investment goods by $26,000 instead of $20,000.

In his Investment Account $26,000 will be credited instead of his legal value of $20,000. At once the banking authorities by its internet mechanism warn both the sellers and law enforcement authorities that a particular man has received bribe to the tune of $30,000 and by which he has purchased consumption goods to the value of $24,000 and has enhanced his investment account by $6,000 in his credit. The person who received and spent the money would be immediately trapped. The man who spends the money today or tomorrow and some months later would be caught at the very moment he attempts to spend the corrupted money.

Since the **Damocles' Sword** is always hanging over the heads of corrupt people, who opt for the bribe and who offer the bribe will be trapped at once.

"Experience demands that man is the only animal which devours his own kind, for I can apply no milder term to the general prey of the rich on the poor".

– Thomas Jefferson

Chapter – 24

How to Eliminate Poverty

Poverty Eradication Technique by Increasing "People's National Profit" (Dual Income to Workers-Wage for Work and Dividend for Investment)

"The poor are human manure in which grow the harvest of life, the harvest to joy which the rich reap"

– **Octave Mirabeau,** The Diary of a Chambermaid

"There are people in the world so hungry, that God cannot appear

to them except in the form of bread."

–Mahatma Gandhi

"It is a tragic mix-up when the United States spends $500,000 for every enemy soldier killed, and only $53 annually on the victims of poverty.

—Martin Luther King, Jr

"Poverty often deprives a man of all spirit and virtue; it is hard for an empty bag to stand upright

— Benjamin Franklin

The **just price** is a theory of ethics in economics that attempts to set standards of fairness in transactions. With intellectual roots in ancient Greek philosophy, it was advanced by Thomas Aquinas based on an argument against usury, which in his time referred to the making of any rate of interest on loans.

Just price - Wikipedia, the free encyclopaedia

https://en.wikipedia.org/wiki/Just_price

1. Just Price Definition: I have already explained in the economic system of Democrism there will be no distinction between consumers and producers. All consumers are producers and all PROducers and conSUMERS. It establishes **"PROSUMER SOCIETY".**

In the PROSUMER society the consumers will produce goods and distribute among them at an acceptable price following certain just guidelines. The price determined by consumers themselves is the JUST PRICE.

Since the goods are produced for consumers, the price of goods should be determined by the consumer on the satisfaction of GENERAL WILL of the people. More reasonably the just price will include certain percentage of profit and it will flow into "People's National Profit Fund". This fund will be utilised to distribute "Dividend" to the consumers themselves. Therefore no dispute will emerge quantitatively in the determination of just price.

The just price is universal and will not vary from person to person or market to market or time to time. Whatever discrepancy arises in the fixation of just price arises it will be immediately automatically settled (self adjustment) on the payment of "dividend'.

In the capitalistic economic systems the price of goods is determined by producers. In India the producers fix the Maximum Retail Price (MRP or Maximum rip off Price) in all packed goods and in other countries, other than India, the producers Suggestive Selling Price (SSP). Many a times if the producers introduce some innovative technologies in the design and production of goods they determine the price (MRPs or SSPs) more than 100-1000 times higher than the cost of production. The huge volume of profit seeks asylum in Swiss banks as black money. According to Stockholm International Peace Research Institute (SIPRI), the blackmoney hoarded in Swiss banks amounts to $1.1 trillion in 2015. Recently a news has burst out the Apple Company (MNC) has paid just $5 as income tax to the profit of $50 million. Now we can deduce how much exorbitant volume of black money is parading as parallel economy. Now the world economy is ruled by these corporate sectors not by the Presidents and Prime ministers as foolish common people believe. These corporate sectors wouldn't pay any "dividend" to their workers. Workers should satisfy with only their meagre wages to regain their lost energy.

The intellectual root of the idea of fixing Just Price goes into ancient Greek philosophy. King **Thomas Acquinas** attempted to exchange goods at Just Price but failed because of non-existence of any planned economic system.

When the attempts made to design economic systems, **Adam Smith** advanced arguments to fix maximum price and to accumulate huge volume of profit to create **"Wealth of Nations"** (1776).

Adam Smith's School of Thought was blindly followed upto 1930 when Capitalism collapsed due to its own policy of **"Maximisation of Profit".**

Even **"Marxian School of Thought"** did not attempt to introduce any theory of "Just Price" for exchange of goods in the market. They simply forwarded "From each according to energy and to each according to need".

Despite the horrendous experience of "Great Depression" of 1930s the present capitalists and corporate sectors don't seem to learn any lesson on avaricious for targeting on "Maximisation of Profit". Maximisation of profit means to fix the price as many times as they can, 100-1000 times, the over Just Price. Since the Capitalists couldn't maximise profit at skyhigh they attempted to implement **Globalisation** of economy and they succeeded; otherwise they would have toppled their own governments. During this period of Globalisation hundreds of Multi-National Corporations emerged like mushrooms. This kind of saturated emergence of MNCs will result in **"bubbling globalisation".** This will have only the "life of rainbow-effect"- beautiful and vanish.Their only aim is Maximisation of profit by dumping their goods all over the world by demolishing all tariff walls. By the power of globalisation the object of MNCs is first murder the culture of other countries, sell their goods, maximise their profit, buy the cheap labour, exploit the scarce resources, and colonise the country economically. In near future this very brutal aim of MNCs will lead to civil wars and ultimately to **World War III**.

Globally all MNCs are interlinked. If one MNC is collapsed the other dependent MNCs will also collapse as it happened during 1930s. People cannot tolerate poverty and unemployment. Countries will open their "**ballistic missile arsenals**" for "end game" (Recently Putin also warned the "Western countries by threatening **'the play game'** is over). If the threatening catastrophy is to being stopped the MNCs should be prepared to change the capitalistic system and prepared to follow a just economic system based on democratic principles.

In the prosumer society of Democrism the consumers (producers) produce goods, fix a price on general will and distribute among themselves. This price is the Just Price.

2. Aim of Just Price: In Democratisation of Economy the **'just price'** means a price determined by the consumers (producers) themselves who consume the goods. The price level will not be determined by the interaction of supply and demand curves of goods. On the other hand it will be determined by an **'economic contact'** drawn among the consumers satisfying the general norms of "**General Will".** On the distribution of goods the just price should not affect any one especially the poor people's standard of living. On the contrary any increase in the price level will make the rich to pay more for elimination of poverty by "Distributive justice" on the dispersion of Dividend". Though it will seem to be a paradoxical concept it is the very aim of the determination of the just price to safeguard the interests of poor.

3. Working on the just- price mechanism: For example, let's assume a particular price is determined as the just price for a commodity in the market. And the poor people consider that the so called just price is higher than their 'expected price'. The 'incremental price' i.e. the **'price gap'** between the just price and 'expected price' will increase the volume of profit. The 'incremental or the marginal price' will operate as a 'stimulator' to enhance the volume of national profit.

We have already discussed that according to **'distributive justice'** the low income group will receive more dividend than the high-income group according to investment burden. Since the incremental price will enhance national profit the poor will receive more dividend than what they paid in the form of 'increased price'. The dividend will compensate the increased price. No one, therefore, blames a particular price level is higher or lower. This neutral price level is the **'just price'.**

In democratisation of economy or in **prosumer society** whenever price level increases it will increase the value of dividend payment to the poor at the resultant distribution of national profit of the people. It will increase the purchasing power of the poor and reduce the income gap between rich and poor. In consequence, the increased price level will lead the people towards an egalitarian society. Hence the price mechanism in Democrism operates for the benefit of the poor. Higher the price level (to a certain extent only) means higher the dividend payment and higher the purchasing power to the poor at the end and vice versa. This strategic operation of just price mechanism is feasible and practicable only in Democrism but not in any other economic systems which are operating for the benefit of rich and vested interests.

Chapter – 25

Price Increase Benefits the Poor the Idea of Democrism

(A Paradoxical Truth)

In Democrism i.e. in Democratic Economy the 'just price is a price determined by the consumers themselves who buy the goods, in the capacity of producers'. The consumers will determine the price at a reasonable level that will not affect their standard of life. Since there is no distinction between producers and consumers, the price determined by the producers for a commodity in the market is nothing but the price determined by the consumers themselves. There will be no interaction between demand and supply forces for the determination of price of the commodities in the market.

In Democrism since all the industries are directly owned by the workers, there will be accountability and transparency and how and the value will be added every process of production and what would be the final production cost.

A 'Market Price Determination Committee' would be established with the cluster of experts and they will determine the 'Just Price' for the commodities to be distributed to the consumers. That price may be, perhaps, higher than the 'expected price' of the poor consumers. This higher margin of expected price may be just over and above the **'just price'** but this 'incremental price' will not affect the poor at any cost. On the other hand, it will help to increase the 'standard of living of people' at the end process. How?

Suppose the expected just price is $10 for a commodity, but it is priced in the market $12. As a producer, the consumer will gain $2. When billions of consumers buy the commodities. A profit of billions of dollars will accumulate in the stock of 'People's National Profit' over a considerable period.

The national profit will be huge when hundreds of goods priced in this way. But this pricing process will not affect the poor people. Because

(a) the doctrine of Democrism is developed as follows:
(4/6 Commandments)
"Work according to Energy;................First commandment
Wage according to Work; ....Second commandment
Investment according to Wage; ....Third commandment
Dividend according to Investment Burden"...Fourth commandment

(b) when the poor workers 'investment burden' in the creation of national capital is higher than other workers they will receive 'higher dividend' than the other high-income group of workers according to 'economic justice'.

(c) therefore when the National Profit increases due to 'incremental or just price', the poor income group of workers will receive higher dividend than what they paid in the form of just higher price.

(d) the higher dividend ultimately will increase the purchasing power of the poor people.

(e) in our example though the poor consumers pay $2 more than the 'expected just price' in the distribution of national profit they will perhaps may get 3 dollars as dividend 'according to **'distributive justice'.**

(f) therefore whatever price rules the market that will soar the standard of poor, will always be the just price.

(g) in this case when the price level increases it benefits the poor because all the poor consumers are producers and the national dividend goes directly to their **'income parentheses'.**

** Economic justice is a component of social justice. It's a set of moral principles for building economic institutions, the ultimate goal of which is to create an opportunity for each person to create a sufficient material foundation upon which to have a dignified, productive, and creative life beyond economics.

Economic Justice Definition | Investopedia

www.investopedia.com/terms/e/economic-justice.asp

Chapter – 26

Property Justice
Property Right to Proletariat Only

"We may have democracy, or we may have wealth concentrated in the hands of a few, but we cannot have both"

– Supreme Court justice Louis Brandeis

"Without property rights, no other rights are possible. Since man has to sustain his life by his own effort, the man who has no right to the product of his effort has no means to sustain his life. The man who produces while others dispose of his product, is a slave." **– Ayn Rand**

"As a man is said to have a right to his property, he may be equally said to have a property in his rights." **—James Madison**

Creation of Property

Property, the material wealth in general terms, is not created by God in the heaven and gifted to some rich at the time of their birth on earth as if decreed by divine providence. Property is the material form of the accumulated labour of the workers, only the workers and nothing but the workers. Property is the rare and exclusive creation of workers by their hard labour. But if the property is now owned by a few capitalists or by the State it implies that it has been tacitly forfeited from the workers without their legitimate permission using their ignorance of human rights and economic justice. The property owned by a few is nothing but a legalised day light robbery. The property that is created from 'labour' is the capital, and if it is created from the 'profit' it is the robbery because profit is the exploitation of labour in the form of money.

Property Right

By the term 'property right' I do not mean in the ordinary sense that is prevailing in the capitalistic societies, which is aggravating economic disparities among the people. In these societies, in the name of 'property right', few people are allowed to accumulate property as much as they can and then legal protection is offered through constitutional authority not to be appropriated by any one. This kind of 'property right' is outrageous to all norms of political and economic justices.

In Democratisation of economy the 'property right' is established on two prerequisite conditions known as **'equal distribution and constitutional protection'.** The equal distribution, first of all, necessitates among other things that the national property should be distributed to all the people equally and then only to sustain perpetually the ownership of property constitutional protection should be endowed with the people as 'fundamental right'. The 'property right' to the people who have no property at all is fraudulent and cheating to the all norms of economic justice.

The Expert Committee of **UNESCO** in its Declaration of Human Rights says that the **'property right'** covers only the value property that is actually required by a person or his family and not more than that. Such excessive property will not come under purview of 'property right'. (UNESCO Symposium: Human Rights: p. 269)

Compulsory Property Ownership

Invariably all the countries have enacted law for compulsory education for the children so that man can understand and protect the value of his liberty and rights. Similarly all the governments enact a law for Compulsory Property Ownership for every worker so that every worker would be assured for 'employment opportunity', 'economic liberty', 'income security', 'economic liberty', 'economic equality', 'economic fraternity' and 'a life without fear of future', and moreover every worker would be able to expose his 'individuality', 'creativeness' and 'originality' in his work. If not though the people get political freedom they would be seen economically slaves everywhere and would be ever fearful of their future, and they cannot plan their future to lead their family towards an ideal life for their children. Considering all these facts Democrism emphasises compulsory property ownership and then 'property right' to protect it. Property right without property is futile; it is like 'work without the right to wage and wage without right to spend'.

In the same line of thought the American philosopher, Russell Kirk (1918-1994) says with historical evidence as follows:

"Private property has been a powerful instrument for teaching men and women responsibility and for giving them the leisure to think and freedom to act with prudence. Where there is no property right human beings are invariably kicked around by the politicians as in Soviet Russia, by military as in any Warlord System, or by a priest craft as in Peru of the Incas".

– **Russell Kirk: 'Economics: Work and Prosperity'** (1988)

If and only if the economy is democratized every one or every worker will be entitled to compulsory property ownership or compulsory direct ownership of capital. This property ownership will provide equal economic power to every worker 1. A happy life in the social segment, 2. A real democratic government in political sector and 3. An economic equality in economic sphere.

Firstly according to Harold J. Laski (1893-1950)

'The possession of wealth means that possessions of such that makes for a happy life, beautiful physical surroundings, leisure to read and to think, a safeguard against the insecurity of the morrow'

– Harold Laski: 'Liberty in the Modern State'
(New York: Harper -1930)

Secondly, Jawaharlal Nehru emphasises the need for distribution of national wealth to the people for the establishment of real democracy in political sector as follows:

"A real government by the people and for the people can be established when all the people really share in the government and the wealth of the country" **– Nehru on socialism**

The French philosopher Rousseau in his book 'Social Contact' the same ideology of equality in wealth as follows:

"Equality in rank and fortune (wealth) without which equality in rights and authority cannot long subsist". **–Rousseau : "Social Contract"**

Thirdly, in the economic sphere Professor Meade insists the equal distribution of wealth for smooth operation of the economy, in the following words :

"In order that monetary and pricing system should work with equity, it is necessary to achieve a fair distribution of income and property"

I have quoted above the philosophical ideas of the famous thinkers on importance of the equal distribution of national property for the establishment a just socio-economic-political order in the world.

Property Right to Proletariat only

It is the prerequisite condition that if the socio-economic-political system of a country should work justifiably for the welfare of the people as a whole first of all the national property should be equally distributed to the people in order to empower them with equal economic power. In democratisation of economy when the national capital is directly owned by the people the national property would be automatically distributed them according to distributive justice. In this context, the property right would be entitled only to the proletariats. This is the concentricity of all economic justices. No one will be allowed to live without work by the income derived from the ancestral property.

Bertrand Russell says that it is the economic justice as follows:

"Economic Justice demands a diminution if not a total abolition, of the proportion of the national income which goes to the recipients of rent and interest"

– ***Bertrand Russell: 'Political Ideals'*** (p. 38)

Since the workers alone are the creators of the poverty, they should have exclusive property right and no one else. J.W. Smith, in his book, 'Economic Democracy: The Political Struggle of the 21st Century, emphatically notes the version with an example as follows:

"The value added to iron of a steel mill becomes the property of the owners of the steel mill. So is the case of all other capital instruments. Property in labour. What is the relationship of the worker which he creates through his work? It has been said that no one has ever questioned the right of a worker to the fruits of his labour. Actually, as was long ago recognised by John Locke and Jean Jacques Rousseau, the right of the worker to the value he creates is nothing more than the particular type of private property applicable to the labour. **Each worker, they said, has of private property in his capacity to produce wealth through his labour and in the value which he creates".**

– J.W. Smith: 'Economic Democracy'

Chapter – 27

Global Justice and Nuclear War Democratisation of Economy Eliminates all Destructive Weapons

Nuclear holocaust

It is the Global Justice that upholds the inalienable right to life of all creatures of nature from the human-made threatenings of all destructive weapons. From World War II the global countries race to adorn their nuclear arsenal to claim "nuclear supremacy and super power". The mad race for nuclear weapons will result in nuclear holocaust along with their parental socio-economic systems of Capitalism and Socialism. In order to save the mankind we, the people should have 'Direct Ownership of Capital'. If the capital is directly owned by the people, they will not permit their own capital to produce the weapons of mass destruction and thereby perish themselves. We don't want neither Capitalism nor Socialism but the Democrism (Democratisation of economy) – the third economic system to ensure the perennial world peace.

"Of all the enemies to public liberty war is, perhaps, the most dreaded parent because it comprises and develops the germ of every other. War is parent of armies; from these proceed debts and taxes ... known instruments for bringing the many under the domination of the few ... No nation could preserve its freedom in the midst of continual warfare".

— James Madison, Political Observations, 1795.

"To me science was a technique to understand a beautiful world."

– Dr John Kogut, scientist, Crusader against 'Star War Program'

"There are plenty of problems in the world, many of them interconnected. But there is no problem which compares with this central, universal problem of saving the human race from extinction."

– John Foster Dulles, Speech to UN General Assembly, 1952

Birth of Nuclear Age

The Nuclear weapons project's roots began in 1939 when at the urging of Leo Szilard, Albert Einstein signed the Einstein–Szilard letter to President Franklin Roosevelt expressing concerns that Nazi Germany might develop nuclear weapons. The copy of the letter is displayed here.(See annexure also)

Einstein and Szilard – Dr Oppenhemer with EinsteinFather of Nuclear Weapon.

Einstein letter to Roosevelt

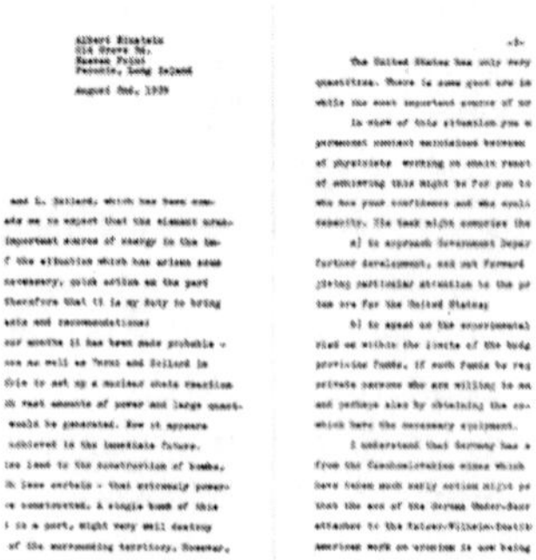

Document 1: Copy of Einstein letter
See: At the end of the chapter also.

The first nuclear device ever detonated was an implosion-type bomb at the Trinity test, conducted at New Mexico's Alamogordo Bombing and Gunnery Range on 16 July 1945.

6 Aug 45. Little Boy was dropped on Hiroshima (war experts said US wanted to show supremacy over Russia)

8 Aug 45. Russia declared war on Japan.

9 Aug 45. Fat Man was dropped on Nagasaki, to compel Japan to surrender to US instead of Russia.

Atom bombing on Nagasaki Aug. 9, 1945 Japan surrendered to US.

02 Sep. 1945. Japan surrendered to America officially.

29 Aug 49. The Soviet Union explodes its first atomic weapon, JOE-1.

3 Oct 52. Great Britain exploded its first atomic weapon.

1 March 1954: US detonated the 'Castle Bravo' the world's most powerful thermonuclear hydrogen bomb device at 'Bikini Atol'.

30 Oct 61. USSR conducted the world's largest nuclear test with 57 megaton device, Tsar Bomba,

Bravo – USA: 1,000 time more powerful than "Little Boy".

Tsar Bomba – USSR 1,400 powerful than 'Little Boy' and 'Fat Man' combined.

18 May 1974..India tested atom bomb "Smiling Buddha" at Pokran.

11-13 May 1998 .. India again tested 5 atom bombs –"Shakthi" at Pokran.

The mankind lives on the brink of nuclear holocaust.

Annihilation of nuclear plants and control the dangerous scientific wisdom"

What we want at present is not 'disarmament', a policy of escapism, but a complete annihilation of all "Nuclear weapons plants and complexes, and the entire delivery system of nuclear weapons. Even if we annihilate nuclear weapon plants we cannot destroy the comprehensive wisdom of scientists and technicians to reconstruct the nuclear plants whenever a governments dem ands. The only solution is to bring the capital required for nuclear plants under the direct control of the people through establishment of "People's direct Ownership of Capital" i.e. **Democrism-The Third theory.**

Delivery Systems of Nuclear Weapons

F 16 Falcon

Submarines

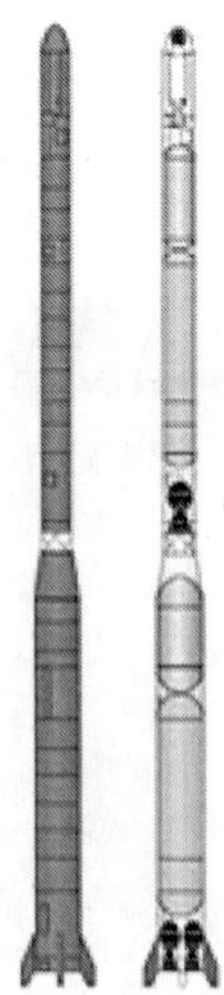

Rockets

Explosion of 'Bravo'

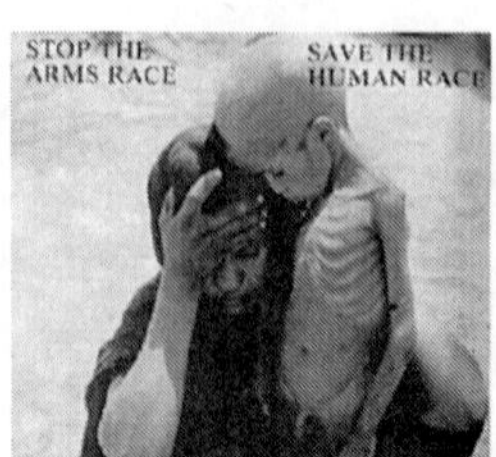

"Hey Poor children! hail
'Bravo & Tsar'
They will save you!!!..."

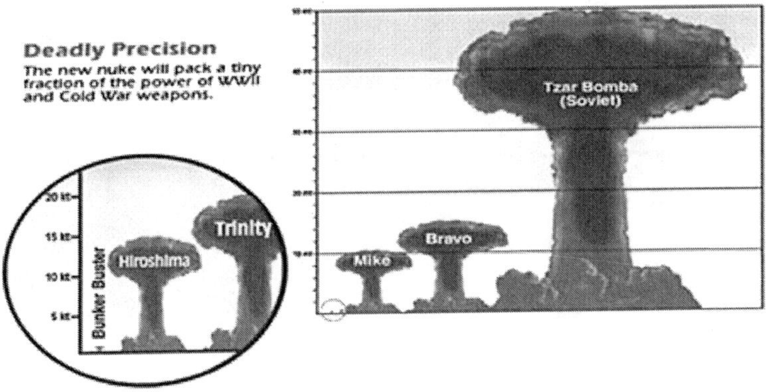

Comparison of holocaust of Bravo and Tsar

"Bravo" Nuclear fallout) (US)...Tsar Bomba the symbol of nuclear holocaust. (USSR)

Explosion of Bravo and its impact

When Bravo was detonated, it formed a fireball almost four and a half miles (roughly 7 km) across within a second. This fireball was visible on Kwajalein Atoll over 250 miles (450 km) away. The explosion left a crater of 6,500 feet (2,000 m) in diameter and 250 feet (75 m) in depth. The **mushroom cloud** reached a height of 47,000 feet (14 km) and a diameter of 7 miles (11 km) in about a minute; it then reached a height of 130,000 feet (40 km) and 62 miles (100 km) in diameter in less than 10 minutes and was expanding at more than 100 m/s (360 km/h, 224 mph). As a result of the blast, the cloud contaminated more than seven thousand square miles of the surrounding Pacific Ocean including some of the surrounding small islands like **Rongerik, Rangeley** and **Utirik.**

Explosion of Tsar and its impact

The **Tsar Bomba** was the largest, (see the picture above) most powerful nuclear weapon ever detonated. It was a three-stage **hydrogen bomb** with a yield of about 50 **megatons.** This is equivalent to ten times the amount of all the explosives used in World War II combined. It was detonated on October 30, 1961, in the **Novaya Zemlya archipelago,** and was capable of approximately 100 **megatons,** but was purposely reduced shortly before the launch. Although **weaponised,** it was not entered into service; it was simply a demonstrative testing on the capabilities of the Soviet Union's military technology at that time. The explosion was hot enough to induce **third degree burns** at 100 km distance [И].

[И] **"The Soviet Weapons Program The Tsar Bomba".**

NuclearWeaponArchive.org. The Nuclear Weapon Archive. Last updated 3 September 2007. Retrieved 23 August 2010.

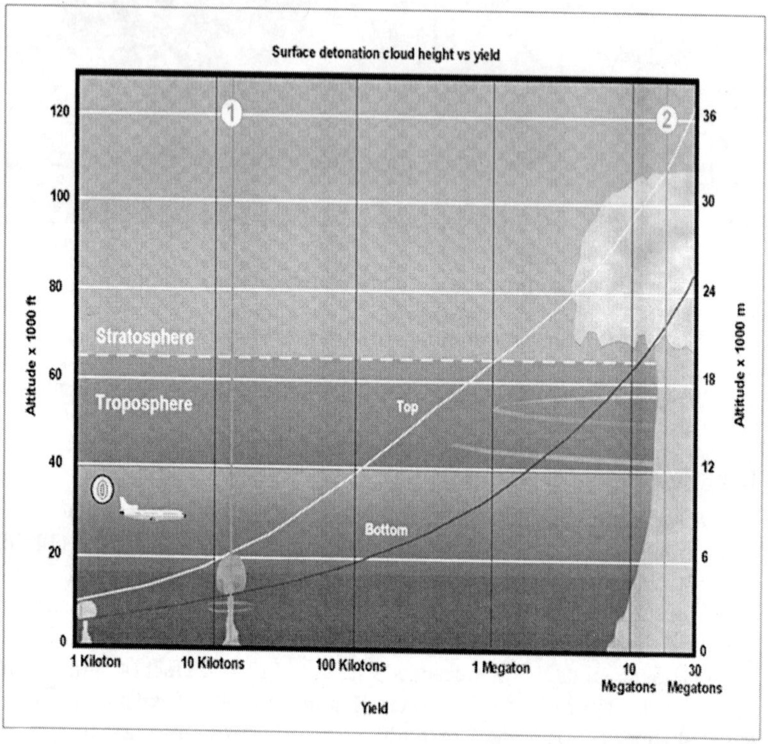

Source: Military history of the Soviet Union the Cold War and nuclear weapons.

Power of Nuclear Weapons

Nuclear Holocaust or One World

We are now living in the fast approaching destruction of nuclear war. In this context I wish to quote the words of Albert Einstein:

"I do not know with what weapons World War III will be fought, but World War IV will be fought with sticks and stones"

In the same wave length of thought William Douglas (Judge, United States Supreme Court), in his book 'Anatomy of Liberty' (p.178) says:

"One's liberty at the community level, no matter how perfect it may seem to be at present, would disappear with nuclear war. Devastation would be so complete that military rule replaces even the free society. Those left would then start anew their search for liberty. But they would

struggle under conditions vastly more difficult than faced Mousterian man when he first emerged from the caves in Paleolithic time"

But the scientists now say that if nuclear war bursts out the whole earth will be engulfed with nuclear winter and all the creatures will perish within a week. So, there will be no question of survival of man.

Global Warheads and World War III

1. Global Warheads: Despite numerous treaties during the Reagan period (1985 -1990) the developed countries (US, USSR, UK, France and China in combine) planted nearly **69,000 warheads on the earth (and the Star War Programme in the sky) which virtually thrust the world towards launch pad of WW III.**

2. Sale of WMD: Moreover during the 1990s the private arms companies in the US and West Europe engaged in the sale of deadly weapons. Today the combined sale of the top 100 arms companies amounts to some $286 billion. **63.3 per cent was accounted for by 40 US companies, and 29.4 per cent by 36 West European companies. (in aggregate: 92.7 per cent)**

3. Exports: During the period between 2000 – 2009 top 15 countries (USA, Russia, Germany, France, UK and others) exported weapons of mass destruction to the tune of $270 billion to the rest of the world.

4. Imports: During the same period between 2000 and 2009 the top 15 countries like India, Singapore, Malaysia, and Korea, Pakistan and so on, imported Weapons of Mass Destruction to the value of $116.197 billion from the US, West European Countries and Russia.

5. The International Trade: The international trade in the military weapons is now aggravating hot tension between the countries and they are engaging frequent wars with conventional weapons at present. (For example; Pak vs. India, N. Korea vs. S. Korea, Iraq vs. Kuwait, Iraq vs. Israel, US vs. Iraq, US vs. Vietnam and so on).

6. Towards WW III: The Military Experts say the regional war between any two countries will gather accelerated momentum with their allies will result in WW III with Nuclear Weapons.

After the WW II right from North Korean War (Communist regime) in 1948 to the Indo-Pak Kargil War in 1999 nearly 20 regional wars have been fought in the world and in which 29,921,942 civilians are killed. The civilian death toll is estimated as higher than the civilian deaths of 27,372,900 during WW. II (1939-1945). These wars are fought with the advanced conventional weapons like AK series, naval systems includes all types of ships like aircraft carriers, submarines, destroyers and frigates.

Encompassing military aircraft, conventional missiles, and military satellites, this is the most technologically advanced sector of the market. It is also the least competitive from an economic standpoint, with a handful of companies dominating the entire market. The top clients and major producers are virtually all located in the western world, with the United States easily in first place.

The Control Arms Campaign, founded by Amnesty International, Oxfam, and the International Action Network on Small Arms, estimated in 2003 that there are over 639 million small arms in circulation, and that over **1,135 companies** based in more than **98 different countries** manufacture small arms as well as their various components and ammunition.*

— *(Debbie Hillier, Brian Wood (2003). "Shattered Lives - the case for tough international arms control" . Control Arms Campaign. pp. 19. Retrieved on 2009-03-28.)

(d) National shares of arms sales of the top 100 arms-producing companies in the world (excluding China).

According to the SIPRI, the top 100 arms producing companies (44 companies are operating in USA alone) have sold $347 billion worth of deadly weapons in 2007. It contributes 63 per cent of total sales.

— National or regional shares of arms sales for the SIPRI Top 100 Companies in top 10 countries during 2003.

Exports (Sales) by 100 companies in 2008 at 1990 prices: USD 384.7 billion

(US 44 and Western Europe 34 Companies)

Imports by top 10 countries in 2008 at 1990 prices USD 10.9 billion

(India : 2.4 billion and China: 2.2 billion)

The Global transference of WMD amounts in 2008 only $395.599 (Exports plus Imports).

(*SOURCE:* SIPRI (Stockholm International Peace Research Institute). 2008. SIPRI Arms Transfers. Database. February. Stockholm. (100 private companies of Top 10 Countries.

Global military expenditure on Warheads

(Capitalism and socialism are dangerous)

The global military expenditure during 2010 amounts to1.575 trillion dollars.

Moreover, during cold war period under Ronald Reagan the global warheads stockpiles (in US, Russia, UK, France and China combined) totaled about **69,490.** According to Barry, in his article **'On Energy'** (Sep.19, 2010), one warhead costs **$70,000** and accordingly one can calculate what would be the total cost each country has to spend for their warheads.

The huge expenditure for military unmasks the fallacy of the capitalism and socialism. Both the systems are very dangerous for the survival of mankind.

Technological development and civilian deaths: According to UNICEF, decade after decade the human causalities in the war increased incredibly. In the regional wars held during 1990s, out of total human causalities 90 per cent were civilians and only 10 per cent were military persons.

"As in any war, there have been dreadful mistakes and civilian casualties. The difference is when Israelis kill innocents they apologise; when Hezbollah kills innocents they celebrate". **–J.D. Hayworth**

"As a civilian during the Second War, I was exposed to danger in circumstances which removed any distinction between the man in and the man out of uniform". **–Lester B. Pearson**

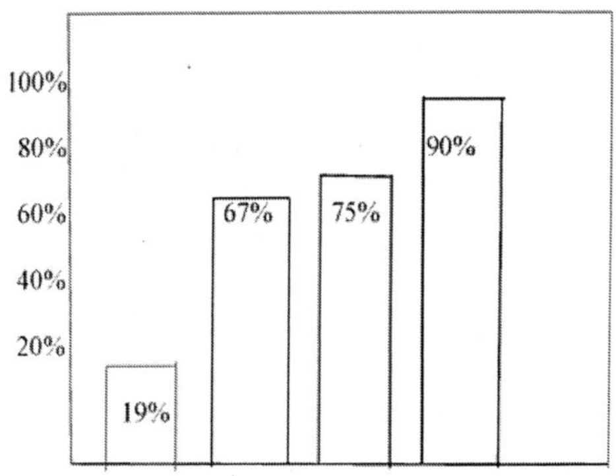

WWI + WWII + 1990s

Civilian Causalities - UNICEF

Unproductive and Waste Capital Accumulation

(a) To produce Hiroshima and Nagasaki type of nuclear weapons (~15 kt each) alone at present cost requires $23 billion[a]. It cannot be produced with bare human hands. It requires a mammoth volume of capital to construct a 'nuclear weapon production industry'. The establishment of Nuclear Weapon Industry requires somewhat between $250 billion and $500 billion depending on the capital-output ratio and the size of the nuclear weapons.

Moreover the 'delivery system' such as military warships, ballistic missiles and rockets and fighter planes (carrier of nuclear weapons) like F-16 costs many times more than the industrial investment. Further, the whole programme requires highly experienced scientists, engineers, technicians and military personnel to work as an elite team. What does the destructive capital, a creation from the tax payments of poor people, produce for the benefit of the people? Nothing and nothing but the annihilation of mankind on the earth forever.

http://wiki.answerscomQ/Howmuch_did_it_cost_to_create_atombomb.

In his Speech before the American Society of Newspapere Editors, on April 16, 1953 President Dwight **D. Eisenhower** said:

"Every gun that is fired, every warship launched, every rocket fired signifies in the final sense, a THEFT from those who hunger and are not fed, those who are cold and are not clothed ....

The cost of one modern heavy bomber is this: a modern brick school in more than thirty cities ..... We pay for a single fighter plane with a half million bushels of wheat. We pay for a single destroyer with new homes that could have housed more than eight thousand people ....

This world in arms is not spending money alone. It is spending the sweat of its labourers, the genius of its scientists, and the hope of children.

This is not a way of life at all, in true sense. Under the cloud of threatening war, it is humanity hanging from a cross of iron ......"

Professor Dallas W. Smyth, Economics Professor at University of Illinois, Urbana, (1963), says:

"Billions for defense but not a cent for Socialism. It is not Socialism to have the government spend 50 billion dollars for weapons; it would be socialism if the government spent the same amount for education or for public works."

But aware of the dreadful consequences of nuclear holocaust the politicians are anxious to spend billions and billions of dollars of poor people's money on nuclear weapons and weapons of mass destruction. President Reagan, in mid 1980s prepared to allocate $ 1 trillion for 'Star War Program'. Why?

Firstly, a deep rooted suspicion prevailed between Capitalist America and Communist Russia on each other due to their conflicting economic systems especially in their 'modes of production of goods and services'.

Secondly, the political as well as economic democracy failed in both the countries. The people lost their birth right to exercise control over their ruling authorities which they elected.

Thirdly, the people were kept in dark chamber to get accountability and transparency regarding how their tax payment was drained out in the military exercises. So that people were unable to check their governments' production of nuclear weapon.

"An Eye for an Eye' makes the world blind"

During the cold war period especially between the era of Stalin and Khuruschev mankind was trusted at the brink of complete annihilation. The first step was put forward by US. On March 1, 1954 President Dwight D. Eisenhower ordered to detonate the 'Castle Bravo' the world's most powerful thermonuclear hydrogen bomb device at 'Bikini Atol' island.

Dwight D Eisenhower

Castle Bravo

To counter the US-Nuclear weapon strategy Khuruschev, the premier of USSR, ordered to detonate the 'Tsar Bomba' the world's most powerful thermonuclear hydrogen device on October 30, 1961, in the Novaya Zemlya archipelago.

Khuruschev

Tsar Bomba

The Tsar Bomba mushroom cloud is seen from a distance of 160 km. the crown of the cloud is 56 km high at the time of the picture.

Nuclear terrorism and annihilation of mankind

Why these two superpowers indulge in nuclear terrorism to threaten the mankind? It is purely on the question of 'capital ownership'.

Primarily they just follow diametrically opposite ideology in the 'ownership of capital'. Capitalism permits that the national capital may be owned by a few capitalists through democratic principles whereas the Socialism insists that the national capital should be directly owned by the State through 'proletariat dictatorship'.

-Khuruschev and Kennedy

Dear Mr.President,

At present I am on the shore of the Black Sea. When they write in the press that Khrushchov is resting on the Black Sea it may be said that this is correct and at the same time incorrect. This is indeed a wonderful place. As a former Naval officer you would surely appreciate the merits of these surroundings, the beauty of the sea and the grandeur of the Caucasian mountains. Under this bright Southern sun it is even somehow hard to believe that there still exist problems in the world which, due to lack of solutions, cast a sinister shadow on peaceful life, on the future of millions of people.

But as you will fully understand, I cannot at this time permit myself any relaxation. I am working, and here I work more fruitfully because my attention is not diverted to routine matters of which I have plenty, probably like you yourself do. Here I can concentrate on the main things.

His Excellency
Mr.John F.KENNEDY,
President of the United States of America
Washington, D.C.

DECLASSIFIED
E.O. 12356, Sec. 3.4

The vibrant soul underlying in these economic systems is the 'economic mechanism' which describes how the goods are produced in factory system. The method of production of goods in factories is identical with the same technology but the capital of the factories varies. For this variation in the capital ownership the global countries fight against each other and spend trillions of dollars for the production of nuclear weapons, weapons of mass destruction and for their delivery systems to fight on the surface and in the space. For this ideological difference these countries prepare to annihilate even the mankind on the earth.

Secondarily these superpowers want to defeat the other country technologically and scientifically to claim that their system is superior to the other system. But both of the superpowers have no interest in eradication of poverty, unemployment, inflation, corruption, economic disparity and so on. If they are inefficient in solving at least the global poverty for more than two hundred years since the outburst of industrial revolution what is the use of these systems? Both the leaders of Socialism and Capitalism accept that they have no solution at their disposal. I present below the historical letter written by Kruschev to John F Kennedy on Sep. 29, 1961.

In his letter Khruschev admits the ineffectiveness of socialistic and capitalistic economic systems to prevent nuclear holocaust.

"Under this bright Southern sun it is even somehow hard to believe that there still exist problems in the world which, due to lack of solutions, cast a sinister shadow on peaceful life, on the future of millions of people."

(i) Does your shoe find solution Khruschev? What does it imply?

at UN General Assembly

Khruschev penned the above letter on Sep. 29, 1961. But exactly a month later on Oct. 30, 1961 Khrushchev ordered to test world's gigantic nuclear bomb 'Tsar Boma'. Was this the solution to establish peaceful life for mankind? We, the people don't trust the words of politicians even if they signed various treats.

The eradication of nuclear holocaust requires short run as well as long run solutions.The short run solution pertains to disarmament of nuclear weapons whereas the long run solution requires the 'reformation of economic system itself.

(ii) Retaliations and annihilation of mankind

The first retaliation resorted to nuclear weapons was launched by US to bombard on Hiroshima and Nagasaki on civilians against Japan's attack on Pearl Harbor. In order to demolish the monopoly in nuclear power of US, USSR tested JOE I. This retaliatory strategy gathered accelerated tempo. England and other western European countries also joined in the mad nuclear race under the guise of the 'policy of deterrence'. When USSR launched Sputnik in the orbit in 1957 President Regan announced 'Star War' programme in 1982. The nuclear war was shifted to outer space.

The global leaders woke up from their deep slumber only after the detonation of 'Tzar Bomba', the king of all atom bombs, on Oct 30, 1961 which was a retaliatory test against 'Castle Bravo' of US on March 1, 1954. **For his part President Reagan announced 'Star War' programme, a complete annihilation of mankind.**

On the other hand India and Pakistan engaged in retaliatory ventures in testing nuclear devices as a separate bloc. India tested nuclear weapons mainly to secure a permanent seat in 'security council' and Pak to occupy the territory of Kashmir despite their people are reeling under utter poverty.

Definition of Disarmament

Disarmament is the act of reducing, limiting, or abolishing weapons. Disarmament refers to a country's military or specific type of weaponry. Disarmament is often taken to mean total elimination of **weapons of mass destruction,** such as **nuclear arms.** General and Complete Disarmament refers to the removal of all weaponry, including conventional arms.

Disarmament can be contrasted with **arms control,** which essentially refers to the act of controlling arms rather than eliminating them. A distinction can also be made between disarmament as a process (the process of eliminating weapons), and disarmament as an end state (the absence of weapons). Disarmament has also come to be associated with two things:

1. **Nuclear disarmament,** referring to the elimination of nuclear weapons.
2. **Unilateral disarmament**, the elimination of weapons outside of the framework of an international agreement, i.e., they are not bound by a treaty such as **START** (Strategic Arms Reduction Treaty).

Disarmament usually prescribes various treaties, bilateral and multilateral. The treaties insist that the terms and conditions should be honoured literally. But the honour of the treaties depend upon the economic and political power of the countries. If a super power dishonours a treaty who will have the courage and strength to punish it and how. The treaties are signed on the optimistic note that the member countries will honour it.

Philosophically, disarmament may be viewed as a form of **demilitarisation;** part of an economic, political, technical, and military process to reduce and eliminate weapons systems. Thus, disarmament may be part of a set of other strategies, like **economic conversion,** which aim to reduce the power of war making institutions and associated constituencies.

Truman's successors recognised the threats posed by the arms race and nuclear proliferation. In September 1961, speaking to the UN General Assembly, a very young and charismatic American President, John F. Kennedy, warned,

"Every man, woman and child lives under a nuclear sword of Damocles, hanging by the slenderest of threads, capable of being cut at any moment by accident or miscalculation or by madness. The weapons of war must be abolished before they abolish us.

Kennedy proposed that to end the nuclear danger

"Disarmament negotiations resume promptly, and continue without interruption. Until an entire programme for general and complete disarmament has **not only been** agreed **but has actually been achieved.**" This programme, he argued, should involve "a steady reduction in force, both nuclear and conventional, until it has abolished all armies and all weapons except those needed for internal order and a new United Nations Peace Force."

(c) Is Disarmament a solution?

The Nuclear Weapons Treaties do not provide any effective solution to establish a Nuclear Weapons Free World. The key Treaties such as Non Proliferation (NPT) and Comprehensive Test Ban Treaties (CTBT) insist the 'nuclear club' countries not to venture any more nuclear weapon tests but not testing of 'ballistic missiles'.

Moreover, these treaties are incompetent to impose strong restrictions on the countries **not to produce** any more nuclear weapons but they only insist on **not to test** any more nuclear weapons. Catastrophically the treaties allow all the countries to produce as many nuclear weapons as they like and compile them in their nuclear arsenal.

European Council -United Nations General Assembly

"We are committed to upholding, implementing and further strengthening the multilateral **disarmament** and **non-proliferation** framework in the fight against threats which are tending to escape the control of national sovereignty, the challenges deriving from destabilising accumulation and spread of small arms and light weapons, from illicit or irresponsible arms trade, and from the proliferation of weapons of mass destruction, which are creating new and growing hot-spots of international tension. In this regard, the EU welcomes the growing support in all parts of the world for an International Arms Trade Treaty and is firmly committed to this process.

EU@UN – EU Presidency Statement – United Nations 62nd General Assembly: General Debate. Europa-eu-un.org. Retrieved on 2012-05-09.

(d) The failure of treaties

Even though the treaties are in force approximately more than $1.5 trillion dollar worth of weapons of mass destruction are transacted between the countries in the international trade every year from 2012 onwards. It is estimated that after cold war in 1991 nearly 30 trillion dollars are spent up to 2012 on military expenditures world wide. When the cold war is over why these countries with accelerated tempo spend such huge volume of money on military expenditure.

World Military Spending.www.globalissues.org. Retrieved on 2012-05-09.

Capitalistic Mode of production and grave military spending:

According to SIPRI (Stockholm International Peace Research Institute), in 2008, 100 companies of top 10 countries export WMD over and above 384.7 billion dollars at 1990 prices yearly to other countries. The exports are stream out by **44 private companies** to the US and **34 companies** to Western Europe. These companies are empowering the Asian and Pacific countries with WMD to the tune of 1.575 trillion dollars approximately every year. India and China are the largest importers (2.4 and 2.3 billion dollars respectively).

Oscar Arias Sanchez, President of Costa Rica (awarded the Nobel Peace Prize in 1987 for his efforts to end civil wars across Central America through the Esquipulas II Accors) has stated:

"When a country decides to invest in arms, rather in education, housing, the environment, and health services for its people, it is depriving a whole generation of its right to prosperity and happiness. We have produced one firearm for every ten inhabitants of this planet, yet we have not bothered to end hunger when such a feat is well within our reach. Our international regulations allow almost three-quarters of all global arms sales to pour into the developing world with no binding international guidelines whatsoever.

Our regulations do not hold countries accountable for what is done with the weapons they sell, even when the probable use of such weapons is obvious.

Anonymous. The Global Arms Trade: Strengthening International Regulations. Interview with Oscar Arias Sanchez. Harvard International Review Date: Tuesday, July 1, 2008, http://www.allbusiness.com/government/government-bodies-offices/11664335-1.html accessed on 10 Feb 2010

Top spending in 2009 ($ Billions, and percentage of total)

Country..............	Dollars (billions)........	of total	Rank
United States	711	41.0 per cent	1
China	143	8.2 per cent	2
Russia	71.9	4.1 per cent	3
United Kingdom	62.7	3.6 per cent	4
France	62.5	3.6 per cent	5
Japan	59.3	3.4 per cent	6
Saudi Arabia	48.5	2.8 per cent	7
India	46.8	2.7 per cent	8
Germany	46.7	2.7 per cent	9
Brazil	35.4	2.0 per cent	10
Italy	34.5	2.0 per cent	11
South Korea	30.8	1.8 per cent	12
Australia	26.7	1.5 per cent	13
Canada	24.7	1.4 per cent	14
Turkey	17.9	1.0 per cent	15
Rest of world	312.6	18.0 per cent	
	Global Total (not all countries shown): 1,735		

Global military spending

The Only Solution To Nuclear Wars

Short-run solution

1. Non-Proliferation Treaty (NPT).......
2. Comprehensive Test Ban Treaty (CTBT) ..
3. Disarmament ....
4. Bilateral Treaties

Long-run solutions

Democratization of Economy (Create "People's Direct Ownership Capital" – Democrism- The Third Theory)

The long run Solution

(a) "People's Direct Ownership of Capital"

Democratic Economy (Democrism-The Third Theory)

The remedy, therefore, in all reasonable respects lies in finding out a "New Economic System" based on socio-economic justices acceptable by the communists as well as capitalists as the ultimate goal. Therefore, we have to establish Economic Democracy, in addition to political democracy, based on the concept of 'Workers' Direct Ownership of Capital'.

The "Workers' Direct Ownership of Capital" will empower the people not to use their capital to produce any destructive weapons to kill themselves. The world peace, therefore, depends on the establishment of 'Democratic Economy' and "One World" but not on the paper agreements on "Disarmaments" or 'Summit' meetings' – the evasive political strategies.

In conclusion, I like to quote the words of Sigmund Freud (6 May 1856 – 23 September 1939), Austrian Originator of Psycho-Analysis:

"..........men are not gentle, friendly creatures wishing for love, who simply defend themselves if they are attacked, but a powerful measure of desire for aggression has to be reckoned as part of their intellectual endowment"

-Sigmund Freud: "Civilisation and its Discontents" (1929)

"Thus" William O. Douglas says:

"our problem does not end with disarmament....The task of our generation is to educate the peoples of the earth on the needs that new community and the ways and means of survival."

-William O. Douglas: "Anatomy of Liberty": p. 176

It is the Law of Nature that dictates all the socio-economic orders to move towards their perfection and eternality. Until they reach perfection change is inevitable. Communism and Capitalism are now changing with rapid pace in the aftermath era of cold war and Globalisation of economy. The wide spread information technology and the powerful domination of computers in every one's life facilitate the world corporate sectors to pave the way for equal distribution of their capital share. In consequence if the Capitalism and communism attain perfection they will conciliate with each other in the concept of Economic Democracy and **"People's Direct Ownership of Capital" (Democrism).** Since there is only one perfection capitalism and socialism should dissolve into Democrism, the ultimate economic justice.

(b) Democratic Mode of Production: I repeatedly emphasise Democratic Mode of Production as early as possible before the nuclear weapons destroy us. In the Democratic Mode of Production the people (workers) would undertake direct ownership of capital of all industries including nuclear weapons production industries (defense industries). Therefore, it is the people have to decide whether they have to allow the 'nuclear weapon- industries' to operate or to dismantle them or to convert them as educational institutions or hospitals, or great stadiums or institutions that would provide socially needed services to the people. The people would not allow these 'destructive industries' to produce 'nuclear weapons' to destroy themselves. The politicians, the bureaucrats, the military brasses and the vested interests should get rid of the decision-making process.

The management of nuclear power industries: The management of these industries and technicians will be entrusted in the hands of the Scientists, professionals of the industries and they will be accountable to the workers of the country. If the people want to produce electricity by nuclear power let they establish nuclear reactors and if not let them dismantle all the reactors and produce the electricity by safe conventional methods. The decision-making authorities should cooperate with people and let the politicians get out of the decision-making processes. People have the absolute right whether they want to use more power of electricity or to live with the limited power of electricity. The decision is always up to their judgement of people. No one can infringe their right.

Plato (428 B.C – 348 B.C), the classical Greek Scholar, nearly two thousand five hundred years ago, insists that the people should be ruled over by the Governing, which represents the head (Rulers or Philosophers Kings) – those who are intelligent, rational, self-controlled, in love with wisdom, well suited to make decisions for the community. He says:

"Until philosophers are kings or the kings and princes of this world have the spirit and power of philosophy, and wisdom and political leadership meet in same man, cities will never cease from ill or the human race".

Though the scientists, philosophers and economists warn the politicians about the holocaust of mankind due to nuclear war, the politicians are spending even now many billions and billions of dollars on nuclear weapons, Nuclear weapon plants and their delivery systems. These politicians are also aware of nuclear holocaust and utter wastage of people's 'tax money' for the production of 'weapons of mass destruction' for nothing. Unless and until we transform the political system of government into economic system of government we cannot inject the 'philosophical form of government' which is advocated by Plato and run flawless government to eliminate nuclear war and create nuclear weapon-free world. I have illustrated the nature of 'economic government' in the 34th chapter.

Annexure: 1

Einstein Letter to Roosevelt (readable version)

Einstein

Old Grove Road

Peconic, Loke

August, 2nd, 1939

To

F.D. Roosevelt

President of United States

White House

Washington, D.C.

Sir,

We recent work by E. Fermi and L. Szilard, which has been communicated to me in manuscript, leads me to expect that the element uranium may be turned into a new and important source of energy in the immediate future. Certain aspects of the situation which has arisen seem to call for watchfulness and if necessary, quick action on the part of the Administration. I believe therefore that it is my duty to bring to your attention the following facts and recommendations.

In the course of the last four months it has been made probable through the work of Joliot in France as well as Fermi and Szilard in America—that it may be possible to set up a nuclear chain reaction in a large mass of uranium, by which vast amounts of power and large quantities of new radium-like elements would be generated. Now it appears almost certain that this could be achieved in the immediate future.

This new phenomenon would also lead to the construction of bombs, and it is conceivable—though much less certain—those extremely powerful bombs of this type may thus be constructed. A single bomb of this type, carried by boat and exploded in a port, might very well destroy the whole port together with some of the surrounding territory. However, such bombs might very well prove too heavy for transportation by air.

The United States has only very poor ores of uranium in moderate quantities. There is some good ore in Canada and former Czechoslovakia, while the most important source of uranium is in the Belgian Congo.

In view of this situation you may think it desirable to have some permanent contact maintained between the Administration and the group of physicists working on chain reactions in America. One possible way of achieving this might be for you to entrust the task with a person who has your confidence and who could perhaps serve in an unofficial capacity. His task might comprise the following:

(a) to approach Government Departments, keep them informed of the further development, and put forward recommendations for Government action, giving particular attention to the problem of securing a supply of uranium ore for the United States.

(b) To speed up the experimental work, which is at present being carried on within the limits of the budgets of University laboratories, by providing funds, if such funds be required, through his contacts with private persons who are willing to make contributions for this cause, and perhaps also by obtaining co-operation of industrial laboratories which have necessary equipment.

I understand that Germany has actually stopped the sale of uranium from the Czechoslovakian mines which she has taken over. That she should have taken such early action might perhaps be understood on the ground that the son of the German Under-Secretary of State, von Weizsacker, is attached to the Kaiser-Wilhelm Institute in Berlin, where some of the American work on uranium is now being repeated.

Yours very truly,

A. Einstein

Albert Einstein

Annexure: 2

Reply from President Roosevelt

THE WHITE HOUSE
WASHINGTON

October 19, 1939

My dear Professor:

I want to thank you for your recent letter and the most interesting and important enclosure.

I found this data of such import that I have convened a board consisting of the head of the Bureau of Standards and a chosen representative of the Army and Navy to thoroughly investigate the possibilities of your suggestion regarding the element of uranium.

I am glad to say that Dr. Sachs will cooperate and work with this Committee and I feel this is the most practical and effective method of dealing with the subject.

Please accept my sincere thanks.

Very sincerely yours,

Franklin D. Roosevelt

Dr. Albert Einstein,
Old Grove Road,
Nassau Point,
Peconic, Long Island,
New York.

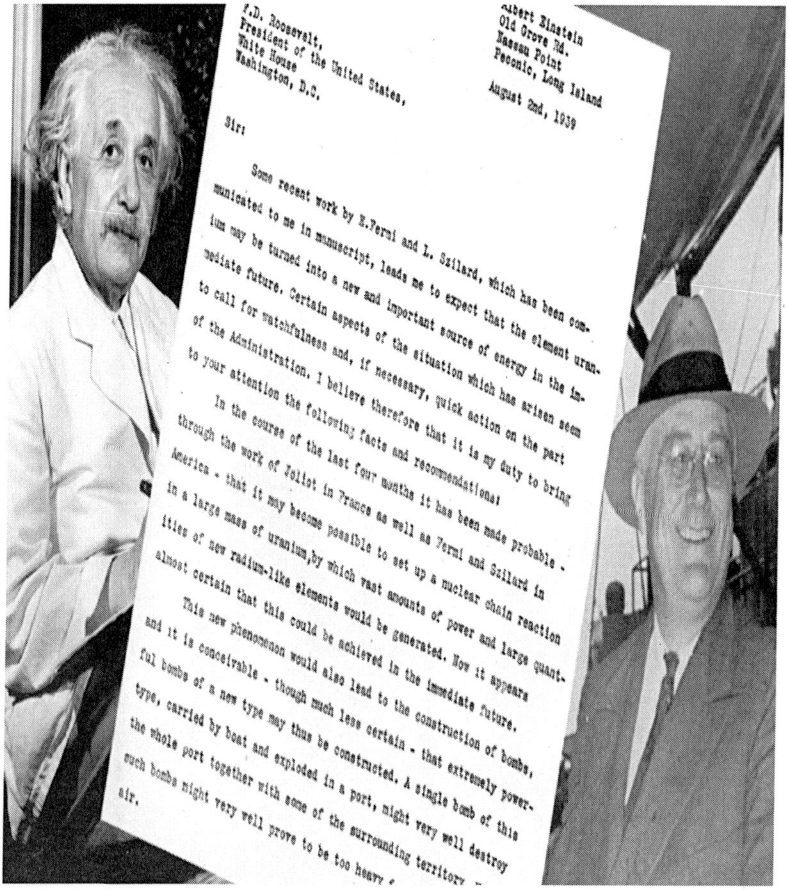
F.D. Roosevelt,
President of the United States,
White House
Washington, D.C.
Albert Einstein
Old Grove Rd.
Nassau Point
Peconic, Long Island
August 2nd, 1939
Sir:
Some recent work by E.Fermi and L. Szilard, which has been communicated to me in manuscript, leads me to expect that the element uranium may be turned into a new and important source of energy in the immediate future. Certain aspects of the situation which has arisen seem to call for watchfulness and, if necessary, quick action on the part of the Administration. I believe therefore that it is my duty to bring to your attention the following facts and recommendations:
In the course of the last four months it has been made probable - through the work of Joliot in France as well as Fermi and Szilard in America - that it may become possible to set up a nuclear chain reaction in a large mass of uranium,by which vast amounts of power and large quantities of new radium-like elements would be generated. Now it appears almost certain that this could be achieved in the immediate future.
This new phenomenon would also lead to the construction of bombs, and it is conceivable - though much less certain - that extremely powerful bombs of a new type may thus be constructed. A single bomb of this type, carried by boat and exploded in a port, might very well destroy the whole port together with some of the surrounding territory.
such bombs might very well prove to be too heavy
air.

Chapter: 28

Global Terrorism: How to Eliminate?

(The blast of twin towers by terrorists killed 2996 people and damaged $3 trillion worth of property)

The Statement, 'One man's terrorist is another man's freedom fighter', has become not only a cliché but also one of the most difficult obstacles in coping with terrorism. The matter of definition and conceptualisation is usually a purely theoretical issue but in the struggle against terrorism, the problem of definition is a crucial element in the attempt to coordinate international collaboration.

The attempt to confound the concepts of "terrorism" and "national liberation" come to fore in various official pronouncements from the Arab world. For instance, the Fifth Islamic Summit in Kuwait at the beginning of 1987, stated in its resolutions that:

The conference reiterates its absolute faith in the need to distinguish the brutal and unlawful terrorist activities perpetrated by individuals, by groups, or by the states from the legitimate struggle of oppressed and subjugated nations against foreign occupation of any kind. This struggle is sanctioned by heavenly law, by human values, and by International Conventions. (Al –Anbaa', Kuwait, January 30, 1987)

The Statement, "One man's terrorist is another man's freedom fighter" justifies "means" (terrorism) in terms of the "end" (national liberation). The former President of the Soviet Union, Leonid Brezhnev, made the following statement in April 1981, during the visit of the Libyan ruler, Muanar Qadhafi:

"Imperialists have no regard either for the will of the people or the laws of history. Liberation struggles cause their indignation. They describe them as 'terrorism'

-(Ray S. Cline and Yonah Alexander,
"Terrorism as State-Sponsored Covent
Warfare"-Virginia Hero Books, 1986, p. 24.)

It is impossible for any organisation to be both a terrorist group and a movement for national liberation at the same time.

Senator Jackson was quoted in Benyamin **Netanyahu's book "Terrorism: How the West Can Win" (p. 18)** as saying:

"The idea that one person's 'terrorist' is another's 'freedom fighter cannot be sanctioned'...It is disgrace that democracies would allow the treasured word 'freedom' to be associated with acts of terrorists."

Without answering the question of "What is terrorism", no responsibility can be imposed on countries supporting terrorism, nor can steps be taken to combat terrorist organisations and their allies (see Security Council Resolution 1269). Without a definition of terrorism, it is impossible to formulate or enforce international agreements against terrorism.

Modern terrorism is increasingly dependent on the support of nations. State sponsoring terrorism use terrorist organisations as a means to their ends, while these organisations depend on the assistance they receive from such countries at the eco, military, and operational levels. Some organisations are so closely dependent on the assistance of states that they become "puppets" functioning at the initiative, direction, and with the complete support of these states. It is impossible to contend effectively with terrorism without severing the close tie between the terrorist organisations and sponsoring states. This tie, however, cannot be severed without agreeing on a broad definition of terrorism, and thus of the states that sponsor it and of the steps to be taken against them.

The struggle to define terrorism is as hard as the struggle against terrorism itself. Under these circumstances, it seems to be difficult to arrive consensus of opinion among the world countries in defining terrorism. Because every country wants to get rid of from the clutches of branding terrorist state. In the absence of universal consensus the affected countries make bilateral agreements to combat terrorism though they know it will not help much in combating terrorism. Though "terrorism is the deliberate and systematic assault on civilians and civilian agents to inspire fear for political ends" the world countries hesitate to take unanimous and strong decision to eliminate terrorism for ulterior motives. If so, how can we eliminate terrorism as mankind badly need it?

Terrorism is a theory and the terrorist is an executor of the theory. A terrorist is a person, armed with destructive weapons, with an aim to kill innocent civilians at large to attract the immediate attention of a state or the world to fulfill his political end irrespective of its worthiness. A person could not become a terrorist until and unless he is equipped with deadly and destructive weapons. At present, the global terrorism is either state sponsored or underworld don sponsored like Bin Laden. In both the cases the terrorists acquire deadly arms and ammunitions, and long range missiles and weapons, and dangerous explosives and poisonous gases directly from the state administration or from vested interests. The world economy is such that its mode of production and distribution is at random and it is for purely profit motive so that the terrorists can conveniently procure the destructive weapons to meet their political motive. In the allocation of scarce natural resources for the production of destructive weapons, the profit motive of capitalists and the political motive of terrorists are in coordination.

The destructive weapons in the hands of wrong persons induce them to indulge in terrorism. If there are no destructive weapons there is no terrorist activities. For instance, the terrorists cannot hijack planes with bare hands with the intention of destroying the twin towers of World Trade Centre in New York and terrorize the whole world by killing three thousand people at a stroke of lightning. In stationary vehicles, in flying planes and in suitcases arms and ammunitions and deadly explosives are used to kill innocent people. We can find no terrorists with bare hands to fulfill his political ends. There is a notion among people that Saudi Arabia is the epicenter of global terrorism where huge monetary resources are available in the name of heavenly law. The arms and explosives constitute the basic element for terrorism.

The production of such deadly weapons cannot be properly controlled and cannot be prevented to pass into hands of terrorists in the capitalistic mode of production whose only aim is profit motive but not social welfare. Before shifting the **epicenter of terrorism** from the Saudi Arabia to other parts of the democratic countries, we have to close all the venues and mode of production and distribution of destructive weapons. Even human suicide bombers cannot turn into terrorists unless they are equipped with explosives. The capitalistic mode of production is never effective to keep the self-interested capitalists under control in the production and distribution of such destructive weapons required by the terrorists. May the aim and pattern of terrorism be any design, the accessibility to the destructive weapons by the terrorists should be wiped out completely for the eradication of terrorism in the world.

Only in the democratisation of economy the people as a whole would have absolute ownership of natural resources and control over the allocation of them for production and distribution of such terrorist weapons. The individual consumers will be served with only consumption goods; no terrorist group or the state will gain access to procure natural resources for the production and distribution of weapons that terrorists require.

Sooner the democratisation of the economy, sooner will be the world peace on the eradication of terrorism. If the views and visions of the people in this regard is clear and courageous, the result will be peace and prosperity.

Volume: VI

Operation of Economic Mechanism

Chapter: 29

Theory of Economic Monetary Equilibrium

Economic Analysis in Real Terms and its Defects

Generally, the economic systems are formulated by the permutation and combination of various 'isms' but the economic analysis are made either in monetary terms or in real terms or in both. Since the producers who initiate production activities are aiming at 'maximisation of profit' only in the form of money we have to scrutinize the operation of economy in monetary terms. Therefore, it is the 'producers monetary equilibrium between their income and expenditure' that plays the pivotal role in the determination of volume of production, employment and income. On contrary the capitalist economist right from Adam Smith to John Maynard Keynes have concentrated on 'real terms' to analyse economic operation to find out solution for economic evils especially for unemployment.

As far as I am concerned if we depend on 'real terms' (aggregate demand for goods and aggregate supply of goods) to analyse our economic problems instead of monetary terms (money income and money expenditure) we will definitely become intellectual bankrupt to find out real economic remedies for our problems. Keynes already dealt with the economic problems in real terms because his real intention was to find out remedies to the problems of rich and developed countries that too during the Great Depression in 1930s. He mainly focused his treatise on how to regain the employment of workers who lost their employment because of market failure due to misdistribution of income and wealth and of low purchasing power of vast majority of people. Keynes never suggested any remedies to solve poverty and unemployment rooted in poor and developing countries. Keynes concentrated his remedial measures to save the rich capitalists from their downfall and to prevent the threatening spread of socialism in USA and West European countries as predicted by Karl Marx that Capitalism would collapse by itself due to its very aim of 'maximisation of profit'. Keynesian ideas in real terms were exaggerated more than reasonable limit by the capitalist advocates. So Keynes advised the capitalists not to produce goods more than the aggregate demand of the people or 'effective demand' for the goods by the people. Though he accepted his theory will not help to attain full employment he forced the thinkers not to deduce their treatise beyond the 'real terms' or 'real equilibrium between aggregate demand and aggregate supply'. To insist his ideology Keynes says:

".....the true law relating the aggregate demand and aggregate supply functions....is a vitally important chapter of economic theory.....without which all discussions concerning the volume of aggregate employment are futile".

Thus, Keynes has misguided the thinkers not to analyse the economic problems beyond the orbit of real terms and has plunged the economic operations into self-defeating mechanism. This is because producers always aims to calculate their success in terms of maximisation of profit but not in terms of volume of goods produced or level of employment created. So he advised the capitalist producers to produce goods only up to the level of 'effective demand' or 'aggregate demand' by consumers and not to employ full production potentialities or all available natural resources. He says when the economy grows richer and richer the economic problems will become more severe and severe. As the economists accepted this kind of the capitalistic mode of production severe unemployment burst out in USA during 1930's (the period of **Great Depression**) due to lack of purchasing power and misdistribution of income. In order to solve this kind of unemployment the US government injected huge volume of money through poor to increase their purchasing power and **effective demand** for goods to stimulate the production in the name of **'pump priming policy'.**

President Franklin D Roosevelt to some extent was influenced by Keynes's pump priming policy to increase the purchasing power of people to conquer the Great Depression. He spent billions and billions of dollars on 'Public Works Administration', on Tennessee Valley Authority and on military to absorb the unemployed workers and thereby increased their purchasing power to clear first the stagnated goods in the market and then to stabilise their employment. The capitalist economists and the American fiscal and monetary policies makers had been targeting the consumers and their purchasing power to clear the market as far as possible.

We are all Keynesians now: Starting from the period of depression (1930s) and still now the US government has been spending huge volume of money for service sector especially military. According to 'Stockholm International Peace Research Institute **(SIPRI)**'s 2006 Year Book on

Armaments, Disarmament and International Security for 2005'[5] and the Centre for Arms Control and Non-Proliferation, 2007 the World military expenditure in 2005 is estimated to have reached $1118 billion in current dollars out of which the USA is responsible for 48 per cent of the world total, distantly followed by the UK, France, Japan and China with 4-5 per cent each. Moreover the US government has spent 41 per cent of her tax revenue to meet military expenditure according to the report of **'Friends Committee on National Legislation, February 15, 2007'**. Such an huge amount has been spent on military not because US in under the threat of any great war but because to redistribute income to the middle class people to increase their purchasing power to clear the consumption goods in the market and to help the capitalists to maintain the level of employment and to achieve their maximisation of profit. Since the fiscal policy has been followed from the outburst of Great Depression President Nixon said in 1971 as follows 'we are all Keynesians now'. This is because the US and other capitalist economies are 'demand side economies' and their economic activities are controlled by the effective demand for goods by the innumerable consumers who are behaving erratically in the market and always threatening the producers not to produce more than their aggregate demand and not trying to solve unemployment and poverty beyond that.

The capitalist economies require innumerable fiscal and monetary policies to exert control over billions and billions of consumers to regulate them to behave rationally in the market in favour of a few producers to achieve their maximisation of profit in order to induce them to venture into further production activities internally and internationally. But it seems to be an impossibility of all impossibilities. On the contrary I advocate an effective economic technique known as Dual Monetary System which will help to establish an equilibrium between the outflow of money and inflow of money in respect of producers which is termed as **producers monetary equilibrium (^{P}Meq).** This technique will operate like crossing a mountain through a tunnel rather than climbing over it. Neither Say's Supply side economics nor the Keynesian Demand side economics will solve our economic problems but my Prosumer side economics will do the miracle within a timeframe.

Economic analysis in monetary terms and monetary equilibrium

Economic Monetary Equilibrium: It means 'a monetary equilibrium between inflow and outflow of money' (i.e. income and expenditure of money) in respect of both producers and consumers to operate production and consumption activities respectively. I have classified this monetary equilibrium into (a) 'Producers Monetary (Money Flow) Equilibrium'(^{P}Meq) and (b) 'Consumers Monetary (Money Flow) Equilibrium' (^{C} Meq) to evaluate in detail.

I. Producers Monetary Equilibrium ($^PM_{eq}$)

Achieving of producers monetary equilibrium at all level of employment is crucially important factor for such as production, employment, income, consumption, investment etc. By this term I mean an equilibrium, in respect of producers, between their outflow of money in the form of wages, interest, rent and profit during smooth and dynamic operation of all economic activities production of goods and their inflow of money during sale of the produced goods (distribution). In simple terms it denotes an equilibrium between money expenditure and money income of producers in their business operations and it may be called as 'Producers Money Flow Equilibrium' (^PMeq). For example, if $100 billion of money outflows as production expenditure from the producers during a particular span of time and the same $100 billion of money inflows towards the producers as sales income during the same span of period this equilibrium between outflow and inflow of money at $100 billion is called as 'Producers Money Flow Equilibrium'. This 'Producers Money Flow Equilibrium' may be sub-divided into three conceptual notions known as

1. 'Producers Positive Money Flow Equilibrium' ($^P_+M_{eq}$),
2. 'Producers Equivalent Money Flow Equilibrium' ($^P_=M_{eq}$) and
3. 'Producers Negative Money Flow Equilibrium' ($^P_-M_{eq}$).

Determination of Employment

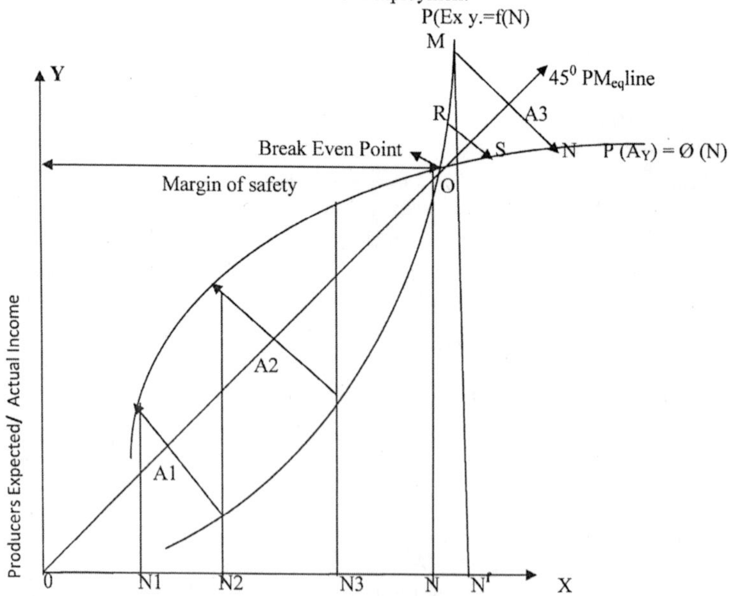

RS=Margin of Insecurity; A1,A2 = Margin of Inducement; A3= Margin of discouragement, N^f= Full employment; OSR = Risky triangle

Producers Positive Money Flow Equilibrium ($^{P}{}_{+}M_{eq}$)

By the term 'Producers Positive Money Flow Equilibrium' I mean the inflow of money towards the producers (income of producers) through the 'commodity market' from innumerable consumers by the their purchase of goods would be greater than the 'outflow of money' from the producers (expenditure of producers) through 'factors market' towards the consumers by the production of goods. In other words in a dynamic economy if the producers increase 'one unit of marginal employment (∂E_{mp})' the producers marginal money income (∂Y) will be greater than their marginal money expenditure (∂E) up to certain level of employment . At each level of marginal employment the producers will receive more than their expected margin of profit and will be induced to produce more and more to maximise their profit. In such kind of a dynamic economy the ratio between 'marginal money income' (marginal money inflow i.e. $\partial M^{\rightarrow f}$) and 'marginal money expenditure'(marginal money outflow i.e. $\partial M^{\leftarrow f}$) in respect of producers may be called **'Producers Money Flow Efficiency'** ($^{P}M^{f}\eta$ where stand for Producers, for Money flow and 'η' for efficiency) and it may be expressed as $\partial Y / \partial E = Ø$.

Generally the producers will persistently wish to keep a positive monetary equilibrium. In other words producers will be keen on their money flow efficiency ($^{P}M^{f}\eta$) (the ratio between marginal income and marginal expenditure or the ratio between money inflow and money outflow) always to be positive i.e. greater than one. We can denote this as follows:

$^{P}M^{f}\eta = \partial Y / \partial E$ or $\partial M^{\rightarrow f} / \partial M^{\leftarrow f} = Ø > 1$

Where Ø is producers money flow efficiency.

In such kind of economic situations producers' 'actual income' will always be greater than their 'expected income' at initial stages of production. It will induce the producers to increase the level of production and employment to maximise their profit. The 'expected income' implies the anticipatory income of producers to cover the 'production cost' including their 'maximisation of profit.

In poor and less developed countries the consumers will naturally have high propensity to consume to meet their bare necessities. They will be eager to spend more than their income by borrowing from financial institutions or from some other sources. This positive economic trend will continue up to certain level of higher income. After that level of income the consumers propensity to spend will decrease as their propensity to save increases and the producers will realise that their 'actual income' will tend to decrease comparing to their 'expected income' and it will result in the reduction of 'maximisation of profit'. To maintain their maximisation of profit the producers will determine the level of employment where their 'actual income' equilibrates with their 'expected income'.Therefore, it is the 'producers monetary equilibrium' that determines the level of employment and volume of production.

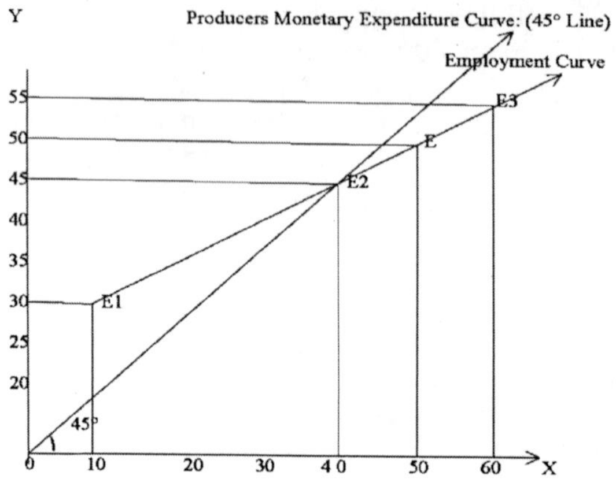

X axis: Producers Expected Income (in billion $)

Y axis: Producers Actual Income (in billion $)

Producers' Monetary Equilibrium

In the above chart the 45⁰ line equilibrates the 'producers expected income' with the 'producers actual income'. So the 45⁰ line is termed as 'Producers Monetary Equilibrium Curve' ($^{P}{}_{Meq}$). The 'employment curve' exhibits various levels of employment at E_1, E_2, E_0 and E_3. Each level of employment coordinates the producers 'expected income' with their 'actual income' when they venture into production activities. For instance, if the producers engage E_1 level of employment and produce goods they expect only $10 billion which will fetch them their expected 'maximum profit'. But in reality the producers realise that they will garner $30 billion for the massive demand for their goods and high 'propensity of consumers'. Since the 'actual income' tends to soar up by $20 billion the producers will be induced to engage more workers to enhance the level of production, ceteris paribus.

At the level of employment of E_1 the 'Producers Money Flow Efficiency' ($^{P}M^{f}\eta$) will be greater than one and they will realise that their profit will be more than their expectations. In our numerical example the $^{P}M^{f}$ç: $30 billion/ $10 billion equals 3. If economic conditions are conducive the producers will be encouraged to increase the level of employment to maximise their profit. And now at E_2 level of employment the producers 'expected income' will be $ 40 billion but they will still realise that their 'actual income' tends to $ 45 billion. The 'Producers Money Flow Efficiency'- $^{P}M^{f}\eta$ will be ($45 billion/ $ 40 billion) 1.125, a positive attitude for producers. Therefore, the producers will pursue the same upward trend and at E_0 level of employment the producers expected income and the actual income will be at equilibrium and the 'Producers Money Flow Efficiency - $^{P}M^{f}\eta$ – will be ($ 50 billion/$ 50 billion) 1. At this level of employment the producers will realise 225 y"lv" maximisation of profit'. If the producers reduce or increase the level of employment from E_0 their profit per worker will fall. Therefore, the producers will not engage more workers than E_0 and the point E_0 will be called as "Producers Effective Monetary Equilibrium" because it the effective point that determines the level of employment.

At the both the levels of employment up to E_0 the producer's monetary efficiency' is always greater than one? I.e. $^{P}M\eta = \partial Y/\partial E > 1$. In poor and less developing countries such kind of economic situation is always prevailing and the economic machinery operating as 'producers-friendly'.

II. Producers' Equivalent Money Flow Equilibrium ($^{P}{}_{=Meq}$)

By the term 'Producers Equivalent Money Flow Equilibrium' I mean an equilibrium between 'marginal rate of outflow of money per time' during production and the 'marginal rate of inflow of money per time' during distribution, at a particular level of employment in static economy or at all levels of employment in dynamic economy.

If such an economic situation prevails that will uphold a sustained monetary equilibrium at all levels of employment and the producers will lead the economy towards 'full employment'. Here the producer's monetary efficiency would be equal to one. In other words,

$$^{P}M\eta = \partial Y/\partial E = \emptyset < 1.$$

In other words we may term it as 'producers' perfect monetary equilibrium'. Such an economic situation is an ideal one but the establishment of which is now a myth like EL Dorado[3] due to our competent economic techniques.

In the chart displayed above when the producers engage 'E_0' level of employment the 'employment curve' interacts with the 45° line i.e. 'Producers Monetary Equilibrium Curve' at E_0. At this point of interaction the producers will realise a 'perfect equilibrium' between their 'expected income' and 'actual income' which will effectuate their 'maximisation of profit'. The point 'E_0' is the 'effective monetary equilibrium' which determines the level of employment in any economy. The producers would not maximise their profit if they fix the level of employment beyond or below the 'effective monetary equilibrium E_0' in monetary terms. J.M. Keynes denotes this same point E_0 as 'effective demand' but in real terms.

On the other hand if the producers increase the level of employment beyond 'E_0' they cannot obtain their 'actual income' to equilibrate with their 'expected income'. For example, if the producers increase the level of employment to E_3 their 'expected income' is \$60 billion but they will actually realise only \$55 billion and the producers volume of profit will fall. Therefore, the producers will not engage more than E_0 level of employment. In other words the producers monetary efficiency will be less than one i.e. ${}^{P}M\eta = \partial Y/\partial E = \emptyset < 1$. (\$ 55 billion/\$ 60 billion = 0.925). Therefore, the producers will reduce the employment up to the level where their 'expected income' equilibrates with their 'actual income' at $E_{0.}$

III. Producers Negative Monetary Equilibrium (${}^{P}{}_{-Meq}$)

By the term 'Producers Negative Money Flow Equilibrium' I mean the producers inflow of money from the 'commodity market' from innumerable consumers will be lesser than the 'outflow of money' through the 'factors market' towards the consumers in a particular period of production of goods. In other words producer's marginal money income (∂Y) would be lesser than their marginal money expenditure (∂E) at certain levels of employment. At these higher levels of employment the producers will receive reduced margin of profit and will be discouraged to produce lesser volume of goods to minimise their loss in profit.

In other words the 'producers monetary efficiency' (^{P}Mn) i.e. the ratio between marginal income and marginal expenditure would always be negative i.e. lesser than one. We can denote this as follows

${}^{P}M\eta = \partial Y/\partial E < 1$ (in our example we can find it as $5/10 = 0.5 < 1$)

In such kind of economic situations producers' actual income would always be lesser than their 'expected income' at any level of production between E_0 and E_3. Between E_0 and E_3 the producers 'expected income' is \$10 billion but their 'actual income' will be only \$5 billion. This trend will discourage the producers to increase the level of employment from E_3 to E_0 because their 'actual income' will be insufficient to cover their 'factor cost'. The producer's maximisation of profit will fall from its previous level at E_0.

In rich and highly developed countries the consumers would have high propensity to save and they would invest it in various 'share markets', 'mutual funds' etc…In the investment sector the producers find insufficient workers to engage their investments. They will realise a lack of demand for investment goods to absorb new employment. This negative economic trend known as depression will pull down the level of employment up to a certain point E_0, in our example, where actual income equilibrates with expected income.

So, in order to maximise their profit, the investors in rich countries like USA, UK, Japan, South Korea want Globalisation and free trade to dump their over-investment goods in less developing countries like India, China, South America etc. where cheap labour is available to utilise their over investment. They heap their investments in these countries stealthily backing up with military might of their countries. The US war on Middle East Countries is the best example. The US wars on these countries are to protect the 'investment of her domestic rich people and to plunder the wealth of these countries in the name of globalisation'.

The poor and developing countries which are unable to solve their poverty and unemployment readily accept the 'over flowing foreign investment' and are slowly becoming their "Economic Colonies". Moreover, the western countries first try to demoralise the people and kill their age long rich cultures to inject their western habits mainly to market their sophisticated goods produced by their over investment goods in order to protect their domestic economic growth and welfare. For example, in India Night Clubs, Call-Girl Centres, Beauty Parlors etc. are rapidly growing more or less in all the towns and sub urban areas; Foreign investments are pouring for the establishment of rich restaurants; richly fashionable variety of goods are heaping in the super markets; a new kind of Am Way and eBay markets are growing everywhere; the electronic media and computers have open up the flood gates of forbidden sexy videos to contaminate the healthy minds of the youth and billions of dollar are spent in sexy ads through TVs to contaminate the minds of youth in their own houses using hundreds of channels. **Bhagavat Gita** says once the family is destroyed the women will become immortalised.

"With the destruction of the family, family order (dharma) and eternal order (dharma) are lost. The whole family transforms itself into adharma (disorder or irreligiousness)."

[Chapter 1 Verse 40]

"With the emergence of adharma, O Krishna, women become impure. And when women fall into bad ways, O descendent of Vrisni, admixture of castes takes place."

[Chapter 1, Verse 41]

On discerning the present day industrial operations the medical experts say the workers are mentally depressed, suffering from hypertension and risking at early cardiac problems. This is the fact how our economic systems are operating now.

In brief

if ${}^{P}M\eta > 1$, the producers will be induced to increase the level of employment up to E_0.

If ${}^{P}M\eta = 1$, the producers will be satisfied to determine the level of employment at E_0.

If ${}^{P}M\eta < 1$, the producers will be warned to reduce the level of employment up to E_0.

The producers perfect monetary equilibrium is restricted at lower level of employment because it has to overcome a lot of impediments on its way towards full employment. The basic impediments are

1. The 'producer's perfect monetary equilibrium' always behaves a dependent factor of 'consumers-perfect-monetary-equilibrium'

$[^{P}pM_{eq} = f(^{C}pM_{eq})]$

2. When the income of consumers increases their 'propensity to consume' falls and they spend lesser amount than their increased income (i.e. $<\partial Y$), and create a monetary gap between income and expenditure.

3. The consumers create time lags in spending the money because the money functions as 'store value' and it induces the consumers to hoard money for its ability to keep the value of money as it is in the short period. This hoarding of money affects the 'expected money income' of producers to put the production activities into operation.

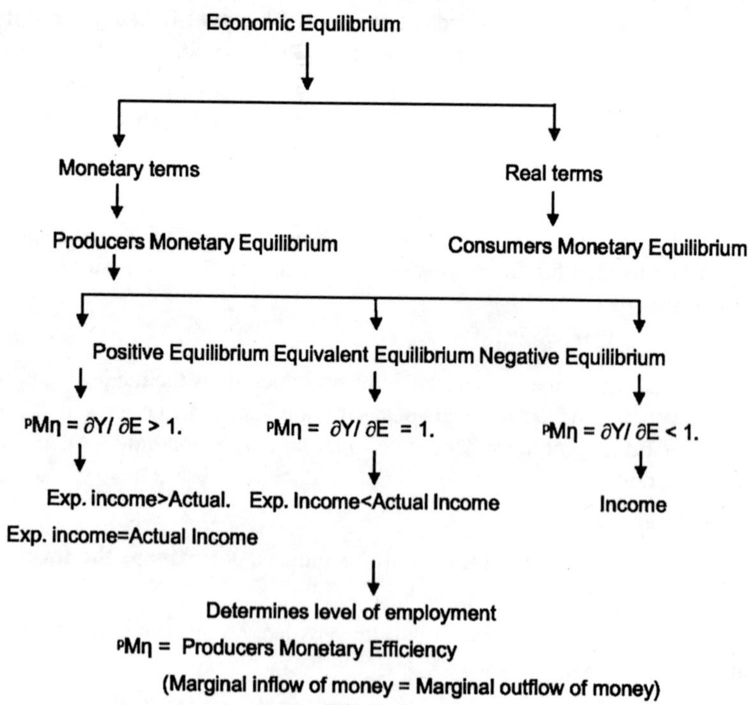

Volume: VII

Operation of Democrism

Chapter – 30

Operation of Democrism at National Level How should an Economy Operate? How would One Rule a Nation

1. In real terms: The operation of economic machinery is usually explained either in 'real terms or in monetary terms or in both terms'. In real terms, according to Keynes, the ultimate object of the operation of economy is to create and sustain 'effective demand' for goods at all levels of production or employment. Keynes accepts the failure of capitalistic mode of production to maintain effective demand at 'full employment level' and the economic operation will move towards chaos and confusion when it develops richer and richer. So he concludes the capitalism will fail ultimately in solving economic problems of mankind. So we have to analyse the operation of economy in monetary terms to find solution for our problems.

2. In monetary terms: In monetary terms the operation of economy denotes 'a perfect equilibrium of circular money- flow between producers and consumers at all levels of employment or production'. The 'money- flow' means 'the rate of outflow and inflow of money between producers and consumers at a given time of production of goods and services and attainment of monetary equilibrium'. Moreover, the money-flow may be bifurcated into 'producers' money-flow equilibrium' and 'consumers' money-flow equilibrium'.

The basically the operation of economy is analysed with reference to 'democratisation of economy' because the capitalistic and socialistic modes of production have been failed in their fiscal and monetary techniques to solve human problems. I, therefore, explain the concept of 'how should an economy operation' by the 'economic technique of **'Dual Monetary System'** with numerical and diagrammatic illustrations.

The law of nature requires free from contradictions in all systems to drive them towards their perfection. But economic systems especially capitalism has many imbibed with many contradictions which tantalize economic activities of man and screwing economic problems in all societies. The contradictions are divided into (a) 'economic class contradictions' and (b) 'economic functional contradictions'.

(a) The economic class contradictions

They may be classified as follows:

1. Capitalists and Workers,
2. Investors and depositors,
3. Sellers and buyers,
4. Producers and consumers,

The above people of different classes now have quite opposite economic interests and struggle constantly in the 'factor and commodity markets' to determine 'just wage', 'just profit', 'just price', 'just rent', 'just interest' etc., in the market by interacting 'demand and supply factors'. Their struggle for obtaining 'equilibrium' and 'economic justice' protracted them into long span of time and retard the requisite economic growth. The poverty and unemployment will not wait for long time to achieve 'just equilibrium' and the people die in appalling poverty and by crushing unemployment.

A well-ordered economic system should be free from all 'economic class contradictions'. Such a well ordered economic system could be established only by **'Democratisation of Economy' (Democrism)** which would lead the people (workers) to empower with 'Direct Ownership of Capital'. The national capital would be owned neither by few capitalists nor by the State. All economic power and decision-makings would naturally be entrusted to the people.

(b) Economic functional contradictions

One of prime economic contradictions is deeply rooted in the functions of money. The existing money in circulation may be called as 'Consumption Money' which has to perform two contradictory functions at the same time. One is 'Medium of Exchange' and the other is 'Store of Value'. Medium of Exchange is dynamic in character and always accelerates the economic activities such as production and consumption. On the other hand the 'Store of Value' is static in nature and keeps the face value of money for ever. This static nature of money creates 'time lags' between income and expenditure. It tempts the psychology of consumers to hoard money not to spend for buying goods and services which are produced for them and to stabilise the level of employment.

Moreover, it tempts the unscrupulous people to indulge in corruption, accumulating black money and to enter in the 'share market gambles' which are considers being economic, social and political crimes. Billions and billions of dollars are dumped in these crimes throughout the world.

In order to eliminate this functional contradiction we have to introduce a new kind of money known as 'Investment Money' to perform only 'store of value'. The present 'consumption money' will perform only 'medium of exchange'. If the consumers at any time have excess of consumption money they may convert into investment money and save them.

In this economic scenario all the commercial banks would be converted into 'investment banks' and the investment money would directly be transferred to 'people's business sector' to buy investment goods only. On the abolition of the economic functional contradiction **'people's direct Ownership of Capital System'** or 'Democratisation of Economy' would be established for creating well ordered economic system. This is the way by which an economic should operate. With the help of a 'circular flow diagram' and a numerical table I illustrate below how the well-ordered economic system would function free from all contradictions.

Generation and flow of money in Democrism

1. In the Democratic Economy: The ideal concept of People's Direct Ownership of Capital' would be brought into operation. By this concept 'all industries will be owned by each worker and each industry will be owned by all Workers'. This is the hub of the just economic system by which I wish to illustrate how an economy should operation.

2. The establishment of industries would be initiated by the workers of the nation as a whole. On behalf of the workers an 'expert committee' by the labour and capital (Binary Economics) from the household sector through the factor market. A requisite volume of consumption money ($\uparrow_{f}^{P}M$) will flow through the factor market (${}_{\uparrow f}^{P}M = {}_{\downarrow f}^{P}M$). Whereas (${}_{\leftarrow f}^{P}M$) is the outflow of money from producers and the (${}_{\rightarrow f}^{c}M$) is inflow of money towards the consumers. (See the above diagram)

3. For the contribution of labour and capital the household sector receive wage and profit (dividend) from the business sector. The flow of dividend is also depicted as an arrow mark in the diagram.

4. All the share markets and the gambling with shares would be abolished in democratic economy and no worker would be allowed to sell their shares. The workers produce not only consumption goods but also capital goods. Therefore they are legally entitled to receive wage for the production of consumption goods and profit (dividend) for the production and contribution of capital goods. Thus, all the workers will acquire a 'dual income'.

5. Now the consumers' aggregate money income would be producers' aggregate expenditure. It would be denoted as $({}_{\uparrow}{}^{c}M = {}_{\downarrow}{}^{P}M)$ in money flow terms.

6. The consumers have provided with dual income to buy goods produced for them but not to hoard the money in any form and not create time lags between their money income and money expenditure.

7. The producers have produced the goods predicting that the consumers would buy the goods at the rate at which they produced to sustain the level of employment.

8. The goods flow towards the consumers through the 'commodity market'. The producers will naturally expect that the expenditure of consumers would equilibrate their **'expected money income'** $({}_{\uparrow}{}^{c}M = {}_{\downarrow}{}^{P}M)$ which denoted an equilibrium between consumers outflow of money and producers expected inflow of money which includes profit of the business.

9. The consumers in the household sector will not spend all the income to buy goods produced for them because when income increases the 'propensity to consume' will fall and 'propensity to save will increase'. When income increases higher and higher the 'propensity to consume' will diminish slowly but the 'propensity to save' will increase rapidly. This psychological behaviour of consumers erupts immense economic problems.

10. Rich Consumers always save or hoard a considerable part of income and cause stagnation of goods in the market and pull down the volume of production and level of employment.

11. In the democratic economy the consumers should save the excess income in the investment bank and no interest would be paid for them. Because this savings become the investment of them and they will receive 'dividend' for their investment according to 'investment burden'.

12. By the 'investment burden' poor consumers would receive higher 'dividend' than the rich consumers to uphold economic justice. This mode of dividend payment would reduce 'income gap' between rich and poor and lead the society towards equality.

13. Now the world is controlled by the supercomputers. The business sector, household sector, factor market, commodity market, government sector, investment bank sector and all other economic agencies are interconnected by 'computer network' and electronic systems. This scientific technology should be used for economic operations to attain their perfection.

14. With this background now we have analyse how the economic activities should operate for the welfare of the society.

15. Under these circumstances when the consumers spend their money income $({}_{\uparrow}{}^{c}M$ = outflow of consumers money income) in the commodity market

they would purchase not only consumption goods but also investment goods. A ratio would have already determined between production of consumption and investment goods. For example, let's assume it may be 10:2. When a consumer spends $120 to buy goods he would receive $00 worth of consumption goods in tangible form and $20 worth of investment goods 'credit form'. This $20 would be credited in the consumer's account in the investment bank implying that the consumer has bought $20 worth of investment goods.

16. On applying this manner of transaction millions of consumers would buy thousands of goods any thereby a huge volume of electronic investment money would be accumulated in the 'Investment Bank'.

17. Now let's presume the average per capita expenditure of consumers in the commodity market amounts to $120,000 per year. The consumers spend this amount in the form of 'consumption money' to purchase $100,000 worth of consumption goods and $20,000 worth of investment goods. The people's business sector would produce $100,000 worth of consumption goods and $20,000 worth of investment goods by utilising 'consumption money' as medium of exchange. The $20,000 credited in the investment bank would assure the consumer that he had bought 'investment goods' to the credited value.

18. If the consumers population of a country figures one billion, it will indicate that $20,000 billion worth of investment goods can be produced to establish industrial units in the given period of time. All these industrial units or business sectors would be owned directly by the workers of the country as a whole. The distinction between capitalists and workers will disappear and a classless society would be established.

19. In the diagram an arrow mark has been drawn to indicate the flow of investment money from the investment bank to the people's business sector. This is only to fulfill book keeping formalities and an authenticate account to the consumers to claim their share of investment in the business sector.

20. The commodity market displays a monetary equilibrium (${}_{\leftarrow f}^{C}M = {}_{\rightarrow f}^{P}M$) between consumers outflow of money and producers inflow of money at a given level of employment or volume of production.

21. Distribution of profit: The aggregate income of people's business sector includes the 'expected profit' also. Since the producers and the consumers are playing the role the 'expected profit' would always coincide with the volume of 'actual profit'. In 'democratic economy' the profit would not be an ugly factor of exploitation of workers. The profit would be apportioned into three domains known as 1. Dividend to workers, 2. Contribution to government – revenue to create 'tax-free economy' and 3. Compensatory income to producers to sustain the level of employment.

21.1. **Dividend to workers:** Since the consumers (workers) contribute a considerable part of their wage to the investment of business sector they are entitled to claim a justifiable portion of national profit. On the contribution to the national capital the low income workers strain to bear more 'investment burden' than the high income workers. The dividend, therefore, should be distributed according to 'investment burden' the economy should operate accordingly to pay more dividends to 'low income workers' than the 'high income workers'. This justifiable distribution of dual income, wage plus dividend, would reduce the income gap between the workers and lead the society to attain equality. Here the profit factor is not playing an unscrupulous role of 'exploiter' but a justifiable part of 'income equalizer'. In the diagram the left side arrow mark exhibits how the dividend flows from business sector to household sector.

21.2. **Contribution to government revenue (Tax-free Economy):** After apportioning dividend to workers reasonably admissible portion of national profit would directly be presented to exchequer of government to meet its expenditure. The direct and indirect tax system would completely be repealed and a tax-free economy would be established. In the diagram it has been displayed as a downward arrow mark (↓) from business sector to government sector. A huge volume of money expenditure and man power would not only be saved but also 'corruption' in the tax-collection system would have been eliminated.

21.3. **Profit in reserve or compensatory income to producers:** The maxim that when increases the propensity to consume diminishes cause severe turbulence in economic activities. The negligence of consumers to buy the consumption goods in the commodity market creates a gap between the 'expected income and actual income' of producers. When the producer's actual income decreases they will reduce the level of employment and production. In order to fill the income gap sufficient volume of profit would be kept in reserve for sustaining the volume of production. This profit in reserve will act as compensatory income to producers to maintain stability in economic activities by equilibrating producers outflow of money with the producer's inflow of money

$$(\uparrow {}^{P}M = \downarrow {}^{P}M)$$

The insufficient purchase of goods would cause a stagnation of consumption goods in the market. Under these critical circumstances the producers should dispose the goods to poor consumers at free of cost or at lower price to suit the consumer's purchasing power. Now the economy would take off into sustained growth. The downward curve from business sector to commodity market denotes theit reaches full employment level, the ultimate object of all economic systems and their policies.

Operation of Economy in Democrism

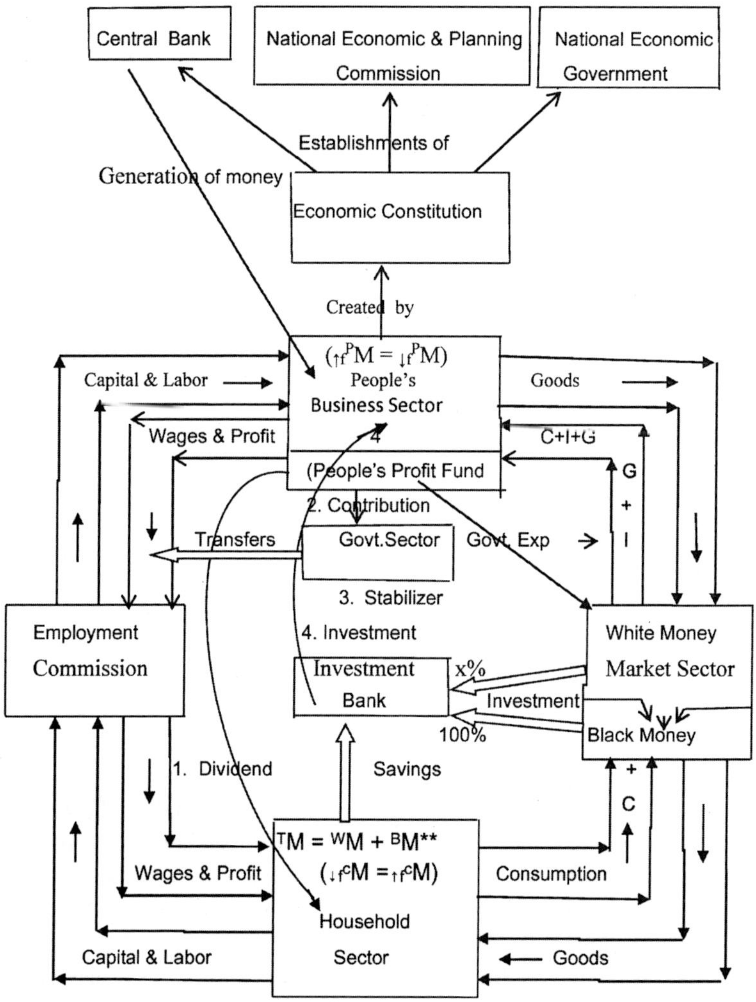

Circular Flow of Money and Goods in Democrism

** ^{T}M = Total Money; $^{W}M + {}^{B}M$ = White Money + Black Money $\uparrow_f^P M$ = Producers' outflow of money; $\downarrow_f^P M$ =Producers' inflow of money; $\uparrow_f^c M$= Consumers' outflow of money; $\downarrow_f^c M$ = Consumers' inflo0w of money

Generation and flow of money in Democrism

Since Democratisation or Democrism – The Third Theory, is the Just an alternative to chaotic and confusing Capitalistic and Socialistic models of economic systems, despite its superiority in theoretical sphere, many a one questions on its functional implementation.

The successful operation of any economic system depends on two intriguing factors, very hard to understand, namely the Generation of Money and Its Flow through various factors of production.

1. Generation of Money: The technique of generation of money differs one economic system to another. The generation of money is nothing but creation of capital to large extend. In capitalistic mode of economies, and its related economic systems. Money is generated by vested interests through "interest bearing debts" from commercial banks owned by private sectors. The commercial banks issue "checks" to these capitalists to acquire billions and billions of dollars. They accumulate huge wealth and controlling economic power over legislature, executive and judiciary. They capture reins of power and become the real rulers of the country, and they grow richer and richer and push down the poor, poorer and poorer.

Now the American elites and economists agitate that the money should not be generated my private commercial banks in the form of 'checks' on viewing the emerging appalling poverty among American people.

Generation of money in Democrism

In Democrism the generation of money entrusted in the hands of working people whenever they initiate production of goods and services. Democrism empowers the working people to frame 'Economic Constitution' focusing mainly on their maximisation of benefits and economic security. On the direction of the rules and regulations instituted by the Economic Constitution, the Economic Government, Economic Commission and the Central Bank will be established in the State. According to the need of production of goods and services, the working people in the Business Sector, will instruct the "Central Bank" to release a required volume of money **(for example, $10 trillion)** through the power and permission of government. The government will act to fulfill the needs of production sector under the guidelines of **"Economic Commission"** framed by the workers.

Diagrammatic illustration: I have illustrated this kind of **generation of money** by the government in the above diagram. The upper part of the diagram appears in triangular form. It emerges from **People's Business Sector** and reaches to **"Economic Constitution".** The "Economic Constitution" creates **"Economic Government"**, "Economic Commission" and "Central Bank" as autonomous power with certain limitations. Especially the **"Central Bank"** is subjected to act according to the "People's Business Sector" by the direction of "People's Economic Government". All the private Commercial Banks in the country will be closed as they are functioning as the agents of Capitalists.

On the contrary all these private commercial banks will be converted as **People's Investment Banks.**

Digital Economy: In Democrism, at the very outset, the Central Bank will be digitalised. As soon as the Central Bank is digitalised, all the Investment banks will also be digitalised. When the banks are digitalised the visible moneys which are in the form of paper will wither away and disappear from circulation and ceased from functioning from certain economic activities such as store of value. Perhaps a moneyless economy will emerge as Karl Marx had visualised.

Flow of money in Democrism: The lower part of the diagram depicts a rectangular form. It consists of **1. People's Business Sector (annexing with People's National Profit Fund) 2. Factor Market Sector (Invisible), 3. People's Household Sector, 4. Market Sector, 5. Investment Bank Sector and 6. Government Sector.**

The interest-free money generated by Central Bank (**say $10 trillion)** will flow out directly to **People's Business Sector** whenever necessary. The Business Sector will distribute the money as **wage for labour and profit for capital to the household sector** thro' the invisible factor market sector. The factor market sector is invisible because labour is not a commodity to bargain in the market by the interaction of demand and supply forces. Labour is dignity, worshipful and national honour in Democrism.

At the same duration of time the **Business Sector** (Production Sector) employing both the labour and capital will produce socially needed goods **(say, $10 trillion**) and set them to flow towards the **Market Sector** at a given price level. This price level will be pre-determined by consumers (Consumers are producers in Democrism) themselves under the guidance of **"Economic Commission for Price Determination".** Since the price level is determined by the consumers themselves it will be the **JUST PRICE**. In any case, the price level will not be determined by demand and supply forces and therefore there will be no question for **Inflation**. The **"Consumer-determined price"** or the Just Price will include a **justifiable share of profit** to flow into "People's National Fund".

Tax-Free economy and Dividend to all: A part of the **Profit Fund** will be allocated for contribution to government directly to meet its expenditure and all kinds of taxes will be abolished. A "Tax-Free Economy" will be established in the country. It has been depicted in the diagram as 'downward arrow' from People's National Profit Fund to Government Sector. Similarly yet another part of Profit Fund will be allocated for distribution of dividend to the whole working class. It has also been displayed as "downward arrow curve" from People's National Profit Fund to Household Sector.

The consumers of the **Household Sector** on receiving wage income for labour and profit income for capital (**say, $10 trillion)** will spend the total income in the **Market Sector** to purchase Consumption as well as Investment goods. The money that issued in the **Market Sector** will be called as **"Consumption Money" ($10 trillion)** and it will **flow** towards the **Business Sector.**

In the **Market Sector,** the flow of money will be bifurcated into **Consumption Money and Investment Money.** Insulating a particular volume of **Consumption Money as** basic structure for **Investment money or Electronic Money($3 trillion)**. The electronic money will digitalize the economy.

The Investment Money, which is based on equal volume of Consumption Money, will be used to buy **investment goods($3 trillion).** Since the Investment goods are in the form of tools, machines, plants, buildings, bridges, dams and so on they can't be purchased in loose and packed material forms as in retail shops. Thousands and thousands of workers cooperating together can purchase investment goods collectively for their proposed construction of industries. Though they buy collectively their individual identity will be established in the capital ownership through maintaining investment account in Investment Bank.

The Investment Money, therefore, for purchase of investment goods will be transferred to **Investment Bank Sector from Market Sector.** In the diagram it has been depicted as x per cent and 100 per cent **leftward arrow marks** from **Market Sector to Investment Bank Sector.** Every worker will have an **Investment Bank Account** and he can verify at any time his share of investment through his credit card, or Investment buyer's dash board or code no received from his bank through SMS or by mini-statements in any ATM centres. There will be perfect accountability and transparency in the investment ownership of every worker. Every worker will be ensured that he will stake a claim his share of investment in every National as well as Global Business units and demand his due **dividend legally and with full legal authority.**

What is x per cent left arrow Mark (Investment): Every worker produces not only consumption goods but also investment goods. Therefore, he is entitled to buy his share of investment goods out of his wage income. Therefore I have perfected the theory from "Work according to Wage and Wage according to Work" to "Investment according to Wage". Therefore, whenever a worker spends his wage income he will not only buy consumption goods but also investment goods by paying a certain percentage of his wage income (say x per cent). This amount will be credited in his Investment Bank Account. For example, we may assume 20 per cent of wage (salary) of every worker may be spent on purchasing investment goods. So if all workers spend $100 tr. in the market, the workers will buy $20 trillion worth of investment goods. To authenticate this purchase, $20 trillion worth of investment money value will be transferred to "Investment Bank" and each worker's "investment Account" will be credited accordingly. In the diagram it has been marked as "left ward arrow" mark from Market Sector to "Investment Bank Sector".

The Investment Account will be transferred from Investment Bank to "**People's business Sector** "and it has been marked in the diagram as "Upward Arrow" mark. Thus, the Business Sector will get **$20 trillion** investment money transfer from the investment bank and **$80 trillion** from Market Sector for sale of consumption goods. In aggregate the business sector will get **$100 trillion** by selling both Investment and Consumption goods, which it spent at the beginning of production of goods.

Democratisation of economy: In Democrism when every year $20 trillion worth of Investment money (20 per cent of wage income) flows to the Production Sector the producers will venture into new production activities, increase volume of employment and income of people. The producers not only utilise the Invest Money for new business ventures but also buy the capital shares of existing corporate sectors to democratize economy as early as possible. This all the industries will be owned by the workers in due course of time in democratic way without harming anyone.

For example, if the **People's Business Sector** has **$20 trillion investment money,** it will invest $10 trillion in launching new industries and will spend the another **$10 trillion** to buy "Capital shares" of existing industries at par value and all share markets would have been abolished. Step by step all existing industries will be bought by the "worker (Consumer) producers". This kind of process of purchasing shares of existing industries ultimately results in "All Industries for Each and Each Industry for All". Moreover, in buying the shares the seller's interests and welfare will also be taken into consideration.

At the beginning the 'people's business sector' backed by Economic Government and the individual corporate sector will also operate simultaneously. Moreover, the Corporate sector will be restricted from issuing new capital shares to expand their business and will also be prevented not to buy any shares from any corporate sector. The amalgamation of corporate sectors will be prevented. Whenever Government needs the private corporate sectors have to transfer their shares to People's Business Sector at par value. Thus, in the process of time "All Industries will owned by Every Worker and Every Worker will own All Industries". This is the basic principle of Democrism.

What is 100 per cent left arrow mark (Black Money): In Democrism the workers will frame an **"Economic Contract"** on the establishment of **"General Will" of the people** and instruct that no one should misuse the money in buying and selling of goods and services and as a means of exchange. Every worker will have to register their annual income range along with their Investment Bank Account Number and primary as well as their secondary mobile numbers. Moreover, the Investment bank and the market sector will have been digitalised. So if any worker or consumer spends more than his registered volume of income in the market, **(say, $1 trillion)** the bank will instantly warn the market sector about the over spending. The market will reject that money and forfeit it as black money or corrupt money. The market will transfer the whole money (100 per cent) and deposit in the Investment Bank. Since the money **($1 trillion)** has been earned by corruption it will be transferred to Investment Bank in the name of **"National Account" and I will be nationalised. In the diagram it has been displayed as 100 per cent leftward arrow mark from Market Sector to Investment Bank Sector.** The corrupt person whoever he may be will be legally punished. Thereby we can establish a **"corruption-free society."**

Morality of society and "Corruption-Free" Economy: Even at the very initial sage if the people realise that they will not spend corrupt money in any form, beyond their registered income, in the market and money will not only be forfeited but also the corrupt person will be arrested. If the people realise the Damocles' Sword is hanging over their heads in the succeeding events of transactions no one even try to dream to get corruption money and spend it. In the very short period the economy will be sanctified and the corrupt practices will be syphoned out. The morality of society will increase. Moreover, nobody will indulge in social evils such as rubbery, murdering for money, depositing the money in Swiss Banks, Stock market gambles and so on. The money one preserves over and above registered income will naturally turn into waste paper.

Purification of political system and elimination of politicians: The most admirable factor I will be that the political system of all the countries will be purified. No political party will be tempted to indulge in corruption. They will be prevented to use black money to buy the vote bank of common people and the whole political system will be purified. A group of people in the name of "politicians" will be eliminated. As soon as politicians disappear and the capitalist class will also be put into tantalisation. The politicians will be replaced by technocrats to rule over the country on the establishment of Industrial Democracy. All the workers (People) will become capitalists and all the capitalists will become workers. No worker who will be able to work will be permitted to get his loaf of bread without producing 'socially needed goods and services'.

Check Mate to Corporate Sectors: On the elimination of black money the big corporate sectors cannot spend billions and billions of dollars to buy the political parties, and tend to hijack legislature, executive and judiciary systems to command the government to dance according to their tunes. Moreover the corporate sectors cannot stimulate with their money power to brain wash the people because all the people would have become capitalists.

Elimination of Black Money: A huge volume of black money is now flooding over Stock Markets, Contract Works, Real Estates, Film Industries, Educational Institutions, Play grounds of football, cricket and so on. This flooding of black money will be shut down as soon as the banking and market sectors are digitalised under supervision of People's government or an autonomous body like Central Bureau of Investigation.

Under the Ultra-modern technology of digitalisation every one, individually or collectively should register his/her official Cell phones numbers, E Mail ids, authorised annual income, his official address and Bank account numbers both in the Investment Bank and Market Sectors of economy. All the banks and market sectors will have been digitally interconnected.

This technique of digitalisation will work effectively even in the present capitalistic mode of economies and we can establish corruption-free Ideal Society if the government is strong enough.

Let's analyse the above diagram. We have already seen the aggregate Investment money **($3 trillion)** accounted in Investment Bank will be transferred to "Business Sector". In the diagram it has been marked as an **upward arrow curve** from Investment Bank Sector to Business Sector.

Peoples Business Sector: I have already mentioned the retail selling price usually includes a considerable volume of profit. So the producers will always keep in mind that his "expected volume of Profit" as a guidance to venture into business. 1. If the "Expected Volume of Profit" is higher than the "Actual Volume of Profit" the producers will be induced to produce more and allocate more profit to the "People's Profit Reserve Fund". 2. If the "Expected volume of Profit" coincides with "Actual Volume of Profit" the producers will maintain the same volume of production and employment and 3. If the "Expected Volume of Profit" falls below the "Actual Volume of Profit", the producers stop the wheels of production. The economy will move towards recession and then towards depression. Under this condition there will be a great volume of unemployment, and poverty will prevail everywhere. Usually one of these three conditions exists in Capitalistic and Socialistic economies in successively and periodically all over the world.

But only in Democrism the first economic scenario, "Expected Volume of Profit" is higher than the "Actual Volume of Profit", will always prevail because in this system all producers are consumers and all consumers are producers. As producers the consumers will always cooperate with economic authorities to uphold the "expected volume of profit" should always be higher than the "actual volume of profit". By his fact the **"People's Profit Fund"**– an annexure to Business Sector – will sufficiently occupy an effective economic role to play. If the "People's Profit Fund" is considerably large, the workers will receive more dividend and the economy will move rapidly towards **"Egalitarian Society".**

Ethics of Wage Variation: The concept of Egalitarian Society should not be misconstrued as equal distribution of wage income to all at work spot, right from chief executive to last grade technician. If so no one goes to educational institutions, strive to increase their knowledge and wisdom, to expose their originality, individuality and creativeness. Morality and civilisation will disappear. Wage differentiation at work spot is a must to run a production unit dignifiedly and efficiently in a civilised manner. Equal wage to all is a purely naked violation of the noble concept of "Work according to Energy and Wage according to Work".

Ethics of Dividend Variation: Distribution of national dividend at the different rates to the various income groups is one of the best economic techniques to create an egalitarian society. In Democrism since all workers assume responsibility to create investment according to their wage, the low income group workers bear more "investment burden" than the high income group of workers. The concept of "distribution justice" insists the national dividend should be distributed according to "Investment Burden". Since the low income group of workers bear more "Investment Burden" they will receive more share of dividend than the high income group of workers. This distribution justice will reduce considerably the wage variation among workers and will lead the economy towards an Egalitarian Society.

As the Wage Variation is justifiable in the production sector so the Dividend variation is equally justifiable in distribution sector.

In the diagram I have pictured the "People's Profit Fund" as an annexure displaying three downward arrow marks. On the left side one downwards arrow mark naming "dividend" reaches household sector. This dividend combining with wage income provides **Dual Income** to the workers. This dual income will reduce the 'income gap' among different income groups.

Thereby Wage Variation in coordination with Dividend Variation justifies the Distribution Justice and leads mankind towards an Ideal Society. Neither Capitalism nor Socialism has any economic technique to create an ideal society except Democrism. Therefore, a person who wants to rule a nation should be well versed with the concepts of how to create interest-free investment and how to distribute national dividend to the people on Distribution Justice.

Government Sector and Tax-free economy: In Democrism the Production Sector has an Integral part of annexure as **People's Profit Fund.** It preserves 1. Economically safe volume of profit in its exchequer for distribution of dividend, 2. Adequate profit fund for contribution to government to meet its expenditure and 3. Necessary volume of fund to distribute to the producers to stabilise their monetary equilibrium ($\uparrow^{P}M = \downarrow^{P}M$) to buy stagnated goods in the market. We may call the third part of the People's

Profit Fund as **"Stabilizer Profit Fund".** It plays strategically important role in stabilisation of economy. The administration of the third part is intrigue and complicated to understand. Overtime if a person understands how to control it to achieve producers' monetary equilibrium he will be able to rule the nation or economy.

(In the diagram I have depicted all these as a downward arrow marks from People's Fund Sector to household sector, Government Sector and market sector). For example, if the Economic Government or any other local bodies need money income for social welfare services from the people, (say $1 trillion) the people will direct their Production Sector to release the money directly to the above agencies from their profit fund (Say, $ 3 trillion). **All direct and indirect taxes and excise duties will entirely be abolished.**

Cost of tax-collection: Moreover we can safely assume that if 30 per cent of total tax income is spent for tax-collection itself only 70 per cent of total tax income will flow towards government exchequer. Apart from the huge cost for collection of taxes, tax-payers have to face hardships for **filing tax returns, calculation of taxes, seeking guidance of auditors and legal opinions. All these complicated processes will put them into great mental depression**. In addition all these hardships unwillingness to give away their income will induce the people for creation of **black money** in billions and billions of dollars and intolerable **corrupt practices, money laundries, depositing in Swiss Banks. All these corrupt practices will be eliminated when in Democrism a part of "People's Profit Fund" is directly contributed to government exchequer.** Moreover the growing **deterioration of moral values** will be absolutely wiped out. The people live in peace with more leisure to spend for developing ones creativeness and originality and to live with reasonable **happiness.**

People's Profit Fund establishes Economic Stability: A portion of People's Profit Fund in kept as standby expenditure (rescue expenditure) to buy goods and services that are stagnated in the market. Since consumers are innumerable, they will behave erratically in the market. They will not usually spend their income to buy goods and services produced for them at the rate at which they are produced. This is natural phenomenon in all the capitalistic modes of production.

In Capitalism the producers "expected volume profit at each will not coincide with their actual volume of profit". When income increases the consumers marginal propensity will fall and they will not all of their marginal income to buy goods and services. As producers experience a negative gap as their actual profit falls down at higher levels of production, they will be prompted to reduce the volume of production and induced to create unemployment.

Keynes emphasises that in the capitalistic mode of production the economic instability will be unavoidable as the consumers will not spend all of their money income to uphold the producers expected volume of profit to be realised. He predicts the consumers will create a lack of effective demand at higher level of employment. If the producers do not realise their expected volume profit to continue the production, they will incur loss because of overproduction at that level of employment. The goods will be stagnated in the market for want of demand for goods. The effective volume of money will be locked or hoarded at somewhere else. Then how to clear the overproduction to stabilise the economy?

Determination of Employment

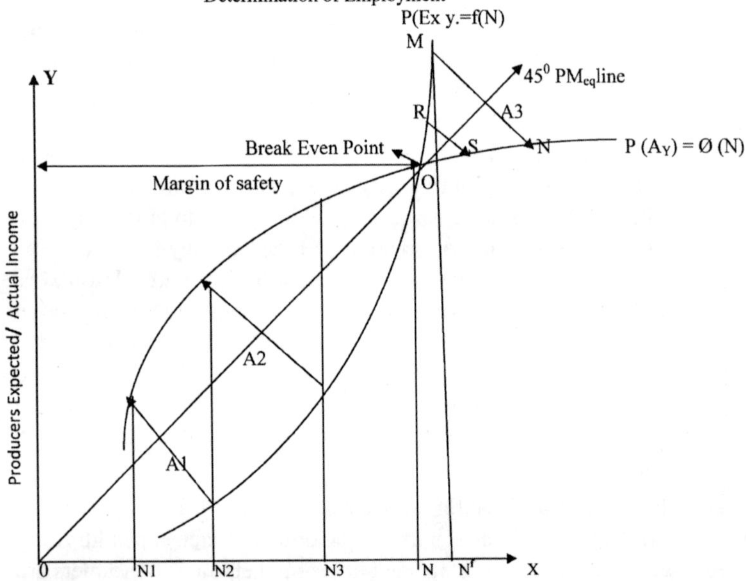

RS=Margin of Insecurity; A1,A2 = Margin of Inducement; A3= Margin of discouragement, N^f= Full employment; OSR = Risky triangle

RS=Margin of Insecurity; A1,A2 = Margin of Inducement; A3= Margin of discouragement. Nf= Full employment; OSR = Risky triangle.

The role of "Stabiliser Profit Fund" and the "tricky triangle" (OSR)

In the above diagram we can notice a "tricky triangle" (OSR) in which all economic problems have been densely thruster in. In the triangle OS denotes downward line of Actual Volume of Profit, OR denotes upward line of Expected Volume Profit and RS denotes **Margin of Insecurity**. As long as "Margin of Insecurity" exist all economic problems will agitate together within the triangle OSR and push the economy towards depression.

At the point of intersection of the actual income curve and the expected income curve at 'O' the producers experience underemployment equilibrium at the level of employment N3. On the other hand if the producers tend to increase the level of employment to **N4,** the producer's actual income will fall well below their expected income. In consequent the producer's maximisation of profit will diminish. Therefore, in order to maintain their maximisation of profit the producers will reduce the volume of production and the level of employment to **N3.** The diminished level of employment will reduce income and consumption of goods. The goods will be stagnated in the market.

The employees who lost their job due to lack of effective demand for goods will have to forgo their income and reduce further consumption. The cumulative trend of diminishing of consumption will force other producers to reduce the level of production, employment, income and further purchasing of goods. It will gain a cumulative process and huge volume of goods will be stagnated in the market, though the goods are socially needed.

If the level of employment is increased to the full employment level at 'N' the economic problems will emerge more severe and severe. The "Margin of Insecurity" (RS) increases and causes to collapse all economic activities. Ultimately the economy will move towards "Great Depression" within short span of time. Then how to solve the problem of depression and make the economy to take off into sustained growth? It is person who knows the remedy will rule the nation. The solution for these problems persists in Democrism and its distribution of "Stabilizer Profit Fund" to wipe out the "Margin of Insecurity".

The vitally of economic stability requires the elimination of "Margin of Insecurity"- SR of the tricky triangle OSR. Technically speaking in the capitalistic mode of production the elimination of Margin of Insecurity has been entangled by two factors. One is the 'expected income curve' OR which is independent variable and the other is 'actual income curve' OS which is dependent variable. The curve OR is independent variable because the 'expected income' is pre-determined or forecast by the producers at level of employment. If they are confident on their 'expected income' would be realised they will venture into business. On the other hand the curve OS is dependent variable because the 'actual income' of producers is influenced by various factors primarily the erratic psychological behaviours of numerous consumers in the market. Secondarily the consumer's marginal propensity to consume will diminish when their income increases. The consumers will not spend all of their income at the rate at which they receive. The consumers in aggregate have no plan of action or economic responsibility to uphold economic stability because there are innumerable and ignorant of the production activities.

There is conflict of interest in the psychology of producers and consumers. The producers always intend to achieve equilibrium between outflow of money and inflow of money. But consumers have no such an economic idea to maintain a monetary equilibrium between their inflow of money and outflow of money. Therefore, at higher level of employment the goods will be stagnated in the market and the producers will reduce the level of employment and production before reaching full employment. It is not the fault of consumers but the fault the economic system.

Therefore, it is advised that the government should interfere in the economic activities to reconcile the conflict of interests between producers and consumers and basically government acts in favour of producers who are few and moreover it is they who initiate production and level of employment. In the capitalistic system the governments will be in favour of national and multi-national corporations because it is they who control the governments.

By the force of producers the governments are induced to enhance the propensity of consumers to buy the stagnated goods to wipe out the margin of insecurity. The governments and central banks initiate various fiscal and monetary policies to control the financial management of consumers to induce to shift the 'producers' actual income cure' to intersect the 'producers' expected income curve' at the employment level of N4 to wipe out the **'margin of insecurity'** to help the producers to enjoy 'maximisation of profit' at full employment level at N4.

In capitalism this economic strategy will fail because at full employment level consumers' income will be high and their marginal propensity to save will also be high. Again the goods will be stagnated in the market due to lack of effective demand and the producers incur loss of income. So, the producers will reduce the volume of production and the level of employment at the point where their 'expected income' intersects their 'actual level of income' at **N3.** This is called 'under-employment' equilibrium. Therefore, in capitalism unemployment cannot be solved and economic stability will not be achieved at any point of time.

In Democrism since all consumers are producers, the consumers will cooperate with the government to take necessary steps to wipe out the 'margin of insecurity' even at the full employment level instead of diminishing volume of production and employment. Practically the innumerable consumers would not have any plan of action to maintain an equilibrium between their 'inflow of money and outflow of money' to help the producers to get their 'expected money income' at full employment level.

In Democrism the consumers' psychology will be not to allow the goods to stagnate in the market because they will not wish the emergence of unemployment among them due to their lack of propensity to consume or purchasing power. Therefore, when the goods tend to stagnate in the market by the ignorance and erratic behaviour of consumers they will prompt the economic authority's to take immediate action to use their "**Stabilisation Profit Fund"** to buy the goods and distribute them at low prices. This kind of 'economic responsibility will help the producers to maintain the monetary equilibrium between their "Expected Volume of Income" and their "Actual Volume of Income" at the level of full employment. This technique will shift the "Actual Income Curve" upwards to intersect the "Expected Income Curve" at that desired level of employment and ultimately try to disappear the "Margin of Insecurity Line" and stabilise the economic activities such as level of production, level of employment and level of income.

The influence of 'time lag': For the lack of effective demand or the lack of propensity to consume if the socially needed goods are stagnated in the market, the economic authorities should not allow long 'time lags' between average rate of goods produced and goods consumed. Due to this 'time lag' if one industry falls itwill gather cumulative process and trigger other industries to fall one after another. Consequently one can witness a large volume of unemployment, appalling poverty and collapse of families and their cultural and moral values. The "Law of Jungle' will occupy the "Law of Democracy". So the economic authorities should not provide much 'time lags' to turn the economic activities ugly. In Democrism, sufficient money will be reserved in "Stabiliser-Profit Fund" to buy the stagnated goods and it will be promptly released, whenever necessary, to prevent the lack of effective demand for goods.

Propensity to consume and Production of goods: When income increases the propensity to consume will decrease. People wish to save money. Saving is private virtue but public vice. If the people attempt to save money (Leakage from expenditure stream) the goods produced will stagnate in the market to that value of savings or hoardings. It is the known fact that the propensity to consume will be low or very low in the upper middle income and rich income groups of people. So the producers plan to produce more goods which have higher propensity to consume than the goods which have low propensity to consume. This kind of strategy of production will be possible only in Democrism which strives for the welfare of people. In the Capitalism the capitalists produce the goods which afford them to attain **"maximisation of Profit".** The producers usually strive to produce more luxurious goods which offer them more volume of profit than the necessities which afford them lower volume of profit.

So in order to reduce the **"Margin of Insecurity**" the producers should be induced to produce the goods which have more propensities to consume. In this regard the poor and low income group of people will naturally have "high propensity to consume". They will spend all of their money income to buy goods and services. Even if the goods are stagnated in the market the "Margin of Insecurity" will be very low and the insecurity can easily be wiped out by utilising **"Stabiliser-Profit Fund".** Basically the "necessities" will not stagnate in the market because they have high propensity to consume and are demanded a very large number of consumers. On the other hand the luxurious foods which have less propensity to consume should not be encouraged to produce more because the stagnating of luxurious will be more risky than the necessities and comforts. The stagnation of necessities and comforts can easily be redistributed at lower prices by compensating "Stabilizer-Profit Fund" and maximise the national aggregate propensity to consume. More the production of necessities and comports less Margin of Risk and the poverty.

Moreover, we should not waste the "People's Profit Fund" to buy the luxuries and the goods which affect one's health like tobacco if they are stagnated in the market. Instead we can reduce the volume of production or put a ceiling for their volume of production.

Allocation of People's National Profit Fund: The allocation of People's National Profit Fund is not established on any mathematical formulae of proportion distribution. The allocation of profit for 'distribution of dividend, contribution to government and to producers' income stabilisation fund will have various volume of amounts as per the needs and intensities of economic problems. Sometimes the ratio of allocation to Dividend: Government Expenditure: Stabilisation Fund may be 50:40:10 and other occasions it may be 50: 40: 10 and so on. So we can reallocate the profit fund to various domains in order to achieve "Producers' Monetary Equilibrium"($\uparrow^{P}M = \downarrow {}^{P}M$) and thereby to rule over the nation and to exert control over the economy.

The most strenuous economic problem is to keep available adequate reserve of "Stabilizer-Profit Fund" to wipe out whenever the "Margin of Insecurity" appears to show its ugly face due to lack of effective demand. The person, in Democrism, who wants to rule over the nation first give more superior priority to allocation of profit fund to "Stabiliser-Profit Fund" than to Dividend and Government contributions. Because the macro-economic equilibrium essentially more important than other contributions. Once we assure the 'producers' monetary equilibrium' ($\uparrow^{P}M = \downarrow {}^{P}M$) at macro-level, the economy will be safe and strong enough to face all other economic problems.

In the above diagram, if the producers produce goods at the level N4 their actual income will fall at 'S' well below their expected income at 'R'. The producers incur loss to the volume of 'OSR' (say, \$ 0.5 trillion) and will reduce the level of employment to N3 where Actual Income Curve intersects the Expected Income Curve at O. In order to sustain the level of employment and to avoid any monetary loss, the producers will stop production at the level of N3 in the Capitalistic Mode of Production. The goods produced beyond N3 will be stagnated in the market. The economy will witness unemployment and the employed workers at N4 will be thrown away and they have to live in poverty. It is the fault of consumers for not buying goods produced for them.

In Democrism in order to avoid such an economic tragedy a portion of People's Profit Fund to the value of $ 0.5 trillion for example, will be utilised by the government to buy the stagnated goods. It will shift both the "actual income curve" to shift upwards to intersect the Expected profit curve at 'E'. The government sells these goods cheaply to the poor and low-income groups of people. The money earned at "Cheap Price Sales Market" will again flow towards "People's Profit Fund" whatever it may be. Suppose if the government sells the $ 0.5 trillion worth of goods to $ 0.1 trillion, this sales income will be reverted to Peoples National Profit Fund. Thus, the level of employment, production income will be stabilised at the level employment N4. At this point the producer's expected income will equilibrate with their actual income. This monetary equilibrium will be called as "Producer's Monetary Equilibrium". Thus, if the "Producer's Monetary Equilibrium" exists at all levels of employment, the economy will move towards **"Full employment",** the ultimate goal of all economic systems.

Chapter – 31

How to Rule a Nation or How to Operate an Economy

How would you rule a country?

Throughout history of mankind many people have ruled countries in different ways. Communism, Fascism, Republics, Democracies, Authoritarianism, and Feudalism are some examples of different types of government. I've narrowed them into four types: Free Democracies, Corrupt Democracies, Modern Dictatorships and Full on Nineteen Eighty Four Style Big Brothers.

So, what would you be? Will you rule fairly or with an iron fist? Is there freedom of speech or is it rates in the eyes for anyone who speaks against you? So take the quiz, so that way should you acquire a small country, you we'll know to do.

Of all the equilibriums so far the mankind discovered in Socio-Economic-Political theories as well as in scientific theories, supreme equilibrium that is directly related to one's day-to-day life is the **"Producers' Monetary Equilibrium at all levels of employment".** It is so simple to say but most difficult and intrigue to achieve. Once you know how to achieve "Producers Monetary Equilibrium" in applying any economic system you will rule the nation to move it towards a Just Society. Because, only this equilibrium is subjected to Natural Law and Natural Justice.

What is meant by Producer's Monetary Equilibrium? When a producer ventures into the production of goods and services he sets out to flow a certain volume of money in the 'expenditure stream' **($\uparrow^{P}M$).** On the sale of such produced goods if he gets the same volume of money in his 'income stream'**($\downarrow {}^{P}M$)** at all levels of employment or production it is termed as "Producers Monetary Equilibrium" ($\uparrow^{P}M = \downarrow {}^{P}M$). This producer's equilibrium seems to very simple. But it is inscribed in the Temple of Wisdom as most intrigue and tantalizing to implement by any economic system. All the existing economic systems have failed in battles of economic techniques to achieve the equilibrium and now they are pushing the world at the verge of collapse.

Scientific inventions relates to what to produce and how to produce. Scientists have no control over their own inventions and on the problems of how and when to use them. For example, atom bombs and the weapons of mass destruction. All their scientific inventions have been nationalised by politicians. They are always at the brutal command of politicians and governments and they kill the people in millions. I deduce these politicians and political governments will be overthrown by technocrats and philosophers and Economic governments in the near future on the advent of digitalisation of economic activities.

The role of scientists: The scientists know the secret of Nature and applying this secret of Nature they help the government and capitalists "what to produce, how to produce, what kinds of goods can be produced irrespective of whether they are socially needed goods or not. Two World Wars were fought using their military inventions. Now terrorism has been emerged using their inventions. If they invent a missile in the name of "defense" of his country they could not exert control over its usage. The military weapons become all the governments' inalienable possessions. When the scientist resists the wrong usage of their inventions they are usually kept in "house arrest" during not only war times but also peace times. They have to lead a life of slaves. They are urged by their governments to invent such dangerous weapons for the sake of money but not for welfare of their mother lands.

It is undisputable fact that the scientist have invented innumerable socially needed goods. They have helped immensely for the growth of the country. They have simplified the day-to-day life of people. But the scientists don't know how to distribute the invented goods justifiably. Even the production of goods on the absence of justifiable distribution is futile. The paradigm is also applicable to the production of weapons of mass destruction. Whether the countries are going to play on the earth with their WMDs like football in a stadium? An eye for an eye is not defense. It will terminate the mankind. However, the capitalists, on occupying inventions of scientists, produce goods to maximise their profit and push the poor still poorer.

The scientists know only how to produce variety of goods cheaply and not how to distribute them justifiably. So the distributive justice rests on the wisdom of economists. Some invention of scientists pushed the mankind at the verge of ultimate determination. The politicians want to exert control over scientists and economists to show their supremacy over other countries but not for the welfare of mankind as a whole.

The creation of just society depends not only on the production of socially needed "goods and services" but also their equitable and justifiable distribution. These scientists and politicians don't know how to create a just society but how to push the world its ultimate termination, the nuclear holocaust. So the responsibility ultimately rests on the wisdom of economists.

As a student of economics I have invented "Democratisation of Economy' or Democrism-The Third Theory to establish an Ideal Society. Not only scientific theories but also social theories are formed by cluster of "Equilibriums". Of all the equilibriums "Producers Monetary Equilibrium" is occupying a reigning position in this modern world to lead mankind towards a peaceful world. So we the people take responsibility and initiation to achieve "Producer's Monetary Equilibrium" ($\uparrow^{P}M = \downarrow {}^{P}M$).

The responsibility, especially the economic responsibility to save the mankind is acquired from the inquiry on "Who should own the Capital". It is the people who are the real creator of capital, should assume the economic responsibility to establish indispensable and unavoidable "Producers Monetary Equilibrium". This equilibrium can be achieved only by "Democratisation of economy i.e., Democrism – The Third Theory". It is a historical necessity for survival of mankind. Now all the global economic systems move towards "Democratic Economy" to achieve their perfection, knowingly or unknowingly, through the "Theory of Evolution" or "Theory of Perfection".

In Democratic economy the national capital will directly be owned by all. So that, "All Industries will be owned by Each Worker and Each Industry will be owned by All Workers". Once this concept is executed the difference between Producers and Consumers will disappear. A PROducer cum conSUMER society will be established in the world. This society will be called as **"PROSUMER SOCIETY".**

The establishment of PROSUMER SOCIETY is a must to realise the "Producers' Monetary Equilibrium". In the PROSUMER society all the producers will strive for the benefits of consumers and similarly all the consumers will cooperate with the producers to uphold the vital equilibrium of "Producer's Monetary Equilibrium" to lead mankind towards an Ideal Society.

If one knows how to implement "Producers Monetary Equilibrium" at all level of employment, he will acquire the knowledge and ability to rule a nation. I have explained the technique of implementation in the above diagram **with numerical example.**

Stabilisation Fund Theory of Profit (MS vs MR)-OSR

Chapter – 32

Ideal Operation of Economy
Monetary 'Circular Flow-Equilibrium' Model
Laws of Nature vs. Laws of Society

Laws of Nature

There are innumerable scientific and natural laws already exist in the universe. It is the man by his intense and constant search for knowing the 'secret of nature' has invented a few laws of nature and converted them into mathematical models or equilibriums. By identifying and sensing the 'secret of nature' man has extracted and converted the 'elements of nature' which have been inherited in the biological, physical and chemical elements. These laws are primarily used by man to produce goods and services to establish a civilised and a wealthy society.

Man has found that the Nature is perfect, eternal and everlasting for billions and billions of light years because he has authentically and experimentally found out that the 'laws of nature' are :

(a) True and not contracting,

(b) Universal and they're applicable anywhere in the universe,

(c) Simple and they can be expressed in terms of a single mathematical equation,

(d) Absolute as nothing in the universe affect them,

(e) Stable from its first discovery,

(f) Omnipotent,

(g) Generally conservative of quality, and

(h) Expressions of existing homogeneities (symmetries) of space and time.

For example, Archimedes' principle, Keller's three laws of planetary motion, Newton's three laws of motion, Euler's laws of rigid body motion, Newton's law of universal gravitation, Newton's law of cooling, Boyle's law, Joule's first and second law, the four laws of thermodynamics, Faraday's law of induction (i.e. Law of electromagnetism), Einstein's theory of relativity, Theories of computer science (algorithmic processes, computer programming, integrated circuits etc.), Cell phone and so on. These laws are mostly satisfying the above mentioned characteristics of 'Laws of Nature' and therefore they are eternal and perfect.

Similarly the Law of Universe requires an equilibrium in the 'earth's orbit around the sun'. The Law of Nature maintains the earth in an accurate 'circular Equilibrium Law' since the genesis of Solar System for its eternality.

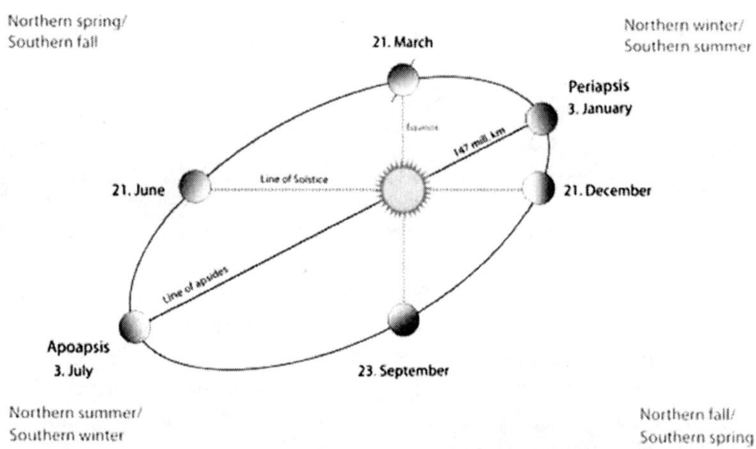

Solar System and Law of Nature

The Earth's orbital path measures 939,336,203.4 km around the Sun. Around January 2nd the Earth comes closest to Sun (Perihelion) and around July 2nd it goes farthest away from the Sun (Aphelion). Whatever it may be if we assume that the Earth starts to travel on its orbital path from a particular point on the orbit on 2nd January, it will reach the same point after 365.25 days. The Earth travels at a constant velocity of 29.77 km/sec (or 67000 miles per hour) for billions of years without any variation. The Law of Universe requires an Equilibrium between the velocities at the starting and terminal points on the orbital path of Earth. Since both the points are coinciding with each other at any particular time the average orbital path of Earth forms a circle. The Law of Universe emphasises the vitality of Equilibrium between the velocities not only for the very survival of circling Earth and other planets but also for the survival of all dynamic factors of any system.

Physiological Law of Nature

The Law of Nature exists in the 'inner organic functions' of all living creatures. These living creatures obeying to natural law have undergone 'an extensive evolutionary process as per Darwinian Theory' on the earth from one organic cell to multi-organic cell like human beings to reach their perfection. In the case of man the Law of Nature exhibits a 'Physiological law' in the form of 'Perfect Circular Flow of Blood' from heart to lungs and to other parts of body.

In the 'perfect circular flow of blood' the 'law of nature' composes 'a natural equilibrium between inflow and outflow of blood' in the heart by continuously expanding and contacting the upper (atria) and lower (ventricles) parts of the heart respectively. This perennial circular flow of "blood – equilibrium" keeps man alive. Once the equilibrium collapses all the organic functions will be pushed at the verge of disarray and ultimate inevitable end of life. In his book 'Physics of the Body' (Madison, WI: Medical Physics Publishing, 1999, p. 182) Cameron, R. James states that 4.4 liters volume of blood (7 per cent of body mass) set into circular motion for a normal adult person (for some authors it is 4.7L to 5L). The more or less volume of blood in circulation is detrimental to health of any person. This limit is determined by the law of nature.

Similarly any variation in the velocity of earth or in its circumference of orbit around the sun will terminate the life of living creatures on the earth. All the systems created in the universe should obey to the Law of Nature. This 'Limits Theory' that exists in nature is also applicable to all man-made-systems which are termed as a constitution of Laws of Society which comprises 'basic economic laws and super structural socio-political laws'.

Laws of Society

Generally all man-made-laws are termed as Laws of Society. Every society has its own laws that can be altered, or deleted or created in order to establish an Ideal Society. The laws of society are classified into 1. Basic Structural Law of Society i.e. Basic Economic Law of Society and 2. Super-Structural Law of Society as already stated. The basic economic law of society narrates the 'function of monetary circular-flow' of any economic system, either capitalism or Socialism or their Chemistry of Systems, and the Super Structural law of society as a dependent factor of the basic economic law of society, illustrates the nature and quality of excellence of laws regarding political system, legal system, educational system, cultural system, religious system etc.

The basic economic law of society primarily relates to the 'Mode of Production' of Capitalism or Socialism or any other economic systems. However whatever the 'mode of production' all the economic systems should accommodate 'the law of nature' in relation to the 'monetary circular-flow equilibrium' between various conflicting factors by applying 'supply and demand forces' of different elements such as capital, labour, volume of production, volume of consumption, revenue and expenditure of government (budgetary equilibrium), and export and imports of goods and services to foreign countries (foreign trade equilibrium).

Let us assume 'other things being equal' and no exogenous factors exert influence on the operation of economy. The above figure is drawn that the 'circular flow of money' operates in harmony with the law of nature and no

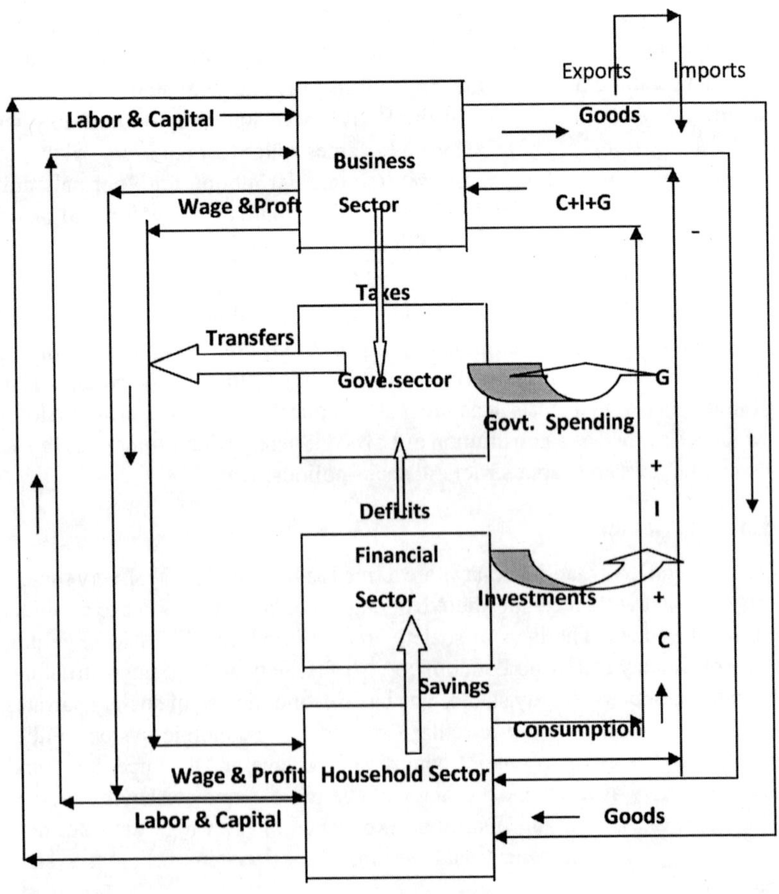

consumers'/producers' erratic behaviour would control or interrupt this circular flow of money.

1. At the very outset the **money will be generated** from **Central Bank** on 'no interest payment' basis and it will be, say for example **$1000 billion,** set to flow towards the producers. All commercial banks operating on 'interest based debt' will be converted into 'Investment Banks' and they will pay 'dividend' instead of interest to the people. **The producers** for the production of goods and services purchase the two basic factors of production, capital and labour, from household sector. say for example, to the tune of **$1,000 billion** which they receive from central bank.

2. **The household sector**, by selling labour and capital will receive wage and profit respectably to the tune of **$1000 billion.** This is the disposable income of household sector to buy goods and services produced for them by the producers. This disposable income includes 'transfer payments' like old age pensions. Unemployment stipends, educational scholarships, healthcare benefits etc. Usually this disposable income may also be called as National Income.

3. Since 'one man's expenditure is another man's income' the producers' expenditure becomes the consumer's income to the volume of **$1,000 billion.** Let's assume that there is no leakage like savings in the consumers' income stream and the consumers spend all of their money income to buy the goods and services in the **'commodity market'.**

4. From the **commodity market** this volume of money flows to **producers** through their 'income stream' to enable them to venture into next round of production. If this 'General or Aggregate circular-flow of money equilibrium' prevails at all levels of supply of money, the economy will move toward 'full employment equilibrium'. This simple equilibrium model resembles 'the circular flow of equilibrium' of the earth around the sun between January 2 and July 2 during Northern Spring(like factors flow from consumers to producers) and July 3 and January 3 during southern Spring (like goods flow from producers to consumers) covering one earth's orbit in 365.256 days by average velocity of 29.783 Km/s.

In the same line of way every successive production that producers will undertake at the same volume of production, depends on the velocity (V) of money (M) in its circular flow between producers and consumers. The volume of production, therefore, emerges as a dependent factor of MV. It may be termed as a linear equilibrium as $P = f(M,V)$, (Where P= volume of production, M = quantity of Money in circulation and V = velocity of money).

For example, if the quantity of money in circulation amounts to $250 billion and its velocity remains at 4, the total volume or value of money will be calculated as $1000 billion. At given price level the consumers will buy

$1,000 billion worth to good produced (P), if there is no leakage (Savings). On the other hand if the quantity of money increases from $250 billion to $300 billion without any variation in velocity the value of money in circulation will increase to $1,200 billion, and it will enhance the price level of goods in the short run immediately and will not increase volume of production because in the short run infrastructure like capital cannot increased in the short run. This inflationary trend will increase production only in the long run by creating competition among producers to achieve maximisation of profit. A reverse trend may also happen if either quantity of money or its velocity or the both diminish marginally.

The quantity theory of money like other economic theories is not constant, accurate and universally applicable like Laws of Nature. So we should not depend upon these theories and their equilibriums to solve human problems.

General Equilibrium Theory and Law of Nature

Now the new macroeconomics strives to build a macroeconomic theory in harmony with Law of Nature or physiological law of equilibrium of blood circulation in human body or circular equilibrium of earth around the sun. In the new economic models, the macroeconomics is assumed to be at its unique equilibrium in harmony with Law of Nature, with full employment and potential output, and that this equilibrium is assumed that it will have been achieved via price and wage adjustments (market clearing). Since the laws of new macroeconomics attempts to coincide with laws of nature, the economists at present have developed a belief that an 'economic evolution' in due course will create a 'general equilibrium' being perfect and eternal and will lead the society to 'Full Employment Equilibrium'.

Jean-Baptiste Say, therefore, in his famous Treatise on **"Law of Markets"** conceiving that the law of nature would prevail in the operation of economy said that 'supply would create its own demand' in real terms and it might be expressed in monetary terms that money circulated from producers to consumers would be in equilibrium with the money circulated from consumers to producers at all level of supply of money.

The **'General or the National Circular Money Flow Equilibrium'** (from the notional vision of classical economists like Adam Smith and Ricardo and neo-classical economists like Torstein Brude Veblen, Alfred Marshall, Hicks, George Stigler etc.,) would be retained or adjusted to any change in the other economic subsystems until a general equilibrium' would be achieved in harmony with the Laws of the Nature. General equilibrium at 'full employment' can be achieved by applying the 'interaction of demand and supply mechanism' or by the theory of 'marginalisation', or through a hypothesised maximisation of utility by money income or by the combination of all of them.

Equilibrium in the interdependent subsystems of economy

The National Circular Monetary Equilibrium is sustained by the strength of equilibriums of various interdependent subsystems such as 'income and expenditure, savings and investment, rate of interest and rate of profit, volume of production and volume of consumption, volume of export and volume of import, revenue and expenditure of government and above all 'producers' expected income and their actual income in their production venture'.

The economists were being confident that the laws of economics would travel in parallel with the laws of nature, due to their automatic adjustment mechanism and the economy would move smoothly towards perfection. During 1930s the blind assumptions were proved false throughout the world. One thing is now clear that if we formulate an economic system that would operate in symmetrical with 'laws of nature' we can establish an Ideal Society. How? Before creating such an economic system let's regain the analysis of the ideal operation of economic equilibrium of subsystems in the following paragraphs.

Equilibriums of Economic – Subsystems

(a) Savings and investment equilibrium: The consumers in the 'household sector' on receiving their disposable money income from producers ($700 billion) after paying taxes ($200 billion) will not spend the whole disposable income for buying consumption goods and services. As the money income increases the 'propensity to save', will increase and the consumers therefore will save (S_{HH} – Household Savings) a considerable part of income (for instance $100 billion) for the sake of earning interest to compensate the loss of value of money due to its 'marginal diminishing utility' and for 'speculative motive' as per Keynes' inference. The consumers will deposit their savings, S_{HH}, ($100 billion) in the financial institutions which will lend the deposits to the firms –investors - in the name of 'investments'(I) ($100 billion) , i.e. injection into income stream, for higher rate of interest to buy investment goods. Let's assume at an optimum rate of interest the 'savings' equilibrates with the 'investments'.

The rate of interest technique prevents the 'leakage' of money from the 'expenditure stream of consumers' in the form of savings and converts it as 'injection' in the form of 'investments' to flow again in the 'income of stream of producers (firms)' to sustain the level of production and employment in all successive rounds of production in a closed economy.

(b) Government's Budgetary Equilibrium: The economic force of gravity on the role of intervention of government was realised only after the 'Great Depression' occurred during 1930s in US and other capitalist countries.

It was John Maynard Keynes who advised that the State should seize economic responsibility though 'budgetary technique' to recover the actual level of employment, production, income and consumption in his revolutionary book 'The General Theory of Employment, Interest and Money' in 1936. The government has two roles to play. One is economic roles and the other is the political roles.

8 (A) The economic roles of government

1. Prevention of Monopoly Power: The government in order to prevent monopoly power should promote effective and workable competition entrepreneurs by encouraging 'individuals' and firms' able to enter freely in the same trade of business.

2. Providing public goods: Public goods are goods whose consumption by one individual does not prevent their consumption by other individuals. An example of a public good is national defense. National defense must protect all individuals in the country. It cannot protect some people but leave others unprotected.

3. Ensuring Economic Stability and Growth: In addition to providing general stability, government has potential role of providing economic stability. If it's possible, most people would agree that government should prevent large fluctuations in the level of economic activity; maintain relatively constant price level; and provide an economic environment conducive to economic growth.

8 (B) The political roles of government

1. Providing for a Fair Distribution of Society's Income: The government should ensure a fair distribution of society's income. In this context the government uses 'taxation' as a technique. So the government has to decide whether it has to levy Progressive tax (income tax – marginal increase in tax rate according to marginal increase of income rate), or Proportional tax (a tax whose rates are constant irrespective of income) or provide tax exemption (for a mother who has three or more children).

2. Discouraging demerit and encouraging merit goods or activities: Another controversial role for government involves deciding what's best for people independently of their desires. The externality justification of government intervention assumes that individuals know what is best for them.

For example, people might know that addictive drugs are bad for them but because of peer pressure, or because they just don't care, they may take addictive drugs anyway. Government action prohibiting such activities through law or high taxes may then be warranted.

Alternatively there are some activities that government believes are good for people, even if people may not choose to engage in them. For example, government may believe that contributing to charity is a good activity. But a very small percentage of the population, even in US, contributes to charity.

However, let's assume the government requires revenue of nearly $200 billion to administer its economic and political responsibilities. The government acquires the money primarily in the form of income tax and corporate tax for national revenues and property tax and sales tax for municipal and county revenues. If any deficit arises the government borrows from financial sector and sometimes from the people directly. Government spends the $200 billion on current goods and services, which economists call government consumption, government investment expenditures such as infrastructure investment or research expenditure, and transfer payments like unemployment or retirement benefits.

Thus, in a closed economy the producers receive $1,000 billion by selling goods and services at a given price level to the consumers ($ 500 billion), to the investors ($200 billion) and to the government ($300 billion) to equilibrate their spending of the $1,000 billion through factors of production in the first round of production.

8 (C) The role of international trade of government

In order to complete the overall operation of an economic system we have to incorporate the international trade. It is exchange of capital, goods and services across international borders. In most countries, it represents a significant share of gross domestic product (GDP). While international trade has been present many centuries of history, its economic, social, and political importance has been on the steep rise in recent centuries.

Industrialisation, advanced transportation, globalisation, multinational corporations and outsourcing all have contributed a major impact on the international trade system. Increasing international trade is crucial to the continuance of globalisation. Without international trade, nations would have been limited to the goods and services produced within their borders.

In the international trade the balance of trade, i.e. net exports (NX), is the difference between the monetary value of exports and imports of output in an economy over a certain period. It is the relationship between a nation's imports and exports.

(Sullivan, Arthur; Steven M. Schifrin (2003). Economics: Principles in action. Upper Saddle River, New Jersey 07458: Pearson Prentice Hall. pp. 462. ISBN 0-13-063085-3).

A positive or favourable balance of trade is known as a trade surplus if it consists of exporting more than importing. A negative or unfavourable balance is referred to as a trade deficit or, informally, living beyond a nation's means, or a trade gap. If the trade gap is zero, the exports and imports are in equilibrium. This monetary foreign trade equilibrium will not make any impact in the economic activities of a country. The marginal increase or decrease in the monetary balance of trade will always be constant in a dynamic economy.

Monetary balance of trade is different from physical balance of trade (which is expressed in amount of raw materials, known also as Total Material Consumption). Developed countries usually import a lot of primary raw materials from developing countries at low prices. Often, these materials are then converted into finished products, and a significant amount of value is added. Although for instance the EU (as well as many other developed countries) has a monetary balance of trade, its physical trade balance (especially with developing countries) is negative, meaning that a lot less material is exported than imported. For this reason, activists talk about the issue of **ecological debt** which implies a sort of predatory economic system. The nature of the trade balance statistics is such that is conceals distorted material flow.

Andrew Simms in his book 'Ecological Debt'. (London: Pluto Press, 2009' p. 200) describes the Ecological debt as the consumption of resources from within an ecosystem that exceeds the system's regenerative capacity. This is seen in particular in non-renewable resources wherein consumption outstrips production. In a general sense, it can be used refer to the overall depletion of global resources beyond the Earth's ability to regenerate them. The concept is based on the bio-physical carrying capacity of an ecosystem; through measuring ecological footprints human society can determine the rate at which it is depleting natural resources. Ultimately, the imperative of sustainability requires human society to live within the means of the ecological system to support life over the long term. Ecological debt is a feature of unsustainable economic systems.]

Dangerous imports: For the sake of simplicity I have assumed 'foreign trade equilibrium' in exchange of goods between countries. But this 'exchange of foreign goods and their consumption' affects lifestyle or the social subsystems of people in the domain of culture, customs and conventions, education, technology, legal system, political aspects etc.

Nevertheless the classical and neoclassical economists strongly speculated that a 'general economic equilibrium'. in the economy as whole would be attained by the operation of 'automatic adjustments' exercising over the conflicting factors by their 'demand and supply' and thereby the economy would function in the direction of perfect equilibrium prevailing in 'laws of nature or the laws of universal science'. The economy, therefore, would attain perfection and eternality in its continuous process of evolution in correspondence with the Laws of Nature.

In conclusion I wish to emphasise two points

The first and foremost point is that in the 'Capitalistic and Socialistic Modes of Production' the General Equilibrium or Full Employment Equilibrium' cannot be achieved even in the long run because of powerful play of conflicting factors of production. In this background I wish to mention the words of Irving Fisher:

"It is as absurd to assume that, for any long period of time, the variables in the economic organisation, or any part of them, will "stay put, " in perfect equilibrium, as to assume that the Atlantic Ocean can ever be without a wave"

Irving Fisher, The Debt-Deflation Theory
of Great Depressions, 1933, p. 339

Secondly, since our goal is to achieve 'General Equilibrium' in correspondence with the 'Laws of Nature' for its quality of perfection we have to replace both the 'capitalistic and Socialistic Modes of Production' by the 'Democratic Mode of Production' which is free from all contradictions of factors of production and distribution. By the term 'Democratic Mode of Production' I mean "PEOPLE'S DIRECT OWNERSHIP OF CAPITAL" or "Democratisation of Economy" (Democrism) the only just alternative system now available in our economic theories. Democratisation of Economy has all characteristic elements to lead the mankind towards an Ideal Society.

Volume: VIII

Chapter – 33

How to Implement the Theory of Democrism

By "Dual Monetary System"

(a new economic technique)

Dual Monetary System – A Solution to All Economic Problems Operation of Dual Monetary System

The creation of capital means the democratic mode of creation of capital by the people, for the people and of the people. The creation of capital would be a continuous process whenever people purchases goods and services. Now on the purchase of goods and services people pay taxes to the government. Instead of paying taxes people would be offered 'Investment Money' to buy investment goods along with consumption goods on every purchase made in the market.

The workers produce not only 'consumption goods' but also 'capital goods' and so the workers are entitled to receive a justifiable wage to buy both the consumption and capital goods. But due to the fault of economic system in the creation of capital the capitalists exploit the workers by appropriating a major portion of their wages in the form of 'interest and profit' and with this 'appropriated money' the capitalists buy capital goods. Since the capitalists are very few they seize a large portion of the wages of millions and millions of workers in the name of profit. With the 'seized the wages of workers' the capitalists purchase all the capital entitled to the workers. (The World Bank statistics say that only 7 per cent-10 per cent of sale price of a commodity is paid to the workers as wages)

It is the economic justice that since the workers only produce the capital goods they should alone be entitled to receive justifiable wages to buy the entire capital goods also but not by any other capitalists or State or exploiters. The execution of this economic justice requires democratisation of economy.

Investment according to wage

Creation of capital by the workers in the form of new investment according to their wage requires the establishment three prerequisite economic structures. It needs only a proper realignment of existing economic structures already functioning. The three prerequisites are:

1. Family-income group structure (Household structure)
2. Bank structure and
3. Market structure – distribution of goods and services.

1. Family-income group structure

The distinction of 'income-group' is not only a prerequisite condition for smooth operation of Dual Monetary System but also indispensable to reduce 'income gap' to establish smoothly an egalitarian society without extorting any income group.

Identification of Income- Group

1. For identification of different income-groups 'Family cards' in different colours would be issued to each family. For instance the families of Low-income group would get Green colour cards, the Middle-income groups Yellow colour cards, the High-income groups the Orange colour cards and Rich and Super-income groups the Golden colour cards.

2. In the family cards as it is existing in India, the name and photo identity of the head of the family and the names of other members of the family with their monthly/annual income would be-printed.

3. Each family card would bear (a) an identity number, (b) an E Mail Id, (c) a password, (d) name of the bank the family should have an account, (e) the account number, (f) House address, and (g) phone number. These particulars are must for the higher-middle class, rich class and super rich class family card holders because it is these families prevent perfect circular flow of money between producers and consumers and cause disequilibrium between production and consumption of goods and services and between income and expenditure of money due to their erratic psychological behaviour in the market which is detrimental to the smooth economic operation. Whereas the low and middle income families (who are economically friendly people) would spend their income as soon as they receive and would maintain equilibrium between income and expenditure for healthy economic operation. All the family cards will be computerised and will be interacted linking with their banks through internet. By the comprehensive usage of internet facilities all banks will maintain the 'income and expenditure account' of all families.

2. Bank structure

"I believe that banking institutions are more dangerous to our liberties than standing armies. If the American people ever allow private banks to control the issue of their currency, first by inflation, then by deflation, the banks and corporations that will grow up around the banks will deprive the people of all property – until their children wake-up homeless on the continent their fathers conquered."?

— **Thomas Jefferson,** 1802

For the smooth and effective operation of Dual Monetary System and over-all economic activities the present age-old bank-structure should be reorganised in scientific manner co-coordinating with market mechanism. At present the banks are treating the 'money' as marketable commodity. They buy the money from the depositors at a price of low interest and sell it to the investors at a price of high interest. Sometimes the banks use 'interest technique' as an indispensable economic strategy to maintain an equilibrium in 'circular flow of money between producers and consumers at all levels of income' but this technique has failed throughout the world. So Dual Monetary System is advocated to save the economic activities from the clutches of incompetent 'interest technique' for which the age-old banking structure requires an integral and inherited reorganisation to face the challenges of intrinsically complicated modern economic problems.

(a) For the effective execution of Dual Monetary System, at the very outset, all the banks will be restrained from using the money as a 'marketable commodity'. There will be no 'deposits' from the savers as well as no 'investments' to borrowers. And thereby as a sequel ' paying of interest' or 'interest phenomenon' would be completely eliminated from the economic structure and in economic literature as a consequence.

(b) As a basic constitution the banks will pursue 'the law of universe' or 'the law of blood circulation' to maintain a 'perfect circular flow of money between producers and consumers' at all levels of money supply or production or employment.

(c) For the purpose of upholding the 'law of perfection' (the law of Universe) The banks would be entrusted with the absolute authority of issuing 'two kinds of money'. One is **'Consumption money'** and the other is **Investment money' (Electronic Money).**

(d) The banks put 'the consumption money' into circulation to 'the extent or volume of coverage' required by the economic authorities. The consumption money is nothing but the 'present money in circulation'. The destructive fault committed by the economists, spreading over a long time until now, is that they have empowered the present money to perform concurrently two contradictory functions, unaware of its dangerous economic consequences; one is medium of exchange and the other is store of value.

As medium of exchange money plays dynamic role flowing incessantly to gear up economic machinery. We may call it as 'active money'(M1) because it effectuates both producers and consumers to exchange goods and services to sustain required level of economic activities such as production, consumption and employment. Contrary to this dynamic character, money has to perform simultaneously the function of store of value and we may call it as passive money (M2) because it is squarely static in nature. By the mental stimulation of money illusion which is naturally inhabited in the minds of all people, the consumers especially those in high income-groups are induced to hoard or store or save the active money for their personal motives guided by psychological factors. They do so because money has store of value and it will not cause to diminish its face value during a considerable period of time. And so the consumers convert the active money into passive money (by hoarding or by saving the active money) not recognising the genesis of economic evils inherited in it, and thus they prevent the active money not being put into 'required volume of circular flow between producers and consumers' to sustain economic activities at all levels of income.

On the contraction of active circular flow of money if the producers will find no prudent approach to maintain monetary equilibrium and they will be inclined to reduce the level of production and employment up to which they will receive money income. The monetary equilibrium at reduced level will, of course, result in unemployment.

Man is born rich in nature and everywhere he is poor in society (God creates man in the midst of abundant natural resources and he is deprived of them everywhere in the world). It is not because of the sin of man in his previous birth but because of the sin that he is avaricious to storing the wealth more than his due. In the evolution theory of money man has assigned money to perform simultaneously two contradictory functions – one is medium of exchange and the other is store of value; whereas the former is dynamic and the latter is static. On the assumption that the money is strictly empowered only to perform 'medium of exchange' function there would be 'perfect circular flow of money at all levels of money supply' or 'perfect real equilibrium between production and consumption at levels of employment' and this attainment of economic perfection would have solved all socio-economic problems of mankind since the genesis of civilisation and we have now been able to live in an well-ordered society.

The concentric economic problem which is exerting more injurious pressure over all other economic problems is to find out an economic technique how to insulate the 'function of store of value' not to interfere with the 'function of medium of exchange'. For the operation of 'store of value' and 'medium of exchange' as well economy requires a 'new economic technique' by which two kinds of moneys would be put into circulation not to interrupt the course of flow of each money in circulation. One money will flow having exclusive character of 'medium of exchange' and the other having with 'store of value' only.

Assigning two different contradictory functions to different kinds of money demands a reasonable but simple reorganisation of the existing banking system. The banks should be entrusted to issue both 'Consumption money' and 'Investment money' into circulation.

(a) The Consumption money at first would flow from producers (production sector) to customers (household sector) in equal value in the form of wages to the services rendered by the workers for the production of goods and services (including capital goods).

(b) It is usually 'expected' that the consumers would spend their wage - income to buy goods and services produced for themselves and set to flow the 'active money' towards the producers to equip them monetarily to sustain the same level of production in the second round.

(c) To mention specifically the consumers in low and middle-income groups would spend their wage-income at the rate at which they receive it from producers. They would constantly maintain a monetary equilibrium between income and expenditure. Since their 'propensity to consume' goods and services is ever in high magnitudes they would spend all their money income and thereby maintain a 'perfect circular flow money between producers and consumers' which would drive the economy in forward motion. For this reason the poor are 'technically friendly but economically collapsing'. Lesser the income, higher the propensity (to consume); stronger the equilibrium but weaker the economy.

(d) But what a strong and sound economy requires is a 'perfect monetary equilibrium at all levels of income'. As a matter of fact when the income of consumers increases beyond a certain level the (marginal) propensity to consume decreases and in consequence it prevents a certain volume of 'active money' not to flow into circulation and instigates the producers to reduce the level of production and employment. As soon as the consumers tend to save money impelled by their money illusion the economy jerks into depression by fits and starts and it is like a straw that breaks the camel's back.

(e) In order to rescue the economy from the stagnation (saving) of active money we have to find out an empirical and scientific technology other than the same age-old economic technique of 'interest'. And so in the reorganisation of banking system a new economic technique known as 'DUAL MONETARY SYSTEM' will be introduced. Under this system a new money by name

'Investment money' will be put into circulation along with the present 'Consumption money'.

Whenever people wish to save a portion of their money income (Consumption money) they can do so with full liberty. But they cannot save it in its original form of Consumption money which has to function as a medium of exchange alone. On the contrary, they can save it in the form of Investment money. For example, if people have an intention to save money they can convert it into Investment money whenever they buy goods and services in the market. Conversion of Investment money means buying of investment goods in the market.

In other words purchasing of goods means purchasing of consumption goods and investment goods at the same time at a particular ratio. Let us assume the 'existing ratio' between the aggregate production of consumption and investment goods is 7:3. And the national income amounts to $100 billion. If the consumers spend $100 billion they will be permitted to get consumption goods to the value of $70 billion and the investment money to the value of $30 billion. It implies the consumers have converted the consumption money into investment money and they have bought investment goods for $30 billion. By means of that the producers of consumption goods will get $70 billion and the producers of investment goods $30 billion in the form of Consumption money. Since the producers realise monetary equilibrium between income and expenditure they will resume second round of production without any time lag.

(a) In the reorganised banking system there would be an 'Investment Account' for all the consumers in their banks and the banks would be called as 'Investment Banks'. There would be no Commercial banks as we have now because all these banks would be ceased to function in the business market for borrowing and lending money for profit motive.

(b) The Investment banks would be spread out throughout the country according to the need of population or number of families. The existing infrastructure of commercial banks would not be abolished but the name board of all the banks would be rewritten as 'Investment banks'.

(c) The consumers who are in possession of $30 billion, as I mentioned in my example, would deposit their Investment money in these Investment banks.

(d) These 'Investment-depositors' would receive 'dividend' instead of interest at a particular interval of time each year according to the value of their investment-deposits. Usually the dividend amount would be higher than the present normal interest amount.

(e) In order to operate the Investment-deposits an Investment account would be assigned to each and every family. The investment account is nothing but a detailed 'pass book' which will exhibit 1. **The name of bank and account number,** 2. The name and photo of the head of the family, 3. The annual income of the family, 4.The name of dependents with age, 5. **E Mail address,** 6. **Ratio of investment deposit especially for higher middle-income and rich families**, 7. Permanent address and above all and 8. **Registered Phone number.** All these particulars would be computerised and stored in a 'database'.

(f) The password and secret code number would be allotted by the banks to the higher middle-income and rich families and their account particulars would be preserved confidentially by the banks. But at the soft touch of the 'mouse' the bank authorities can bring into light all monetary transactions of these families for economic scrutiny and detect whether any economic scandals are committed by them to devastate economic stability.

(g) The Investment banks could not entertain the depositors to withdraw any amount of investment money, in view of the fact that they have already bought 'investment goods' out of the money and in order to substantiate that the consumers are entrusted with 'investment money'. And the consumers can assert their legal right in the stock of national capital up to the value of their investment money savings.

(h) The banks would not accept the 'Consumption money' as deposits and so that they wouldn't pay any interest to the depositors. But for safekeeping of money the consumers can hire the banks as 'custodian of money' and they can withdraw and deposit money whenever they desire by using checks, credit cards and other monetary tokens as usual. For the purpose of rendering these services the banks will charge its customers a reasonable amount as 'bank charges' to meet their expenses. Moreover on the deep and wide utilisation of computer and phone services it is said that the banks will come at the door steps of customers to render their services.

(i) Hereafter there would be only Investment banks which would use money only as "dynamic economic equilibrator" to maintain perfect circular flow of money. The present characterisation of money as a 'commodity' in the credit market would be completely abolished forever.

(j) The circular flow of money would be classified into two segments: one is 'circular flow of consumption money' and the other is 'circular flow of investment money'. The former would manage to sustain 'an equilibrium between production and consumption of consumer goods in respect of consumers' and the latter 'an equilibrium between production and consumption of investment goods in respect of producers' at all levels of employment to lead the economy towards full employment.

(k) The primary function of Investment banks is to ensure and give producers a guarantee for future certainty that a monetary equilibrium in circular flow of consumption money and of investment money would be maintained at all levels of money supply. If producers have such a guarantee to attain monetary equilibrium despite a time lag prevails in the production and sale of goods, they will drive the economy towards full employment within a prescribed period. I call this monetary equilibrium as “Producers’ Monetary Equilibrium” which means ‘an equilibrium between expenditure and income of producers’ at a particular level of employment.

There is another monetary equilibrium known as “Consumers’ Monetary Equilibrium” which I mean ‘an equilibrium between income and expenditure of consumers’ at a particular level of income.

In general terms I wish to name the combination of the two monetary equilibriums as ‘Economic Monetary Equilibrium’. Between the two the Producers’ Monetary Equilibrium is the prime mover of economy because it is the producers who organise economic activities and therefore if they attain monetary equilibrium between expenditure and income they will maintain the level of production, employment and income and take off the economy into sustained growth.

The most horrible of all the economic defects of our present economic system is the interdependency of the Producers’ and Consumers’ Monetary Equilibriums. Primarily the Producers’ Monetary Equilibrium is depending on the ‘Consumers’ Monetary Equilibrium’. Because, if the consumers fail to spend their money income at the rate at which they receive it from the producers by purchasing the goods produced for them, the producers could not get their ‘expected income’ to meet their expenditure and thereby fail to attain their monetary equilibrium. In consequence of that they could not sustain the level of employment and production. Therefore, what we now need is an economic technique that would liberate the interdependency of the two monetary equilibriums. In other words producers would get their monetary equilibrium even if the consumers do not spend their income to buy the goods produced for them. To put in other terms the producers would get their ‘expected income’ to sustain the level of employment and production even though a certain volume of goods are stagnating in the market. It is a must because maintaining of employment is vital to ensure one’s ‘right to live’ than material goods that are stagnating in the market for time being or going waste. Man is gift of the God and his life is more valuable than goods.

On account of this fact if we discover an ‘economic mechanism’ that would liberate ‘Producers’ Monetary Equilibrium’ from the dependency of ‘Consumers’ Monetary equilibrium’ that mechanism would be the turning point of the history that would solve all socio-economic problems of mankind.

What is the ‘economic technique? How to execute it by renovating the present economic systems? The economic technique is a mechanism to control all economic activities like volume of production, volume of employment, volume of income, establishing price level, creation of adequate investment, establishing economic equality and economic security, preventing circulation of black money, eliminating corruption and solving other economic problems to order to lead the economy towards its perfection. It consists of two economic techniques. One is **'Mono-Economic Technique'** and the other is **'Multi-Economic Technique'.**

The Mono-Economic Technique refers to the application of only one economic technique to solve all socio-economic problems of mankind at a single stroke and the Multi-Economic Technique refers to the application of multitude of economic techniques even to solve a single economic problem in the name of various fiscal and monetary policies which we are now practicing. For example, even to control the price level of a commodity the government uses various fiscal policies like taxation and correspondingly the central bank uses various monetary policies like credit control. In consequence the combination of both the policies go futile in controlling the price level of a commodity and the economic problems are becoming too complicated for the people to understand what is happening in the economic sphere.

Mono-Economic Technique and Investment Money: By the term Mono-Economic Technique I mean an economic-mechanism that will solve all the socio-economic problems by executing only one economic technique. This economic technique stresses the necessity for putting into circulation a new money known as 'Investment money' in association with the present 'Consumption money'. To maintain a perfect economic operation the 'role-play' to be undertaken by Investment money seems essentially strategic. Because for nearly two hundred years we have over-burdened the Consumption money to execute various functions primarily 'medium of exchange' and 'store of value' which are self-contradictory with each other by which we are still suffering for not solving our problems.

Producers' consistent economic responsibility: The producers are the initiators who are venturing in the production of goods and services and creation of employment, of course, for profit motive. In order to the accomplish their venture they are always in profound thought of equilibrating their productive expenditure and income to sustain the level of production in the next round. It is the producers alone who will have ardent impulse that the money should function only as 'medium of exchange' because money will flow with full steam from consumers to equilibrate their expenditure. The profit motive of the producers prompt them to behave with a sense of economic responsibility and induce them to keep abreast a perfect circular flow of money between producers and consumers.

Consumers' erratic psychological behaviour: On the other hand the consumers are always guided by their erratic psychological behaviour to act in the market to spend their money income. They are many and not coordinated. No one can guide them or control them how to spend their money income in the manner in which the economy requires. They have absolute economic liberty in spending their income despite economic consequences. It is not their economic responsibility to watch over whether they maintain a circular flow of money between their income and expenditure to navigate the economy sail smoothly and steadily. Since a consumer is one among million buyers and he is in the midst of numerous surging commodities he is always economically inconsistent to spend his income in the way in which various producers expect for.

The consumers behave erratically in the market as the money has 'store of value'. It prompts the consumers not to spend their money income at the rate at which they receive from the producers because they are aware of the fact that their money income will not diminish in value if they store it or hoard it or save it. So when millions of consumers make delay or create 'time lag' in spending their income it directly affects the producers by not selling their goods at the rate at which they produce and prevent them to receive their 'expected income' to continue the next round of production and to sustain the same level of employment.

Economic Strategy of Investment Money: The economic strategy that I want to maneuver for the stable and smooth operation of economy at all levels of production is to rescue the monetary equilibrium of producers (i.e. equilibrium between income and expenditure of producers) from the dependency on the monetary equilibrium of consumers (i.e. equilibrium between income and expenditure of consumers). In other words producers' monetary equilibrium and consumers' monetary equilibrium will operate independently. In the money flow independency the producers will get their expected income even if the consumers fail to spend money for purchasing the goods produced. (in the words of Keynes, even if there is a deficiency in effective demand the producers would get their 'expected income'). Since the producers get their 'expected income' as if they have sold the goods at the rate at which they have produced the economy will operate smoothly with accelerated momentum towards full employment. One's employment is infinitely superior than waste of goods. Man is God's creation but goods are man's creation. Which do 'You, the people' want? Man or goods? Which do you want to sacrifice a man's life or goods' life?

Both in Capitalism and Socialism 'the right to live and the right to work' of man has been directed to sacrifice for the sake of the produced goods that are not sold. Our present economic systems are such that if the goods are not consumed at the rate at which they are produced the workers are ordered to go out of employment for the blunder committed by the consumers and producers. Millions of workers are unemployed, living in poverty and their children are dying in hunger and malnutrition because of the fact that producers don't want to produce goods more than the demand of the consumers who fail to equilibrate their income and expenditure to satisfy their money illusion.

For the sake of maximisation of profit the producers throw out the workers out of employment in order to save the goods from stagnation and decay. For producers goods are more important than the life of workers. Is it not shameful when we are mutely watching our neighbours dying in poverty for someone's profit motive? Is it not offensive as our society is loosely textured where the people have no right to live? Is it not against the will of God when His children's 'the right to live' is forfeited as the goods are not sold at the rate at which they are produced? Can we punish those people who deprive 'the right to live' of God's children for the sake of greedy consumers who have money illusion to store the money? Yes we can punish the greedy people not the poor workers. But in our present economic systems we are punishing the honest workers whom the God loves them very much. The workers only duty is to produce the socially needed goods but not selling the goods in the market. As soon as the workers have accomplished their 'production-duty', they should not be overthrown out of employment as waste paper if their 'sister and brother consumers' do not buy the goods produced for them? So we have to reorganise the economic system in which everyone will cooperate with each other to uphold everyone's 'the right to live'- the God's supreme commandment of all Ten Commandments? How is it possible?

It is possible if and only if the economy uses the Investment money as Rescuer or Pilot money. As Rescuer the Investment money will absorb the Consumption money that is saved by the consumers. In other words if the consumers wants to save money they can do so by exchanging their Consumption money for Investment money when they buying goods and services in the market. The producers will get their required Consumption money to proceed with perpetual succession of production at all levels of employment. And the consumers will deposit their Investment money in the banks which will offer them dividend to increase their purchasing power.

As Pilot money the Investment money will lead the Consumption money protectively into the 'income stream' of producers by blocking any leakage in the form of savings usually made by consumers in their 'expenditure stream'. Since the 'income stream of producers and expenditure stream of consumers' are free from any obstruction there will be perfect circular flow of money between consumers and producers at all levels of production.

The genesis of consumption and investment moneys

The Consumption money originates from the producers through central bank first and foremost and flow in the form of wages and profit towards consumers (household sector) when they sell their services, labour and capital, for the production of goods and services. In response the consumers (household sector) set in motion the same volume of consumption money to flow towards the producers (producer sector) by buying the goods and services they have produced in a static economy. Over again the producers on receiving their 'expected' volume of consumption money they will spend it to the consumers to buy their services to continue the second round of production and so on. In general perception it is expected that a particular volume of consumption money will flow from producers to consumers and from the consumers to producers to sustain a particular level of production and employment.

On the other hand the Investment banks will set to flow 'Investment Money' towards the commodity-markets where the consumers will buy consumption goods in exchange of consumption money and receive a certain quota of investment money to stake a claim that they have bought investment goods. The consumers will deposit their investment money in the banks. Once again the investment money flow towards the markets and from markets to consumers and to banks. Briefly speaking whenever consumers execute purchases they have to purchase not only consumption goods for their immediate consumption but also investment goods for the future capital accumulation for the marginal increment of level of production, employment and income.

3. MARKET STRUCTURE

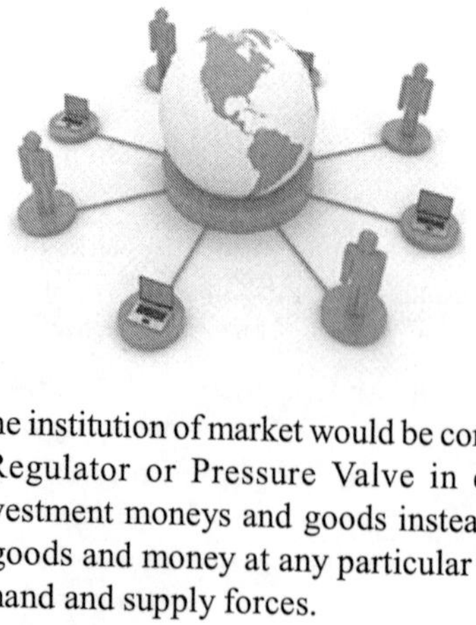

In Democrism, the institution of market would be completely restructured to play a role of Regulator or Pressure Valve in controlling flow of Consumption and Investment moneys and goods instead of a merchandiser for the exchange of goods and money at any particular price determined by the interaction of demand and supply forces.

(a) Ownership of Market Centres: The market i.e. market centres would be exclusively owned by the people, neither by the State nor by a few individuals. The market centres would function as 'Distribution Industries' and they are owned by all the consumers. Hence every consumer will own a share in all the Distribution industries and each such industry will be owned by all the consumers.

(b) Market Centres: The market centres would be classified into three categories – namely, 1. Super Market Centre, 2.Discount Market Centre and 3. Low Price Market Centre. These three centres may operate under one roof or under separate roofs.

(c) Just price and Market democracy: In the market the price of commodities will not be determined by demand and supply forces. Since the consumers are the producers the consumers themselves will determine the price of commodities and distribute them among themselves and so that the price would be the Just price. It would be the just price because no consumer can accuse that a particular price is higher than their expectation in view of the fact that the price has been determined by the consumers.

The just price will naturally uphold Distributive Justice. For fixation of just price the consumers will execute an 'Economic Contract' to adjust themselves and not to allow their erratic psychological behaviour to perturb the smooth operation of market activities and to harass production forecasting. For the execution of 'Economic Contract' the consumers will establish an 'Economic Commission' consisting of market experts.

The Economic Commission will deeply watch the economic activities and fix the price of commodities periodically or whenever necessity demands to maintain monetary equilibrium between producers and consumers and basically the monetary equilibrium of income and expenditure of producers to sustain the level of production and employment. Now let me explain how the Economic Commission will utilise the Investment money in the market for smooth operation of the economy.

(d) Establishment of Market Centres: For effective and free flow of distribution of goods adequate market centres would be established according to number of families in line with cooperative stores or super markets or ration shops. These market centres would be called as "Consumers' markets" after the name of the area.

(e) Item of goods for sale: In the market centres one can buy from safety pin to automobiles. In special cases a separate market centre will operate for sale of specific goods like timbers, jewels, garments, construction materials, petroleum products etc. No market center will be allowed to sell any explosive materials like dynamite, TNT, nitrate compound, Trinitrotoluene, gun and nitrate cotton, explosive powders and the other explosive materials needed for terrorists and suicide bombers. These explosive materials are not consumption goods and the production and distribution of these goods would be strictly controlled by the 'Consumer-vigilance Centres' and the 'Economic Commission'.

(f) Dual Prices: Moreover in all packed and non-perishable goods two prices would be printed- one is the price of consumption good and the other is the price of Investment good. For example, if a consumer buys a fan he will notice the consumption price of the fan to be ₹ 750 and the common investment price ₹ 250 and the total maximum price ₹ 1,000. When the consumer pays ₹ 1,000 in the form of consumption money he will get the fan for his consumption and for the remainder of consumption money ₹ 250 he will get Investment money to assure him that he has purchased investment goods in the common pool of national capital. Both the prices includes a certain ratio of profit determined by the **'Economic Commission'**. Usually the shopkeeper would give the investment money in the form of or check and in special cases in liquid cash. The consumer will deposit the investment money given in his Investment bank.

The shopkeepers can use Electronic Money in the place of investment money. Electronic Money is the money used by electronic media through internet for exchange of investment goods. Electronic money will operate as a medium of exchange for investment goods but it will not be in form of liquid cash or check. For Example, when the shopkeeper is bound to pay the investment money to the consumer he will not pay it in the form of liquid cash but will send a message to the consumer's investment bank with the help of internet all the transaction particulars regarding 1. the date and time of purchasing, the code number and amount of consumption goods purchased and the value investment price ₹ 250 that the shopkeeper has to pay to the consumer and the bank will automatically credit ₹ 250 in the customer's investment account. The customer will get a receipt for the transaction and he can verify it with the help of his own computer and even in the bank. Every month the bank will send a detailed report to the customer as it has been sent my Telephone Department to the customers. The electronic-investment money will simplify the transaction of investment goods.

(g) Computerisation: Both the Investment Banks and Consumers' Markets nationally and internationally should be computerised. There would be foolproof and indestructible internet link between all Consumers' Markets and Investment banks. A consumer can buy any commodity (those are covered under internet web) anywhere in his country or anywhere in the world using his Credit/Debit Card and pin code or secret password exclusively allotted for him but each consumer would be allotted only one bank for all his transactions to keep his account properly and to avoid double-accounting. If a consumer wants a carbon copy for all his transactions the shopkeeper would send it simultaneously with the bank as we are now sending E Mail messages.

Furthermore the consumers need not feel any agony or desperation if he happens to lose or misplace his Credit Card.

The consumer can demand as many proxy 'Investment credit cards' as the number of his family members in order to use them by other family members for smooth operation of family transactions but all the family credit cards will have the same pin number and secret password to keep a single investment account. No family member can use the investment credit card unless he pays consumption money to buy consumption goods. In other wards no one can buy any consumption goods which are indexed under internet web. In addition the head of the family can change his secret password once in three months, for example, to avoid misappropriation.

In line with Investment Credit Cards the consumers can demand as many Family Cards in par with the number of adult members of his family. The family code number of the Family Card and of the Investment Credit Card will be identical. When a consumer wants to buy a particular consumption commodity he can buy it on presenting his Family Card along with the Investment goods on displaying his Investment Credit Card to get his investment money. Both the code numbers should be identical whenever transactions made. Otherwise he cannot buy neither the consumption goods nor the investment goods. So the no consumer can misuse the Investment Credit of others. In order to facilitate the consumers a ' folder type money card' may be used. On the top half of money card the 'family card code number' may be printed and on the bottom half of money card the 'Investment Credit Card Code Number' may printed. So a consumer need not bring two cards to buy a specific commodity.

Since the Investment Credit Card is functioning as money we may use only one Money Card in the form of present money. The 'Family Code number' of family card and the 'Investment Credit Code Number' are identical we can print the same number on both the faces. Since the Money Card has two faces we can use one face for the identification of consumption money to buy goods and services and the other face for the identification Investment money to buy investment goods. The Money Card will function only as an 'identity card' of a consumer and therefore no face value would be printed on both sides.

So we can leave to the judgment of the 'Economic Commission' whether they want to use 1. Two distinct Money Cards or 2. Folder Money Cards or 3. Only one Money Card for the identification of Consumption Money and Investment Money.

One point is crystal clear that whenever a consumer wants to buy a specific commodity he has to pay the price in the form of Consumption Money (or a check) and also register the code number of 'Money Card' to buy 'investment goods'. The Money Card would be used only to buy Investment goods in a particular ratio with the consumption goods prescribed by 'Economic Commission'.

(h) Specific item of commodities: It would be intolerable and outrageous to carry with the Money Card to buy all kinds of commodities. To buy petty goods like a note book, a pencil, a candle, an electric bulb and such commodities which are selling in loose with insignificant price one need not to carry Money

Card. We cannot force the petty shopkeepers and street vendors to computerize their shops. Some categories of goods and services must be exempted from the coverage of Internet web.

The Economic Commission or the 'Consumer Committees' would decide which commodities should be brought under Internet Web. For example, the commodities being sold in super markets and those commodities whose price is higher than a certain value and the commodities which are harmful for one's health and all explosive commodities may be brought under Internet Web. So if a consumer wants to buy packed materials, or a Television set, or Intoxicants like alcoholic drinks he has to present Money Card to buy simultaneously investment goods. The economic authorities should strive to computerize more or less all the market centres and endeavour to bring maximum items of commodities under internet web so that all consumers will become investors by having credited their Investment accounts. For establishing an healthy economy the economic authorities may fix higher investment ratio on buying luxurious and intoxicant goods. It will force the high income groups to pay more investment money for economic development.

(I) Protecting village and cottage industries: Virtually around 70 per cent of population of less developed and developing countries live in villages. Their survival solely depends on agriculture and village and cottage industries. For example, what volume of agricultural goods that 70 per cent of farmers can produce that the same volume of goods can be produced just by 20 per cent of farmers alone. The agriculture is over burdened by 50 per cent of farmers and they are unemployed or under employed. They are in utter worst destitution, malnutrition and illness. Most of the African Countries, South East Asian Countries and India are shining and scintillating examples. It is profoundly pathetic to note that even in India more than 230 million villagers live in destitution and die in poverty though India is considered to be highly powerful and technologically competitive with western countries.

Nearly 70 to 90 per cent of villagers are almost solely depending on village and cottage industries apart from agriculture for their employment and sustainable surveillance. Since they are illiterate and technologically raw hands they could not compete with modern and large scale industries. Just acquiring a loan from a bank to start village and cottage industries cannot solve their unemployment. As soon as the villagers get a bank loan they can start a cottage industry but their sustainability of employment depends on the demand for their goods produced. They have to market their goods mostly in towns and cities where they have to face stiff competition from highly sophisticated large scale and medium scale industries. Moreover these village and cottage industries are lacking guidance from well trained managers. The sustainability of village employment depends on the real equilibrium between the rate of goods produced and the rate of goods sold or on the monetary equilibrium between the 'expected income and expenditure' at all levels of production. In the absence of managerial skill, adoption of ever changing technologies, marketing facilities, extensive advertisement and substantial prospective consumers it would be Herculean task to rope the village job-seekers within the circle of 'permanent employment' and 'stable income'.

It is not socio-economic justice; it is not efficient and morally justifiable government and it is not renowned economic system that permits a few city-workers to lead a comfortable life abandoning a vast majority of village people in destitution. It is undisputed truth that no one is in favour of such drastic economic disparity to prevail within a country (and between the countries). If so then what is the remedy? Where the solution lies? Then I have to turn towards 'Democrism' and 'Dual Monetary System'.

(1) In Democrism or in 'democratic mode of production' the people will contribute a share of capital from their 'Investment Account' to venture as many village and cottage industries as possible every year. All these industries will be owned by everyone and every industry will be owned by all. Since every cottage industry is owned by all it can be taken for granted (assumed) that the people as whole will authorise economic authorities to take suitable steps to sell the goods at the rate at which they are produced to sustain employment.

(2) The village industries will be organised into 'village communes' which will be under the management of well-trained industrial managers. These managers take responsibility of marketing the goods in super market-centres, discounted price market-centres and low priced market-centres in the towns and cities and wherever than can sell them on behalf of the people as a whole because these socially needed goods are owned by the people.

(3) For the sake of argument if the goods are not sold at a reasonable price an 'industrial subsidy 'would be given to the village industries to sustain the level of wage- income of workers and to maintain the level of production.

(4) **Investment money and industrial subsidy:** The industrial subsidy would be created from the flow of investment money specially generated by the society (consumers) as a whole for the purpose of upholding the 'right to live' of fellow citizens living in the villages. It is the society that has established the village industries and it is the same society that has ordered the village workers to produce the socially needed goods and hence it is same society that is morally bound to absorb the goods at the rate at which they are produced. On the other hand if the individual village worker himself ventures an industry with his own capital then it will be his individual responsibility to decide what to produce and where to market and how to stabilise his employment and income. The economic responsibility will be individualised and the worker has to bear all risk factors. He is therefore separated from the society and cannot expect any economic support from the other members of society.

Such an '**Economic Isolation**' threatens the village workers not to venture into 'self-employment' and coerces them as unemployed or bonded labourers. This 'economic isolation' of workers is a common factor in all the countries which follow 'Capitalistic mode of production'. This Economic Isolation develops an attitude of non-cooperation among the workers and 'don't care' attitude on the suffering of other workers. The Economic Isolation is horribly threatening the village workers to venture in self-employment. Unless and until 'Social Involvement' is injected in the establishment of village industries, the villages cannot develop economically and socially. The Social Involvement among the workers can be cultivated if and only if the people (worker-investors) as a whole contribute a share of investment in the creation of village industries. This is what Democrism advocates.

We can presume that if a village industry is owned by all the workers of a nation there will emerge a social involvement or social interest among the workers in all the activities of the industry. And it may also be presumed that the whole nation (all workers) will show utmost interest on the sale of village industrial goods at a reasonable price. Perhaps if the goods are not sold at the expected price the 'Economic authorities' will give money subsidy to the village industries and sell the goods at discounted price. The money subsidy will function as **'income stabilizer'.**

For example, if the 'monetary subsidy' requires ₹ 10,000 million in a particular year to stabilize the wage- income of village workers, the economic authorities will increase the price of luxurious and inelastic goods and services that would fetch ₹ 10,000 million. The buyers of these goods would pay ₹ 10,000 million in the form of 'Consumption Money'. In order to compensate their increased monetary (consumption) expenditure they would be paid 'Investment Money' to the same value. The 'Economic Justice' pervading in this operation is that it is same consumers who have invested capital in their own village industries and their prime motive will be stabilisation of such industries. By exchanging the consumption money into investment money no one will be exploited. This money conversion technique underlies as one of the rules of Economic Contract conceived implicitly among the consumers.

Patron Industry: It means a strong and powerful large scale industry that can protect a weak or infant industry without trouble by providing monetary help. For example, Electricity, Railway and Airway are strong and powerful service industries and they can perform as Patron Industries. In order to save village industries from want of 'expected' income, instead of increasing the price of so many goods we can, for example, increase the electricity charge per unit of power consumption. For the increased charge the consumers will get investment money in par. The income derived by the marginal increase of electrical charge will be utilised as subsidy to fill the deficiency of 'expected income'. Since electricity is widely used by all the consumers a meager increase in the electrical charges per unit will save millions of villagers from poverty. Hence this Electricity industry will be hailed as Patron Industry of Village industries and the industry which receives financial support will be called as Beneficiary Industry. Since both the Patron and Beneficiary industries are owned by the one and same identical person no one will be oppressed or exploited. It is necessary that the patron industry should be a single powerful industry but it may consist of some industries like Electricity, Railway and Airway industries to share burden of financial support for beneficiary industry.

According to the census of 2003 nearly 585 million people in India i.e. 86.2 per cent of Indian population live in penury and destitution whose daily income is less than $2 a day. Sixty per cent of these people live in villages and 80 per cent of them are artisans or underemployed or unemployed.

Indian poverty is primarily attributed to village poverty. A country is poor mainly because its villages are poor. A vast majority of Indian villagers are artisans and hence they can be employed in village industries. Their stability of employment and income depends on the monetary equilibrium between their production expenditure and 'expected' income. Since the worker-investors as a whole in general or the worker-investors of Patron industries in particular are the same investors of village industries. These worker-investors of patron industries should assume the economic responsibility of procuring the goods for marketing at the rate at which they are produced. In other words there should be 'required' or "equilibrating' producers'- money-flow" between the Patron industries and the village industries, whether it is in the form of subsidy or financial support, to sustain the level of income of villagers.

On procuring necessary village- industry- products the Patron industries will market them in the Supermarkets or Discounted price-markets or low price-markets to sell them at justifiable or agreeable price. Due to erratic psychological behaviour, if the consumers show disregard in buying the goods these goods may be offered as free goods to low-income consumers at low price-market centres or other market centres by increasing the price of other fast moving goods. For the payment of the 'increased price' these consumers could be compensated by offering investment money. The consumers i.e. the worker-investors must purchase the village-industry-goods because it is they who have not only invested their money in the village industries but also ordered them to produce such socially needed goods for them. Therefore, it is their implied economic obligation to buy them through any market manipulation recommended by economic authorities.

This justifiable economic operation cannot be executed neither by the Capitalistic nor by the Socialistic Mode of Production but only by Democratic Mode of Production in which all the people of the nation as a whole take direct initiation and responsibility in all economic activities.

Volume: IX

Formation of Economic Constitution

Chapter – 34

Constitution of National Economic Government

"Constitution is not an instrument for government to restrain the people, it is an instrument for the people to restrain the government"

— **Patrick Henry**

Preamble

We, the people, declare under the economic system of Democrism "all the industries are owned by each worker, and each worker will own all the industries". To administer the principle of the economic system the power of the economic government is divided into three separate powers such as Legislative, Executive and Judiciary. The Judiciary is the highest and its Supreme Court has the power to pass ultimate order to rectify the mistakes committed by legislative and executives and interpret the meaning of the laws framed by "Economic Constitution". Though the government is created by the workers under presidential form of government or parliamentary form of government, the people should not misconstrued that will lead them ultimately to "proletariat dictatorship". The tyrannical form of government emerges only and if only if the three powers of government are encroached by a single person or single group or single party. To illustrate comprehensively it is necessary for us to quote the words of James Madison, the American Fourth US President (1809-17) here under:

"The accumulation of all powers, legislative, executive, and Judiciary, in the same hands, whether of one, a few, or many, and whether hereditary, or elective, may justly be pronounced the very definition of tyranny". On account of preserving the sanctity of democracy, we, therefore, proclaim the separation of powers of democratic government.

The capital has massive economic power that can effortlessly control the three powers of government. Since more or less the whole national capital is directly owned by a few in capitalism and by a single party or a group in Socialism, the global economy is crushed under tyranny and the people have been squeezed by appalling poverty for nearly two hundred years when two economic systems emerged in the world. Considering the historical facts in whom the capital should be entrusted?

The 'natural law and natural justice say that every creation is owned by the creator and therefor the global capital should be owned by the people who are the creators. Therefore, we uphold the direct ownership of capital by the people.

"Because it is man who is perfect and eternal by evolution of mankind; because it is man who forms the societies to secure his 'right to live'; because it is man who transforms the societies on denial of his 'right to live'; because it is man who creates all the things, philosophies, and executions; because it is man who constitutes the laws of society; because it is man who transforms the laws of society; because it is who elects the governments; because it is man who rejects the governments. Man is supreme ; man is omnipotent; man is the greatest.

Man is 'social justice'; man is economic justice; man is political justice; man is natural justice; man is above all controversies and man is peace loving creature. Man is superior to Capitalism; man is superior to socialism; and man is embodiment of Democrism. The capital, therefore, should be entrusted to him. He knows how to create an ideal society. Capitalism knows only how to create profit; Socialism knows only how to impose dictatorship; but Democrism alone knows how to create 'just society'. All the philosophies lead to Democrism. It is the only just alternative for mankind to live in the world peacefully.

Introduction

1. At the advent of the **French Revolution** 'Democracy' spread all over the world with accelerated tempo toppling all the monarchical and dictatorial governments in Europe. The principle of 'Democracy' proclaimed by Abraham Lincoln at his Guttenberg address was considered to be the most energetic, virtual, universally acceptable and most quoted dictum by the people.

The principle was highly esteemed by the vested interests in political arena who wanted to demonstrate **'Capitalistic Mode of Production'** because it paved the way for upholding 'Property Right' to the rich capitalists. And the principle was deceitfully used, against the honest expectations of Lincoln, as a powerful weapon to protect 'capitalism' and its aim of 'maximisation of profit'. These rich capitalists exploited the poor people by influencing the 'democratic governments' with their money power by corrupting the politicians, bureaucrats and common people. Since the very aim of **'French Revolution'** for upholding the three fundamental rights of Equality, Liberty and Fraternity, it was the Karl Marx, who strived to save the people from exploitation, advocated 'proletariat Dictatorship' on the basis of 'Socialistic Mode of Production'. Instead of creating an Ideal society the 'government of proletariat dictatorship' led by the 'politbureau' of communist party for the imposition of a 'Society of Slaves' in their countries which was more horrible and ruthless than the previous monarchical governments. So Harold J. Laski in his book 'Liberty in the Modern State' rightly said as follows:

"Russian working-men have probably often tempted to the view that their Bolshevik masters mistakes communist dogma for the social truth".

2. The World governments shuttled between 'non-equality democratic governments' and 'non-liberty proletariat governments'. Between the tussle of these governments 'Fraternity', the third principle of Democracy was squashed and terminated in the world and 'terrorism' occupied its place to command the world governments to reign the people by dreadful of frightens. A cold war emerged between these governments and the mankind has been now threatened to live under the shadow of third world war which may annihilate the whole humanity within seconds by bombarding nuclear weapons like 'Tzar Bomba' and 'Castle Bravo', on waging nuclear war intentionally or by triggering accidently or by waving wrong combating signals from any one side.

3. **Third World War:** In 1992, on the collapse of Soviet Union, the cold war vanished from the views and visions of global politics.

On the contrary some Muslim scholars and elites have developed with utmost sincerity a political concept on the platform of religion, a 'Union of Islamic Countries' comprising Iran, Iraq, Egypt, Turkey, Saudi Arabia, Pakistan, Bangladesh, Indonesia, Libya, Malaysia, Afghanistan, Kuwait, Qatar, Oman, Yemen, Sudan, Algeria, Morocco, Tunisia, Nigeria, Uzbekistan and other Muslim nations in Asia to fight against US and Western Christian countries for the cause of spreading religious dogma, protecting Islamic customs and conventions and preserving Islamic civilisation. Some Muslim elites say that they first muster military personnel for training their fundamentalists to spread terrorism for uprooting the basic economic structure of their enemy countries and then to occupy nuclear weapons to wage full-pledged war on non-believers of Islam. Perhaps it may result in the burst out of 'Third World War'.

4. All the politicians use the word 'Democracy' mainly it appears as a convenient resort to intoxicate the minds of people to exploit the poor and innocent people through their own political parties, various forms of Medias and the government agencies. So a maxim was brought into existence that 'power tends to corrupt and absolute power corrupts absolutely' (**Lord Acton**).

5. On the backdrop of these detrimental scenarios what form of government we, the people, at present want immediately for the establishment of an ideal society.

6. **The form of governments:** Both Democratic theory and democratic governments are the general terms in the pages of political dictionary. More or less all the countries claim that they have democratic governments because they are most fascinating doctrine to divert the rational thought of common people to escape from tight corners. We, the people, want an effective and energetic government which has full potential power to establish an ideal society. The governments existing at present on the basis of Capitalistic Mode of Production or Socialistic Mode of Production have failed to satisfy the long pending aspirations of people. So we are ardently strive for establishment of a government that is based on Democratic Mode of Production, the only alternative to lead the mankind towards an ideal society.

7. **Economic Government:** For establishment of an 'economic government' we have to ensure the following inalienable legislative rights and powerful directions with strong approval of 'General Will' of the people for:

(a) Identification of 'Fundamental Rights'
(b) Identification of 'Economic Constituencies'
(c) Identification of 'electorates',
(d) Identification of 'legislators',
(e) Identification of 'head of the government',
(f) Identification of 'Council of ministers, and
(g) Identification of the powers of Judiciary and Executive systems.

8. **Definition of Fundaments Rights:** Fundamental rights mean those legal entitlements without which man cannot live (right to live) with Liberty, equality, fraternity, justice, economic security, economic power by which one can able to expose one's originality, creativeness and individuality for the benefit of his own and his fellow members of society, and last but not least, free from fear of future

9. **Virtue of Fundamental Rights:** The fundamental rights have legal enforcements enacted by the legislature. The fundamental rights are common to all citizens irrespective of any social, political and economic status. It is, therefore, proclaimed that all are equal before law. On analysing fundamental rights deeply we can classify them into (a) active or economic fundamental rights and (b) passive or political and social fundamental rights. Between the active and passive fundamental rights it is the passive fundamental rights that have been effectuated by all constitutions as the only source for the creation of just society. This is because any fragile economic system can reign the country without assuming any economic burden and any illiterate can become head of the State.

10. **Active or Economic Fundamental rights**

(a) From very birth of a child these rights are universally prevalent and inalienable and no one can forfeit these rights from the people as these rights are endowed by the law of nature.

(b) These rights are 'active or economically powerful' because the implementation of these rights costs the society monetarily forever and for implementation of these rights the countries must bear economic burden for which economic system must be basically very strong inherently.

(c) The society assures that it will endure necessary monetary cost perennially to uphold the inalienable 'right to live' of every citizen. Among these rights the first and foremost is 'right to work'.

10.1. **Right to Work:** The right to work means that a worker first seeks an opportunity, according to his education and experience, to produce goods or services which are socially needed and then he demands equivalent wage to consume the goods or services to establish his 'right to live' because of the fact the society in which he lives has assured him 'right to work' according to 'social contract' created by the 'general will' of the people.

On the other hand if the society fails to provide him his 'due work' or employment it should assume 'constitutional responsibility' to pay him adequate monetary compensation to lead him a decent and economically secured life without fear of future.

Technical definition of 'right to work': It is technical because it introduces some rules and regulations in the definition of 'right to work'. These rules and regulations may change from society to society due to power of economic scenario of a country. For example, some countries may enact a law that if a worker has registered his name in 'employment exchange', the government is obliged to offer him a job within six months in satisfaction of his education and experience and moreover according to the need of 'production necessities' of a country. On the other hand if the government is inefficient to fulfill his legal obligation, the affected worker may file a suit in the court of law against the government as it fails to honour his 'fundamental right to work'. Under these circumstances the court may direct the government to pay the 'affected worker' a reasonable compensation that will secure him to lead him a life of decency still he get his due or justifiable job for the satisfaction of the judiciary. Among all fundamental rights the 'right to work' is indispensable because it only ensures person to exercise his 'right to live' which is endowed by 'Law of Nature'. Otherwise the very basic purpose of creating a civilised structure of human society as well as human morality will also collapse together.

In conclusion, I wish to say that the right to work is the concept that people have a human right to work, or engage in productive employment, and may not be prevented from doing so. The right to work is enshrined in the Universal Declaration of Human Rights and recognised in international human rights law through its inclusion in the International Covenant on Economic, Social and Cultural Rights, where the right to work emphasises economic, social and cultural development

10.2. **Right to Wage:** Every citizen has right to wage for his production of socially needed goods and services. Every worker should be paid equal wage for equal work without any discrimination on the basis of gender, race, religion, migration, physically handicapped and so on. Child and bonded labour should be abolished by exploiting their poverty and by inducing for payment of wages.

No Work, No Wage: Those who are physically and mentally fit to produce socially needed goods and services and those who want to be voluntarily unemployed for upholding for their family and social prestige should not allowed to receive any income from any source like rent from estate and ancestors property. They have to work or forgo the income.

10.3. **Right to Production:** Every worker has right to produce socially needed goods and services engaging his capital and his labour in the factories or cottage and village industries or agricultural farms for the socio-economic needs of society. The workers get wages according to their work to uphold their 'right to live'. The workers only duty is to produce socially needed goods for the consumers and it is the utmost responsibility of the society as a whole to distribute the goods justifiably to the consumers. In turn it is the economic duty of the consumers to buy the goods at the rate at which the goods are produced for them.

On the contrary, if the consumers due to their erratic psychological behaviour fail to create adequate demand and cause stagnation of goods in the market, it will induce the producers to reduce the volume of production and create 'unemployment'.

This kind of unemployment due to 'lack of effective demand', in terms of John Maynard Keynes, will forfeit the workers 'right to live'. For the reckless fault of consumers, the workers should not be punished as they have accomplished their 'economic duty'. Even though the 'lack of effective demand' prevails in the economy. The workers **'right to production'** should be saved as long as they wish to work. For the misconduct of consumers in the market it is the consumers should be punished if there is over savings or hoarding. This volume of over savings should be extracted in order to flow towards producers for sustaining the volume of production to save the workers' income and their right to live. Then the dictum that 'punish the consumers and save the workers' will become the principle of production.

In the Democratic Mode of Production the consumers, in the capacity of workers, punish themselves and the workers, in the capacity of consumers, save their 'right to work'. This is the entitlement of 'right to production' Consumers as workers may suffer but not the workers as consumers.

10.4. **Right to Investment:** Every worker has right to create new investment out of his known legal source of income, especially S of labour to stabilize his own employment and also to provide opportunity for creation of new employment by equilibrating his 'savings' into 'investment'.

Workers' investment is a perennial flow towards accumulated stock of national capital by increasing its marginality. When the marginal income of present workers increases it results in increasing marginal stock of capital which the workers will utilise it primarily to enhance their standard of living and to open the flood gate of employment opportunities for their future generation.

On the other hand if the private corporate sector creates 'capital wealth' by inducing the private 'Capital-providers' or 'Stock-holders' on the sale of 'equities', assuring a huge volume of profit or 'dividend'. These stock-holders 'create' wealth without lifting a finger.

We call this dividend as 'return on equity' (ROE). The ROE is deliberately devised to continue its value to infinity in the 'stock market gambling' to attract more and more people to play in the financial sector and ultimately push them to perish into the deep sea of debt.

In the capitalistic mode of production (or in the democratic capitalist countries) it has been made the law of the land as equivalent as the divine right of kings, that was once the law of land in ancient times. Indeed, "maximising returns to shareholders" is universally exalted as divine law or mandate.

10.5. **Right to justifiable dividend:** The poor and low-income workers for contributing investment by certain ratio, say 10 per cent - 20 per cent, for capital accumulation and development of economy, they have to sacrifice some volume of consumption of bare necessities. In this regard their "Investment Burden" is high.

In the case of 'middle-income workers' their contribution for 'investment', say 20 per cent - 30 per cent, for capital accumulation they need not sacrifice any necessities or comforts but certain luxurious goods. Their "Investment Burden" will be less than the investment burden of poor and low income workers even though their contribution for national welfare is higher.

Similarly in regard to 'rich and high- income workers' their contribution for 'investment', say 30 per cent - 40 per cent, for capital accumulation for their country's development they need not sacrifice any of their consumption of necessities, comforts and luxurious goods, except certain portion of their 'savings'.

Economic Patriotism means carrying on certain burden for the economic security of fellow citizen. For this noble cause in Democrism "People's National Profit" would be created in the "People's business sector" by selling goods and services at 'just price' without any taxation.

Tap the Rich, Pat the Poor: Tap the rich respectably and pat the poor acceptably to reduce the margin of income between poor and rich, step by step, is vital factor of patriotism by fraternity justice. The national dividend will be distributed according to investment burden; since low income workers investment burden is high they will be paid higher volume of dividend than other two income groups. This distribution justifiable method will be followed to all income groups. This distribution justice will narrow the ultimate income gap without interfering in the 'wage distribution' in the work place that is established by 'wage justice'.

In this strategy of income distribution every worker has the 'right to wage' justice (wage according to work) and 'right to justiciable dividend' (dividend according to investment burden).This 'dual income' – lower the wage and higher the dividend – will eliminate income gap and lead the workers to establish 'egalitarian society'.

10.6. **Right to Economic, Health and Mental Securities:** Senior citizens, widows, orphans, and mentally retarded persons should be provided with adequate economic security by money and kind and the State should offer adequate and best medical care at first priority by considering them as rare social property up to their death in full satisfaction of judiciary. These persons should not be wounded by others physically and mentally by using indecent words and deeds publically or privately in their homes. All the persons should use respectable words to call them considering their age, past social and job position, and now their physical inability.

11. Passive Fundamental Rights

List of important Passive or Political fundamental rights:

Right to equal protection under the law

Right to freedom of thought

Right to freedom of speech and press (cf. freedom of expression)

Right to freedom of association

Right to freedom of movement within the country

Right to vote in general election

Right to direct a child's upbringing

Right to privacy

Right to marry

These passive Fundamental rights are ensured to all the people in all the constitutions because by exercising these fundamental rights, people cannot control the government to uphold their 'right to live' but the governments can easily keep the people under their control.

Moreover the governments will not carry any economic burden if the people exercise these fundamental rights.

Right to vote: More or less in all the democratic countries it not the people but the some vested interests and corporate sectors by using the their money power and by buying all kinds of media and propagating impossible advertisement to elect the governments which they function for their benefits after the elections. Billions and billions of dollars are spent to brain wash the people by vested interests and the 'fans of cine heroes' who are considered to be demigods. Even an illiterate charismatic leader by using his cine field, caste, race, religion and so on are adoring the head of state by on the manipulation or big corporate sectors. The people's 'right to vote in general elections can be made a 'stock of mockery' and the people's 'ballet paper', the only democratic power to elect their leader and ruling themselves has now become 'salable commodity' in 'election super market'. It has been actualised for many decades even in USA and India, the biggest democratic countries. This is one of the reasons for emergence of 'terrorism' even in democratic countries.

Since the most of the fundamental rights are passive, fragile, and powerless the a large majority of electorates, including elected representatives in the legislature want to be bargained themselves to get small or huge monetary and other kinds of benefits according to their capacity even in the form of black money in the 'election super markets'. In the 'commodity super markets' the buyers are paying money and in 'election super markets' the sellers are paying money.

Since most of the fundamental rights are passive, inactive and having limited operational usage by the people, we have to empower them by transforming the passive fundamental rights (political) into active fundamental rights (economic). Therefore we have to establish 'Economic Government' (Industrial Democracy) in the place of 'Political Government' (Political Democracy). How to establish **'Economic Government' or 'Industrial Democracy'.**

I have already mentioned in item No.10 the 'Economic Fundamental Rights' on which the 'Economic Government' would be established. Now I have to specify the other elements of economic government.

12. Identification of 'Economic Constituencies'

We know that in politics the country is divided into various kinds of constituencies according to area-wise. For instance in India the electorates exercise their franchise into various kinds of constituencies. They are 'National Parliament Constituencies, State Legislate Constituencies, City Corporation

Constituencies, Town Municipality Constituencies, and Village Panchayat Constituencies and so on according the need of service of the people. These constituencies have a head known as prime minister for the nation, Chief Ministers for States, Mayors for Corporations, Chairmen for municipalities and Panchayats. They serve for the people to uphold their passive fundamental rights and to provide some welfare services, from village to national level within the powers offered by constitution.

13. In the formation of 'economic government' the constituencies are established by 'industry wise' and not area wise. The industries are classified by heavy industries, medium scale industries, small scale industries, village and cottage industries. In these industries the working populations may be distributed into various magnitudes and proportions.

The heavy industries constitute railways, airways, surface or road transports, IT industries – both hardware and software industries, postal departments, petroleum industries, nuclear power industries, thermo and hydraulic power industries, fertilizer industries, textile industries, food industries, agro industries, automobile industries and service industries like government workers, military and police securities, college and university education, higher and primary education, health care – hospitals, legal services, places of worship and so on. Accordingly the medium, small and cottage and village industries and self-employed industries will be classified as per the existing procedures.

14. Identification of electorates

All the working people are electorates irrespective of the size of the industries. These electorates their representatives 'national economic parliament, State economic legislature, city economic corporation, small scale and village and cottage industry councils. The number of 'worker representatives' will be elected according the worker population, to each 'economic ruling bodies' from economic parliament to village councils.

14.1. Formation of 'National Economic Parliament'

For instance let's assume a country's aggregate worker-population amounts to 200 million workers. They may be divided into 200 'national economic parliament constituencies' and each constituency contains one million workers. These workers elect 200 representatives to national economic parliament according to prorate of workers working in each industries i.e. industrial constituencies. For example, if the national railways contains five million workers, the railway workers will elect five representatives and if iron and steel industries conation three million workers, these workers will elect three representatives and this election procedure will be followed from national heavy industries to national village and cottage industries.

14.2. Election of National Economic Prime Minister

These representatives will elect their nation's Economic Prime Minister who should belong to working class. Perhaps if a nation wants a 'presidential form of government', the 'Economic President' may directly be elected by the workers of the nation as a whole.

14.3. Council of ministers: The prime minister will send a list of ministers whom he thinks efficient and cooperative with him to a specially appointed 'economic and planning commission' to get its advice for the appointment of his council of ministers. The prime minister take due consideration whether his ministers belong to their respective 'industrial constituencies' and well versed about the problems of the workers who elected them. Moreover the prime minister will have prerogative power to select or oust any minister considering their ability of function.

15. Identification of powers of Judiciary and Executive

The Judiciary body of any democratic country is an independent body and separate from the Executive and Legislative bodies of both 'economic and political governments'. The judiciary will keenly watch through the Supreme Court and all other courts up to district courts whether the 'Economic Executive and Legislative bodies' sincerely and honestly endorse the 'economic fundamental rights' of people. These courts as usual take care of maintenance of law and order in the country along with solving problems related to civil and criminal offences.

The 'executive body' is always under the direct control of 'legislative body' in the national economic government. The duty of executive body, from chief secretary to municipality chairman', is to accomplish the orders, especially economic fundamental rights, passed by the 'economic legislative body'.

16. Financial Administration by Budget

In Democrism the budget, an instrument of financial administration, will reflect the values and priorities of a nation and its people. In Economic Government the priories are framed as follows:

1. **Stability of economy:** The economic government will give first priority for stabilisation of economy by 'equilibrating the expenditure and income of producers' at all levels of money supply, or all level of employment and income. Once the stability is assured the economy will 'take off into sustained growth'.
2. **Creation of egalitarian society:** When the economy is stabilised it is easy for the government to lead the people to achieve 'egalitarian society' by distributing a considerable volume of 'national profit' according to the 'investment burden of the workers' that will reduce the income gap between rich and poor.

3. **Fulfillment of necessary basic needs of people through central and local bodies:** In the rural areas people need various basic necessities like primary schools, proper roads, street lighting, drainage, clinics, brick houses and so on.

17. Revenue and Expenditure of Economic Government

The budget primarily concentrates the acceptable sources of revenue and justifiable streams of expenditure to provide maximum welfare to the people in order of priority of income groups.

Revenue: In respect of the fact that all the industries are owned by all the people the 'People's National Profit' (PNP) will directly flow in the income stream of working people or 'People's Economic Government'. The national people's profit is dependent factor of 'cost price' (Cp) and 'Just price'(Jp) of aggregate goods and services produced in a given period of time, say one year. It can be written as:

$$PNP = f(Cp, Jp) \ldots\ldots\ldots(1)$$

We can bifurcate the above function as follows

$$PNP = \text{Ø}(Cp) \ldots\ldots\ldots\ldots(2) \text{ and}$$

$$PNP = \Omega\,(Jp) \ldots\ldots\ldots\ldots (3)$$

(a) People's National Profit and Cost of Production.

When $PNP = \text{Ø}(Cp)$

At a given volume of production people's general national profit will enhance by decreasing cost of production. The cost of production will decrease when the productivity of labour increases due to experience, education, proper training, working environment and by injecting newly discovered technologies. On the increase of productivity the volume of employment should not be reduced at any cost but volume of working hours should be reduced and the workers should be allowed to gain more leisure.

The workers will utilise the leisure hours to increase and expose their originality, creativeness and individuality which are essential for enriching civilisation. More the leisure means more the productivity, more the national profit and more the cultural activities.

(b) People's National Profit and Just Price

When $PNP = \Omega\,(Jp)$

Since all the consumers are the producers the price of the commodities will be determined by the consumers themselves. That is the 'just price'. Consumers, on the principle of transparency, will have the commanding authority to know the 'cost price' of commodities in the capacity of producers.

The consumers will provide authority to 'economic commission' to fix just price for commodities to adequate 'NATIONAL PROFIT' for redistribution of income for their own benefit. Higher the Just price, higher the national profit and higher the dividend. Higher the dividend means lower the 'Income Gap' between poor and rich and it will not only increase the 'purchasing power' of people but also lead them as quickly as possible towards an 'egalitarian society'.

(c) Gap between marginal cost price and marginal just price

When the economy develops or takes off into sustained growth the marginal cost price of a commodity will not increase in the short period because labour productivity and introduction new production technology will not take place within short period say five years. On the other hand the marginal just price can be increased by consumers/producers on the advice of their 'economic commission'. The marginal gap between the two prices will be going on increasing and thereby 'marginal profit' will also increase continuously.

The marginal increase of national profit should not be construed as exploitation of consumers or workers because within very short period say once in six months the consumers will paid as 'dividend' (higher refund) from the stock 'national profit' at a particular ratio. The marginal dividend received by the consumers will always be higher than what they paid for 'marginal just price' for any commodity.

Only at the very first instance the consumers will suffer by paying higher 'marginal just price' than 'marginal cost price'. On getting 'dividend according to their investment burden' the bubbling market condition will vanish and the economy will grow with a speed of accelerated temp.

It is known fact that the 'People's National Profit' is the dependent factor of the combined variable factors of cost price and just price. The cost price may be stable or decrease due to application of new technologies and production of goods by large scale industries and this trend continue up to certain point and it may be called it 'decreasing marginal trend' and it will not continue towards as no one can produce any goods at 'zero cost'. But in the case of 'social services' I may serve to the societies at 'zero cost' and it is known fact that all mothers serve to their families at 'zero cost'. Some times the cost price tend to increase due to scarcity natural resources. But the 'just price' will always move on the path of 'increasing marginal trend' because it is determined by the consumers according to the need of the economy. In the consequence of the decreasing/stable cost and the increasing price the national profit will increase considerably and it ultimately benefit the people.

Since PNP = f(Cp, Jp), when the factors of 'decreasing marginal cost' and 'increasing marginal just price' operate simultaneously the people's National Profit will increase significantly and considerable amount may be allocated for 'people's dividend', contribution to the government expenditure and to keep adequate reserve to stabilise the economy.

18. Expenditure

The Economic Government fixes the just price to all goods and services. The just price includes cost price and affordable 'margin of profit'. The consumers will pay only the cost price for every purchase of the goods and services and the 'margin of profit' will be returned to the consumers in the form of 'investment money' which will be deposited in their 'investment bank'. The 'consumption money' equivalent to the 'investment money' will be in the possession of economic government that will decide how to spend the money with the approval of the people's representatives in the parliament. The government expenditure will chiefly include 'contribution to new investment in goods and service sectors', contribution to the political government by abolishing all taxes, contribution to national dividend fund to distribute dividend to the workers. contribution to "people's business sectors" to stabilize their income and employment and contribution to the precautionary reserve fund to meet unforeseen endogenous and exogenous calamities. And last but not least a contribution to parliamentary fund to drive government machinery to uphold democratic system of the country.

18.1. Contribution to new investment

In its yearly budget the Economic Government will allocate a certain percentage of People's National Profit for creation of new investment. The volume of creation of new investment depends on the volume of the national profit and the structure wage between various income groups. [$I = f(w,PNP)$]. If the government strives to increase wage income of poor and middle income groups of workers who occupy major portion of buyers in the market, the national profit will boost up and it will help the government to expedite to create higher volume of new investment.

On the absence of erratic influence of 'interest and taxation techniques' the government can create yearly investment with mathematical accuracy. For example, Mrs Joan Robinson in her book 'Accumulation of Capital' illustrated that if the investment increases at the rate of 1/multiplier x acceleration i.e. (multiplier x acceleration)"[1] every year, it will lead the economy towards golden age. Since the national profit is directly owned by the people the workers will accept to create investment with mathematical accuracy.

18.2. Contribution to National Dividend

One of the vital expenditures of Economic Government is to make adequate contribution to national dividend. The government will distribute the national dividend to the workers according to their investment burden. In coordination with the wage income the dividend income strives to compress the income gap between various income groups to create an egalitarian society. It is the utmost duty of government to create an egalitarian society by using 'dividend technique' without crushing the rich people by levying high income taxes. The 'taxation technique' has failed as it creates very huge volume of black and induce the rich to run a parallel economy. Being rich is not a sin but it is the sin to humiliate other fellow citizens.

18.3. Contribution to the government

Government's Property is Nobody's Property

At the present economic scenario more or less all the political governments - capitalistic and socialistic – are depending heavily on taxation to run their economic machineries. Since the tax payers are not directly involving in the construction government properties they infer that the government's property is nobody's property. This kind of unpatriotic inference induces the vulgar sentiments of people to destroy or damage the government's properties of billions and billions of dollar whenever the people want to demonstrate their angry on the government's policies.

Even the newly installed ruling party construes that all the constructive projects, completed or in progress, of previous government are unproductive and anti-people and want to derail or destroy them, though billions of dollars are invested in them. It is because of the fact that the previous government's property is nobody's property. There is no constitutional power to prevent these political governments to waste the huge volume of tax money of the people, collected mostly from poor and middle classes. People can witness such kind of 'economic crime' in India both in Centre and State governments. What is the punishment for them or what is the remedy to stop such kind of horrifying 'national economic crimes'?

Abolition of Taxation Technique and Application of People's National Profit Technique

In the political governments taxation is the main source of income. The government invests the 'tax-income' in many profit yielding projects like railways. Though the investment is made out of people's taxation the profit earned is not distributed to the taxpayers. Therefore, the people infer that government's poverty is nobody's property.

In the Economic Government it's required income is directly contributed from the 'people's national profit fund'. When the economic government invests this people's income in various 'profit yielding projects' the taxpayers will be entitled to receive 'dividend' from the aggregate profit of these projects. Since some of the government undertakings are 'dividend yielding projects' the people will certainly believe that the government's property is their own property. So that they will not damage government's properties when they are compelled to demonstrate agitations against their government. Moreover, the- law of Democrism insists not only the -industries but also the governments should maintain accountability and transparency to the people to all the industrial activities. Considering all the facts of economic activities the 'People's Profit Technique' is occupying supreme position.

Chapter – 35

Operation of Global Economy in Democrism World Economic Government and One World

Introduction

Towards One World

Preamble

We, the people of all the sovereign States refer to the noble belief of all humankind united primarily under one common economic authority. Debatably, it has not materialised so far in the human history, yet proposals for a unified global economic authority have existed prominently since the period of Karl Marx, by his passionate call for "workers of all the countries unite" for the establishment of 'One Economy' and 'One World'.

Since Socialism, the theory of Karl Marx, -though a fascinated term of working class, was operationally incompetent under 'proletariat dictatorship'. It, therefore, steered the Russian people toward 'Prison economy' instead of 'One Economy' and 'One World'. For inherent fallacies of operational techniques of socialism the Russians had to sacrifice their liberty, equality, fraternity and above all their right to live in the 'prison economy' constructed by the Dictator Stalin behind the 'iron curtain'.

The Russian working class was gripped by terror and awesome through out their lifetime. When 'Perestroika' (Reconstruction) and 'Glasnost' (Openness) were introduced by Premier Gorbachev the myth of the socialistic pattern of 'One Economy' and 'One World' concepts were shattered not only in Russia but also throughout the Western Europe.

The establishment of 'One World' concept was first attempted in politics to prevent war between the countries. Since various attempts in politics failed now we attempt in economic sphere mainly to enrich the globalisation of economy, to eradicate poverty and to prevent war between countries and to eliminate differentiation in economic systems.

One World concept before two world wars: Various proposals for the establishment of a unified global political authority to create 'One world' existed since ancient times—in the ambition of kings, popes and emperors, and the dreams of poets and philosophers.

World government – retrospection

1. World government is the notion of a single common **political authority** for all of humanity. But it emerged due to subsequent struggle between secular authority, represented by the Holy Roman Emperor, and ecclesiastical authority, represented by the Pope.

2. **Hugo Grotius** in his book **'On the Law of War and Peace' (1625)** presented an idea of having an 'international law' to establish a world government. For his ideas he was from many countries from Paris.

3. **Joseph Smith and Theo democracy: Joseph Smith**, in early 19th century, taught that a Theo democracy would guide and direct the **Kingdom of God (Zion)** on the earth during the end times. On March 11th, 1844, Smith organised a **Council of Fifty,** who was to work under the direction of the Priesthood authorities of his church, along with a **Council of Friends.** This group of three organisations was expected to rule as a world government just prior to the Millennium.[1, 2, 3]

4. Karl Krause

In 1811, German philosopher Karl Krause, suggested, in an essay titled **"The Archetype of Humanity",** the formation of five regional federations: Europe, Asia, Africa, America and Australia, aggregated under a **world republic.**

5. Ulysses S. Grant on the necessity of world government

Ulysses S. Grant commented, "I believe at some future day, the nations of the earth will agree on some sort of congress which will take cognizance of international questions of difficulty and whose decisions will be as binding as the decisions of the Supreme Court are upon us".[4]

Formation of World Government

The First pragmatic approach

Immanuel Kant

The concept of a peaceful community of nations had been proposed as far back as 1795. Immanuel Kant's essay **'Perpetual Peace'**(1795) was considered to be the pioneer of all concepts to creating world government.

He illustrates three basic definitive articles for organising human affairs to permanently abolish the threat of present and future wars, and to help establish a new era of lasting peace throughout the world. The three definitive articles are:

(i) "The Civil Constitution of Every State Should Be Republican"

(ii) "The Law of Nations Shall be founded on a Federation of Free States"

(iii) "The Law of World Citizenship Shall Be Limited to Conditions of Universal Hospitality".

The Second pragmatic approach

Karl Marx: Marxian political slogan **"labour of all counries! unite"** is one of the most famous rallying cries not only of *communism,* but also of world government. It is found in *The Communist Manifesto* **(1848),** by *Karl Marx* and Friedrich Engels. A variation ("Workers of all lands, unite") is also inscribed on Marx's tombstone.

V.I. Lenin: The staunch follower of Marx and the Russian most revolutionary, V.I. Lenin, never attempted to establish a **world government** despite Marx's appeal for "Workers of All countries Unite". Lenin forcefully worked for the establishment of a 'world socialist economy' governed by a "Bolshevik World State" (Goodman, 1953, 231). Similar to capitalism, socialism had neither action programme nor economic technique to operate its economic machinery except the political rude idea of 'proletariat dictatorship' under one party rule.

Both capitalism and socialism followed a policy of 'hatred' and 'killer instinct'. So in communist ideology, ultimately, balance-of-power politics between states enjoying unrestricted sovereignty did not cause war; **the real cause of war was capitalism.**

In practice, the Soviet Union's internally and externally repressive policies made a mockery of socialist ideals of a classless society, or a world of peaceful socialist republics. Its cold war policy resulted in the disintegration of the Soviet Union itself in 1991 during the tenure of Michael Gorbachev.

The Third pragmatic approach by Woodrow Wilson

First World War and League of Nations

Industrial revolution converted regional wars into world wars by the invention of weapons of mass destruction. The world became "Open War field". He "War Machines" were able to pierce through oceans and open air. The protective barriers of countries like forts, forests, mountains, and rivers became idle spectators. War became instead of soldiers against soldiers but soldiers against civilians.

The Industrial Revolution changed the entire face of the world. Especially the industrialisation of Western Europe promoted mass production. This mass production had been dedicated to First World War between 1914 and 1919. The result of this industrialised warfare was an unprecedented casualty level: eight and a half million soldiers killed, an estimated 21 million wounded, and approximately 10 million civilian deaths.[5, 6]

The horrendous of war such an extent, hitherto mankind never witnessed, and the dreadful impact of weapons of mass destruction, produced in industries, forced world leaders especially then US President Woodrow Wilson to seek a permanent solution for survival of mankind in future. The world leaders decided to establish a **world government** in the name of League of Nations.

The League of Nations was an intergovernmental organisation founded as a result of the Paris Peace Conference that ended the First World War. It was the first international organisation whose principal mission was to maintain world peace. Its primary goals, as stated in its covenant, included preventing wars through collective security and disarmament, and settling international disputes through negotiation and arbitration.[7]

Other issues in this and related treaties included labour conditions, just treatment of native inhabitants, human and drug trafficking, arms trade, global health, prisoners of war, and protection of minorities in Europe.[8] At its greatest extent from 28 September 1934 to 23 February 1935, it had 58 members. But these countries didn't have any agenda to creation of a powerful world government.

The diplomatic philosophy behind the League represented a fundamental shift from the preceding hundred years. The League lacked its own armed force and depended on the Great Powers to enforce its resolutions, keep to its economic sanctions, or provide an army when needed. However, the Great Powers were often reluctant to do so. Sanctions could hurt League members, so they were reluctant to comply with them. When, during the Second Idalou-Abyssinian War, the League accused Italian soldiers of targeting Red Cross medical tents, Benito Mussolini responded that "the League is very well when sparrows shout, but no good at all when eagles fall out."[9]

The fourth pragmatic approach by

Adolf Hitler's racial superiority

Nazi Germany, Second World War and World government:

The ruling Nazi Party of 1933-1945: Germany envisaged the ultimate establishment of a world government under the complete **hegemony** of the **Third Reich.**[10] In its move it overthrew the post-World War I Treaty of Versailles and withdrew itself from the League of Nations.

In his desire and stated political aim of expanding the "living space" (*Lebensraum*) of the German people by destroying or driving out "lesser-deserving races" in and from other territories dictator Adolf Hitler devised an ideological system of self-perpetuating expansionism, in which the expansion of a state's population would require the conquest of more territory which would in turn lead to a further growth in population which would then require even more conquests.[11]

In 1927, Rudolf Hess relayed to Walter Hewel Hitler's belief that world peace could only be acquired "when one power, the racially best one, has attained uncontested supremacy". When this control would be achieved, this power could then set up for itself a world police and assure itself "the necessary living space.... The lower races will have to restrict themselves accordingly".[11] This policy of supremacy ultimately led the mankind to Second World War.

The fifth pragmatic approach by

Roosevelt, Churchill and Stalin

World Government and United Nations

World War II, 1939–1945, resulted in an unprecedented scale of destruction of lives (over 60 million dead, most of them civilians), and the use of Weapons of Mass Destruction. At the conclusion of war many international leaders called for the establishment of institutions able to permanently prevent deadly international conflicts.

This led to the founding of the United Nations in 1945, which adopted the Universal Declaration of Human Rights in 1948. Many, however, felt that the UN, essentially a forum for discussion and coordination between sovereign governments, was insufficiently empowered for the task.

A number of prominent persons, such as Albert Einstein, Winston Churchill, Bertrand Russell and Mohandas K. Gandhi, called on governments to proceed further by taking gradual steps towards forming an effectual federal world government.

The United Nations main goal is to work on international law, international security, economic development, human rights, social progress, and eventually world peace. The United Nations gather regularly in order to solve big problems throughout the world but in the direction and satisfaction of US. It is because the United Nations is financed by some of the wealthiest nations especially by US...

Still now there is no functioning global international military, executive, legislature, judiciary, or constitution, with jurisdiction over the entire planet. So UN is unable to function as a strong world government and it fails to create 'One World'. While the United Nations exists, its authority is limited to a mostly advisory role, and its stated purpose is to foster cooperation between existing national governments, rather than authority over them.

World Government, Globalisation and World War III: World War I was fought for four years. World War II was fought for six years. But the World War III would be fought for 60 seconds at the most when 'Castle Bravo' and 'Tsar Bomba' are detonated against each other. It will be fortunate enough for world people who will disappear within a few twinkles of eyelids. The earth would become a great 'fireball'.

How to save the mankind? It is in our hands. At least now itself we, the people, have to capture the 'global capital' without any hesitation and to establish 'democratic mode of production' (i.e. Democrism) which is our-birthright.

The sixth pragmatic approach by

Wendell Wilke and Garry Davis

World Federalist Movement

Wendell Wilkie expanded on the notion of World government in his book "One World". He didn't believe that communism would be incompetent to establish 'One world government'. He advocated an alternative system to replace 'proletariat dictatorship' with a powerful democratic system. In 1943 his book was widely accepted throughout the world. He says:

"The best answer to Communism is a living, vibrant, fearless democracy — economic, social, and political."

—Wendell Wilkie, "One World"

The years between the conclusion of World War II and 1950, when the **Korean War** started and the Cold War mindset became dominant in international politics, were the "golden age" of the world federalist movement. Willkie's book **"One World"**, first published in 1943, sold over 2 million copies. In another, Emery Reves' book **"The Anatomy of Peace"** (1945) laid out the **arguments for replacing the UN with a** federal world government and quickly became **the "bible" of world federalis**ts. The grassroots world federalist movement in the US, led by people such as Grenville Clark, Norman Cousins, Alan Cranston and Robert Hutchins, organised itself into increasingly larger structures, finally forming, in 1947, the United World Federalists (later renamed to World Federalist Association, then Citizens for Global Solutions), claiming membership of 47,000 in 1949.

Similar movements concurrently formed in many other countries, leading to the formation, at a 1947 meeting in Monteux, Switzerland, of a global coalition, now called World Federalist Movement. By 1950, the movement claimed 56 member groups in 22 countries, with some 156,000 members.

Garry Davis

In France, 1948, **Garry Davis** began an unauthorised speech calling for a world government from the balcony of the UN General Assembly, until he was dragged away by the guards. Mr. Davis renounced his American citizenship and started a **Registry of World Citizens,** which claimed to have registered over 750,000 people in less than two years. **Opinion polls carried out by UNESCO in 1948-1949 found world government favoured by a majority of respondents in six European countries and rejected in three other countries (Australia, Mexico and the United States).** On September 4, 1953, Davis, from the City Hall of Ellsworth, Maine, announced the formation of the **"World Government of World Citizens"** based on 3 **"World Laws" — One God (or Absolute Value), One World, and One Humanity.**[12]

Following this declaration mandated he claimed by Article 21(3) of the Universal Declaration of Human Rights, he formed the United World Service Authority in New York City as the administrative agency of the new government. Its first task was to design and issue a "World Passport" based on Article 13(2) of the UDHR. To date over 800,000 of these documents have been issued to individuals worldwide. They have been recognised de facto by over 180 countries.

The seventh pragmatic approach by US to establish the 'world government' through Wal-Mart:

Wal-Mart Stores, Inc. was founded by American retail **legend Mr. Sam Walton** as purely a retail shop **in Arkansas in 1962.**

Today, with over 2.2 million associates worldwide, Walmart operates over 10,000 units in 27 countries under 69 different banners, and serves more than 200 million customers per week. Walmart recorded $419 billion in annual net sales in fiscal year 2011 (FYE10, Feb. 1, 2010 to Jan. 31, 2011). It earns a profit of 25 per cent of net sales, i.e. $105 billion. The huge volume of profit inflows to US.

Control of world economy: John Maynard Keynes and Wal-Mart: Wal-Mart and its sister concerns like Sam's stores have 8970 (2011) locations in 27 countries world widebut under 69 different names. By 2050 it spread all over the world.

The company operates under the Wal-Mart name in the United States, including the 50 states and Puerto Rico. It operates in Mexico as Wales, in the United Kingdom 9n he name od Assad, in Japan as Seiyu, and in India as Best Price. It has wholly owned operations in Argentina, Brazil, and Canada. Wal-Mart's investments outside North America have had mixed results: its operations in the United Kingdom, South America and China are highly successful for short term, whereas ventures in Germany and South Korea were unsuccessful.

It controls the markets of 'end – consumers'. In terms of Keynes it is the market that determines the **"the aggregate effective demand"** for more than thousand kinds of goods and services which determine a country's 'aggregate production', 'aggregate employment', 'aggregate consumption', 'aggregate income', and 'aggregate investment'. So it is said, "Wal-Mart could take over a country".

Inclination on military: It is predicted that by 2050 the Wal-Mart will spread its wings world wide and infuse more than one trillion dollar into US GDP. To maintain such a great 'economic empire' it may requires the support of US strong military power. US will readily rush to support with nefarious designs to establish its 'economic empire and imperialism' throughout the world and strive to impose one world government.

There are a historical evidences all over the world. When 'East India Company' had come to India for trading it ultimately conquered India, Pakistan, Ceylon, Myanmar, Singapore, Malaysia, South Africa and so on. These countries had to struggle more than 200 years for their freedom. Wal-Mart is not exempted from 'East India company' and US is not exempted from Britain.

All these economic tragedies will be staged in the name of 'globalisation' and the mankind will witness innumerable 'Chinese like massacres'.

The eighth pragmatic approach by Globalisation

Globalisation is eternal evolution towards the World Economic Government

Law of Nature and evolution: The Law of Nature demands that every system should undergo evolution towards its perfection to sustain eternality. Both Capitalism and Socialism have not evolved in coordination with Law of Nature. So they are still undergoing evolution to attain their perfection. But they are always stumbling throughout the world. No doubt the ultimate end point rests on 'globalisation of economy'.

Globalisation will confidently lead the economic systems towards their perfection not through the chaotic Capitalism and Socialism but through establishment "People's Direct Ownership of Capital" (i.e. Democrism). Let's take Wal-Mart for example.

Wal-Mart and Globalisation: Since the Wal-Mart is spreading over all kinds of 'end-consumers' it has wide influence on the people to buy one good or other. But Wal-Mart is owned by a single family of Sam Walton. When it spreads throughout the world it will be as dangerous as Capitalism and Socialism in the management of economic activities. At any time the US government or any other country may take over the company and exert control over world economy with the help of mighty military power. There are lot of instances in history. It may result not only in 'economic imperialism' but also in World War III. The fact prompts the experts to alarm that if **7-Eleven will destroy 30 stores Wal-Mart will take over the country.**

No doubt that Wal-Mart paves way for globalisation. But it should not be owned by a family or a few capitalists. It should be directly owned by the people to demonstrate the real goal of globalisation.

The only solution

(a) The capital stock of Wal-Mart (like other Companies) should be divided into billions of shares. These shares should be distributed at 'par value' to all the people throughout the world. Right from top most managerial staff to low grade associate should not be disturbed at any cost. Only the distribution of capital share should be democratized as per law of 'One Share to One Person'. This democratic law will work in comply with the 'Law of Nature'. On the implementation of this law 'globalisation' will lead mankind towards an Ideal Society.

Globalisation is a process by which the experience of everyday life is marked by the diffusion of commodities and ideas, is becoming standardised around the world. Factors that have contributed to globalisation include **increasingly sophisticated communications and transportation technologies and services**, mass migration and the movement of peoples, a level of economic activity that has outgrown national markets through industrial combinations and commercial groupings that cross national frontiers and international agreements that reduce the cost of doing business in foreign countries.

Globalisation offers huge potential profits to companies and nations but has been complicated by widely differing expectations, standards of living, cultures and values, and legal systems as well as unexpected global cause-and-effect linkages.

The proponents of global governance face a similar challenge. It remains to be seen whether the developing agents, networks and structures of global governance can effectively promote environmental protection; will be able to develop authoritative mechanisms for disciplining the use of force, by non-state actors as well as by the world's most powerful states; and will serve the interests of the bottom half of humanity barely seeking out a living, even if it means demanding a small sacrifice from the fortunate fifteen per cent of humankind living in the world's high-income economies. For those who lament present day conditions, Wendt's teleological theory of world order development might provide some comfort and inspiration in reminding us that history is not over.

One World concept in the event of Globalisation in Economics

Proponents of world government offer distinct reasons for why it is an ideal of political organisation. Some are motivated negatively and see world

The tenth and the ultimate pragmatic approach by Democrism World Government under Democrism. Operation of Democrism – The Third Economic System (The Tax-free, Interest-free and Corruption-free Economy) It is an idea of How to rule a nation

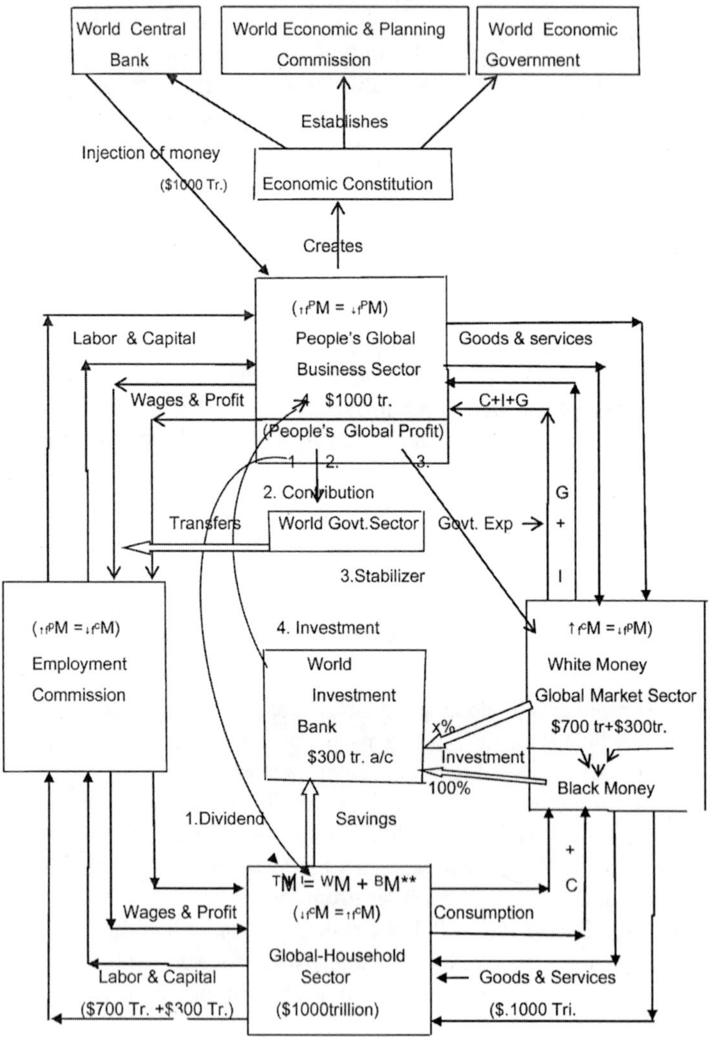

Circular Flow of Money and Goods in Democrism

** ^{T}M = Total Money; $^{W}M + {}^{B}M$ = White Money + Black Money
$\uparrow_f^P M$= Producers' outflow of money; $\downarrow_f^P M$ =Producers' inflow of money;
$\uparrow_f^c M$= Consumers' outflow of money; $\downarrow_f^c M$= Consumers' inflow of money

government as the definitive solution to old and new human problems such as war and the development of weapons of mass destruction, global poverty and inequality, and environmental degradation.

In Democrism the operation of Global Economy is replica of operation of National economy. I intend to explain the operation of global economy in two distinct models for the benefits of my readers. The first model, Global Macro Level, assumes each country in the world as independent consumer in the Global Household Sector. If there are 200 countries in the world, it may be presumed that there are 200 consumer countries in Global Household Sector and each country will operate distinctively as an individual consumer in the global economic activities.

Operation of Democrism at Global Level Model

The diagram displays five distinct but indispensably interdependent economic sectors for the operation of global economy such as 1. World Production Sector, 2.World Household Sector, 3.World Commodity Market Sector, 4.World Investment Bank Sector and 5.World Economic government.

Now I illustrate the operation of global economy diagrammatically with hypothetical data in coincidence with world bank statistics of 2012. Basically I take the circular flow of both the consumption and investment moneys between the household sector (200 countries) and production sector globally as a whole.

It is not necessary to establish any fresh prerequisite infrastructures for the operation of global economy. The World Bank and IMF may be converted as **'World (Global) Central Bank'**, World Trade Organisation as **'World (Global) Commodity Market** and the UN as the **'World (Global) Economic Government'**, all the member countries of UN as **'World (Global) Household Sector'** and all the National and International Corporate Sectors irrespective of their size as **'People's World (Global) Production Sector'**. Moreover all the national and international Commercial Banks will be transformed into as **"World (Global) Investment Banks**'. There will be no commercial banks in the world. This present structural transformation will lead the global economy to move smoothly towards Globalisation i.e. one world and one economy.

Let's assume the Gross Global Income would be $1000 trillion which includes $700 trillion as consumption money and the rest $300 trillion as investment money. Further, assume each country as a distinct consumer irrespective of its size of population. In other words there are only 200 consumers who will buy globally produced goods from the global market for their consumption and investment purposes. For example, India may be constituted a separate entity or a single consumer unit and it buys goods in the global market for the sake of its 1.2 billion people as a whole. This concept of transaction will apply to all 200 countries.

Generation of Money: There will be only one kind of money, say dollar. If the countries want distinct kind of money to suit their transactions, they may have and they transfer the dollar into their native money value as it now in operation to satisfy their local consumers and for smooth operation of economy and it is possible as the world is rapidly digitalizing.

The money (say dollar) will be generated by the **"Global Central Bank"** on the direction of **Global Economic Government** and on the guidance of **Global Economic Commission** whenever necessary. When the **Global Production Sector** needs $1000 trillion for the production of goods and services, the Global Central Bank will release the money on piecemeal method. The 'Interest based loan' system of commercial banks would have been abolished. There would be no 'stock market gambles' all over the world.

1. Global Production Sector: The global production sector by acquiring labour and capital, for example $700 tr. and $300 tr. respectively, from the global household sector which consists of 200 countries, will produce socially needed goods and services for the consumption of global workers. For the payment of money, the global production sector would have received adequate money from global central bank. These goods will flow towards household sector towards global market sector. For the contribution of labour and capital the household sector will receive money income to the tune of $1000 trillion equivalent to the value of goods produced at about $1000 trillion in the form of wage and profit. See the diagram.

2. Global Household Sector: The global market sector would have received periodically the consumption and investment goods from global production sector to meet the aggregate demand of the household sector (200 countries). I have already specified that the household sector would spend their Gross Global Income ($1000 tr.) to purchase consumption goods ($700 tr.) as consumers and investment goods (300 tr.) as producers. In Democrism all consumers are producers, and all producers are consumers. It will be called as Global Prosumer Society.

The consumption goods will flow directly towards the global household sector (200 countries). Since the 'investment goods like machines and plants couldn't be bought in retail shops like that of consumption goods, an "Investment Account" would have opened for all 200 countries in the 'global investment bank". When the global household sector pays the "Consumption Money" to the worth of $1000 trillion, $700 trillion will directly flow towards "Global Production Sector" for the purchase of consumption of consumption goods and the remaining $300 trillion will be converted as "Investment Money", in the form of "Electronic Money", and the amount will be credited in the "Global Investment Bank account" of each country. On the conversion of Investment Money, the Consumption Money $300 trillion will directly flow to the Global Production Sector along with Consumption Money. Now the

Global Production Sector will get \$700 trillion for sale of consumption goods and \$300 trillion for the sale of investment goods.

The amount \$300 trillion credited in the Global Investment Bank Account will be transferred to the account of Global Production Sector. In consequence the Global Production Sector will get \$1000 trillion consumption money to complete the circular flow of money. It will establish the producers circular equilibrium between "Producers' Outflow of money and Producers' Inflow of money" ($\uparrow^{P}M = \downarrow {}^{P}M$). This monetary equilibrium satisfies the basic condition of Natural Law.

I wish to state that the price of consumption and investment goods includes a certain value of profit. The rate of profit will be determined according to the needs of the economy.

The \$1000 trillion worth of Net Global Income will flow from the 'Global Commodity Market' towards the 'Global Production sector' to boost the marginal increase of production, employment and income.

To promote the effective operation of global economy all the basic sectors would be digitalised and interconnected.

3. Global Market Sector: The Market sector operates as fulcrum (in the lever system) between the 'weight' of the household sector and 'effort' of the production sector. Like a 'balance' it tends to maintain equilibrium between the marginal rate of expenditure of household sector and the marginal rate of income of production sector. In the words of Keynes, it acts as a determinant factor to sustain or assert the volume of 'effective demand' that determines the level of employment, production and income.

The diagram illustrates the enterprise of the following three distinct functions of market sector: 1. The transfer of goods from production sector to household sector at a given price level, 2. The transfer of the Gross National Income of household sector to production sector for purchasing consumption and investment goods and 3. The transfer of a part of Gross Global Income in the form of 'electronic money' (Investment money) to the 'Global Investment Bank' to maintain the 'Investment Account' of each country. This transfer is a legally justified acknowledgment that each country has bought its due share of investment goods from aggregate global investment stock.

The market sector acts as a filter or a check valve to permit to flow in only he white money for buying goods and services and retains all black money to stagnate as dirty element to be thrown out of 'transactions' with the help of digitalised "Investment Bank". The circulation of black money should be eliminated from exchange of goods and services by 'economic techniques' and not by political rules and regulations introduced day in day out. Who are these framers of 'political rules and regulations'? The corrupt politicians and the capitalists behind the curtain. In consequence all the political rules and regulations have been rusted and failed in the elimination of black money. So the parallel economy run by black money has been more forceful and greater than the visible economy run by white money.

Transfer of Investment Money to the workers: Subsequently each country will transfer its 'aggregate investment money' accounted in its 'global Investment Bank' to the individual 'Investment Account' of its workers in order ensure that each worker has an investment share in all the global industries.

Global Dividend (Income Equalizer): On the contribution of global investment each country will claim 'dividend' (Income equalizer) according to their 'Investment burden'. The workers will earn their legally entitled 'dividend' from stock of People's Global Profit gained by the global industries through their countries' 'Global Investment Bank'. It will create a sense of legal authentication among the workers that they are inalienable shareholders of all the global industries. This power of mental substance will accelerate the force of necessity for globalisation. In the diagram the flow 'dividend' from 'People's global Profit Fund' to 'Global Household Sector' is displayed by a downward arrow mark.

Investment burden: I have mentioned the dividend as 'income equalizer' because the global dividend will be distributed according to 'investment burden' of each country. The poor countries have to shoulder heavy burden more than the rich countries for the creation of global investment. According to distributive justice the poor countries will gain more volume of dividend than the rich countries. This marginal increment of dividend will reduce the income gap between poor and rich countries and in subsequent years the income gap will vanish and the countries will become equal economic partners in the global economic growth. So we may call the dividend as income equalizer.

Global Market Sector and the elimination of 'Black Money': In the diagram I have exhibited the operation of the Global Market Sector as a controller and an administrator of the flow of white and black money from the countries of Global Household Sector to the Global Production and Global Investment Bank Sectors whenever consumption and investment goods are bought by global countries.

Let's assume the Global Household Sector spends $1000 tr. to buy $700 tr. worth of consumption goods and $300 tr. worth of investment goods through the Global Market Sector. The Global Market Sector would transfer directly the $700 tr. to the Global Production Sector for the sale of consumption goods. The value of money spent for purchasing investment goods would be credited to the Investment Account of each country maintained in the Global Investment Bank. Value of money received for the sale of investment goods would be transferred in tangible and visible form to the Global Production Sector. In consequent the Global Production Sector would receive $1000 tr. from the

Global Market by the sale of consumption and investment goods. The Global Production Sector would ultimately attain equilibrium between the outflow and inflow of moneys at particular level of employment or production or money supply.

In the diagram I have marked the flow of investment account from Global Investment Bank to the Global Production Sector by an upward arrow mark. It will inform the Production Sector that each country has investment share in the global capital stock.

Black Money becomes Investment Money: In the diagram I have bifurcated the Global Market Sector into two segments. The upper segment denotes 'white money' and the lower segment denotes 'black money'. Both the segments are connected digitally with the Global Investment Bank by two leftward arrows marked as 'x per cent investment' and '100 per cent investment' from white money and black money segments respectively.

The Global Market Sector will also operate as a check valve to separate the flow of white and black moneys towards the Global Production Sector. It will retain the black money and permit only the white money to flow towards the Global Production Sector and filter the black money at the lower segment. For instance, if a country's legally declared Gross National Income is $10 tr. and it has secured $2 tr. in excess by manipulating corrupt practices. With this $2 tr. black money if the country spends $12tr. in the market to buy consumption and investment goods. The Global Market Sector will permit only $10 tr. for purchasing goods and services and reject $2 tr. from business transactions. It is possible because the Global Market Sector and the Global Investment Bank Sector would have been interconnected by computer network technology. As soon as the country spends more than $10 tr. the internet network system will alarm both the Market and Investment Bank sectors about the legally declared National Income of the country'which would have accounted in the Investment Bank Account.

The Market Sector will forfeit the black money $2 tr. and transfer it to 'Global Investment Bank' for crediting the "Common Investment Fund Account'. In the diagram it has been displayed as 100 per cent Investment leftward arrow mark. The country cannot claim any volume of divided for this black money investment. Out of the $10 tr. white money, $3 tr. (30 per cent) will be transferred to the Investment Bank for crediting the country's 'Investment Bank Account' as the country's contribution to aggregate investment fund. For this contribution the country I will be entitled to claim dividend. It has been depicted as 'x per cent Investment arrow' from Global Market Sector to Global Investment Bank Sector. The Investment $3 tr. will be transferred as "Electronic Money" not in the tangible form of Consumption Money. The rest $7 tr. white money will flow towards the Production sector for purchasing the consumption goods along will $3 tr. for purchasing investment goods. The Global Production Sector will altogether will receive $10 tr. in the form of Consumption Money.

The black money would be eliminated even internationally only by digitalizing the economy. It is possible, one day or another or even after some decades after, if the countries are willing to adopt the democratic system of economy i.e. Democrism-The Third Theory.

People's Global Profit Fund Sector: Every sale of goods and services, nationally or internationally, whole sale or retail, includes a huge volume of profit. More the middle men between producers and final consumers mean more the exploitation. In the capitalism profit means exploitation. In Democrism profit means a technique of income equalizer and economic stability. How?

In Democrism all the consumers are producers. The consumers in the capacity of producers earn profit they will transfer the profit to the "People's Profit Fund" for redistribution among themselves. There will be no exploitation. Here the "Profit" is not one means profit but people's profit. People's profit will flow into the 'Income stream of people' but not into the pockets of a few capitalists.

In Democrism, when Global Production Sector earns profit it will transfer the profit to the 'People's Profit Fund' for redistribution. The redistribution of profit has been classified as distribution for the 'dividend', contribution to the Govt. expenditure and reservation of fund for economic stabilisation of employment and income of workers.

In the diagram I have depicted it in the form of three 'downward arrow' marks from 'People's Profit Fund', in the name of "Dividend", "Contribution" and "Stabilisation".

For example, let's assume that the producers in "Global Production Sector" derive $1000 tr. from the sale of goods and services and they receive $600 tr. profit out of it and they transfer this $600 tr. profit to the "Global People's Profit Fund" which is exclusively entitled to consumers. Let's further assume that this $600 tr. will be allocated as follows: (a) $300 tr. for distribution of 'dividend' to the workers, (b) $250 tr. for contribution to the government on behalf of consumers on abolishing all kinds of taxes and (c) $50 tr. for stabilisation employment and income of workers whenever certain volume of goods tends to stagnate in the market for lack of effective demand.

Since the consumers would not exploit themselves, as one wouldn't dig his own eyes, the volume of profit would be returned to the consumers according to "Distributive Justice". This is the credo of Democrism.

Operation of Global Economy in Democrism

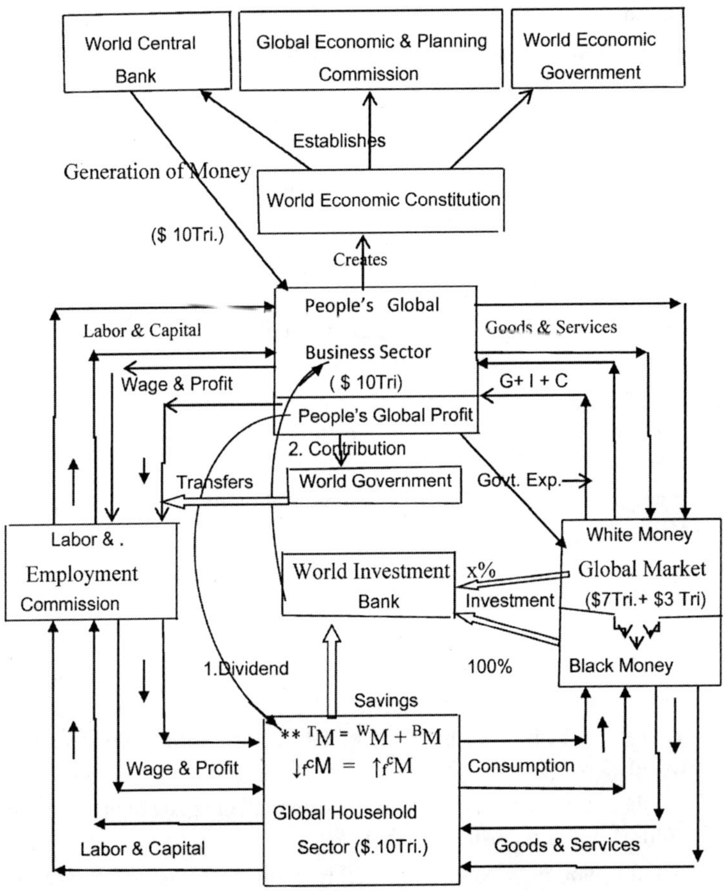

Circular Flow of Money and Goods in Democrism

** ^{T}M = Total Money; $^{W}M + {}^{B}M$ = White Money + Black Money
$\uparrow_f^P M$ = Producers' outflow of money; $\downarrow_f^P M$ =Producers' inflow of money;
$\uparrow_f^c M$= Consumers' outflow of money; $\downarrow_f^c M$ = Consumers' inflo0w of money

The operation of national economy in Democrism in the context of globalisation can be illustrated on the following hypothesis.

1. The economic system 'democrism' should be in operation in some or various countries.
2. These countries should be incorporated as one bloc like European Union.
3. There should be numerous multi-national corporations in the world within and without the bloc.
4. The workers of all countries should have absolute freedom to share their wage income in all the multi-national corporations.
5. At present there should be some billion workers **(say, 500 billion)** engaged in all small, medium, large scale business units.
6. All the workers should have a bank account and credit/debit card at the maximum possible extend.

Now I can explain the operation of global economy and the elimination of all economic evils including black money with help of the above diagram.

1. In the diagram I have assumed a particular multi-national business unit like Microsoft has approximately 100 branches all over the world.
2. It acquires necessary capital and labour globally to the value of **$10 trillion.**
3. The industry pays **$7 trillion as wage** for the labour and **$3 trillion as profit** for the capital. Thereby the workers receive $10 trillion money income.
4. This business sector produces goods worth of $10 trillion annually equivalent to the combined value of wage and profit
5. There should be free mobility of labour and capital all over the world.
6. All the workers should have an Investment Bank Account with any volume initial deposit even about $0.
7. All the workers should have debit/credit card and a **registered phone numbers.**
8. All the workers should mention their legally accepted annual income with small variation of 10 per cent.

I. Production Sector of global industry: We know that there is no distinction between workers and capitalists in Democrism or Democratic mode of Production. In our study a particular production unit spends **$10 trillion** to utilise labour and capital from household sector. For which it pays **$7 trillion** as wage for labour of I million workers for example, and $3 trillion as profit for capital. It produces **$10 trillion** worth of goods/services and sells them through global or national market sector. The production unit will try to operate to sustain a required monetary equilibrium between its marginal rate of outflow of money (wage and profit)($\partial\uparrow$PM) and marginal rate of inflow of money ($\downarrow$PM) (sales income received from consumption, investment and government expenditures) at a particular level of production/employment/money supply. ($\partial\uparrow$PM$=\partial\downarrow$PM) i.e., Producers marginal monetary equilibrium)

Factors of Production: Democrism recognises only two factors of production, Labour and Capital. The production sector receives labour and capital from household sector, for which it pays wage and profit to the workers of the household sector. The value of wage will not be determined by the demand and supply forces of labour because labour will not be a tradable commodity in Democrism. Here labour will be treated as national dignity, honour, reverence and respect. The value of labour will be determined by an economic agreement or economic contract derived by the general will of the workers. Since in democrism there is no distinction between workers and producers we may safely conclude that the workers themselves will determine their wages. The workers in the household sector will receive dual income by the way of wage for labour and profit for capital.

The Household Sector: The household sector consists of all the global workers individually with separate identity. All the workers will have a distinct identification card exhibiting his (1) Registered mobile number, (2) Name, (3) Photo, (4) Unique identification number, (5) Legally approved monthly/annual income, (6) Name and address of Investment bank, (7) Investment bank account number, (8) Email address, (9) Date of birth and age, (10) Residential address, (11) Occu-pation, (12) Address of work place. Moreover, if necessary the identification cards may be issued in three distinct colours as green, yellow and orange. The green for low income group people, the yellow for middle income group people and the orange for high income group people. Whatever may be the colour the personal particulars will be the same.

[The workers may be classified into 'consumer-workers and producer-workers'. Both the workers belongs the same category. But they perform different works in different sectors. In the household sector they perform as 'consumer-workers' and in production sector as 'producer-workers'. The 'producer-workers' will produce goods and services and distribute them among themselves as consumer-workers at a given price level. There will be no exploitation and no taxation in the process of distribution. Since the price of commodities is determined by the consumer-workers themselves that price will be called **'Just Price'**]

The workers should always keep with them the identification card or a small statement that will exhibit 1. Registered mobile number, 2. Photo, 3. E mail id if any, 4. Name of the investment bank, and 5. Account no., wherever and whenever he goes for purchasing. These particulars are required to sign up his account and to login. He can buy goods and services anywhere in the world by using this Identification card especially his registered cell number and he may simultaneously use his debit/credit card for his online business transactions.

Operation of Democrism at National level: Both the consumption and investment goods are produced by the workers themselves. Therefore, the workers alone are entitled to buy the consumption and investment goods in the capacity of consumers and producers respectively. The workers will buy consumption goods directly from the consumer market but how they will buy investment goods like tools and machines, plant and machineries, land and buildings in the producer market?

Suppose a worker buys a commodity at maximum retail price **(MRP) $10** by issuing consumption money. The price of the commodity contains not only the cost of the consumption commodity at $6 (60 per cent of MRP) but also the cost of the investment commodity at $3 (30 per cent of MRP) that is used to produce the consumption commodity or future investment, and a contribution fund at $1 (10 per cent of MRP) payable to government to meet its expenditure. This government expenditure is also called as 'government investment' for welfare and public work schemes. This contribution will replace all kinds the Goods and Services Taxes and income taxes too.

On receiving the consumption money to the value of **$10** the seller in the market sector, for example, will give the worker **$6** worth of consumption goods and $4 worth of investment goods. The consumer can buy the consumption goods in tangible and visible form but the investment goods in invisible form. The investment goods can't usably be sold in small units. The investment goods will be stocked in huge quantities in the form of machines, plans and, land buildings. The consumer can claim a minute share in the sock of investment but can't claim the share of investment to be transferred to his household sector. So, instead of transferring investment goods, an equal value of 'investment money' i.e. 'electronic money will be transferred to every worker's investment account' in his 'investment bank'. The transfer of investment money will be a continuous and perennial process in the infinitely long time whenever the consumers make purchases, small or large quantities in the market. Though the investment of **$4** per transaction may be very small, its value in aggregate stock in accumulation of numerous buyers, created in numerous transactions will be significantly large and will empower the workers to gain economic security to play with equal power in the economic field. It has been displayed in the diagram in the form of an arrow that connects 'market sector' with 'investment bank sector'. Basically the two sectors will digitally be connected and this computerisation will control all economic activates.

The investment money $4 in the form of electronic money will be transferred to the worker's 'investment account' in the investment bank from the market sector. It has been exhibited in the diagram by a leftward arrow mark of x per cent. The transfer of investment money is a self-realistic and a legal proof of authentication that the worker has bought $4 worth of investment goods from the aggregate capital stock. A worker can make thousands of such transactions in a year and will stake an ownership right on his aggregate value of investment goods credited in his investment account. For example, if a worker has $25,000 in his investment account it will imply that he would have investment ownership right to that value in the national or global capital stock of all national/global industries. The worker is entitled to claim his share of 'dividend' from the national/global profit fund created for the assignment.

In the same line of interpretation if billions of workers nationally/globally create 'investment' the economy will acquire adequate capital not only to launch new industries but also procure the share capital of already existing industries to implement 'people's direct ownership of capital' and for the establishment of "Democrism", the new third economic system.

Global /National Market Sector: In Democrism the two primary and distinct functions of market sector are to administer the perfect transfer of consumption and investment goods from producers to the consumers for the exchange of consumption money. The first primary function is that the consumption goods will be exchanged directly through transfer of consumption money. Second, the investment goods will be transferred to the consumers through **"electronic money"** and that will be credited to the consumer's "investment account". The aggregate value of consumption and investment goods in the form of 'consumption money' will directly flow towards producers to stabilise the economic activities.

Though consumers pay **'consumption money'** to buy investment goods the market will convert it into 'investment money' and credit the amount in the consumer's 'investment account'. In consequence the producers will receive the aggregate volume of consumption money which they spent for buying labour and capital from the consumers in the household sector.

The second primary function is that the market sector will take on the flow of black money at its very origin. If a consumer, where ever he may or at any corner of the world, spends in excess of his legally declared annual income the market will reject the 'transaction as over spending' because it may be earned by corruption. This corrupt money would be transferred to 'investment bank' and it will automatically be passed over the producers for investment purposes.

In some indispensable cases the excess money will be permitted for purchasing life-saving medicines, healthcare materials and educational purposes, and for purchasing other necessities to uphold one's right to live. In curbing the circulation of black money the application of 'digital technology' will play a vital and active role. Without the help of 'digital technology' then elimination of corruption will be impossible. The criminal laws and judiciary will play only passive role with lot of loopholes. Further, the introduction of numerous laws will shrink the liberty of people and lead the society towards dictatorship and democracy will peril at the end. Economic problems should be solved by economic techniques only. "The best government is that govern least" with minimum rules and regulations.

Global Production Sector: Global production sector will accommodate worker-producers only. The producers receive aggregate sales income primarily by selling consumption and investment goods and secondarily the money income from government sector and black money forfeited by the market sector as well. (See the diagram)

The aggregate sales income of producers naturally includes a substantial volume of 'profit' . This volume of profit will be transferred to the "People's Global Profit Fund, a sub-division of production sector (See the diagram). The global profit fund has been exhibited as rectangular shape in the production sector. I have already explained the global profit fund will be employed to perform three strategic activities namely (1) distribution of dividend to the workers of all the countries according to distributive justice, (2) contribution of fund to the governments to meet their public work expenditure by abolishing all kinds of taxes and (3) stabilisation fund to compensate producers income when they experience deficiency in their sales income to maintain the level of production and employment.

Effective role of profit: In democrats the profit would be used for distribution and for contribution purposes. In regard to distribution purposes, a considerable portion of profit would be reserved for the payment of **dividend** to the workers.

Similarly in regard to contribution purposes a reasonable portion of profit would be utilised for the contribution to government to meet its expenditure on abolition of all kinds of taxes.

Moreover, an adequate portion of profit would be retained for bridging the income gap between "the producers' expected income" and the "producers' actual income". Due to this income gap the producers would incur loss as the consumers' fail to buy the goods already produced for them. Naturally to prevent such loss (due to lack of effective demand) the producers would be induced reduce the level of production and employment. Therefore, in order to prevent the producers' income gap, in Democrism, this remaining portion of profit would be utilised to buy the stagnated goods in the market. It would equilibrate producers' monetary income to their monetary expenditure. This portion of profit would play a strategic role to stabilise the economic activities at all levels of employment.

For example, let's assume the volume of **national profit** amounts to **$3 trillion.** Out of which **$1.5 trillion** is allocated for distribution of dividend to the workers. The workers will get the dividend according to their 'investment burden'; by which low income group workers will get more dividends per share than high income group workers. This justifiable model of distribution will reduce the income-gap among the workers and it will drive the society towards egalitarianism.

Let's assume out of the remaining national profit of **$1.5 trillion, $1 trillion** will be directed to flow towards the government exchequer to meet its expenditure. All direct and indirect taxes will be abolished. There will be direct flow of money from the 'people's profit fund' to the government exchequer. All kinds of cost incurred for the collection of taxes will be eliminated. Thereby the corruption or black money involved in the process of collection of taxes will absolutely be terminated.

The third and last portion of national profit, **$0.5 trillion,** will be retained by the 'Economic Commission' as a strategic reserve fund for stabilisation economy. Whenever the producers experience lack of demand for their goods they will be forced to reduce the volume of production and employment to maintain maximisation of profit. Suppose the producers realise $0.5 trillion worth of goods have been stagnating in the market due to lack of demand. The lack of demand is attributed to erratic psychological behaviour of consumers and their irrational decision-making in the market. Since in Democrism all the consumers are the producers and vice versa, the consumers themselves will be affected by the resultant lower level of employment and production. In order to prevent the depression trend of the economy and to stabilise the level of employment and production, this $0.5 trillion will be spent to buy the stagnated goods. The producers will receive adequate income and continue the production in the next round at the same level of employment.

Thus, in Democrism, the profit factor will be employed as 'stabiliser' of the economy and the stagnated goods that are purchased for $0.5 will be distributed to the low-income group or poor people at concessional rate or free to increase their standard of living. It would be utilised to buy the stagnated goods in the market. It would equilibrate producers' monetary income to their monetary expenditure. This portion of profit would play a strategic role to stabilise the economic activities at all levels of employment.

For example, let's assume the volume of national profit amounts to $3 trillion. Out of which $1.5 trillion is allocated for distribution of dividend to the workers. The workers will get the dividend according to their 'investment burden'; by which low income group workers will get more dividends per share than high income group workers. This justifiable model of distribution will reduce the income-gap among the workers and it will drive the society towards egalitarianism.

Let's assume out of the remaining national profit of $1.5 trillion, $1 trillion will be directed to flow towards the government exchequer to meet its expenditure. All direct and indirect taxes will be abolished. There will be direct flow of money from the 'people's profit fund' to the government exchequer. All kinds of cost incurred for the collection of taxes will be eliminated. Thereby the corruption or black money involved in the process of collection of taxes will absolutely be terminated.

The third and last portion of national profit, $0.5 trillion, will be retained by the 'Economic Commission' as a strategic reserve fund for stabilisation economy. Whenever the producers experience lack of demand for their goods they will be forced to reduce the volume of production and employment to maintain maximisation of profit. Suppose the producers realise $0.5 trillion worth of goods have been stagnating in the market due to lack of demand. The lack of demand is attributed to erratic psychological behaviour of consumers and their irrational decision-making in the market. Since in Democrism all the consumers are the producers and vice versa, the consumers themselves will be affected by the resultant lower level of employment and production. In order to prevent the depression trend of the economy and to stabilize the level of employment and production, this $0.5 trillion will be spent to buy the stagnated goods. The producers will receive adequate income and continue the production in the next round at the same level of employment.

Thus, in Democrism, the profit factor will be employed as 'stabiliser' of the economy and the stagnated goods that are purchased for $0.5 will be distributed to the low-income group or poor people at concessional rate or free to increase their standard of living.

In conclusion, I emphatically advocate that all global industries should be owned by each worker and each global industry should be owned by all the global workers. This wills be the only solution to the problems of mankind hitherto experiencing since the genesis of civilisation. I assure Democrism will lead the mankind towards "One World, One Government and One Humanity".

References

1. Andrus, Hyrum Leslie (1958). *Joseph Smith and World Government.* Salt Lake City, Utah: Deseret Book. OCLC4146522.
2. Riggs, Robert E. (Winter 1959), Joseph Smith and World Government, "Book Reviews", BYU Studies: 71–73.
3. Bradley, Don (April 2006), "The Grand Fundamental Principles of Mormonism: Joseph Smith's Unfinished Reformation", Sunstone: 32–41.
4. Schwartzberg, Joseph E. (2004). "Reform of the General Assembly" (PDF). *Revitalizing the United Nations: Reform through Weighted Voting.* New York and The Hague: Institute For Global Policy, World Federalist Movement. pp. 3. ISBN0-9710727-4-4.OCLC56124473.

5. Bell 2007, pp. 15-17.
6. Northedge 1986, pp. 1-2.
7. "Covenant of the League of Nations". The Avalon Project.http://avalon.law.yale.edu/20th_century/leagcov.asp. Retrieved 30 August 2011.
8. See Article 23, "Covenant of the League of Nations". http://avalon.law.yale.edu/20th_century/leagcov.asp.,"Treaty of Versailles". http://en.wikisource.org/wiki/Treaty_of_Versailles.andMinority Rights Treaties.
9. Jahanpour, Farhang, "The Elusiveness of Trust: the experience of Security Council and Iran" (PDF).Transnational Foundation of Peace and Future Research.p. 2.http://www.transnational.org/Area_MiddleEast/2008/Jahanpour_SC-Iran.pdf. Retrieved 27 June 2008.
10. Weinberg, Gerhard L. (1995), *Germany, Hitler, and World War II: essays in modern German and world history*. Cambridge University Press, p. 36.
11. Weinberg, Gerhard L. (1995), *Germany, Hitler, and World War II: essays in modern German and world history*. Cambridge University Press, p. 36.
12. Worldservice.org

Chapter – 36

Constitution of World Government

The world economic government will operate under Democrism as per the Articles prescribed below:

Article: 1. We, the people of all countries, tirelessly endeavour for the establishment of 'One World' from the genesis of civilisation. On account of our faith, enriched from the time immemorial, that the creation of 'One world' would eradicate war between countries, appalling poverty of the people, unbearable torture of unemployment, the horrifying pollution of earth and so on.

Article: 2. In the pursuit of our noble cause we, the people, trust the immediate establishment of 'One World' despite the futile and trivial criticisms flowing here and there for personal motives enclosed by bias fundamentalism and narrow minded walls. This clotted darkness of history will always prevail.

Article: 3. By the term 'one world' I mean 'one world government'.

Article: 4. Here and ever I use only **'world economic government'** as designation instead of 'world political government' which is entrenched with full of corrupt practices at all levels of hierarchy.

Article: 5. The 'Economic Government' will occupy like the position of proton of nucleus of an atom and all other forms of governments will revolve like electrons around the nucleus. This is 'Law of Nature'.

Article: 6. The establishment of 'World Economic government'.

This government would be established only by the adult the 'worker-representatives' irrespective of gender who have completed 18 years old.

Article: 7. There are at present 164 sovereign countries in the world. These countries would send the representatives to the economic government according to their population.

Article: 8. As the member countries represent on the basis of worker population the bigger countries should not claim special privileges in decision-making process. They should not exhibit egoism, bias, superiority complex, money and muscle power over the representatives of small countries. All the members should be treated 'equal and indispensable members' of the government.

Articles: 9. The rights and liberties of minorities should be protected at any cost.

Article: 10. Duties of rich countries: Execution of International Fraternity: The countries which are inherently put at more advantaged position than the less advantaged countries should help the latter countries to bring them up to their standard primarily in the domain of education, standard of living, nutrition, and other basic necessities of livelihood.

Article: 11. Legislature: The head of the government called as 'President of World Economic government'.

Article: 12. The legislature or Senate would consist of 'President', 'Vice-President', 'Chairman and deputy chairman' of the legislative assembly, 'council of ministers' and other indispensable authorities if necessary.

Article: 13. Expert Committee: An expert committee of at least 10 members would be appointed to select the president of economic government. The expert committee consists of 75 per cent members from developed countries and 25 per cent members from less developed countries. In aggregate at least 15 per cent of members should belong to judiciary. If the committee fails to appoint the president unanimously then the majority of members would decide the president by secret ballot.

Article: 14. The number of contenders for the post of president should not exceed three who should have at least 30 per cent of member countries.

Article: 15. Qualification: The president contenders should have attained at least 40 years and have minimum prescribed educational and moral standards. They should not have any stigma of criminal prosecutions adjudged by court of law.

Article: 16. Office of the world president: The tenure of the office of the world president would extend for only four years. If the president or the vice-president intends to administer the office for another four years they may contest the election without obtaining the approval of the 'expert committee'. On the other hand if any one intends to fight for presidential post he or she should get not only the approval of 'expert committee' but also obtain the backing of 30 per cent of member countries. No president should occupy more than eight years continuously or intermittently.

Article: 17. Council of ministers

Prerogative of president and Universal representation: The selection of 'council of ministers' comes under the purview of president. Since the world economic government embodies inherently a non-political and regional body the president should be cosmopolite in the selection of his council of ministers. He should not select his council of ministers from the nation to which he belongs to exhibit his regional affinity or from any political party he may have leniency.

He, therefore, should be justifiable in covering all the nations to have representation in the council of ministers. In this aspect his council of ministers should be a combination of 'cabinet ministers' and 'State ministers'. For example, the council of ministers may have a berth of cabinet ministers up to 40 per cent and the remaining 60 per cent to state ministers in the council of ministers that should shelter all the nations.

Executive powers of economic government and capitalism

Article: 18. Portfolios: The government would function through its various portfolios with collective responsibility under the chairmanship of president. The major portfolios are:

(a) Foreign affairs,
(b) Public finance, banking and investment,
(c) Internal defence, (police),
(d) External defence (military),
(e) Industries, -large, small, medium, micro,
(f) Multinational Corporations,
(g) Food and Agriculture,
(h) Transport - surface, sea and air,
(i) Communication,
(j) Labour and employment,
(k) Education-primary and higher,
(l) Health,
(m) Research and Development including space research,
(n) Preservation of natural resources – national and intercontinental and so on.

The above portfolios are not listed on their merit of importance. All the portfolios are equally valued as essential as others because they are interred mingled in the modern world of global village.

19. Globalisation: The globalisation has its own merits and demerits in its application through Capitalism and Democrism.

First, the developed capitalist countries, impose 'globalisation' on poor and developing countries to merchandize their 'over production' for stabilising their own economy.

Second, these countries not only buy cheap labour but also extract rare and scare natural resources from these developing countries like India and other middle east countries and market the finished goods at least 1000 times higher than labour cost within seconds by using credit cards through 'online trade'. The buyers are under strong influence of convenient to the buy the goods at their doorsteps with easy money transfer.

Third, the multination corporations who have stretched their market wings sell their goods at international platform at the least hundred to 1000 times more than the 'wages' paid to workers.

Fourth, these MNCs spread and deeply root their 'economic colonies' throughout the world with powerful support of military of their 'mother land'. Once they entered a country it would be hazardous to drive them out unless and until the economically subjected countries engage in World War III.

Fifth, The MNCs exploit trillion and trillions of dollars from the workers of foreign countries will sole motive of profit illusion and store the money in various bank especially in Swiss. They measure their business success in the 'balance of profit' and therefore they are unceasingly 'bulling' the value of their shares between thousand and ten thousand times more than their 'par value' or 'intrinsic value'.

On creating 'bubbling market', 'bubbling price', 'bubbling investment' and 'bubbling profit' the MNCs are forecasting to attract gigantic projects beyond their capability and competency. In the stock market the 'bulls' are bubbles'. The bubbling economies are volatile and evaporative even by the slightest impact of economic turbulence. The stock markets have converted a vast majority of people as gamblers. They are ardent to earn treasure without shaking even their little finger. Consequently, the bigwigs will disappear with their bounty and the workers will be thrown out on the streets with begging bowls as it became apparent similar to the 'great depression' of 1930s. John Maynard Keynes, now, has no remedial measures to save these kind unemployed workers of MNCs. What prudential system will now protect the mankind? It is the bewildering problem now to surface over the international economic government to seek for a permanent solution.

Article: 20. Globalisation and Democrism: Globalisation of economy is the scorching problem for the very survival of economy and for the eradication of poverty but it should not be within the orbit of capitalism. It is well established fact that capitalism is a self-propelled and self-centred system that is always concerning the interests of a few capitalists by compromising the welfare of people.

On the intellectual perceptive of the history of economic thought since Adam Smith the only alternative to capitalism and socialism remains before the mankind is the establishment of 'Democrism' or 'People's direct ownership of Capital'.

Article: 21. Global Investment of the Workers and Establishment of Global Industries (MNCs)

The dawn and realisation of industrial globalisation of both in goods and service sectors is a long awaiting aspiration of modern world on the failure of political attempts (League of Nations and UNO) after first and two world wars. Basically the UNO after striving for more than 50 long years and spending billions of dollars utterly failed in the eradication of poverty, preventing numerous regional wars, stopping the killing of millions of innocent civilians and reducing the huge income gap between rich and poor. More or less it has become the string-puppet of US interventionism. The world accepts UNO on the concept of 'something is better than nothing'.

Then what is the remedy? Since the political strategies have failed we have to sincerely attempt to establish 'globalisation of economy' not under the thumping pressure of capitalism but the self-governing power of 'Democrism' i.e. 'People's Direct Ownership of Capital'. Sooner is the construction, later is the destruction.

(a) Establishment of MNCs: Under influence of Democrism all the defective and damaged economic activities such as investment, production, employment, income distribution, industrial management, pricing system, banking structure, circulation of money and so on should undergo systematic renovation and reformation. Fortunately the seed for such renovations is already strewn due to the economic evolution towards its perfection as per natural law.

(b) The establishment of the MNCs would be undertaken as per the guidance of the **'global industrial experts and promoters'**. These industries may be projected and proposed anywhere in the world after due consideration of national interest and feasibility. They may be launched in any country in the world. Perhaps it may be US, UK, Russia, China, India, Iran, Pakistan, Ceylon, South Africa, Brazil, Israel, Palestine, Egypt, Australia, Germany or any country in the world.

(c) Investment: The investment for the establishment of a new MNC would directly be contributed by the 'workers of all the countries' as a whole. Suppose there are 300 billion workers in the world. The 'global industrial experts and promoters' have planned to construct a MNC in Singapore with aggregate investment of 300 billion dollar. The required investment would be acquired as follows:

If a consumer buys a commodity in the market he would buy not only consumption goods but also investment goods. Suppose if he pays $10 he will buy $9 worth of consumption goods and the additional $1 that he pays is the contribution for purchasing investment goods. The $1 would be considered to be 'Investment money'. The investment money would be transferred to his 'investment account' in the 'investment bank'. All commercial banks would subsequently function as 'investment banks'. As soon as he purchases the 'investment goods' he would receive a SMS from his banker and from the seller whether he buys 'online' or not, beside with his 'balance statement'.

For every purchase of $10 worth of goods by 300 billion consumers in a day the 'global industrial experts' would accrue $300 billion to start the work immediately. Moreover these promoters are not going to investment the money in a single day. They will disperse the investment money in a 'piecemeal' method or step by step. Therefore they start two or three MNCs simultaneously or utilise the money to buy the existing shares directly from the MNCs at par value. Thereby the global workers can acquire the already functioning MNCs also without harassing the capitalists.

(d) Management of new industries: The global workers as a whole cannot participate in the management of industries directly. They will entrust the management of every industry to a 'managerial committee' comprising of elite and experienced worker-managers to supervise and to run the industry efficiently. They should maintain accountability and transparency and present a 'white paper' to all the workers of the company and to the council of ministers.

(e) Management of existing industries: The management of newly acquired industries would be administered as usual by the 'committee of existing managers'. Not only the incumbent managers but also the previous owners or the managing directors or the president of the company can take part in the management of the company. No managerial staffs are permitted to claim more numbers of shares than the number of shares of ordinary workers.

(f) Salary and honorarium: The managers, professionals, technical persons etc. would be paid higher salary considering their responsibility, qualification, experience and merit they enjoy. Otherwise not only the efficiency, the supervision and the respect of the workers but also the production and income, and competitiveness of the industry will collapse.

(g) Just price: Just price is the price determined by the 'general will' of the consumers who are authorised to distribute the goods and services among themselves disregarding the demand and supply forces.

The price – gap: Since all consumers are the producers they will fix the just price over and above cost price. The price-gap is for providing adequate margin for distribution of global dividend, for contribution to global government expenditure, for compensation of deficiency in producers' income to stabilise global employment, and for provision of adequate investment to initiate new national and multi-national industries and for the acquisition of shares of existing global industries, and for creation of reserve fund to meet natural calamities.

(h) Distribution of global dividend: The global dividend may be distributed to the workers in two means. One is the direct distribution through global business sector or global government and the other is representative distribution through national business sector or national economic government.

(a) Direct distribution of dividend: In the case of 'global direct distribution' the global dividend earned by all the global industries would be deposited in a 'global dividend fund'. Some rich countries may contribute a considerable volume of amount to the 'global dividend fund' for prompt eradication of global poverty. The global economic government through its global business sector distribute the dividend to the working class according to their investment burden. The low income workers would receive higher dividend whereas the higher income group workers would get lower dividend.

This distributive justice not only reduces the 'income gap' between workers but also increase the purchasing power of low income group workers. This increased purchasing power of poor would lead the economy to eradicate poverty as swiftly as possible.

(b) Representative distribution of dividend: Apart from distribution of national dividend reserved in the national dividend fund, the national economic governments may request the 'global economic government' to transfer the 'global dividend' to their 'distinct national dividend fund' for the distribution of 'aggregate dividend' to the workers. The 'aggregate dividend' combines both the 'national dividend' earned from national industries and 'global dividend' derived from multinational corporations. Both the dividends would be combined together and distributed to the workers according to their 'investment burden'. It should be specified here that the 'share capital' invested in 'national' industries as well as in 'multinational corporations' is directly owned by the global workers as a whole. No distinction should be drawn between 'national workers' and 'foreign workers'. All the workers should be merited and honoured as 'global workers'.

(i) Global Tax-Free Economy: To meet the expenditure of the global economic government a considerable proportion of 'global dividend fund' would be apportioned without taxing the people through its member countries. The global government should present its budget by portfolio-wise periodically for the ratification of its member countries.

(j) Corruption Free – Global Economy: Money is not a commodity to buy cheaper and to sell dearer. To materialise this fact all the commercial banks should be converted into 'investment banks'. The workers would deposit their investment money in these banks which will transfer the investment money to the 'global or national investment fund' to start new industries or to buy the shares of existing industries at their par value.

On the other hand all the commercial banks especially Swiss banks accept the black money for mala fide intention against the morality of honest citizens. These banks should be treated more criminal than the corrupt depositors. Some reports claim that Indians alone have deposited more than US$1.4 trillion in Swiss banks. But the Swiss Bankers Association reports that Indians have about US$2billion. ("White Paper on Black Money". Ministry of Finance, Government of India, 2012.)

Short-term remedy

(a) Whatever the volume of money the very accepting of black money as deposit primarily by the banks or by any agency or by any person should be treated a severely punishable crime and treason against the country which spoils the economy. To stop the flow of black money immediately there should be a statutory or mandatory condition that depositors should submit an endorsement received from government authorities, to the Swiss and other foreign banks when huge volume of money, more than $100,000 is invested. The endorsement should be in quadruple - the first to the bank, the second and the third to the 'income-tax department' and the central bank of respective countries and the fourth for the safe custody of the government. The endorsements should be compatible with requisite identification cards of depositors. These transactions may be carried out by 'online' also. All these deposits should be renewed every five to ten years.

The enactment of anti-corruption measures and bank deposits

The **United Nations Convention against Corruption (UNCAC)** is the first legally binding international anti-corruption instrument. In its 8 chapters and 71 Articles, the UNCAC obliges its States Parties to implement a wide and detailed range of anti-corruption measures affecting their laws, institutions and practices. These measures aim to promote the prevention, criminalisation and law enforcement, international cooperation, asset recovery, technical assistance and information exchange, and mechanisms for implementation.

The UNCAC has passed statutory authority to all 'State Parties' to enact such anti-corruption laws. The UNCAC was adopted by the United Nations General Assembly in Mérida, Yucatán, Mexico, on 31 October 2003 by Resolution 58/4. The convention was signed by 140 countries. As of 12 July 2012 (2012 -07-12)[update], the convention had been ratified, accepted, approved or acceded to by 161 countries (which became thus States Parties to the convention) as well as the European Union and applies to most of the world population.

The **International Court of Justice** (French: *Cour Internationale de Justice*; **World Court):** Provided any 'State Parties' fail to enact a stringent 'anti-corruption act' the world court may be approached for remedy. But the court will not pass any 'direction' on 'state Parties' to implement its order because it will lead to encroach the sovereignty of the 'State Parties'. Therefore, the main functions of World Court are restricted only to provide advisory opinions on legal questions submitted to it by duly authorised international organs, agencies, and the UN General Assembly.

Therefore, the long term and pragmatic solution is to convert all commercial banks into 'global investment banks of people' and replace capitalistic and socialistic systems by democratic system i.e. Democrism.

VOLUME: X

Theories of Employment

Chapter– 37

Four Basic Theories of Employment

(A Critical Review)

Among the most indispensable human rights such as liberty, equality and fraternity the first and foremost right that a society should provide to every worker is his 'right to work'. By the term 'right to work' I mean the stability and security of employment as long as a worker is willing to work to order to uphold his 'right to live'.

At present there are only two basic theories of employment in the economic literature: One is Say's Law of Markets and the other is Keynesian Theory of Employment. Both the theories have failed to provide 'right to work' and thereby 'right to live' to the citizens of society in the constitution as one of the 'fundamental rights' because of the ineffectiveness of economic systems. So in order to empower the economic systems I classify the theory of employment into four groups as follows:

1. Say's Market Theory of Employment,
2. Keynesian Effective Demand Theory of Employment,
3. Producers Profit-Motive Theory of Employment and
4. Producers Money Flow Theory of Employment.

However, it is known that Keynes has already proved that Say's Law is futile and Keynes himself is accepting that his theory of employment is ineffective to lead the economy toward 'full employment equilibrium' under the 'capitalistic mode of production'. In order to ensure 'right to work' and thereby 'right to live' we have to formulate a new theory of employment and to drive the economy to reach 'full employment equilibrium'.

Therefore, I have formulated a new theory of employment based on my new found 'Law of Producers', 'Effective Monetary Equilibrium' or Producers

Money Flow Theory of Employment. The distinction between Keynesian theory and of mine is intellectually contradicting. Keynes has approached the employment theory in real terms whereas I analyse it in monetary terms. According to Keynes, the level of employment is determined the 'effective demand for goods' which is decided by the point of interaction of 'aggregate demand for goods' and 'aggregate supply of goods' and it is called 'real equilibrium'. The real equilibrium between aggregate production and aggregate distribution (aggregate selling) of goods by the producers cannot be achieved independently at all levels of employment.

The achievement of real equilibrium has great hurdle as it depends on money expenditure of billions of consumers in the market, who behave according to their erratic psychology in the market. In other words the 'producer's real equilibrium' depends on the 'consumers monetary equilibrium'. Moreover 'consumers (workers) money equilibrium between their money income and expenditure' settles at lower level, for example, at 1 trillion dollars whereas the producers (capitalists) want their 'real equilibrium' to settle at higher level, for example, 1.5 trillion dollars because of their avaricious desire for maximisation of profit. With 1 trillion dollars of wage income how can the consumers buy 1.5 trillion worth of consumption goods which the producers fix for their goods? Since the consumers do not have enough money to buy the goods for the satisfaction of fulfilling producer's maximisation of profit, the volume of production and level of employment are determined at lower level. The very greediness of capitalists for maximisation of profit leads to the destruction of capitalism. So that Keynes advises the intervention of State to control the capitalists desire for maximisation of profit and redistribution of income to pave the way for workers or consumers to get higher level of wage income as much as possible to save capitalistic mode of production. Keynes has not any intention to change the very basic structure of capitalistic mode of production but he wants only the intervention of State through its budgetary technique to control the capitalists. He allows the capitalism to march on its way as usual.

Keynes, therefore, restricts and misguides the thinkers that they should analyse the economic problems only in real terms of aggregate demand and aggregate supply. He demarcates the area of thinking by advocating as below:

"...The true law relating the aggregate demand and aggregate supply functions is a vitally important chapter of economic theory...Without which all discussions concerning the volume of aggregate employment are futile"

'The General Theory of Employment, Interest and Money'

Though it is undisputable fact that Keynes is the greatest revolutionary economist that the world has ever produced, his advocacy to analyse economic problems in real terms, especially the theory of employment has been trembling in the global economy still now.

Since the economic analyses in real terms have failed in determination the level of employment as well as in solving the unemployment in poor and developing countries I wish to scrutinize the theory of employment in monetary terms.

According to monetary terms, the level of employment is determined as follows: When the producers venture into production they will expect different monetary equilibrium between the rate of outflow of money and rate of inflow of money for different levels of employment. But at a particular supply of money there will be a one monetary equilibrium that will determine a particular level of employment. It may be termed as **"Producers' Effective Monetary Equilibrium".** This monetary equilibrium will lead the producers to equate their "actual monetary equilibrium with their 'expected monetary equilibrium'. This effective monetary equilibrium of producers not only determines the level of employment but also stabilises it at that particular supply of money.

In other words, the "Producers effective monetary equilibrium (${}_{eff}^{P}E_{q}$) is the functional equilibrium (F_1) between producer's outflow of money (${}_{\leftarrow f}^{P}M$) and producer's inflow of money (${}_{\rightarrow f}^{P}M$)". Or it may be termed as functional equilibrium (F_2) between "Producers actual monetary equilibrium (${}_{A}^{P}Eq$) and Producers expected monetary equilibrium (${}_{Ex}^{P}Eq$)"

$${}_{eff}^{P}E_{q} = F_1\left({}_{\leftarrow f}^{P}M = {}_{\rightarrow f}^{P}M\right) \text{ or } F_2\left({}_{A}^{P}Eq = {}_{Ex}^{P}Eq\right)$$

(Left arrow indicates the outflow and the right arrow the inflow)

It is well known fact that Say's Law and Keynesian Law of Employment have been widely illustrated in economic literature. However, in order to complete the theory of employment I like to explain them briefly before I put forward my monetary theory of employment.

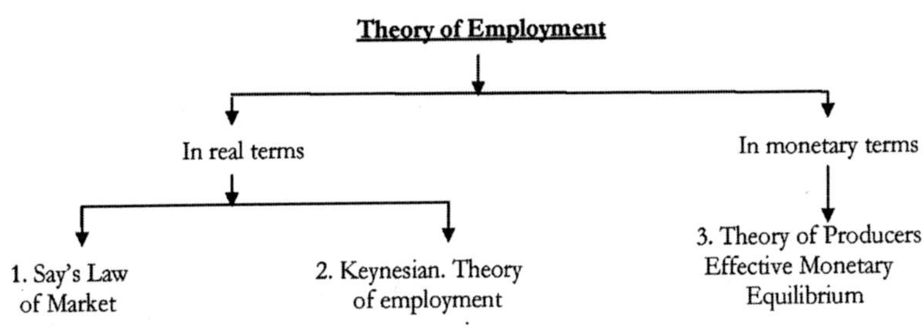

Chapter – 38

Producers' Profit-Motive Theory of Employment

The producers before venturing into production they will ascertain two kinds of profits. One is their minimum expected profit (P_E) and the other is their expected or realised actual profit (P_A). Producers have no other motive to enter into business except to accumulate wealth by maximisation of profit. In the capitalistic mode of production both the State and the consumers should leave way to the producers to exploit workers for providing adequate employment opportunities to the people. Therefore, Keynes says the consumers should assure the producers that they will provide adequate 'effective demand for goods produced' to determine the volume of employment in a country. However, Keynes warns the producers that their greediness for maximisation of profit will hamper the purchasing power of consumers and it will pull down the 'effective demand' for goods to uphold the level of employment.

To control the capitalist producers motivation Keynes directs the State to intervene in the economic activities to maintain a justifiable balance between 'maximisation of profit' and 'purchasing power of consumers'. He intends that the balance of economic power between producers and consumers should target in reducing the 'maximisation of profit' and enhancing the 'purchasing power of consumers' to maintain 'effective demand' for goods as high as possible to solve unemployment. Keynes warns in the same line of thought of Karl Marx that the very aim of uncontrolled 'maximisation of profit' itself will destroy the capitalists as it will demolish the purchasing power of people and reduce the effective demand for goods.

Despite the Great Depression of 1930s which forced the capitalistic mode of production to disappear in the world due its uncontrolled greediness for maximisation of profit and misdistribution of income, even now the money illusion capitalists enchant them to determine the volume of employment by calculating their 'maximisation of profit'. Therefore, the producers determine the volume of employment where the 'aggregate supply curve' intersects the 'aggregate demand curve' at E in the graph drawn below. The capitalist producers calculate their success in the business by the sin of the volume of exploited profit only. This psychology of producers forces them to correlate the volume of employment with their profit income.

The producers compose their objects into two parts. One is their 'minimum expected profit' and the other is the 'actual expected or realised profit'. The 'minimum expected profit' guide them to venture into business with certain volume of employment and the 'actual expected or realised profit' induce or discourage them to determine the volume of employment to harvest their aim of 'maximisation of profit'.

Minimum Expected Profit (P_E)

In order to venture into business the producers expect a minimum profit for various levels of employment (or volume of production). The minimum expected profit is included in the 'aggregate supply price' in addition to the factor cost. It may be written as

Aggregate Supply Price (Z) = Factor cost + Minimum Expected Profit (P_E)

In this aspect the producers will determine the value of minimum expected profit over and above the prevailing market rate of interest. Otherwise the producers will not invest their capital for production of goods. Keynes terms the minimum expected price as the income of entrepreneurs. Moreover the 'minimum expected profit' will be going on increasing in correspondence with the increasing level of employment as the other factor costs of production, especially the labour cost and the cost of scarce natural resources, will also be increasing in due course of time. Since there is a functional relationship between 'minimum expected profit' and level of employment it may be written as $P_E = Ø(N)$ and it may be called as 'Expected Profit Function'.

Actually Expected Profit (P_A)

The second major factor in addition to 'aggregate supply price' is the 'aggregate demand price' for determination of volume of employment. When the aggregate supply price is determined by the producers in the factory, the aggregate demand price is influenced by the consumers on buying the goods produced in the market. The aggregate demand price comprises both the factor cost and the actually expected profit of producers. It may be written as:

Aggregate Demand Price = Factor cost + Actual Expected Profit (P_A)...(2)

In both the equations the factor is the same. If we deduct the factor cost in both the equations the aggregate supply price becomes the function of the 'minimum expected profit' i.e. $Z = \text{Ø}(P_E)$ and the aggregate demand price as the function of 'actual expected profit', i.e. $D = f(P_A)$.

At the initial stage of production the 'actual (expected) profit' should be greater than the 'minimum expected profit'. On the existence of such economic condition the producers will be induced to increase the level of employment to achieve maximisation of profit.

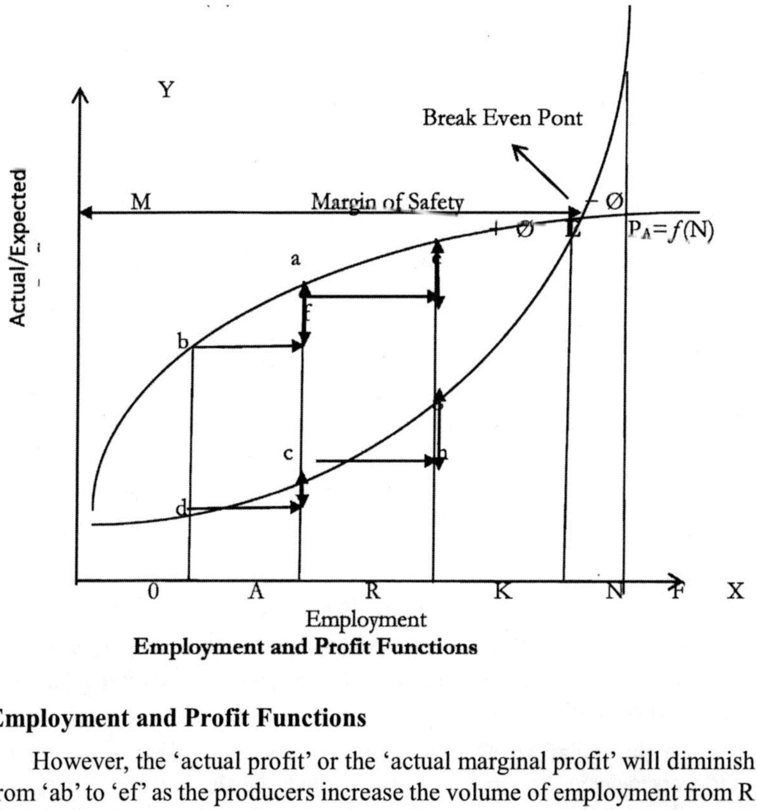

Employment and Profit Functions

Employment and Profit Functions

However, the 'actual profit' or the 'actual marginal profit' will diminish from 'ab' to 'ef' as the producers increase the volume of employment from R to K. It has been explained in the above diagram. Assuming the technology and other factors are stable, there will be competition among the producers and it will increase the 'factor cost' especially labour cost and the cost of scarce natural resources and infrastructures. These factors determine the "producers' actual profit curve" to descend towards x axis when the level of employment increases. The nature of "producers' actual marginal profit curve" is determined by the 'consumers diminishing marginal propensity to consume'.

The producers would have an estimated schedule of 'expected marginal profit' at increasing level for every 'marginal increase' in the level of employment. For example, if the level of employment increases from R to K, the producers expected marginal profit 'gh' would higher than 'cd'. Therefore, the 'producers expected profit curve (P_E) curve is drawn upwards towards Y axis.

Since producers actual profit is the determinant factor the level of employment would be determined where P_A curve intersects PE curve at E where producers will maximise their profit. On the other hand if the producers increase (or decrease) one more employee from N to F they will incur loss and their aim of maximisation of profit will suffer.

Moreover, when the income of consumers increases along with the level of employment, their propensity to consume will not increase at equal rate. Since the consumers spend less on goods produced the rate of actual profit of producers will naturally diminish. All these facts will create a negative functional relationship between 'actual profit' and 'volume of employment'. It may be termed as 'actual profit function' i.e. $P_A = f(N)$.

In order to achieve maximisation of profit the producers will determine the level of employment at N where 'actual profit function' intersects the 'minimum expected profit function' at E. The point E is called 'break-even point' because at that point the producers will undergo neither gain nor loss. If the producers engage more employees or less employees than the volume of employees at E they will experience diminishing marginal rate of actual profit (double headed arrow) and it will move toward zero profit. Therefore, E is the 'effective profit point' that determines the volume of employment. It has been illustrated in the above diagram.

Margin of Safety and Angle of Incidence

The margin of safety and the angle of incidence are the two guiding concepts designed for the producers and policy decision-makers to administer the economy to function smoothly.

Margin of Safety: Margin of safety is the guiding principle for the producers to decide how much volume of goods they have to produce in order to stabilise the volume of employment and income or to realise maximisation of profit. Longer the margin of safety line is the higher the maximisation of profit at higher level of employment. If the producers are able to get a longer margin of safety line they can play in the market with higher volume of production.

In the above graph AE is the margin of safety at N level of employment and the producers will determine the level of employment at that point. Before venturing into business the producers will calculate the strength of their margin of safety to encounter the competition in the market.

The policy decision-makers of the economy also should endeavour to keep the country's margin of safety to be lengthier as far as possible to stabilise the economy in terms of employment, production and income.

However, it is not necessary for all the producers to employment workers up to the end point of margin of safety to achieve their maximisation of profit. Some producers may fix the volume of employment at any point on the line of margin of safety to stabilise their business strongly in the market any thereby they will leave a considerable volume of employment to stagnate in the economy.

In such cases the State should interfere in the decision-making policies of producers in order to maximise the utility of workers to march towards full employment level.

Angle of Incidence: The angle of incidence is formed on either side of 'E' where the producers' actual profit curve intersects their expected profit curve. In fixing the angle of incidence the producers' actual profit curve plays a dominant role. It is because of the fact it is the ultimate profit that produces will realise at point E. The shape of the curve is decided by the consumers and the producers cannot exert any control over it. The curve starts from left and travels towards right but at downwards trend. For the consumers income increases their propensity to consume will diminish.

On the other hand the producers' expected profit curve is an estimated curve designed by the producers by analysing the present and future factor costs, availability of natural resources and government policies. Therefore, the curve always goes upwards from left to right. It denotes that producers 'expected profit' will increase when the level of employment increases.

The angle plays a strategic part in deciding an economy's both underemployment and full employment equilibriums. In capitalistic mode of production the angle (Tan Ø i.e. actual profit/expected profit)) will be anywhere between 'more than zero and less than infinity' i.e. Ø = >0° and <90°. Greater the value of angle means greater the profit in the short run. In the long run a lot of competitors enter into the industry and push down the producers' aggregate profit. Moreover the 'margin of safety' for all industries will prevail at underemployment equilibrium. This is the fate of capitalistic mode of production.

How to achieve full-employment equilibrium? By implementing effective fiscal and monetary policies the 'economic authorities' should strive to reduce the angle between 'actual profit curve' and 'expected profit curve' towards zero step by step but with accelerated tempo. It can be made in three ways.

1. 'Ceteris paribus' keeping the "producers' expected profit" to be stable at all level of employment, the economic authorities or the State should strive the "producers' actual profit curve" to shift below towards the "producers'

expected profit curve". But controlling producers' actual profit is difficult because it is determined by innumerable consumers and, their income and diminishing marginal propensity to consume in capitalism. Or

2. Protecting the "producers actual profit curve" to be stable at all level of employment, the economic authorities should execute economic strategies to shift the producers' expected profit curve upwards to tend to coincide with the producers' actual profit curve. This will also be very difficult because the producers are economically very powerful by their capital ownership though they are very few. Or

3. We have to adopt some economic strategies to shift both the curves to move towards each other simultaneously at all level of employment. This economic maneuver will make both the curves to become a single straight line and the angle of incidence will disappear or become zero. This strategy requires the elimination of class distinction between workers and capitalists or consumers and producers. This will be feasible only in the economic system of Democrism or democratisation of economy. In the democratic mode of production the 'margin of safety' will protract up to the level of full employment. Therefore, I venture to state that Democrism is the only alternative system to Capitalism and Socialism to solve unemployment and poverty.

Sin of the Capitalistic Mode of Production

1. Selfish motive: The greatest sin of the capitalistic mode of production is its driving force for realisation of maximisation of profit instead of welfare of society to venture into economic activities for generating employment opportunities and production of goods and services.

2. Abdication of right to live: The operation of economic machinery in capitalism requires 'maximisation of profit' of few capitalists. The exclusive aim of the operation of all economic machineries is to assure 'right to live' to all members of society. The right to live of a person depends on his 'right to work' or his persistence of employment. The economic systems that we formulated force all the people of country to uphold its 'right to live' on a few capitalists' or some vested interests' aim of 'maximisation of profit' is utterly frightful and intolerable.

3. Surrender of consumers' sovereignty: Consumers may have all rights to exercise their sovereignty in the market in buying goods and services. But if the consumer's sovereignty is encountering with the aim of the producers' maximisation of profit, the producers will suspend all of their economic activities by reducing volume of production and level of employment. Since the producers invest billions and billions of dollars in the business they will not allow the consumers sovereignty to surpass their aim of 'maximisation of profit'. Because of that fact the producers administer sexy advertisements and other malpractices to fool the innocent consumers to buy the goods at the exorbitant price.

4. Compromising the quality of goods: The aim of the maximisation of profit compels most of the producers to supply not only inferior quality of goods but also adulterated goods. It is the money greedy producers who pollute the air, water and land and endanger the health of consumers. Most of the governments are controlled by these producers as the politicians have hidden agenda with these corrupt people. If and only if the manmade calamities occur worse than war crime, then alone the governments stage a drama that they are exercising stringent action on them to pacify the agitating people. The governments are coerced to act in harmony with the aim of the producers to reduce poverty and unemployment to some extent. Billions and billions of dollars are spent by the corporate sectors to the political parties even in the democratic elections to form puppet governments. After the elections these puppet governments extend helping hand to the corporate sectors to earn their money in excess as compensation by allowing free hand to exploit the consumers nationally and internationally by supplying inferior goods gambling on the healthcare and life of poor people. For example, the World Bank Report says if US alone just spend two per cent of her military expenditure ($1.75 trillion which is more than combined military spending of G7 countries and more than half of global military spending) for poor people; the global poverty will be wiped out immediately. But US cannot do it because it will not encourage the poor countries to become as competitors to her corporate sectors in future.

5. Maximisation of profit creates Corrupt Societies: Irrespective of Capitalistic or Socialistic or any kind of ideological societies, their socio-economic-political activities consist of two structural functions. One is their basic structural functions of economy and the other is their superstructural functions of socio-political formations. The basic structural functions determine the spectrum of superstructural functions of societies and differentiate them to vary from one another.

The basic structural functions of any society are its economic activities of the economic system that a society follows. The basic structure is laid on the foundation of 'Capital Ownership' of the economy. The fact that 'who owns the capital' determines the economic system of the country, whether it capitalism or socialism or any other 'ism'. In the capitalistic mode of society the capital is owned by a very few families or capitalists. We know that the propelling force of these capitalists to venture into production is to acquire 'maximisation of profit'. The government through its fiscal and monetary policies should assure the capitalists to reap their maximisation of profit to uphold the volume of production and the level of employment perpetually. Otherwise industries will be collapsed and the economy will be driven to face depression and there will be unprecedented unemployment everywhere.

In order to avoid such kind of economic collapse the superstructural functions of society will be transformed to satisfy the whims and fancies of few capitalists. The constitutional law of the society, the customs and convention of the people, the literature of society, the religious norms of the devotees followed so far, the curriculum of education, the electoral system of the country, the method of formation of government, the life style of the people etc. which have been cherished beautifully for a long time as 'superstructural functions' and the 'identification of society' will be reconstructed or transmuted in the manner in which to satisfy a few capitalists ambition of 'maximisation of profit' which forms the basic structure of economic activities of society. If not, the capitalists refrain from production activities and create unemployment. In other words in the capitalistic mode of society the volume of employment is determined by the ambition of 'maximisation of profit' of few capitalists.

Therefore, there would be a 'class struggle for ever and ever always between a few capitalists who are in possession enormous economic power in the form of capital and the vast majority of working class in solving unemployment or acquiring 'right to live'. The attempts and struggles for creation of just society will only be a fantasy. In this context the only solution left before us is to transform the brutal capitalistic mode of production to the justifiable 'democratic mode of production'. In the democratic mode of production all the national capital will be distributed directly to all the workers equally. It will transform the basic structure of society to uphold the eternal concept of **'Each Industry for All and All Industries for Each'.** This is the only alternative to lead the mankind toward an Ideal or Just Society.

In brief, if we permit the 'maximisation of profit' of a few capitalists to be the driving force of socio-economic-political activities, the mankind will perish very soon.

Chapter – 39

Say's Law of Market - I

In his reputed book 'Treatise on Political Economy' J.B. Say, the French economist, says as follows:

"......a product is no sooner created, than it, from that instant, affords a market for other products to the full extent of its value. When the producer has put the finishing hand to his product, he is most anxious to sell it immediately, less the value should vanish in his hands. Nor is he less anxious to dispose of the money he may get for it; for the value of money is also perishable. But the only way of getting rid of money is the purchase of some product or other. Thus, the mere circumstance of the creation of the product immediately opens a vent for other products"

-Say J.B., "Treatise on Political Economy" pp. 78-79

The crux of the treatise is that supply creates its own demand.

1. Production offers sufficient purchasing power: In other words what Say believes is that the producers provide adequate wage income or purchasing power to the people to buy all the goods at the rate at which they are produced. Therefore, the producers will sell the total volume of goods at the rate at which they produce in the market. There will be equilibrium between rate of production and the rate of selling of the goods. Therefore, the goods-flow equilibrium will not cause to any reduction in the level of employment. The producers will have strong belief that the consumers will maintain effective demand with their adequate purchasing power and therefore no reduction in the level of employment will emerge due to stagnation goods in the market.

But Keynes views the above statement of Say is impracticable in the real world. Keynes argues that when production increases the money income of people will also increase accordingly. The consumers' psychology is when money income increases their propensity to consume will decrease. Therefore, the consumers will not buy all the goods produced and Say's law of market will not operate. As the propensity to consume decreases overproduction will emerge either in the market or in the industry. In order to eliminate the overproduction the producers will decrease the level of employment and it will result in unemployment due to lack of effective demand.

2. Automatic equilibrium between Savings and Investment: J.B. Say believes the consumers will spend their money income as the rate at which they earn it. The consumers will not hoard any money income. And if they do so the money income will lose its value when price level increases. Therefore, the consumers will lend the money to the investors to earn interest. If the depositors do not lend the money to the investors the money income of consumers will lose its value. In order to prevent the loss of money value the consumers will either spend all the money income to buy the goods produced or lend it to the investors to help them to buy investment goods. Therefore, J.B. Say argues that the level of employment will not decrease and there will be always sufficient effective demand in the market for goods.

The above argument is not applicable to the practical world of economic operations. The interest technique will not convert all the deposits into investment. The producers who acquire savings at a particular rate of interest will not convert it into investment unless they realise the rate of profit i.e. the marginal efficiency of capital in terms of Keynes; will be sufficient enough to cover the rate of interest to be paid. In other words the investors will expect that their volume of profit earned from investment should be greater than the volume of interest payable to depositors. On the other hand if the investors forecast that the rate of profit would be less than the rate of interest they will not borrow savings from depositors. Therefore, the investment goods that the investors have to buy in the market will stagnate. Before borrowing savings the investors not only scrutinize the rate of interest but also the reliable rate of profit. If the investors do not satisfy on the rate of profit, they will not buy investment goods in the market. The stagnation of investment goods will cause to reduce the production and level of employment. Therefore, it will be erroneous to believe that the economy will move toward full-employment on the false statement of J.B. Say that supply creates its own demand.

Keynes rejects the Say's assumption that supply creates its own demand because it requires that 'the aggregate demand price should be equal to the aggregate supply for all levels of output and employment' Keynes argues that this factual condition is not possible in the present capitalistic and political systems.

-Keynes, John Maynard: "The General Theory of Employment, Interest and Money" pp. 21-22.

3. Wage cut policy: One of the recommendations of Say to solve unemployment is 'wage-cut'. According to Say, if unemployment prevails in a country it is due to the fact that 'supply of labour' exists greater than 'demand for labour'. Hence the producers cut wage rate of workers to absorb excessive workers for production. This wage cut is one of policies of Say to solve unemployment. But this wage-cut policy is not practicable in industries for the following reasons:

(a) **Trade Union:** Throughout the world the trade unions are very strong and they will not allow any wage cut.

(b) **Minimum Wage Act**: Apart from influence of trade unions all the governments in the world have enacted 'minimum wage act'. Therefore, no producer can reduce the wage of workers and provide employment to unemployed workers.

(c) **Reduction of purchasing power:** The frightful fact is that the wage cut of workers will lead to reduction of money income of people and it will naturally decrease the purchasing power of people. Less purchasing power means a great fall in the demand for goods; and it will reduce the sale of goods. Produced goods will spontaneously stagnate in the market and it will reduce the level of employment but not increase the volume of employment. Moreover according to John Maynard Keynes the volume of employment of a country depends on 'effective demand' for goods but not the wage-cut of workers.

4. The Great Depression: In 1776, Adam Smith (1723-1790), the father of economic, wrote his famous book 'Wealth of Nations'. Considering him as beacon J.B. Say (1767-1832), Ricardo (1722-1825), Malthus (1766-1834), J.S. Mill (1806-1873), A.C. Pigou (1877-1959), and the contemporary economists of John Maynard Keynes developed economic theories in logical point of view. To our surprise no economists had been illustrated how the volume of production, volume of consumption, volume of investment and volume of employment of a country were determined for 150 long years still the publication of the book 'General Theory of Employment, Interest and Money' by Keynes in 1936. They concentrated only on the micro level of economics (taking a single industry and single consumer) and never considered the macro level or taking the country as a whole.

(a) Automatic Adjustment: They never explained 'how the economy was operating'; 'how should the economy operate' and 'what should be the role of government' to maintain smooth operation of economy. They believed there would be an 'Automatic Adjustment' between conflicting variables like demand and supply of goods to fix the price, and the interest would lead to equilibrium between savings and investment, the wage rate would equilibrate the demand for and supply of labour etc. Their logical view did not apply in the real world.

(b) Maximisation of Profit: No doubt in the capitalistic mode of production it is the capitalists who take initiation for creation of employment and produce goods with an exclusive object of maximisation of profit. The capitalists, who are very few, appropriate huge volume of national income and provide very meager volume of national income to the billions of workers for whom goods are produced. The misdistribution of national income drastically reduces the purchasing power of people. Though the goods are heaped in the market the people have no money to purchase them. Due to the bitter fact the goods are stagnated in the market and the producers reduce the volume of production and level of employment. This kind of unemployment still reduces the income of people, which still causes for further reduction of production. One industry after another industry has to be closed in cumulative manner. The misdistribution of national income in favour of capitalists' maximisation of profit destroys not only the capitalistic mode of production but also throw away the employees on the streets as beggars. It has happened in US and it is called as 'Great Depression'.

(c) Keynesian approach: During the period of Great Depression the economists could not deduce what factor that determines the volume of employment and volume of production. The economic literature maintained dead silence on these economic problems. The economists were searching a solution in the dark chambers as they have experienced such terrible problems ever before.

In 1936, Keynes shined as guiding star to navigate the world from depression to recovery by publishing his book, 'The General Theory of Employment, Interest and Money'. Keynes pointed out that it was 'effective demand' that plays the role of 'determinant factor' in deciding the volume of employment, volume of production, volume of income, volume of consumption etc. The global economists thrilled on his timely exposure of wisdom, otherwise communism would have haunted the world which would have led the world to its worst collapse.

There were two fallacies in Keynesian doctrine: 1. Keynes analysed his theories in 'real terms' and. He explained only the redemption of unemployed workers to gain their employment by redistribution of income, increasing the purchasing power of people by undertaking public works and by enhancing the 'level of effective demand' by budgetary techniques inviting the State intervention.

Keynes never advocated any 'theory of employment' to create new employment opportunities in poor and developing countries. The crux of his employment theory was to regain employment for those who lost employment due to lack of effective demand in developed countries during Great Depression.

Chapter – 40

Say's Theory of Employment – II

2. Say's theory of market or Say's theory of employment

The phrase of Say's theory of market that 'Supply creates its own demand' had been considered to be truism for a long span of period still Great Depression swayed the world into great agony. More or less all the economists assumed the catchword to be practicable and built up their theories of employment. During the period of Say most of the economic theories were formulated on basis of pure 'economic logics'. Say, therefore, believed that whatever socially needed goods at whatever volume the producers supplied them that would be demanded by the consumers in the market by automatic price adjustment mechanism.

Since there was no State intervention, no influence of trade union and no 'minimum wage act' at that time Say, like other economists, also believed there would be automatic adjustment between aggregate demand for and aggregate supply of goods. In other words, Say took as true that there would be an equilibrium between aggregate supply function and aggregate demand function, i.e. $\varnothing(N) = f(N)$, at all level of employment. His faith on the operation of the market led him to emphasise that the producers 'expected minimum proceeds of income' would equilibrate with their 'expected proceeds of income' at all volumes of production and employment. By his notation we could derive a conception that the curves of $\varnothing$ (N) and f (N) would coincide with each other i.e. the gap between them tends to zero. It has been presented in the graphical form below.

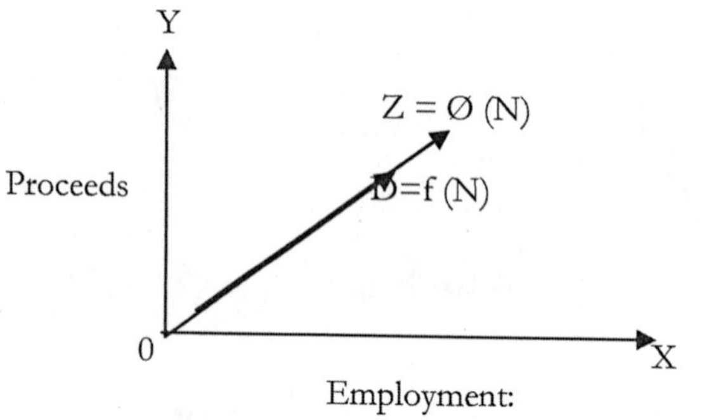

Employment and Proceeds of income

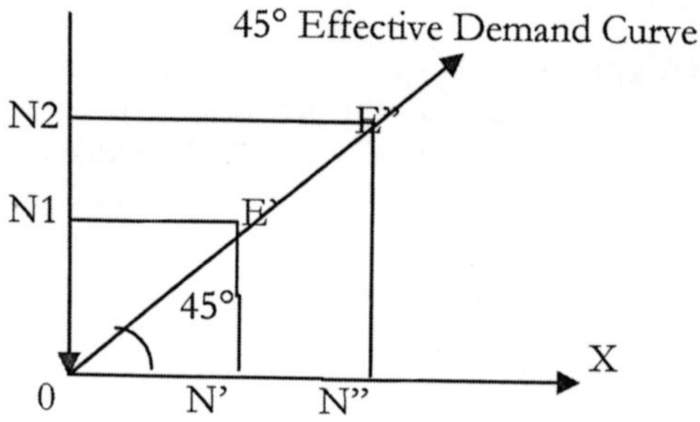

X axis: Aggregate supply Function [Z=Ø (N)];
Y axis: Aggregate Demand Function [D=*f* (N)];
Aggregate Demand/Supply Functions.

I. Application of Say's Theory of Market in Democratisation of Economy

In the present economic complexities and the structure of both capitalism and socialism Say's law cannot be implemented forever. But we can deem that Say's theory of market may be executed when the economy is democratised i.e. when national capital is made to be directly owned by the people. It is because of the fact that when the people own direct ownership of capital, (1) there would be no State intervention in the economic administration, (2) there would be no distinction between producers and consumers, (3) there would be no trade unions as all the industries are directly owned by the people, (4) there would be amicable wage policy formulated by the workers themselves,

(5) there would be an economic situation that the workers in the capacity of capitalists maintain equilibrium between production and sale of goods at all levels of employment, (6) there would be no greedy 'profit motive' to drive the economic machinery to operate and (7) there would be just price as the price of goods is determined by the consumers themselves.

1 (a) Democratic Economy and Say's Law: In the above diagram: (17) I have attempted to illustrate the survival of Say's 'Theory of Market' on the execution of 'democratic economy'. It is well known fact that not only the economic techniques but also scientific market systems and globalisation have developed rapidly. In the modern era of 'communication technology'.

1 (b) 'Monopoly Capitalism' and 'Democratic Economy': It was John Maynard Keynes who exponentially proved that in the development of corporate sector or 'monopoly capitalism', the profit greedy producers indulged in 'over production' which prevented all the wheels of production units and resulted in 'Great Depression'. It has ben explained in the diagram: 16.

1 (c) Aggregate Demand and Supply Functions: In the diagram (18) the X axis denotes 'aggregate Supply Function' and the Y axis the 'aggregate Demand Function'. The aggregate supply function is a set of numerous points and each point specifies a particular volume of employment. The producers cannot fix the highest value of point to employ huge volume of employees in order to maximise their profit. They can fix only a particular point at which the aggregate demand function intersect up to which the buyers will purchase goods produced. Otherwise the producers incur heavy monetary loss due to 'over production'. This is called 'effective demand' and there will be only one 'effective demand' on the 'aggregate supply function'. On the other hand if the producers produce 'more than or less than' the **effective demand their 'maximisation of profit' will also descend adversely.**

1 (d) The 'Law of Market – Blunder' committed by Say: Due to analytical and circumstantial error Say emphasised that the 'effective demand' will intersect on all points of 'aggregate supply price' if adequate inputs are available and the producers will lead the economy towards 'full employment'. This economic blunder led the Say to indicate that the 'aggregate demand function' will always overlap on the 'aggregate supply function' and I have explained notion in the diagram (15). After applying deep contemplation not only Keynes but also Prof. Mrs. Joan Robinson and like other thinkers warned that the present 'corporate and monopolistic capitalism' would not solve any basic human problem like poverty, unemployment, economic disparity etc., and advised the future generation to find out an alternate economic system.

"The profound conviction that the economic problems of want and Poverty and economic struggle between classes and nations is nothing but a frightful muddle, transitory and unnecessary muddle."

– Keynes, John Maynard: "Essays in persuasions"

"The outstanding faults of economic society in which we live are Its failure to provide for full-employment and its arbitrary and inequitable distribution of wealth and income."

– Keynes, John Maynard: "General Theory"

"It is true, with adequate organisation there need be no unemployment. There is always something useful that can be done even with a man's bare hands. The massive unemployment and underemployment that afflicts the world today shows a defect in social and economic institutions".

– Professor Mrs. Joan Robinson:
(Economic Philosophy – p. 114)

1 (e) Democratic Economy and 'continuous process of effective demand'

Every point on the effective demand curve determines the volume of employment, production and income. In monopolistic capitalism only one point of effective demand determines the level of employment. But in democratic economy all points that flow on the effective demand curve determines not only the level of employment but also stabilises it.

1 (f) The formation of effective demand curve

In democratic economy the position and formation of effective demand curve occupies a vital position in determination of level of employment. I have, therefore, in the diagram (20) drawn the curve being 45° line. It is because of the fact that every point on the effective demand curve 'aggregate demand function' equilibrates the 'aggregate supply function' at every level of employment. In other words [Z = *f* (N)] = [D=Ø (N)] at all level of N.

N="

Σ [Z=*f* (N)] = [D=Ø (N)] "N

N= 0

For example, at N' level of employment the E' on the effective demand curve equilibrates 'the aggregate supply function or (price) which is the 'producers' expected money income' with the 'aggregate demand function (or price) which is the producers' actual money income, i.e. N'E' = N1E'. At this stage the producers will maximise their profit and thereby they will be induced to employ more workers to enhance the production. This market or economic condition will induce the producers to increase the level of employment to N" and the producers will experience the equilibrium between aggregate supply and aggregate demand. This is the 'theory of market that 'aggregate supply creates aggregate demand' under the democratic economic system. In fact, such market condition can be materialised only in democratic economy because in this economic system all producers become consumers and vice versa and no one in either capacity wish to be self-suicidal.

1 (g) Say forecasted the market theory of employment in the ambit of classical, neoclassical and monopolistic capitalism that supply would create its own demand. Eventually he was proved wrong by John Maynard Keynes... During 'Great Depression' it was John Maynard Keynes who had thrown all the capitalistic and socialistic theories in the dustbin of economic thought by his advocacy of macroeconomics. But Keynes accepted the inefficiency of the capitalistic system that would create or reinstate employment only to those who lost employment due to lack of effective demand. At last he too advised the all the economist to establish an effective and forceful economic system for future survival mankind. So, on my part I advocate 'democrism-the third theory' or 'democratic economy' to solve all socio-economic problems.

Chapter – 41

Producers' Monetary Theory of Employment

The theory of employment can be classified into Primary theories and Secondary theories. The primary theories consist of Keynesian Theory of Effective Demand in real terms and Producers Effective Monetary Equilibrium Theory of Employment in monetary terms whereas the secondary theories though they are not so significant, relate to Producers Actual Profit and Margin of Safety of Production.

The producer's effective monetary theory of employment depends on two 'circular flow of money functions' at different levels of employment (or production). One is 'producers minimum expected circular flow of money' $({}_{\copyright f}{}^{P}M)_{min,ex}$ and the other is 'producers actual circular flow of money $({}_{\copyright f}{}^{P}M)_{actual}$. The producers determine '$({}_{\copyright f}{}^{P}M)_{min,ex}$' at various levels of employment in prior of production as a schedule of employees but '$({}_{\copyright f}{}^{P}M)_{actual}$' is though predicted by the producers it is exclusively influenced by the consumers behaviour in the market. It transforms '$({}_{\copyright f}{}^{P}M)_{min,ex}$' as dependent factor of '$({}_{\copyright f}{}^{P}M)_{actual}$ ' and for that justification consumers are called 'king of the market'. It may, therefore, be inferred that '$({}_{\copyright f}{}^{P}M)_{min,ex}$' $= f$('$({}_{\copyright f}{}^{P}M)_{actual}$') and $N = f$('$({}_{\copyright f}{}^{P}M)_{actual}$'). Now let's us explain the employment function with a diagrammatic representation.

1. In the above figure the producer's circular flow of money is divided into two segments. One is 'productive out-flow of money' i.e., out-flow of money from producers to consumers and the other is 'consumptive our-flow of money' i.e., out-flow of money from consumers to producers. On the whole the combination of both the flows of money (1) and (2) creates one simple circular flow of money between producers and consumers.

Simple model of producer's circular flow of money

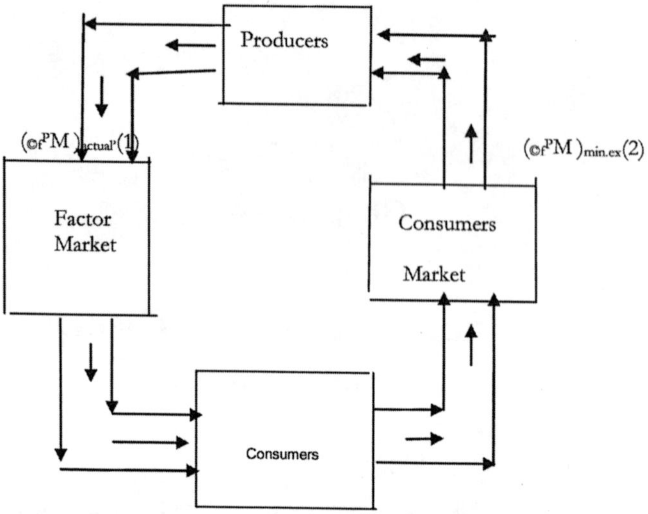

2. Productive out-flow of money

It may be highly relevant to call it 'producers minimum expected circular flow of money' $({}_{©f}{}^{P}M)$ min.ex in relation to volume of employment (or production). The producers will prepare a schedule of 'minimum expected money income' at each level of employment in prior to entering into production. A sample schedule is presented below. At the outset, the out-flow of money is actually originated by the producers through factor market to buy factors of production especially 'the labour' in order to produce goods and services. The in-flow of money indicates the producers 'minimum expected money income' which includes their profit also. It is semi-circular flow of money [(1) at the left side of the above figure] because it passes from producers to consumers though factor market only. The following table will illustrate the process of flow of money at various levels of employment:

Table 4: Relationship between N and '$({}_{©f}{}^{P}M)$ min.ex'.

Relationship between N and '$({}_{©f}{}^{P}M)$ min.ex'
Flow of money in billion dollars (in '000)

Vol.of employment	10	20	30	40	50	**60**	70	80	90
Producer's min. exp. Cir. Flow of money $({}_{©f}{}^{P}M)$ min.ex.	60	120	200	300	430	**570**	720	900	1100

3. Consumptive out-flows of money $({}_{\copyright f}{}^{P}M)$ min.ex)

It may be aptly called 'producers actual money income' or 'producers actual circular flow of money' on sale of goods to the consumers in the commodity market. It is consumptive semi-circular flow of money [(2) at the right side of the figure] because it flows out from consumers to producers on buying the goods and services. At the beginning as the consumption for goods is very high the producers usually receive more actual income than what they spent for production of goods because of the fact of high propensity to consume at lower income or employment level. The producers will also prepare a schedule of actual income on sale of goods after the production because the consumers are not only numerous but also usually behaving erratically in the market.

4. Consumptive out-flows of money $({}_{\copyright f}{}^{P}M)$): actual (in '000)

Vol. of employment	10	20	30	40	50	**60**	70	80	90
Producers actual Cir. Flow of money '$({}_{\copyright f}{}^{P}M)$ actual'	60	200	230	400	540	**570**	600	550	500

Relationship between N and '$({}_{\copyright f}{}^{P}M)$ actual'.

The producers are always intensively keen on the trend of the two schedules. If $({}_{\copyright f}{}^{P}M)$ actual' is greater than '$({}_{\copyright f}{}^{P}M)$ min, ex' the producer will be induced to enhance the level of employment to maximise their profit. The producers will continue in engaging more and more employees up to the point where '$({}_{\copyright f}{}^{P}M)$ actual' equals '$({}_{\copyright f}{}^{P}M)_{min,\ ex}$'. In the given table it is illustrated clearly that at the level of employment 600 workers the producers actual money income equals with their 'minimum expected income' of \$ 570 million and the producers will maximise their profit. In contrary, if the producers increase the level of employment to 700, their 'minimum expected income' will be \$ 720 million but their 'actual income' would be only \$600 million and the producers will be succumbed into heavy loss of \$120 million.

Employment and monetary relationship

Relationship between N and '$({}_{\copyright f}{}^{P}M)_{min,ex}$' and ('$({}_{\copyright f}{}^{P}M)_{actual}$')

Flow of money in billion dollars ('000s)

Vol. of employment	10	20	30	40	50	**60**	70	80	90
Producer's min. exp. Cir. Flow of money $({}_{\copyright f}{}^{P}M)$ min.ex	60	120	200	300	430	**570**	720	900	1100
Producers actual Cir. Flow of money $({}_{\copyright f}{}^{P}M)$ actual	60	200	230	400	540	**570**	600	550	500

Relationship between N and '$({}_{\copyright f}{}^{P}M)_{min,ex}$' and ('$({}_{\copyright f}{}^{P}M)_{actual}$'

Therefore, the producers will determine the level of employment where ('$(_{©f}{}^{P}M)_{actual}$') curve intersects the '$(_{©f}{}^{P}M)_{min.ex}$' curve at E. 'E' is called the **'Producers effective monetary point'.** This is the only point on the curve ('$(_{©f}{}^{P}M)$ actual') so effective that determines the level of employment where producers maximise their profit.

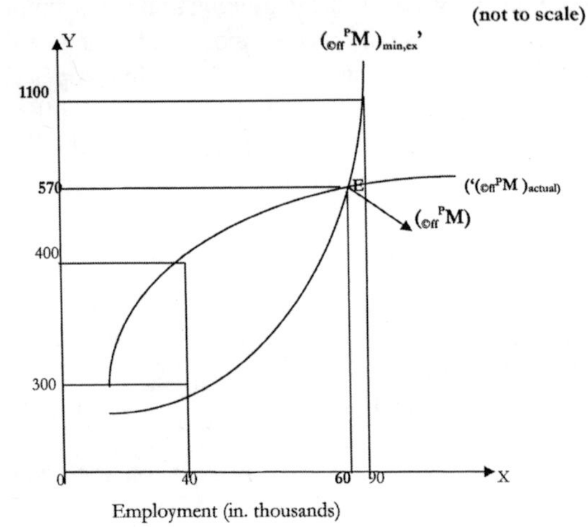

Producers Effective Monetary Equilibrium

Solution on its wings: "Towards Full Employment"

1. In order to achieve full employment if the producers enhances the level of employment from 60,000 to 70,000 the producers will find that their actual inflow of money will fall to $600 billion from their expected money inflow of $720 billion.

2. The producers will experience a loss of revenue to the tune of $120 billion which is nothing but a loss of revenue of consumers themselves in the 'prosumers society' of democratic economy.

3. In order to avoid the huge loss the producers (consumers) will convert the 'consumption money' into investment money' in the 'investment bank account' of consumers.

4. The stored 'consumption money' will now be released and it will be propel to flow towards the producers to stabilise the 'level of employment' at the level of 70,000. This is nothing but helping the consumers themselves from incurring heavy loss.

5. The consumers 'investment account' will be credited by $120 billion more. Since the investment is created within the internal investment banking system operating within the country, it will be termed as 'Convertible Exogenous Investment'.

6. This is the 'convertible Investment' because the consumers can exchange the 'investment' into 'consumption money' whenever they desire but within in a prescribed period, and buy the consumption goods in the market.

7. If such consumers do not operate promptly the stored goods will be valued less and will be sold to poor whose propensity to consume is very high or issued at free of cost, if possible, to clear the market and to prevent the wastage of goods.

8. The money income is usually hoarded by the rich people because their 'propensity to consume' 'the value of money' will diminish when their income increases. Due to the fact when the Exogenous Investment is created, it should not be used to produce more consumption goods. On the other hand the exogenous investment money may be treated as **'Green Capital investment'** and may be utilised for the development of renewable energy and **'green technology'.** Thus, we can create a clean, green, and pollution-free nation.

9. On the advent of widespread and sophisticated internet technology 'the producers cum consumers' can get adequate money income to stabilise the level of employment by interacting investment and consumption money with each other in the market and banking sectors within seconds under 'Dual Monetary System'.

10. By this way of conversion strategy the producers can lead the 'under – employment equilibrium' to 'full employment equilibrium'.

11. On the other hand, if the investment is overflowing at the 'full – employment level', the excess investment may be converted into 'Endogenous Investment' and may be exported to foreign countries without interest exclusively to create a 'poverty-free and pollution-free' world.

12. The theory of Democrism (The Third Theory) i.e. "Peoples' Direct Ownership of Capital" under its strategic economic technology of Dual Monetary System not only stabilise the volume of employment at full-employment level but also create a 'war-free world' and endeavour to establish an ideal and peaceful society in the world.

Index

D

E

M

N

O

P